# THE ROLLING STONES IN THE SIXTIES A PEOPLE'S HISTORY

Richard Houghton

Spenwood Books
Manchester, UK

First published in Great Britain 2022
by Spenwood Books Ltd
2 College Street, Higham Ferrers, NN10 8DZ.

Copyright © Richard Houghton 2022

The right of Richard Houghton to be identified as author of this work has been asserted in accordance with Section 77 of the Copyright, Design and Patents Act 1988.

A CIP record for this book is available from the British Library.

ISBN 978-1-9168896-5-1

Printed and bound by Sound Performance Ltd, 3 Greenwich Quay, Clarence Road, Greenwich, London, SE8 3EY.

Design by Bruce Graham, The Night Owl.

Front cover image: Stanley BieleckiASP/Getty Images
Rear cover images: Clockwise (from top left): Barry Denman, Laurie Stead, Martin Culleton, Richard Houghton, Richard Houghton, Brenda Parker

All other image copyrights: As captioned.

# BY THE SAME AUTHOR

You Had to Be There: The Rolling Stones 1962 - 69

The Beatles - I Was There

The Who - I Was There

Pink Floyd - I Was There

The Rolling Stones - I Was There

Jimi Hendrix - The Day I Was There

Led Zeppelin - The Day I Was There

The Smiths - The Day I Was There

The Jam - The Day I Was There (with Neil Cossar)

Black Sabbath - The Day I Was There

Rush - The Day I Was There

The Wedding Present - Sometimes These Words Just Don't Have To Be Said (with David Gedge)

Orchestral Manoeuvres in the Dark - Pretending To See The Future

Simple Minds - Heart of the Crowd

Shaun Ryder's Book of Mumbo Jumbo

Cream - A People's History

Queen – A People's History

Jethro Tull – Lend Me Your Ears

Thin Lizzy – A People's History

The Stranglers - Live (Excerpts)

For Bill

# CONTENTS

Introduction ............................................................................................. 9

1962 ...................................................................................................... 13

1963 ...................................................................................................... 17

1964 .................................................................................................... 104

1965 .................................................................................................... 280

1966 .................................................................................................... 453

1969 .................................................................................................... 458

Postscript ............................................................................................ 473

Acknowledgements ........................................................................... 474

# THE ROLLING STONES IN THE SIXTIES: A PEOPLE'S HISTORY

THE ROLLING STONES IN THE SIXTIES: A PEOPLE'S HISTORY

# INTRODUCTION

The Rolling Stones first performed in 1962 and, 60 years later, are still going strong. Their history as a band is well documented. But much of what has been written about their live shows up to 1967, when they largely withdrew from performing until they re-emerged as a live act in 1969 following the death of Brian Jones, is drawn from newspaper accounts of the time. This book shines a new light on that period of the Stones' history. It uses first hand interviews and completely fresh material, garnered from people who saw them as they graduated from performing before a handful of people in small clubs to packed theatres and arenas around the world.

This is not a definitive history of those early concerts and neither does it pretend to be. As an original member of the group, Bill Wyman's account of the band's early days in his autobiography *A Stone Alone*, drawn from his diaries and supplemented by press reports, is as close as we are likely to get to an accurate historical record. Keith Richards' *Life* is a more impressionistic account of those formative years, while Mick Jagger, who reportedly returned a £2m publisher's advance when he couldn't remember certain details of the band's career and Bill declined to help him fill in the blanks, seems unlikely to write his own autobiography. As for Charlie Watts, who we sadly lost in late 2021, he generally shunned the spotlight throughout his Stones career, and Brian Jones, of course, is long since gone… more's the pity.

This is also not a definitive history of the band's early shows, because it comprises over 600 individual recollections of encounters with the Stones and it would be unrealistic to expect everyone who saw them or dealt with them in some way to have perfect recall. In some instances, the accounts I have reproduced contradict each other. Some tales will have been embellished over the years and other memories will be incomplete. The Rolling Stones have not, of course, been averse to being economical with the truth themselves over the years, and their manager Andrew Loog Oldham famously engineered early headlines for the band by encouraging outrageous stories in the popular press. But what I have been most struck by is the number of people who, on seeing my plea for stories, contacted me and began their communication with 'I saw your letter and it brought the memories flooding back' or similar.

# THE ROLLING STONES IN THE SIXTIES: A PEOPLE'S HISTORY

The memory can play tricks and support acts or venues will have been misremembered. Where possible I have tried to correct such errors. In a handful of instances, I have had to triangulate the information provided by a contributor (the date, the venue and the supporting artists) to successfully identify a show and have edited the entry accordingly. I was unable to verify one enticing account suggesting that the Stones, Jimi Hendrix, Cliff Richard and Olivia Newton John all appeared at the same small club in the west of England and so have omitted it. Everything else is how it has been told to me. I have tried not to rewrite history as it has been recalled.

From their first show outside South-East England, at the Outlook Club, Middlesbrough on 13 July 1963 to topping the US Billboard charts with '(I Can't Get No) Satisfaction' on 10 July 1965, took the Rolling Stones just two years. This phenomenal rise was achieved in an age where there was no YouTube, Internet or *X Factor*, when - to begin with, at least - there was in Britain no Radio 1 or *Top of the Pops*, and when the music industry was still controlled by record company moguls who thought they knew what young people should be listening to better than the young people themselves. The Beatles had opened people's eyes and ears to the possibilities but were, to many teenagers, nice boys and part of the establishment. The Stones were different.

That the Stones achieved their stellar success so rapidly is testament to a number of factors. Not only was Britain ripe for change culturally and socially, emerging as it was from a period of post-war austerity, but the band had a wealth of material to draw upon. They played a phenomenal number of concerts, racking up over 800 shows around Britain by the end of 1966, along with countless TV and radio appearances. In this period, they were to learn the stagecraft that was later to earn them the accolade 'Greatest Rock'n'Roll Band in the World'.

It is perhaps hard now to understand the impact the Stones had on teenagers in the early Sixties and the extent to which their arrival challenged the established order. As Tom Wolfe said, 'The Beatles want to hold your hand, but the Stones want to burn your town.' This was certainly the view held by my father, who repeatedly stated that there were 'only three things wrong with this country – ITV, Harold Wilson and Mick Jagger'. Dad's sentiments are reflected in the parental opinions of many of the book's contributors.

## THE ROLLING STONES IN THE SIXTIES: A PEOPLE'S HISTORY

This book, therefore, is not just about the Rolling Stones. It is a window on the past, a book about what it was like to be a teenager in early Sixties' Britain, when you couldn't do things without your parents' permission, when the pubs – if you were old enough to go in them - shut at 10.30pm and when there were only two TV channels. BBC2 did not begin airing until 20 April 1964 and Channel 4 was more than 20 years away. Britain in 1962 was still in the clutches of post-war austerity, with rationing coupons still a live memory for many. Teenagers hadn't really been invented until the Rolling Stones came along and opened people's eyes to what was possible.

This book also contains accounts of their early appearances elsewhere in the world, including their first US tour and the impact they had on teenagers there. In the US particularly, the impact of the Stones on teenage perspectives on life comes through in people's recollections.

A couple of housekeeping issues:

Keith was born Keith Richards but dropped the 's' from his surname in 1963 at the suggestion of the Stones then manager Andrew Loog Oldham to sound more hip. He only reinstated it in the 1970s. I refer to him, as have most of my contributors, as Keith Richards.

Although ticket prices were and are still often set by the promoter, the Rolling Stones have regularly attracted criticism for the admission prices they charge. The stories from my contributors demonstrate that this has been a feature since the beginning of their career, whether because ticket prices in the Sixties seemed great value than they do in the modern era or because even then the band could command a premium.

So – this is not a definitive history. It is the recollections and remembrances of the people who were there – in the front row, in the wings, in the side alley waiting for autographs – from 50 or more years ago. Time will have blurred some memories and polished others. But the stories are fascinating, whether you are a Rolling Stones fan or a social historian. They paint a picture of a more innocent time, when five young men from London and the South-East of England exploded onto the British music scene and shared their enthusiastic for R&B and the blues with an unsuspecting world. This is the story of what it was like to see the Rolling Stones perform in the early Sixties.

Here it is. How it was. Ladies and gentlemen, the Rolling Stones...

**THE ROLLING STONES IN THE SIXTIES: A PEOPLE'S HISTORY**

THE ROLLING STONES IN THE SIXTIES: A PEOPLE'S HISTORY

# MARQUEE CLUB
## 12 JULY 1962, LONDON, UK

*The Rolling Stones perform as a group for the first time with a line-up containing Mick Jagger, Keith Richards and Brian Jones. The band go on to play a further twelve times in the period to the end of October 1962, principally at the Ealing Jazz Club.*

# STUDIO 51, KEN COLYER'S JAZZ CLUB
## NOVEMBER 1962, LONDON, UK

**I WAS THERE: BRIAN ROBINSON, AGE 17**

When I started getting into music at school I was into blues and, earlier, rock. I'm talking about Jerry Lee Lewis, Little Richard and people like that. But then I got into trad jazz when I started work. There was a place called the Abracadabra Jazz Club in Coventry, near where the old Coventry City FC ground was. I remember going there and seeing people like Acker Bilk, Ken Colyer and Chris Barber and I was very much into that. With Chris Barber I ended up getting into skiffle with Lonnie Donegan. And, being into that, me and some lads went down to London and went to Ken Colyer's Jazz Club, near Leicester Square. It was a Sunday and there was a door open and we went in. There was no one there but we could hear this music downstairs and went further down, opened this door and it was a bit like I assume the Cavern was, where The Beatles played - a big basement place, you know, with a stage. And there was no one there except this band at the end, obviously practicing or whatever, and my two mates said, 'Eugh, we're not staying here.' Anyway I walked right down to the front, in front of them, and the guy was sitting down playing slide guitar fantastically.

I was the main one interested in that sort of blues music then. When he'd finished I was stood in front of him and said, 'You're really good, you are. What's your name?' He said, 'Brian.' And I went, 'Oh, that's my name. Brian. What's the name of your band?' He said, 'We are going to be the Rolling Stones.'

# THE ROLLING STONES IN THE SIXTIES: A PEOPLE'S HISTORY

## I WAS THERE: NIKKI BENNETT

I grew up in Sidcup, north west Kent, and my father was a teacher at Dartford Grammar School, with Mick Jagger one of his pupils. In later years, my father sometimes got called by the press to make a comment on Mick for an article. I remember one account of Mick quickly ditching his school blazer and putting on a shiny jacket just before going on stage to receive a school prize from the headmaster.

Nikki Bennett's father taught Mick Jagger at Dartford Grammar School

I was a great Rolling Stones fan and I and my friends used to see them locally, before they became really well known, plus a girl in my class went out with Mick's brother Chris for a while. Another girl's parents knew Mick's parents quite well and remembered seeing Marianne Faithfull there, having tea once. My father taught French and German and often wondered if Mick's French had come in useful when he married Bianca!

# THE RED LION
## 23 NOVEMBER 1962, SUTTON, UK

## I WAS THERE: JOHN HINTON-STYLES

I was in a band called the Presidents and we played in Sutton in Surrey every other week with the Stones for about two years. It was the back of a pub called the Red Lion. I went back there fairly recently and couldn't believe how small it was! It was quite the thing in Sutton at the time, they had two damn good groups playing in a pub back room. It was very, very small – a couple of hundred people. They were shoulder to shoulder. You couldn't move and it was very, very hot in there. My wife used to do the handbags. She used to turn thruppence. We had a manager who was also very involved with the Stones, Glyn Johns. He was the recording manager at Decca and later did a lot of their sound work. He was our manager and was also one of our vocalists. He got us in there but of course we were doing quite a lot of work. We were probably working four or five times a week playing all over the South East and earning quite well, but we all had other jobs. I was a hairdresser. We were all zonked out when we were finished because we were working during the day and playing during the night. We played all the latest pop stuff. Being the pianist, I did a lot of Jerry Lee Lewis stuff. At that time the Stones had a pianist. They were playing sort of more rhythm and blues. The place was packed solid. They would never allow it these days. You couldn't move in there.

## I WAS THERE: ROBIN MAYHEW

I was lead guitar with the Presidents and our link with the Stones goes back to their beginnings. The late pianist Ian Stewart was a good friend of ours and our original bass player Colin Golding often helped out when the Stones did the odd gig. We knew Stu before. Stu the Chin. He was always noted for his huge chin. The Harlequin coffee bar in Cheam was a great centre for all the local music fans. Stu would come to the Harlequin and we would be talking about gigs and music and things. We saw each other outside the music side of it, because he was a keen cyclist and we had all our bikes and pushbikes and motorbikes and that sort of thing.

He had this embryo of a band that he was working in with Jagger and Richards and he was always talking to us about it, because we were already well established. He'd say, 'I've got this band starting and it sounds pretty good but come and sing some harmonies for us. That would be good.' He said to me a couple of times, 'I wish you'd come and teach our guys how to sing harmony, because they can't. It's hopeless.' The Presidents did lots of gigs all around South London. We had a residency which all came about because of a 21$^{st}$ birthday party at the Red Lion in Sutton. The guy who was having the party booked us to play there because we were the local talent. We decided, after the gig, which had gone down so well, 'We'll see if we can book the hall every Friday.' So we did, and the landlord was delighted because every Friday it was rammed with people. And Stuey – Ian Stewart – pleaded with us because our bass player used to play with the Stones now and again, because they had no bass player on the odd gigs they did. Stuey said,

'Any chance of us coming down and playing at the Lion?' So we thought about it for a bit and then we thought, 'OK.'

We were so busy we had lots of gigs to do so we weren't going to miss out. We said, 'We can do it for a few weeks every other Friday. And you can come in and do it.' At that time Bill Wyman had come down and he'd seen the Stones or he might have seen us. He came down probably one night when they were playing bass-less, because we were playing elsewhere. When the Presidents played the Red Lion, because we were already quite well established and had a good following, it was bursting. It was absolutely rammed. And Mr Edwards the landlord loved it because he was taking loads of money. I remember one Friday night we weren't gigging so a couple of us went down to see the Stones. And there was about six people. We were getting a full house. It was a bit of a joke. It would be unmiked of course. In those days they used the house PA there, which was really crummy. It was just a couple of twelve-inch speakers hanging on the wall, so it was very poor. Stu's piano playing - which you don't really hear on any of the early Stones stuff, it's not sort of there in the foreground at all - was just brilliant.

The Red Lion had a crummy old upright piano and he would be great. I went up to the stage because one of the numbers we did was 'Sweet Little Sixteen' by Chuck Berry. And I said to Mick Jagger - I'd never met him or spoken to him - 'Can you play 'Sweet Little Sixteen'?' and they did. And Keith Richards in his autobiography mentioned the Red Lion and said, "Sweet Little Sixteen' went down well', which made me chuckle because, you know, I'd requested it but there were only a handful of people in there.

# WETHERBY ARMS
## 7 DECEMBER 1962, CHELSEA, LONDON, UK

*Following an audition at the Wetherby Arms pub in Chelsea, London, Bill Wyman is hired as the Rolling Stones bass guitarist.*

THE ROLLING STONES IN THE SIXTIES: A PEOPLE'S HISTORY

# EALING CLUB
## 12 JANUARY 1963, EALING, LONDON, UK

*The Rolling Stones play their first gig with Charlie Watts on drums.*

# RICKY TICK CLUB, STAR AND GARTER
## 25 JANUARY 1963, WINDSOR, UK

### I WAS THERE: STEVE TURNER

I was buying singles by the age of 10 and like millions of others, can still remember all the words to 'Rock Around the Clock'. My early and only attempt at musicianship floundered when I insisted my piano teacher try to teach me Elvis' 'Are You Lonesome Tonight?'. I remember the excitement of the Beatles' first album in '62, and it being lent around the class during the long freeze of that winter. The turn towards black R&B and Blues was doubtless influenced by the exotic nature of the people who were into it – the beats. R&B from the Marquee (Alexis Korner, Cyril Davis, etc) was the first English product of the R&B boom, but still with a heavy influence (and personnel) from the fading trad jazz scene.

The Windsor Ricky Tick Club was a cornerstone of the vigorous Blues and R&B scene that emerged in the early Sixties in and around West London. It started in the back upstairs room of the Star and Garter on Peascod Street, a stone's throw from the main entrance of Windsor Castle. There were also Tick off-shoots in High Wycombe and Hounslow, which covered the same musical ground, but the Windsor one was the first, established by Philip Hayward and John Mansfield.

The Star had a history of boxing and other entertainments in the upstairs back room, where the club set up, which was entered along an alleyway. The front room of the Star hosted Trad Jazz several nights a week. I first went there in 1962, aged 14. Gigs were advertised by little cardboard flyers given out or left on the pub tables. I think the normal price was four shillings (20p).

There was a bar at the Tick, but it was mainly an underage crowd.

# THE ROLLING STONES IN THE SIXTIES: A PEOPLE'S HISTORY

Underage drinking was safest in the Queen Vic, run by an irritable old guy and found down a backstreet behind the Star. Cider was 10p a pint, and on occasional police busts we would claim innocently that we were 'only' on cider. I went with there with Rusty, two years above me at Slough Technical School.

It was a 40-minute walk to Windsor from our end of Slough. We would meet up with Ivor, who lived in Burnham, Delia Shepherd from Wraysbury (Rusty's girlfriend), her friend Felicity and local girls Jenny (who I remember as a long-haired beauty in the Jane Birkin mould) and Sheila (who was heavier, good fun and beehived). The older, hip Windsor scene included Dickie Dee, Cornflakes (a mate of Mick's) and Ginevra. We wore duffle coats or black oil-skin, three-quarter length coats, jeans and Dunlop Green Stripes.

The Stones started playing there regularly in January 1963, a few months after forming and shortly after getting their residency at the Station Hotel, Richmond.

I think I was there the first time the classic Mick, Keith, Brian, Charlie and Bill line-up appeared at the Tick, and certainly no-one can say I wasn't. The Stones didn't open the Tick and I saw each of Zoot Money, the Cyril Davies All-Stars, the Graham Bond Organisation and Georgie Flame and the Blue Flames there at different times.

By about Easter 1963, the people running the Tick were producing heavy two-colour oil-paper posters with bold, rounded lettering and an anonymous silhouette of a singer, which they fly-posted around town. We soon started tracking them and peeling the posters off, sometimes before they dried, sometimes in several torn bits, to be reassembled on bedroom walls. This continued for several years and covered American Blues artists brought over as part of the Blues boom as well as groups like The Who, The Yardbirds and Spencer Davis.

Why did we first go? Did we hear the Stones at the back of the Star when we came to the front Trad room? More likely Delia, already an authority on blues artists like Lightnin' Hopkins and Robert Johnson, led us there. Delia, deep voice and eyes, straight black hair, big dog, duffel coat and duffel bag.

It was a Friday night residency, with a capacity of maybe 100. You got your wrist stamped with indelible ink as a pass-out. Occasionally the one who had paid would pass out to have the night's stamp copied in ballpoint onto the hands of others still in the Vic. The oldest looking would go to the bar in the corner to try to fool the barman.

The Stones had a small ill-lit stage area (powerfully evoked for me on their *No Security* tour nearly 40 years later, when they marooned themselves on the B-stage in the middle of the crowd at Murrayfield Stadium and sang Chuck Berry numbers). I remember the Tick as always being full, sweaty, noisy, two deep by the middle of the evening as people climbed on shoulders, dancing on the spot only. It must have got busier during their residency, which stretched beyond the release and success of 'Come On' in the early summer.

I can remember one night where Brian didn't appear, Mick making a lame joke about him being 'in bed with Flo, I mean 'flu'. Maybe he was right the first time. Rust and I re-constructed the playlist a few years ago, reasonably accurately I think ('Mashed Potato' anyone?). Apart from those details I can't remember much change over the six months and maybe dozen nights.

# EALING CLUB
## 9 FEBRUARY 1963, EALING, LONDON, UK

**I WAS THERE: TREVOR BAVERSTOCK**
Dave and I first saw the Stones in early '63. We moved into digs, just a room really, near Ealing Common station and were working at an insurance company in Harrow. We could go one stop to Ealing Broadway. I remember a fellow there called Bob Jacques saying, 'There's a good club you should go to in Ealing', and he mentioned the Ealing Club. I remember queuing outside. We were both very familiar with Chuck Berry and Bo Diddley and we had a lot of American records.

I heard someone singing 'Bye Bye Johnny'. I turned to Dave and said, 'Sounds like a good group and she's got a bloody good voice.' I thought it was a woman singer. I don't know if it was the pitch of his voice. It was very crowded – hot, smoky and generally not much air. We'd go in the entrance and the stage was on our left. I think there were just seats around the wall. I don't think there was any seating apart from what was stuck to the wall.

# THE ROLLING STONES IN THE SIXTIES: A PEOPLE'S HISTORY

## I WAS THERE: DAVID COLYER, AGE 18

The Ealing Club was absolutely packed. The group was the Rolling Stones and they were fantastic and did a load of Chuck Berry and Bo Diddley numbers. We had a few drinks then found we had no money left for more. However, we stayed until 11pm and I was exhausted after some mad dancing.

Trevor Baverstock and David Colyer enjoyed 'mad dancing' to the Stones

## I WAS THERE: TREVOR BAVERSTOCK

Although Dave has written the name of the group in the diary, I think he added it afterwards. At the time I'm sure he wrote, 'We don't know the name of the group.' There was no way we knew their name at the time.

# EALING CLUB
## 16 FEBRUARY 1963, EALING, LONDON, UK

## I WAS THERE: DAVID COLYER

We went to the Ealing Club again and paid the four shillings (20p) entrance fee. The Rolling Stones were there again and after getting our drinks we just managed to find a place to stand on the dance floor, as it was packed.

## I WAS THERE: TREVOR BAVERSTOCK

During the intermission was the only time you could really buy drinks. So I was queuing for a drink and looked behind me and one of the guitarists had come down. It was Keith Richards. He was standing behind me in the queue for the drinks and I turned around and said, 'Oh, do you want to get in front of me, mate?' I thought it was a nice gesture. He just walked in front of me. He didn't say thanks or anything. I felt like I wished I hadn't bothered.

THE ROLLING STONES IN THE SIXTIES: A PEOPLE'S HISTORY

# STUDIO 51, KEN COLYER'S JAZZ CLUB
## 3 MARCH 1963, LONDON, UK

**I WAS THERE: GINGER MATTINSON**

One of my earliest recollections is seeing Alexis Korner performing above the Roundhouse pub in Wardour Street, with Charlie Watts on drums and Mick Jagger on vocals. When the latter pair subsequently formed the Rolling Stones I was a regular visitor to Studio 51, aka Ken Colyer's Jazz Club, in Great Newport Street, where they belted out renderings of Chuck Berry, Bo Diddley and Coasters hits. Their performances at Great Newport Street were in two parallel vault-like subterranean rooms with rounded ceilings, the rooms joined by a wide archway in the central wall, and the band played at the far end of the left-hand one. The Stones were extremely popular there. It was always packed with young people, to the extent that there was not really space to dance.

I always felt the band members were a bit aloof, they seemed to keep themselves to themselves and didn't interact or socialise with their fans. Perhaps even in those early days they were aware of their importance.

My two best friends and I had girlfriends out of a group of girls from Maidenhead/Marlow way. That group included sisters Jean and Chrissie Shrimpton, the latter being Mick Jagger's girlfriend at the time. In spite of this, we never crossed paths with the Stones.

**I WAS THERE: ANDREW CRISP**

One of the great names in old style jazz in the Fifties and Sixties was Ken Colyer. In fact, he was a sort of God amongst the purist enthusiasts. He had a club called Studio 51 in Great Newport Street in the West End of London. As well as regular evening jazz sessions they had R&B on Sunday afternoons. The

Andrew Crisp moved like Jagger after harmonica lessons from Mick

Stones usually featured. Naturally, being a blues lover, I tried to get up to London as often as possible. At the time I was trying to learn to play the harmonica – the 'harp' – but not making much headway. I just could not make that whining, bending sound that the greats of the instrument such as Little Walter made. So in the interval of a Sunday afternoon Stones session, I asked the singer and harp player, whose name wasn't really known then, for some tips. He invited me into the rudimentary dressing room and we sat down and traded harmonica licks. I learned to play the harp thanks to Mick Jagger.

## I WAS THERE: ADELE TINMAN, AGE 16

I was quite lucky in my family in that my uncle was a pianist and had a lot of jazz records, and I was into jazz strangely enough, sort of, more than I was into anything else. There were people like Alexis Korner who were around then, and Cyril Davies. Alexis was a bluesman, and it was him more than anyone else who first introduced people to Muddy Waters and all the American blues legends. I suppose the Stones picked up on that. Alexis was very well known as a bluesman. I certainly remember also seeing Cyril Davies. They were all around, playing that sort of American blues. The other person who brought people over was Chris Barber. They had these early packages where they had people like Sonny Terry and Brownie McGhee. It was so uncommercial then. It was like an underground.

I would have been at college with my friend Barbara Heasman at that time. Barbara mentioned there was this band and she was going out with this bloke called Keith and that they played every Sunday afternoon at this club off Leicester Square in Great Newport Street. I said, 'Oh, that sounds good' and that's why I went. All Barbara said to me was, 'I'm going out with this bloke called Keith who plays the guitar.'

It was No.51, and a basement, virtually next door to the Photographer's Gallery. It was a Sunday afternoon. It wasn't even a Sunday evening. It was an afternoon session at Studio 51.

Why did we go to see them? For me it was always the music. Whenever Mick used to introduce a number, he'd always say, 'This is a Muddy Waters number' or, 'This is a Howlin' Wolf number.' In other words, he'd always mention where he got it from. I always remember them doing that and thinking 'yeah', then of course it encouraged you to go out and find the originals.

It was very different in those days - we didn't have that much American music on radio. There was a chap I used to go out with who was a harmonica player called Ray and he used to play in the intervals. He used to start playing when we were all standing there in the interval and I think Mick didn't like that very much. It was competition! I was quite underage for going in clubs. I think they weren't licensed because I remember people used to go to the pub next door. Certainly Studio 51 in Great Newport Street wasn't licensed. That was Coca Cola, you know? That's why I probably went – because I didn't have to pass the 'are you 18?' test.

*In the early months of 1963, the Rolling Stones played a circuit of club and pub gigs. They held a weekly residency at Ken Colyer's Jazz Club from March 1963 until September 1963. Three to four times a week they would appear at one of Studio 51, the Ealing Jazz Club, the Red Lion in Sutton, the Ricky Tick Club at Windsor's Star and Garter, Harringay Jazz Club at the Manor House pub, the Crawdaddy Club at Richmond's Station Hotel, and the Wooden Bridge pub in Guildford.*

# THE WOODEN BRIDGE
## 30 MARCH 1963, GUILDFORD, UK

### I WAS THERE: STUART FARROW, AGE 24

I was 16 in 1957. We were in our garage with a friend of mine, John Hammond working on our scrambling bikes and suddenly this Bill Haley and the Comets came on with 'See You Later Alligator'. And we both looked at each other. It was that good. It was absolutely amazing, the music. Then of course it was all rock'n'roll up until the early Sixties. And then R&B came along. Somebody said the Rolling Stones were at

The Wooden Bridge so we just went down. I went with my brother and his friend. It was all this type of music that we liked. It had a very good rhythm to it. It wasn't very busy. You had your good-looking Billy Furys and people like that, but they were a scruffy group and a lot of people didn't bother. I remember standing around, jigging around to the music. It wasn't tremendously busy and the music was very loud. We were actually talking to Brian in between numbers. We just had a few words with him. 'Where are you playing next?', 'Are you playing so and so?' We talked to him about what they were doing and things like that. It was a good atmosphere in the pub. The music was very good. I remember Paul (Samwell-Smith) telling me he used to go over to Mick Jagger's place at Richmond. He had a flat there. And he said it was the most disgusting flat he'd ever been into. He said it was absolutely filthy. They weren't as big as people think now. I don't think Brian, my son-in-law, believed me when I said they were playing in a pub. He said, 'I'll go and have a look online so see whether they did.' I said, 'I know they did. Because we were there!'

*The Rolling Stones appeared for the first time at Eel Pie Island.*

# EEL PIE ISLAND
## 24 APRIL 1963 TWICKENHAM, LONDON, UK

**I WAS THERE: ROBIN MAYHEW**
And then, I don't know how it happened, but Stu negotiated - now with Bill Wyman in the band - to get to Eel Pie Island. And the guy there took them on, and they got a residency there. From then it took off. For a while we thought we were unlucky that somebody from Eel Pie Island had come, because they'd heard the Red Lion was cooking on a Friday night and they came on a night when the Stones were on, and they got the gig. If they'd come on our Friday, we might have got it! I think they got it through Stu's diligence and his negotiating the gigs. And they lived over that way, more towards Richmond. So they probably had a little bit of a following locally, and they could do a bit more, you know.

# EALING CLUB
## 27 APRIL 1963, EALING, LONDON, UK

### I WAS THERE: DAVID COLYER

We saw them a lot at the Ealing Club, plus the Station Hotel in Richmond, Studio 51 in Leicester Square, and The Marquee in Wardour Street. Their music was great and reproduced the sounds of rhythm and blues classics from America, and sometimes sounded better than the original recordings. I didn't always feel their recordings lived up to their live performances, and they used to have an excellent piano player in the band - Ian Stewart - but he didn't take part in their success.

### I WAS THERE: TREVOR BAVERSTOCK

We saw them nine times at the Ealing Club. They also had a pianist, who we learned later was Ian Stewart. He was one of the ones who winged it. We also saw them in a pub opposite Richmond station - the Station Hotel - once or twice.

# CRAWDADDY CLUB, STATION HOTEL,
## 12 MAY 1963, RICHMOND, LONDON, UK

### I WAS THERE: TONY DONALDSON, AGE 20

I was living in Twickenham and working in Richmond as a hairstylist in a top hairdressing salon. One lunchtime I was in the L'Auberge coffee bar by Richmond Bridge when somebody, possibly the Stones' manager, was handing out tickets to see the group play in the back room of The Station Hotel, opposite Richmond Station. I went along with my girlfriend to see them that weekend and we were blown away as to how good they were.

The music they played was mainly rhythm and blues, as they were very influenced by Chuck Berry, and to this day my favourite song is 'Mona'.

Within weeks the queue to get in went from the entrance and along the street. It only cost a few shillings to get in. I can't remember exactly how much it was but possibly no more than 25p in today's money. Within a month it became so packed inside they then moved on to the legendary Eel Pie Island in Twickenham, famous as a traditional jazz venue. I had been going there for a couple of years already as I was also very keen on trad jazz and used to go along with my best mate, whose uncle, Arthur Chisnall, ran the venue, and we used to get in for free. It was perhaps the most atmospheric venue for live music and dancing you were ever likely to see, and I feel privileged to have been there so often. However, within a short time this venue also became so packed that they were again forced to leave, going on to the Athletic Club at Old Deer Park, Richmond.

Suffice to say, within a short space of time they left here as their records had started to become hits and they were internationally famous. During all this period you didn't go along just to listen to the Stones - you went to dance as well. Unfortunately for spectators, once they started doing 'proper' concerts this exciting aspect of seeing live bands was lost.

# EEL PIE ISLAND
## MAY 1963, TWICKENHAM, LONDON, UK

### I WAS THERE: JACKIE HANKINS, AGE 24

I lived in Epsom then. They lived in Epsom at one time on Upper High Street. They had a bungalow up on the hill and used to jam out there in the evenings. The youngsters knew where they were. They were just beginning to have a following. I remember going to see them in Eel Pie Island. It was a hall, quite large, and had quite a name. There was always a crowd of us. It wasn't a place you'd want to go on your own. There weren't fights, but people had a drink and were high-spirited. I've got to be honest, although I liked them it wasn't really my type of music. They weren't my favourite band. I liked The Hollies and The Searchers and Gerry and the Pacemakers.

I didn't like the jumping around. It was a bit loud and a bit in your face. Whereas the Hollies and all those were always dressed in suits, always suited and booted. Then you got to Keith and that lot, and they looked like they'd just got out of bed. They didn't look like they'd washed for a month. You see, 17-year-olds and 18-year-olds, they'd like them because it was all a finger up to society. I was a bit older.

THE ROLLING STONES IN THE SIXTIES: A PEOPLE'S HISTORY

# RICKY TICK CLUB, STAR AND GARTER
## 28 JUNE 1963, WINDSOR, UK

### I WAS THERE: DAVE DOMONE, AGE 19

It was a building behind a pub in Windsor. My memories were that we paid to get in, had our foreheads - or maybe arms - stamped so we could go back into the pub to get drinks and then return to the music. They were on a low stage in a corner and people would ask for requests of particular numbers, especially Chuck Berry and Bo Diddley, which they dutifully played. As I was, and still am, a fan of rock'n'roll, blues and R&B of the Fifties and Sixties, we were mightily impressed by the fact they knew all these numbers and could play them in what sounded to us then an authentic manner. It's a pity we didn't have mobile phones or video cameras then.

Dave Domone, rear left, with a ciggie, was mightily impressed

### I WAS THERE: ROBIN MAYHEW

Stu used to live in Pittenweem. That's where he was born. He came and stayed with my wife Nadia and I. We had a small hotel in the Scottish borders for a number of years. Stu stayed one or two nights, and we walked along the river because we were right by the Tweed and talked not about music but about life in general. It was lovely. And he went on up to Pittenweem and his friends and family. And then he sadly died. Stu was a lovely man and sadly missed. We were living in Scotland at the time and came down for the funeral in Randall's Park, Leatherhead. And there was a wake held at the Caddington Golf Club, and Jagger and Richards were there. No words were exchanged.

The only other opportunity I had to speak to Mick Jagger was when David Bowie executed Ziggy Stardust at the Hammersmith Odeon – 3 July 1973. There was a great big party afterwards at the Café Royal. Jagger was there with Bianca, and Angie Bowie and Bianca were dancing around, and Bowie was with Jagger, and I went to say goodbye. It was time to go and I went to see David to say, 'Good luck, mate, whatever you do. It's been great working for you,' and Jagger went, 'Neh neh neh

neh neh.' Taking the piss, you know? I felt like saying to him, 'Remember when I requested 'Sweet Little Sixteen'?' It was very crummy - that first gig I saw of the Stones. That early time at the Red Lion - you wouldn't have thought they were going to go anywhere.

*The Rolling Stones released 'Come On', a cover of a Chuck Berry song, on 7 June 1963. It was a recording the band was later to disown, complaining that it didn't reflect their sound. But it was their first single and the first opportunity for many people outside the club circuit in London to hear them on national radio.*

### I WAS THERE: JOHN HINTON-STYLES
We got to know each other quite well. But when they actually started to get somewhere and get a record out, that was when it all changed.

## SCENE CLUB
### 11 JULY 1963, LONDON, UK

### I WAS THERE: TREVOR BAVERSTOCK
There was hardly anybody there. The place was empty. There was a stage at the end of a sparse hall-like area. The Stones came down from the stage and were standing around. We were standing very close. They came down for a break and Jagger, speaking in a sarcastic tone, said, 'Oh, Brian Jones - the greatest jazz guitarist in the world!' I heard it clear as a bell. Jones had obviously said something, and he was mocking him, you know. We thought Brian Jones was the main man with his guitar work.

*Although they continued to gig primarily in clubs around London and the South East, the Rolling Stones began making forays into the Midlands and the North of England. Their first gig outside of the Home Counties was in Middlesbrough.*

THE ROLLING STONES IN THE SIXTIES: A PEOPLE'S HISTORY

# OUTLOOK CLUB
## 13 JULY 1963, MIDDLESBROUGH, UK

### I WAS THERE: PETER WILKINSON, AGE 21

I am the same age as Mick Jagger, give or take a month or two. I've been fortunate enough to see them twice - once in the US - but the first time was at a wonderful club in Middlesbrough called the Outlook, run by a friend of ours called John McCoy who also had a band called the Crawdaddies. The Stones played on a double bill with The Hollies. Mick Jagger sat at the back of the stage on a stool and played and sang from there.

### I WAS THERE: DAVE CONNOR, AGE 17

Middlesbrough in them days was so vibrant. It was just unbelievable. The Outlook was on Corporation Road. There used to be a crowd of mates went. That was like our 'in place' at the time. I lived just round the corner. It was only three, four minutes' walk. It was downstairs and they only had soft drinks, no alcohol whatsoever.

The Outlook was only a very, very small place. It was classed as the North vs the South. The Hollies were classed as being the North. And the Rolling Stones did their first gig outside London. The place was chock-a-block. At that point in time The Hollies were the known people. The whole place was just buzzing, completely. Years later my friend Barry Falconer bought the place. When he went into it, it was three feet deep in water. There were all these bills, bill heads - everything was just floating about in the water. Because when they moved out of the building they just left it. He even found a receipt there. If they'd paid half a crown more, they could have had The Beatles rather than the Stones. It's been knocked down now, and there's law courts there.

### I WAS THERE: BARRY JONES, AGE 16

I was an apprentice at Pickerings Lifts and there was a gang of us worked there. There was a lot of clubs around the area you needed membership for. Obviously, all of us couldn't afford them so what we did was split it so we would get different clubs'

Barry Jones loved old style R&B

membership cards. There were about 40 or 50 apprentices all around the same age. And the majority of us were into music so, on a Friday, we used to get the *NME* (*New Musical Express*) and sit outside with fish and chips then talk about, 'Is there anything on in our area?', because sometimes they advertised in the paper. And then you would say, 'Well, I'd like to go and see them - can I borrow your membership card?', so, 'Yes, you could borrow my membership card but I fancy going to the KD Club - can I borrow your membership card?' That's how a group of us worked, because we just couldn't afford it.

We did as much as we could in terms of helping each other get to see these groups and bands. In 1963 Luxembourg would be the main radio station but that one used to go off its station every now and again. In Stockton we had a shop called Leslie Brown's, predominantly a toy shop, but in the front of the shop they had two booths so if you heard a record or you knew the group's name you could go in and say, 'Have you got the latest Shadows record?' and you could go into the booth and listen to it. So when you heard something like 'Come On' by the Rolling Stones on the radio and you'd think, 'Whoa, that's different,' you'd go to Leslie Brown's, say, 'Can I have a listen to it?' That's how we got into a lot of the groups in the very early days, before they were mega.

I was right into the music, I knew both The Hollies and the Rolling Stones at that time. The atmosphere in our clubs was absolutely electric, to go and see these fellows who had a single out. For that particular night at the Outlook Club there was two of us went. We went into town first in Stockton, to a pub called the Jockers, and we had a couple of drinks in there then we got the 55, a United bus – it was red, I'll always remember that – and we went direct to the club itself. On the night we had to be there by half past seven. The Hollies came on first. The three songs I remember them playing were their hit of the time, '(Ain't That) Just Like Me', 'Rockin' Robin' and also another called 'Little Lover'. Eric Haydock played a six-string bass and got a helluva sound out of it. When the Rolling Stones came on it was the old-style rhythm and blues, how I like it. They were quite smart that night. They played 'Mona', and Mick Jagger mentioned, 'This was one Bo Diddley did', and 'Carol' and 'Come On'. And when you'd go back into work on a Monday, before you started work, everyone would be saying, 'I went to see so and so at Redcar Ballroom' or the Astoria Ballroom or The Globe, things like that. That's how it was back in them days. It was just fantastic.

# THE ROLLING STONES IN THE SIXTIES: A PEOPLE'S HISTORY

**I WAS THERE: MIKE GUTTERIDGE, AGE 17**

I can remember the date exactly, because it was my 17th birthday. I was in a band called The DenMen, a really popular local band in the North East. It was ten shillings (50p) to get in and that was one of the advantages of being in a really popular band. We got in these places for nothing. I doubt it held more than 150 people. The Stones were paid £35. There was no alcohol. It was orange or coffee or tea. So we got in late – The Hollies were on as well - and this was really just a very small coffee bar. It was quite incredible. It was the Stones' first booking outside London. After it finished Brian Jones gave me a giveaway record of 'Come On' signed by all of them, which, unfortunately, a lodger I had decided to sell down the pub a few years ago.

After that, when everybody had gone, me and the other guitarist in my band sat and had an orange juice and coffee with Jagger and Richards on this little stage, literally just sat having a chat and a coffee with them. I remember asking Keith Richards about the start of 'Down the Road Apiece'. It was a little bit of an anathema at the time, so he said 'yeah, sure I'll show you.' He demonstrated it, not plugged in, with the Epiphone Riviera he used, then said, 'Here', so I tried it on Keith's guitar. It's just a triad formation on A, which is pretty commonplace now, but the Stones had it off to a tee at the time. And they were wearing these boots and of course I was in this band from Middlesbrough Art College, so I said, 'I like those boots' to Mick Jagger, and he said 'Yeah, man, these are Chelsea boots.'

# CORN EXCHANGE
## 20 JULY 1963, WISBECH, UK

**I WAS THERE: BRIAN THURLEY**

I saw the Rolling Stones in 1963. They played Wisbech Corn Exchange, not far from me. I admit to not remembering much about the gig, but they played 'Come On', which they had recently released and which is still my favourite from the Stones' catalogue. Brian Jones has always been my favourite of the Stones. Their earlier recordings, mostly covers, are still so exciting for me.

At that time, we had a local band called the Tea Time Four (although there were mostly five or six of them) and for a couple of years I regarded them as 'our' Rolling Stones, with longish hair and a set that was predominately Chuck Berry, Jimmy Reed, Muddy Waters and the usual American bluesmen. I remember Fats (on bass and vocals) being excited about the Rolling Stones being from London. Leader of the Tea Time Four was Boz, who was also an admirer of the Rolling Stones. He went on to play bass with King Crimson and Bad Company. Fats eventually joined Brian Auger's band on bass.

# RICKY TICK CLUB, STAR & GARTER
## 26 JULY 1963, WINDSOR, UK

**I WAS THERE: STEVE TURNER**
Late on in the Stones' residency at the Tick, while 'Come On' was still in the charts, we met Mick. Rusty, Delia and I caught the last train home from Windsor to Slough, with not many other passengers. Mick was at the end of the carriage on his own. He came over to get a light - none of us would think of approaching him, you had to be cool! Here's a rough reconstruction of the conversation:

Mick: Have you got a light? (Delia gave him a light)
Rusty: Any ideas what your next record will be?
Mick: No, we might do a live song. Y'know, we sound better live.
Me: What do you think of The Beatles?
Mick: Fucking Beatles! No, they've been very good to us. They might write a song for us for the next single.
Me: Do you think of yourselves as an R&B band? (The current argument was could an authentic R&B band have a hit record without being a pop band, selling out, etc?)
Mick: Yeah. (He then gave us a mini lecture about R&B's origins in race music in the States)
Me: How old are you all?
Mick: I'm 19, Keith's 19... Brian's... Bill's... and Charlie's 21!

The train arrived in Slough and Mick legged it to catch the connection to Paddington.

# THE ROLLING STONES IN THE SIXTIES: A PEOPLE'S HISTORY

# CALIFORNIA BALLROOM
## 27 JULY 1963, DUNSTABLE, UK

### I WAS THERE: DAVID ARNOLD, AGE 17

I can't recall who amongst my group of friends developed an interest in the Rolling Stones, but one of us read about them in early summer 1963. Their unkempt appearance and the fact that they played a lot of Chuck Berry and Bo Diddley songs proved to be a lot more appealing than the more conventional image of The Beatles. Five of us went in a car. We were all living in Bedford, 20 miles away. They performed on the second stage - the opposite end of the hall to the main stage - and apart from the girls that were with them there was just the five of us standing at the stage looking at the first half of their performance.

I remember they did 'Jaguar and the Thunderbird', a Chuck Berry song. They used to do 'I'm Moving On' as well, and 'Walking the Dog', 'Hi-Heel Sneakers' and 'Can I Get a Witness?'. At the interval they came and sat in the seats down at the side of the hall and we sat next to them. My friend sat next to Bill Wyman and we were just talking about how things were going and 'what time are you on next?' Bill was very co-operative and talkative and happy to exchange pleasantries.

The second half of the performance attracted a few more people. People from the other end of the ballroom thought 'this is quite interesting.' They sang 'You Better Move On' and they must have mentioned that it was an Arthur Alexander song. One of the guys remembered Arthur Alexander had written the song 'Anna' on The Beatles' first album and so after that we developed an interest in Arthur. It's strange. I probably saw them nine or 10 times but didn't buy one of their records. I've never really gone back and picked up on the Rolling Stones stuff. Looking back on it now, what jumps out at me is the fact that we saw the transformation, because the first time we saw them they were at the secondary stage rather than the main stage when there was literally no one there looking at them. Needless to say, the subsequent shows at the Cali became more and more manic. We were lucky in as much that we saw the transformation from virtual unknowns to idols in a period of a couple of months. They never did appear on that minor stage again.

# THE ROLLING STONES IN THE SIXTIES: A PEOPLE'S HISTORY

## I WAS THERE: GERRY PARKER, AGE 19

I was a vocalist in a group called the Mavericks in 1963. Top of the bill were Russ Sainty and the Nu-Notes. Second on the smaller side stage were the Stones, with us as backup. I remember Bill Wyman had a home-made bass guitar. They played their hit record 'Come On' and the crowd went mad. At the time I thought, 'What a scruffy lot we have here,' but the young girls loved the casual way they dressed. It was the start of a new era.

Gerry Parker and his group The Mavericks

## I WAS THERE: MARGARET SENIOR, AGE 18

The California Ballroom was a big dance venue. I sat next to Mick on the corner of the stage while he took a break. I talked to him for a while - I think he was interested in what we thought about them. The place was packed. It was one of the best dance halls around then. He was very friendly and I was flattered, I suppose. Little did anyone know how famous they would become in less than a year.

# THAMES HOTEL
## 30 JULY 63, WINDSOR, UK

## I WAS THERE: STEVE TURNER

The Star isn't there anymore – it was closed overnight in the mid-Sixties and then demolished to make way for new shops. The Stones' residency moved to the bigger Thames Hotel after the Star and Garter room was closed for safety reasons (the worry was the ancient floor couldn't take the bouncing crowd).

At the time we felt the closure was an authority conspiracy to kill the Windsor R&B scene, which always sat uncomfortably with the conservative royal town and the squaddies from the barracks. But the Tick was reincarnated in a condemned Victorian mansion in Clewer, down by the River Thames, a black-painted labyrinth also long demolished, although a mock-up of the interior appears in Antonioni's 1966 film, *Blow-Up*.

We followed the Stones over to the Thames Hotel for the summer residency. It was after one of those summer gigs that we sat at the end of a short wooden jetty on the Thames and agreed to meet in Trafalgar Square on New Year's Eve in 2000. I had forgotten all about it until Rusty brought it up in '99. I didn't go.

## EEL PIE ISLAND
### 14 AUGUST 1963, TWICKENHAM, LONDON, UK

**I WAS THERE: JIM MILROY, AGE 15**

I'd just started working in London. We'd heard this was the place to go. It was an old hotel, which they turned into a music venue (it had been a brothel as well in its past). You used to get there by footbridge and Eel Pie Island is not the easiest place to get to if you haven't got transport. It was called the Crawdaddy Club. I can't think who else was on the bill but there'd be a main band and two or three support bands.

They were going through all the old proper R&B and blues stuff. What people appreciated was that they explained whose stuff they were playing, like 'Little Red Rooster' by Big Mama Thornton, then say, 'And this is our version.' They were really informative. You got the impression they were enjoying it as well. With a lot of other bands you'd go and see, they'd just crib off everybody else and not tell you about it.

## WINTER GARDENS
### 16 AUGUST 1963, BANBURY, UK

**I WAS THERE: PETER JONES, AGE 16**

I was involved in the music industry. There was a band in Warwick called the Talons. They were a couple of schoolmates, a couple of other people, and their mum who used to drive the van. They had a Bedford van in those days and I was their roadie. Their music was very much blues-based so they knew of the Stones. I think they'd been down to see them play in Richmond so when we saw they

*The Talons' manager come roadie, Peter Jones*

were playing in Banbury we persuaded their mum to drive us. When I told my dad I was going to Banbury he tried to stop me because Banbury was a really rough town in those days. Ethel Usher was the lady who owned the Winter Gardens. Ethel was a great promoter and really far-sighted. She told a story that the Stones that night cost her £200. That's how much she had to pay the band. And they tried to wriggle out of the booking, because within a week or two of that they were a household name.

### I WAS THERE: TREVOR NEVETT, AGE 22

Mrs Usher was the person who owned the Winter Gardens, she used to book loads of names besides the Stones - Freddie and the Dreamers, Helen Shapiro, Chas and Dave when they were with Cliff Bennett and the Rebel Rousers. It was quite the 'in' place. They had boxing, roller-skating, everything there. You'd get about 380, 400 in there easily. They were going to have the Beatles there, but they were too much money - about four or five hundred quid. So she had the Stones. The Stones weren't a big thing, but they were on the way up. They were a bit scruffy. Ethel Usher sent them off to get haircuts. Mick borrowed a leather jacket off a chap who was a friend of mine called Bruce Cox. Banbury would never have got them if they'd been big, they were just about making it, really. It was a sell-out.

### I WAS THERE: DOREEN WASSELL (NÉE CLUTTON), AGE 17

I lived in Croughton, about nine miles from Banbury. A crowd of us would pile into one car for the trip there and back. The Winter Gardens was a very popular dance venue drawing teenagers from far and wide, including American servicemen from the airbases of Croughton and Heyford. I would have enjoyed wild rabbit stew and dumplings before going out for the evening. The Winter Gardens had a very strict code of dress at that time. If you weren't dressed to the mark, you weren't allowed entry. The girls wore pencil-slim skirts and the dapper boys wore winkle-pickers. After a warmup by the local band, on came the Rolling Stones. Shock and horror went across the dance floor. This group of lads were wearing jeans and looked like they hadn't changed their clothes for weeks. They had scruffy hair and were generally very untidy. How could the management allow these youngsters in and on stage when there was such a strict code of dress?

# THE ROLLING STONES IN THE SIXTIES: A PEOPLE'S HISTORY

## I WAS THERE: ELIZABETH BELCHER, AGE 17

I was at the concert in Banbury Winter Gardens. I went with a schoolfriend who had previously lived in Cheltenham and knew Brian Jones. I have an autograph signed by them all. I remember they did not seem to go down that well. Ann and I chatted to them afterwards by the cloakroom, Ann talking to Brian about life in Cheltenham.

*Elizabeth Belcher's schoolfriend knew Brian Jones*

## I WAS THERE: KEN PRATT, AGE 15

Dressed in smart casual wear, I was amazed to see this group on stage not in suit and ties, as all groups tended to dress, but in similar clothes to which we would wear during the week. At the time my hair was fairly blond, and to see this guy on stage with blond longish hair ... well, Brian Jones straight away became my hero.

That night I went into their dressing room after the show and they all managed to cadge one of my Senior Service cigarettes, and I had a good chat to them. I never saw them live again until they appeared in Coventry. Dusty Springfield was on the same bill, but when the Stones performed you couldn't hear the songs due to all the women screaming. I let my hair grow long and became a fervent fan of the Stones from then on, buying their first single, EP and LP. I must admit my love for the group faded when Brian left the group.

## I WAS THERE: JOE FREEMAN, AGE 16

The price of the tickets was 7/6 (37p). It sold out in four days. The Winter Gardens were owned by Mrs Ethel Usher, who also owned the Inn Within pub just 20 feet from the dance hall. It was designed in a Spanish style and was a popular watering hole before going to the dance hall. Mrs Usher was a very successful businesswoman. She would say about an artist, 'If they're out there I can get them.'

In 1961 she refused to book The Beatles because they were scruffy. When the Rolling Stones arrived on the Saturday morning to unload their gear and to meet Mrs Usher she told them to all go and get their hair cut or she would not let them perform. This they all promptly did.

At six o'clock that evening the Stones visited a small nightspot just 150 yards from the Winter Gardens called The Gaff. Georgie Fame played piano there before he hit the big time. They only played for one hour but for a treat Mick Jagger got up on stage and sang 'Whole Lotta Shakin' Goin' On'. The Gaff was packed to the door as usual and they gave him a great reception. The Astranaughts were Mrs Usher's resident band. They were the best band in town at the time. The Stones came on stage at about 9.15pm. They were dressed in very smart suits and ties. But Jagger soon removed some of his attire as the sweat started to flow. At the end he shouted to the audience, 'Give me a song to go out on,' and someone shouted 'Shake, Rattle and Roll', Bill Haley's big hit, this time accompanied by the Astranaughts. Jagger took it on and put it over very well using the full length of the stage. At the end they gave him a chorus of 'For He's a Jolly Good Fellow'.

**I WAS THERE: COLIN HUCKINS, AGE 16**
I was overwhelmed to be seeing them live. They performed very well and the only disappointment for me was that they were only on for a short time in the middle of the evening, whereas I expected them to come back on and close the show.

## MEMORIAL HALL
### 17 AUGUST 1963, NORTHWICH, UK

**I WAS THERE: GAY JINKS**
My boyfriend Tony (now my husband) read about a new group in the *New Musical Express* or the *Melody Maker*. As a result, we went to see the Rolling Stones at Northwich Memorial Hall.

When they came on stage we moved to the side of the hall and just watched. Most people were dancing but it wasn't too long before they stopped and moved to the edge of the stage to watch. We were all mesmerised by the group, especially Mick Jagger. After a while we noticed a young chap standing watching just by us. He was smartly dressed and wore glasses. At the interval he started to speak to my boyfriend and I, asking if we were enjoying the group and did we think they stood up to The Beatles and other Mersey groups? After a minute or two he said he had to go to the dressing room to see the boys. At this point I asked him who he was. He said his name was Andrew Loog Oldham and that he was their manager.

After a while he came back and asked if I would like a signed photograph. I said 'yes please' and he then asked my name and returned to the dressing room. When the second part of the show started, he returned and gave me a signed photograph. They wore black cord trousers, blue gingham shirts with button-down collars, black knitted ties, black leather waistcoats and Cuban heeled boots. For the second half they wore black cords, black and white dog-toothed check jackets, shirts and ties and Cuban heeled boots. We have always remembered the show and my husband has been a fan ever since, although we've never managed to see them live since.

## ATALANTA BALLROOM
### 19 AUGUST 1963, WOKING, UK

**I WAS THERE: ANDY SYLVESTER, AGE 14**

I was lucky enough to meet them soon after 'Come On' had been released at the back door of a fleapit Surrey dancehall. I chatted with Bill, Charlie and Keith before Mick and Brian pulled up in a Mini with two leggy blondes. They went straight to a coffee bar across the street called Crowns. I got their autographs, which I then lost! It was in the thick of the Mod era and nearby Guildford had a very healthy R&B scene, especially at the Ricky Tick Club.

## RICKY TICK CLUB, THAMES HOTEL,
### 20 AUGUST 1963, WINDSOR, UK

**I WAS THERE: MARTIN OSBORN, AGE 18**

One of my older brothers was working and living in the area at that time and he knew I liked bands that played Chuck Berry's music so invited me down to see the Stones. The venue was like a wooden-built village hall in the garden of the Thames Hotel pub, next to the Thames, with a lofty raftered ceiling. The Stones had recently signed with Decca and, as part of the deal, must have received new Vox AC30 amplifiers and these had been roped up in the rafters. The stage was a raised wooded area about a foot high, just about big enough to hold the band and their gear but not large enough for Mick to run around on, so he had to be content with his strange jigging and clapping semi-static dance.

Martin Osborn saw the Stones in Windsor

Bill, who I had the opportunity to chat to in the break, mostly about equipment and set-lists, only needed about a square foot to operate in so space was not a problem. There were no tickets for the night. You paid on the door about 2s 6d (13p) and the back of your hand was stamped with a rubber stamp as proof of payment.

# IL RONDO
## 24 AUGUST 1963, LEICESTER, UK

### I WAS THERE: SUSAN ALCOCK (NÉE MEASURES), AGE 17

It was quite a small venue but one my friends and I visited most weeks. It was the highlight of the week. Six of us went – myself, Joan Brown, Pamela Blakesley, Christine Hunt, Angela Bowey and Lyn Heath. The Stones were dressed alike in dark trousers and leather jerkins. I can't believe how lucky we were because even at the back of the ballroom we had an excellent view. Who would have thought at that time they would turn into the legends they are now?

### I WAS THERE: SUSAN O'LEARY

I saw them at the Il Rondo and asked Mick why he had brown suede shoes on when the others had black leather. He said some girl had kissed his black shoes and he couldn't get the lipstick off!

# THE ROLLING STONES IN THE SIXTIES: A PEOPLE'S HISTORY

## I WAS THERE: MARTIN OSBORN, AGE 18

The Il Rondo was a dance venue. I went there with my girlfriend - now my wife - and our drummer and his girlfriend. The Stones appearance had been somewhat tidied up from when we saw them at the Station Hotel and they all wore the same outfit, which consisted of a blue open-neck shirt, little black leather waistcoat, smart trousers and black Cuban winkle-picker boots. They looked like Paso Doble dancers. The music was just as good, and they still played Chuck Berry songs better than Chuck himself.

## I WAS THERE: TED GARRATT, AGE 15

When I went to see the Stones the first time, it was one of those evenings where you didn't tell your parents where you were going, and it came out afterwards. And I got the immortal line when I grew my hair that, 'You look like one of those bloody Rolling Stones.' Which wasn't meant as a compliment, but it was the best thing they could have said to me.

'Come On' was out. Aged 15 in rural Leicestershire, my background was going to De Montfort Hall in Leicester and pretty much seeing packages with The Shadows. My hot band were a band called Peter Jay and the Jaywalkers, who were always bottom of the bill. You saw Billy Fury, you saw Eden Kane and you saw Cliff Richard as well. And then in Hinckley there was a place called the George Ballroom which pretty much everybody played at – the Cream, Rod Stewart when he was in Steampacket ... everybody except The Beatles and the Stones. I went and saw Gene Vincent – I can only have been about twelve or 13 – and thought he was absolutely wonderful.

But in July 1963 or thereabouts, my father bought the *Daily Mirror*. Their pop music guy, a suit called Patrick Doncaster, did an article on the Rolling Stones with a photograph. There they were, in one of the biggest-selling national newspapers, leaning against the wall and looking what nowadays would be considered fairly respectable but wasn't at the time. I'd never heard of them before but read the article and was fascinated. A number of my friends all read the same article and then by magic the wonderfully named *Leicester Mercury* advertised that a place in Leicester called the Il Rondo on Silver Street had got the Rolling Stones appearing on August 24, 1963. We caught the bus there, sat upstairs at the Il Rondo and, as they say in all the movies, my life changed forever.

It was one of the first gigs the Stones played outside London. They kept talking about what they did 'back home' and I remember them doing 'Johnny B Goode' and how we all had to spiral our arms up in the air because that's what they did at the Eel Pie Club or the Crawdaddy or wherever. That night was absolutely fantastic. That night at the Il Rondo, they were a tidy group of boys. I don't think anybody should underestimate the absolute passion that came across, mainly from Jagger, Richards and Jones. It was pulsating. It was raw. It was exciting. After watching Eden Kane and Billy Fury at De Montfort Hall, you were absolutely gripped. It was almost like a physical sensation and got your head as well as your throat.

Just after that, they released 'I Wanna Be Your Man' and in November they played Nuneaton Co-op Hall and I went with some of the same people, again on the bus, and we were pretty sure Keith Richards was wearing the same shirt he'd worn back in August! He was dishevelled. That was a much, much bigger venue – a hall – and it was fantastic. A few weeks either side of that appearance, The Beatles played the Co-op Hall and all my friends went and – sad thing that I am – I didn't. Because I wasn't interested in The Beatles.

The Stones were based on the blues and, while at that age I didn't know a lot about it, I knew of Howlin' Wolf and Sonny Boy Williamson and John Lee Hooker, and I always think of the Stones as part of those magical threads, whereas The Beatles were more Little Richard and American pop, good as that was.

I don't remember them playing any self-penned stuff, but I was absolutely fascinated seeing the development of the Stones, both in terms of their personalities and musically. That night at the Il Rondo, Mick Jagger didn't move around very much. As I recall it, he was pretty much static. He played quite a lot of harmonica, although Brian Jones played a lot of harmonica as well at that time. And Keith Richards looked like your best friend at school. He was quite neat and tidy. So when we saw them the second time at Nuneaton Co-op Hall and thought he was wearing the same shirt, he'd become one of the Bash Street Kids in no more than three or four months.

That launched me into people like The Yardbirds, John Mayall, Graham Bond Organisation, Clapton and Beck, Page, etc. They all played in

# THE ROLLING STONES IN THE SIXTIES: A PEOPLE'S HISTORY

Hinckley. They were all part of this movement that I and my friends were leading the charge on, even though the Stones were the most popular of all of them. In our little part of the world, the Stones were considered a Mod group and were owned more by Mods, whereas The Beatles were seen as more of a rocker group, not because of their personalities but because of the music they were playing. They became a life movement of which the music was a key component. For me and my little gang, if you were coming from a blues background, it was partly an open door. It was a cultural movement. Yes, it was anti-parental. Yes, it was anti-authority. And it hit us at 14 and 15 and onwards and gave us a badge of honour, as something to aspire to in terms of attitude. My parents hated it. They didn't like any pop music.

## OASIS CLUB
### 30 AUGUST 1963, MANCHESTER, UK

**I WAS THERE: CHRISTINE MURPHY, AGE 15**

My very special memory of them was cycling after school to Manchester, locking my bike up in the city centre near a club called the Oasis then going to Kendals department store where I changed. I wore a red maxi skirt, a navy and white striped shirt which I'd attached a man's starched collar to, and patent shoes. So

Manchester Oasis Club ticket

*Christine Murphy got changed at Kendals before going off to see the Stones*

me and my friend waited outside the Oasis, autograph books in hand, and next minute there they were - our heroes! They wore elephant cord jackets with round necks, college scarves, shirts and ties, jeans and pointed shoes. We went over and they signed our autograph books and we thought how posh they were and how polite too. And, of course, so cool. I got Mick, Keith and Brian's autographs. Next minute they had gone. My autograph book, which I still treasure, is full of groups' autographs. They were always called groups. We never used the word 'band' in those days.

### I WAS THERE: GEOFF BULLOUGH

I have only seen the Rolling Stones once and that was at the Oasis Club. It was a very small club and I always stood close to the stage before any band started playing. The crowd would surge forward as the music started so I was often pushed up and found myself standing at the side of the stage. When the Stones played and this happened, I looked at Mick Jagger and Mick looked at me. Nothing was said and the show went on. The same thing happened with Manfred Mann. And for Memphis Slim, my head was pushed up against the end of his keyboard as he played his baby grand piano. He just acted like it was a normal gig.

*On 31 August 1963, the Rolling Stones played their first show outside England.*

# ROYAL LIDO
## 31 AUGUST 1963, PRESTATYN, UK

### I WAS THERE: TREFOR JONES, AGE 14

I had already bought the Stones' first single 'Come On' but was too young to attend the gig that Saturday night at the Royal Lido. However, my mates, John Ottley and David Owens, and I knew from previous Saturdays that the artistes usually arrived during the afternoon so we made our way to the Lido and stood near a cafe window which overlooked the beach.

# THE ROLLING STONES IN THE SIXTIES: A PEOPLE'S HISTORY

I think the cafe was closed to the public at that time of day because we never went inside. Inside we could see all the members of the Rolling Stones. The group came to the window grinning and waved to us. My mates and I went home having decided to return to the Lido that night because there was a place to stand outside which was at the back of the stage.

We were able to hear the band playing as a window was open, although the sound was a bit muffled. We couldn't really see them. Eventually a jobsworth came along and told us to go or he would get the police. I think he thought we were trying to play on a nearby children's amusement ride. A family friend called Bill Baines worked as bouncer at the Lido and I had already asked him to try and get autographs, the next day I had all the Rolling Stones' autographs!

Trefor Jones had already splashed out on 'Come On'

I gave half of them away to my girlfriend in 1965 and lost my own half over the years. However, when I met my wife to be in 1970, she had an autograph book. She lived in Chester and her grandfather worked at Chester Royalty Theatre so besides the Stones, the book had many Sixties artists' autographs in it, including The Beatles. I forgot to smuggle that book away after my divorce, so I'm doomed never to have those autographs.

## I WAS THERE: IAN JONES, AGE 16

My wife to be and I saw the Stones at the Royal Lido. It's now known as the Nova. We saw all the top groups of that golden time, including The Beatles, Gerry and the Pacemakers, Dave Berry, Johnny Kidd and the Pirates, and loads more. They were introduced as coming from the Crawdaddy Club in Richmond, Surrey. All of them were untidy but that was becoming the trend with long hair. Jagger wore a grey round-neck jumper. My wife commented that he had unkempt teeth.

# THE ROLLING STONES IN THE SIXTIES: A PEOPLE'S HISTORY

## I WAS THERE: RICHARD AUSTIN

I was working at Prestatyn Holiday Camp during the 1963 season. I recall the concert was advertised around Prestatyn as being 'London's answer to The Beatles' and it was well attended.

When the Stones came on everyone clustered to the stage. I recall thinking that this group were rather ugly looking and not well dressed. I was brought up in Liverpool attending events featuring The Beatles, The Searchers and Billy Fury, all quite well dressed. It was usual for rock bands at the Lido between sessions to have a drink at the bar and I remember trying to speak with the lead singer there (I didn't know who Mick was at the time). He came across as quite stand-offish and aloof. At that time the power in England rested in London and the Home Counties, so anyone coming from up North was looked down on.

*Richard Austin and friends outside Prestatyn Holiday Camp*

## I WAS THERE: ROB DAVIES, AGE 15

I was staying with my parents in my aunt's caravan on the Bastion Road site, just behind the Lido. That night I set off for a walk with my friends

Jeff and Ken, who were staying in the next caravan. We were walking along the promenade when we heard music coming from the Lido ballroom so decided to take a look.

When we reached the Lido, we noticed a large poster saying 'London's answer to The Beatles - the Rolling Stones.' We all laughed at this as we had never heard of them and at the time The Beatles were at No.1 with 'She Loves You'. But we went to investigate. Luckily, the curtains of the ballroom had not been closed properly so we could see inside. I'll never forget that first look through the window, seeing the group on stage. I had never seen anyone dressed like that in my life. Their long hair was incredible. It was right at the end of their performance, so we only heard a couple of songs, neither of which we knew.

They then left the stage and we wandered off around the back of the Lido. At the back there were bins, empty beer kegs and assorted crates. We sat down and chatted for a few minutes. Suddenly, a door opened just to our right and down the steps came the group. There wasn't much room to get past us so at least two of them (if only I knew who!) brushed against my legs as they walked to their van a few yards away. Some of the group were carrying their guitars - no roadies then - and there were no autograph hunters or girls waiting to mob them, just three 15 year-old boys staring in amazement at these strange young men as they went on their way. Little did we know what was just around the corner for them.

## 10 SEPTEMBER 1963

*The Rolling Stones were still playing club gigs at Ken Colyer's Studio 51 in Great Newport Street, London. The Beatles dropped in on rehearsals on this date and, on hearing the Stones were struggling to decide what their next single should be, John Lennon and Paul McCartney retired to Colyer's office and finished writing 'I Wanna Be Your Man', which was to become the Stones' next 45.*

# THE RITZ
## 14 SEPTEMBER 1963, KINGS HEATH, BIRMINGHAM, UK

**I WAS THERE: TONY LEE, AGE 18**

My fiancée Joy and I danced regularly at the Elite in Handsworth and the Ritz in Kings Heath, both converted cinemas, and enjoyed upcoming British groups and occasional American artists. We were so lucky to see Gene Vincent and his Blue Caps, Frankie Valli and the Four Seasons, and - oh, I wish I could remember them all. However, the most mesmerising of them all were The Beatles and the Rolling Stones - both of whom had that special quality and excitement that captured the audience. No one danced when they were on. The Ritz had a bar beneath the dance floor where the turns often went for their drinks. Mick Jagger, waiting to be served by my side, cadged a Disque Bleu cigarette, which he still owes me!

# BRITISH LEGION HALL
## 17 SEPTEMBER 1963, HARROW, LONDON, UK

**I WAS THERE: BARRY MARSHALL, AGE 17**

The British Legion Hall had a bar and there was a hall at the back. I saw the Rolling Stones there. I think I'd bought 'Come On'. We all wore suits and stuff and I remember they had a light and it made the white collars and shirt-sleeves always come out blue. I went to Carnaby Street and bought, and still have, a black leather waistcoat and black leather tie. I bought them because the Stones had them.

**I WAS THERE: VALERIE DUNN**

I was already a very keen fan of theirs. I think they'd already brought out one record by that stage. When the gig was over, my friend, myself and my sister hung around and when they were leaving, I remember the exit backstage took you up the side of the hall.

I don't remember anyone else hanging around. We started chatting and walked to South Harrow station with them. I talked to Charlie

Watts. My dad was a jazz drummer and I remember talking to him about his drum kit, asking what make it was, him saying, 'What do you know about drums?' When I said 'Well, my father was a percussionist,' he said, 'Oh.' So I asked, 'Do you use Zildjian cymbals?' because I remember my father saying Zildjian had got rivets in them. I managed to have a reasonable conversation with him about kits. I didn't want him to think I just wanted to get off with him, I wanted him to think I was there because I respected them as musicians. I didn't talk much to the others, they were trailing along behind.

*Valerie Dunn chatted to Charlie about drumming*

When they got to the taxi rank at the station, they said, 'OK, bye sweethearts' and they waved and got in a cab. And we were, 'Oh, my God.' We were chuffed that they were happy to walk along with us. Then we got the train from Harrow back to Rayners Lane.

A friend of ours who was at the gig took photographs of them. We were still at school and I remember we met him after school and he sold us the photos for sixpence a copy.

# PALAIS
## 21 SEPTEMBER 1963, PETERBOROUGH, UK

### I WAS THERE: NICK BASFORD
Their hair was long, but neat and clean. They wore grey shirts with rounded collars, black wool ties, leather waistcoats, black bell-bottom trousers and Cuban heeled boots. Jagger was much given to bopping a tambourine or shaking maracas as he sang. 'Come On' was out but the band's repertoire was mainly covers of Chuck Berry, Bo Diddley, Buddy Holly and various Chicago or Louisiana bluesmen.

THE ROLLING STONES IN THE SIXTIES: A PEOPLE'S HISTORY

# ASSEMBLY HALL

## 28 SEPTEMBER 1963, WALTHAMSTOW, LONDON, UK

**I WAS THERE: ALAN MILES**
When the Stones played the Walthamstow Assembly Hall it was packed to capacity. The Stones could not get into their van afterwards due to the masses of fans, so they all ran for it up Farnham Avenue along Forest Road and past The Bell pub. They sat on the wall of the car park, obviously waiting for their van, until 1am in the morning, signing autographs and cuddling the girls.

*In October 1963 the Rolling Stones embarked upon their first UK tour, which was a package tour featuring a number of acts. Each group or artiste would perform twice nightly. Headliners were the Everly Brothers and, depending on the running order, the Stones were advertised as low as fifth on the bill below Bo Diddley, Julie Grant and – when he was added to the tour to help boost flagging ticket sales – Little Richard.*

*The venues were cinemas and theatres in the Gaumont and Odeon chains with a capacity of around 2,000. The tour took in 31 venues in 36 days. The Stones would play a short set of five songs before making way for the next act. Each performer played twice nightly, an early evening show typically starting at 5.45pm or 6.15pm and concertgoers ushered out of the building in time for a second house at 8.30pm or 9.00pm.*

# THE ROLLING STONES IN THE SIXTIES: A PEOPLE'S HISTORY

# ODEON THEATRE (AKA ASTORIA)
## 1 OCTOBER 1963, STREATHAM, LONDON, UK

### I WAS THERE: SUSAN MCLAREN, AGE 13

Before the concert at Streatham Astoria, I saw Brian Jones leaning out of an upstairs window. He threw a photo out, which I later got signed by Keith, but also an apple core, which I kept in a tin in the shed until it was full of maggots and my dad made me throw it out! Later I met them all and got their autographs.

Susan McLaren kept an apple - eaten by Keith Richards - in a tin

# ODEON THEATRE
## 4 OCTOBER 1963, GUILDFORD, UK

### I WAS THERE: VERONICA SEWELL, AGE 14
I went with my mother as she wouldn't let me go on my own. The Everly Brothers topped the bill and the Stones were first on. It was brilliant and I loved them from that day. They all came on and were all dressed the same in black ties, black trousers and black and white jackets. I can't remember who

else was on, but I wasn't interested. I liked the Everly Brothers but the Stones were who I wanted to see. After seeing them I used to go regularly to Guildford Odeon to see lots of people. Got lots of autographs doing all sorts of stupid things like nipping round the back, laying under coaches and things. It's horrific when I think of it now. But we loved it! I met lots of the stars round the back there. I was in love with Mick Jagger, like millions of other girls!

## GAUMONT THEATRE
### 5 OCTOBER 1963, WATFORD, UK

### I WAS THERE: DIANA WHITNEY, AGE 22

My mother-in-law had a neighbour called Queenie who worked as an usherette at the Gaumont. The Rolling Stones decided to go for a break in the town after rehearsing and when they came back they tried to get in a side entrance. Queenie would not let them in as she thought they were a scruffy bunch of boys that were trying to sneak in. They had to get hold of the manager, who let them in.

*Diana Whitney's mother-in-law's neighbour disliked those 'scruffy' Stones*

### MY WIFE WAS THERE: GERRY PARKER, AGE 19

My wife went to the Gaumont concert. She said the Stones were hard to hear from the screaming.

### I WAS THERE: BARRY MARSHALL

I had a Saturday job in a record shop and because of the trade connection I managed to get backstage at Watford. I couldn't meet the Everly Brothers but did meet the Rolling Stones, Little Richard

THE ROLLING STONES IN THE SIXTIES: A PEOPLE'S HISTORY

and Bo Diddley. I remember getting Bo Diddley's 'Pretty Thing' single autographed. I really liked Bo Diddley and Chuck Berry. They recorded for Chess and their stuff was issued in this country on the Pye R&B label. I had a long chat with Bill Wyman - it wasn't until later that I realised that he was that bit older - he actually behaved that bit older. I got the first Stones single autographed by Bill and by Mick Jagger and Brian Jones. I think Keith and Charlie had gone off somewhere.

# GAUMONT THEATRE
## 9 OCTOBER 1963, WORCESTER, UK

### I WAS THERE: SANDRA LONGMIRE, AGE 14

The Stones appeared in Worcester twice within the space of three months. My personal memories are of both Mick and Keith being very friendly and approachable, nothing like their bad boy image.

My friend and I were only 14 at the time and I remember that we ran home from school that day and quickly got changed from our school uniforms, probably into something black as that seemed fashionable at the time. Our main aim was to meet the bands and get autographs. We were really Beatles fans, but they now seemed out of our reach as the whole country was going Beatles mad.

We saw The Rolling Stones arrive on the tour coach and got them to sign our autograph books. When they came out between shows, they asked us where the nearest pub was. We walked with them, feeling very grown up, and took them to a pub called Dudfields. We then had to wait outside as we were only 14. There were two performances, their slot probably lasting no more than 20 minutes, and we used to listen with our ears pressed against the exit doors. It was quite loud and there was lots of screaming.

### I WAS THERE: ROY TAYLOR, AGE 16

My pal Phil and I were both 16. We left school early that day to see what we could see in the build-up to the concert, which we were going to that evening. We were in a local band, The Mohawks, and primarily went to see the Everly Brothers, although we were fans of this new band called the Rolling Stones too.

We went to the car park behind the Gaumont at about 4pm. Mick and Keith were sat on a wall, chatting to several girls. The stage door was open and I could hear the Stones' music being played inside. Brian, Charlie, and Bill were running through the backing of 'Fortune Teller', which I recognised as a Merseybeats song and which I think they were considering playing. Anyway, the three of them then walked through the stage door and I managed to have the briefest chat with Brian, who was carrying his green Gretsch Anniversary guitar. All I could think of to say was, 'Where did you get your guitar?' He replied, 'Sound City, man! Good place.' It was hardly earth-shattering stuff, but it made my day.

Roy Taylor, far right, with his group, Bumbly Hum

The concert was great. I remember: The Rattles, a German group who sang 'Zip-a-Dee-Doo-Dah', Bo Diddley, the Duchess and Jerome, who produced that wonderful Bo Diddley beat and the Everly Brothers, who closed the show. The Stones closed the first half. I remember 'Come On' and then a fantastic sound as Brian played slide on their current single, 'I Wanna Be Your Man', which The Beatles had given them. There was a lot of screaming, but nothing like what it was for The Beatles, who I had seen at the same venue in May.

## GAUMONT THEATRE
### 10 OCTOBER 1963, WOLVERHAMPTON, UK

**I WAS THERE: IVAN JACKSON, AGE 19**
I went with a schoolfriend who I lost touch with many years ago. It was possibly the first or second gig I ever went to. The Stones were bottom of the bill, which also included Chuck Berry, Little Richard, Bo Diddley, plus others. In those days sets were short - often 20 minutes from

the top act. But even at that stage the Stones were so different and a force to be reckoned with, and certainly a band with a big future, an alternative to The Beatles, who were getting a bit too much attention.

It was a super line-up. That was the only time I have seen the Stones live as I never have been a large venue follower of anyone. Last year I was looking at some Ronnie Wood prints in a local gallery and the gallery assistant asked if I liked the Stones and if I had ever seen them live. I answered, that although I had followed the Stones for many years, I hadn't seen them live. Prompted by my wife I was able to put the record straight.

*Ivan Jackson saw the Stones at the bottom of the bill in Wolverhampton*

## GAUMONT THEATRE
### 11 OCTOBER 1963, DERBY, UK

**I WAS THERE: MOIRA ALLEN, AGE 15**

As a schoolgirl I wasn't allowed to go to the shows, although I didn't have the money anyway, but was able to go down after school to wait at the stage door, see who ventured out after the matinee and collect as many autographs as possible. On this particular day a group of young lads from a group we'd vaguely heard of came out of the stage door, signed a few books, chatted a bit, then casually strolled over to the Wimpy Bar across the road and sat enjoying their coffees. No one had followed them in or approached them inside - perhaps we were too polite in those days. Afterwards they got into the minibus to return to their hotel, which would have been either The York or The Clarendon, both on Midland Road. Of course, it was the Stones.

We had an advantage over those who'd been at the concert as by the time it was over they were too late to get autographs and have 'real' contact with their idols. I remember thinking Brian Jones was the best looking and of course when I decided to sell those autographs a few years ago his signature and the anecdote helped a lot. The fact that when I'd said, 'Thank you' to Mick Jagger for signing he looked straight at me and said, 'No, thank *you*!' had me telling the tale for ages.

When they became so famous within the next couple of years, it was great to realise that I was there when they were first starting out. I had many other autographs in my book and sold one or two more, but that encounter made the deepest and most lasting impression on me.

### I WAS THERE: COLIN BROWN, AGE 17

When the Rolling Stones appeared at the Gaumont I was living at home. I was into all the latest groups. Other people I remember on the gig were Julie Grant, The Flintstones and Bo Diddley with Jerome and the Duchess. A mystery surprise guest came on and it was the great Little Richard. The Rolling Stones were very good, with Mick as usual full of energy and of course Brian Jones on guitar. They played their latest release, 'Not Fade Away'. Good times. Good gigs.

### I WAS THERE: BARBARA CASTLE

Me and a group of friends went to the Gaumont in Derby to see the Rolling Stones. They came on the stage dressed in black trousers and little black and white checked waistcoats. We thought they were fantastic. My friend who was sitting in the row in front turned around and said, 'Shall we scream?' We all fell about laughing.

### I WAS THERE: BARBARA ZOPPI

The Stones were bottom of the bill. The Everly Brothers were at the top. I remember they played four songs and bowed, because The Beatles bowed. Their hair was just past their ears, which was very long for those days, and they wore leather waistcoats like window cleaners. They did 'I'm a King Bee', 'Come On', 'Not Fade Away'. I remember Little Richard stripping, taking his shirt off, and my friend said, 'If my mum had known he was going to do that she wouldn't have let me come.' It was very risqué for those days. It's the best bill Derby's ever had.

THE ROLLING STONES IN THE SIXTIES: A PEOPLE'S HISTORY

# CITY HALL
## 15 OCTOBER 1963, KINGSTON-UPON-HULL, UK

**I WAS THERE: COLIN ALLAN, AGE 14**

I was at the concert at Hull City Hall. They played two shows and I attended the earlier house. I had bought the group's first record, 'Come On', and persuaded a few schoolmates to go to the City Hall to see them play. We were all 14. The Stones were well down the bill, below Johnny Kidd and the Pirates and Heinz. In fact, for the first house performance, there was a very small audience. Once on stage, Mick Jagger turned to us (we were on the closest bit of the balcony) and seemed genuinely pleased to acknowledge true fans. Afterwards, we went backstage and - despite being boys - were invited into their dressing room. We talked to Mick and I got the autograph of drummer Charlie Watts. Do I wish I'd kept it? You bet, it would be worth good money these days.

We were so inspired by their earthy R&B music that we formed what must have been their earliest tribute band. The only problem was that we couldn't really play, despite many hours' practise on acoustic guitars. Still, that didn't stop us miming to their records at the school's Christmas concert. As I could do a passable imitation of his dance shuffle, I was out front, gyrating like Jagger. Our act that night was to prove the highlight of my short 'pop' career, but I remained an avid fan of the Rolling Stones for the remainder of my schooldays. I like to think I was one of their first disciples … in Hull, anyway.

The second time I saw the Stones perform was at Old Trafford, Manchester in June 2018 - a gap of nearly 55 years.

**I WAS THERE: GRAEME MIDDLEYARD, AGE 17**

The Stones were supporting Heinz and main act, Johnny Kidd and the Pirates, at Hull City Hall. The concert took place a matter of weeks after I started my second and last year in the sixth form. I recall the impact the Stones had on me, and my fellow sixth-formers, certainly as far as hair was concerned. On one memorable occasion at the end of morning assembly the school Head left us in no doubt that, if the hair remained as long after the forthcoming weekend, action would be taken. Needless

# THE ROLLING STONES IN THE SIXTIES: A PEOPLE'S HISTORY

to say, the barbers in Hull were kept very busy the following Saturday.

*Graeme Middleyard had not long since started in the upper sixth*

## I WAS THERE: PETER ALTON GREEN

I saw the Rolling Stones twice in the Sixties, first in 1963 and again in 1964. Earlier the same year, The Beatles played the Majestic in Hull and the promoters probably thought a seated audience would be better for the Stones as the Beatles gig was difficult to control, probably because of the low stage. The full artist list was Eric Lee and the Aces (a local Hull group), Heinz (ex-Tornados) with backing band The Saints, whose lead guitarist Roy Phillips later became lead singer and organist with The Peddlers, Johnny Kidd

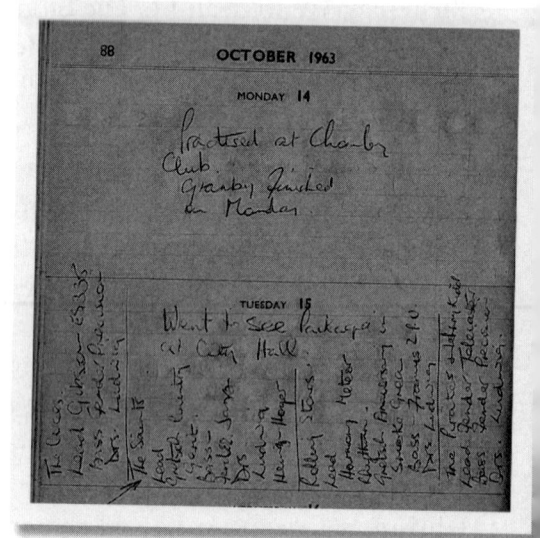

*Peter Alton Green's diary entry for the Stones' City Hall show*

and the Pirates, and the Stones. At the afternoon sound check, both the Stones and Kidd opted to use the Aces' PA system, comprising a Leak 30 Varislope Hi Fi amplifier with four-into-one custom-built mixer and two 2 x twelve inch custom built cabs with no tweeters. I had no difficulty hearing the vocals from the acts that used this PA. The actual show went very well, all the acts being well received. I do not recall the Stones facing the amount of screaming The Beatles endured at the Majestic. Gear-wise, the Stones were using Vox AC30s for the guitars, Keith playing a Harmony Meteor and Brian a smoke-green Gretsch Anniversary, while Bill had a two pick-up Framus Bass and Vox amp. They opened with 'Come On' and, according to Eric Lee, singer with the Aces, performed 'I Wanna Be Your Man' for the first time on a stage.

THE ROLLING STONES IN THE SIXTIES: A PEOPLE'S HISTORY

# ODEON THEATRE
## 16 OCTOBER 1963, MANCHESTER, UK

**I WAS THERE: LEENA TRUDY**

I skipped school to travel to Manchester to meet my friend, Marji. We had tickets for both houses. In those days there were two shows a night. But first, we had to transform ourselves from schoolgirls into at least 16-year-olds. So we made for the posh Midland Hotel and marched through the lobby to the ladies powder room. There, the transformation would take place with make-up, back-combing, and hitching our skirts up into minis, much to the amusement of the attendant. We were now ready to rock. The Rolling Stones were the opening act. After their four-song set, we didn't stay to watch the rest as we had only come to see them. We went to the bar across the road for a cola (we were only 13, going on 18). Lo and behold, we walked right into the Stones. They were eager to know how they sounded. Could we hear the bass? Was the rhythm okay? Were the drums too loud? How was Mick's voice? We sat at their table and were offered a drink. We chose vodka and lime as it sounded cool - our first alcoholic drink in a bar. They were amazed we hadn't stayed to watch the other acts; missing the Everly Brothers, Bo Diddley, etc. We said we were also going to the second house, again just to see them. We were asked to meet them again afterwards, back in the bar, to let them know if they sounded better - how did they look, were they really ok? We said we would, but we didn't. We were keen to get to t'chippy before catching the last bus home. Chips or Stones? Stones or chips? The chips won. We must be the only girls that stood up the Rolling Stones.

**I WAS THERE: JIMMY MURPHY, AGE 21**

I went with my girlfriend Pam Felstead, who was 23 at the time. Top of the bill were the Everly Brothers, who were excellent. Bo Diddley was next – OK, but repetitive, although his sister had wonderfully tight trousers. The Stones were on but, apart from 'Not Fade Away', were poor.

**I WAS THERE: STEVE BERNING, AGE 11**

My mother took my brother and me - I would have been 11 and Pete was 7. I remember them playing Bo Diddley's 'It's Alright' in a set of around 25 minutes. They had a backline of Vox AC30s and not much else. Their sound was almost overwhelmed by the sound of screaming teenage girls. My mother thought it was extremely funny when theatre staff pulled back girls, who had been hanging over the edge of the royal boxes, by hooking a yard brush over each shoulder.

## ODEON THEATRE
### 18 OCTOBER 1963, NEWCASTLE-UPON-TYNE, UK

**I WAS THERE: BRIAN SWALES**
I saw the Stones at Newcastle Odeon. Also on the bill was Bo Diddley and while he was on, a couple of the Stones came and watched his act, sitting in empty seats in front of us. Sadly I can't remember which two it was! Three of us travelled up to Newcastle, mainly to see the Everly Brothers and Bo Diddley, and we weren't impressed with this new group supporting the headliners. They appeared lost on the big stage and we thought their sound wasn't good.

*Brian Swales watched as a couple of Stones watched Bo Diddley*

## GAUMONT THEATRE
### 19 OCTOBER 1963, BRADFORD, UK

**I WAS THERE: KEN DORRINGTON, AGE 19**
By the time the tour got to Bradford, Don Everly had gone home ill, Phil carrying on alone. The rest of the bill consisted of Bo Diddley, who was very good, Mickie Most, who sang 'Sea Cruise', and The Flintstones and Julie Grant, of who I remember nothing at all. I think we paid twelve shillings and sixpence (63p) to see the concert. I remember vividly the Stones performing 'Come On' and Keith's little run across the stage, a feature at

that time. The crowds in those days mostly stayed seated and I don't recall too much in the way of screaming. It was a very different matter when The Beatles appeared at the same venue.

*Ken Dorrington recalls Keith's little run across the stage*

## GAUMONT THEATRE
### 22 OCTOBER 1963, SHEFFIELD, UK

### I WAS THERE: GILLIAN SCAIFE (NÉE BUNTING), AGE 16
I was there that day with Ann and other friends from sixth form at High Storrs Grammar School. I remember we sat upstairs and I think we went to other shows. Over the years I began to doubt it was the Rolling Stones I saw as they went on to be such global stars, but I definitely remembered Little Richard.

### I WAS THERE: DAVID ROE, AGE 22
The thing that sticks in my memory is the fact that they were all dressed in identical black-and-white dogstooth suits.

### I WAS THERE: DAVID ARNOLD
I had a houndstooth jacket made. I binned it some time ago. I did actually get one of those made at a local tailor's because I'd seen the Stones wearing them.

### I WAS THERE: BOB MILLER, AGE 16
Myself and my girlfriend Jenny Holmes went to one of the shows. I was still at Carlton Grammar School. The Stones looked great and their performance was fantastic - what we could hear of it. Jenny was focused on Brian Jones though. We went on to get married in October 1967 and are still together now.

## ODEON THEATRE
### 23 OCTOBER 1963, NOTTINGHAM, UK

**I WAS THERE: MARTIN OSBORN**
My girlfriend, my band's drummer, his girlfriend and I saw the Stones at the Odeon Theatre, Nottingham. We all had dental appointments or some other excuse and set off from Leicester to Nottingham (no motorways then) in the drummer's dad's Hillman Minx, arriving late. We asked the man on the door if the Stones had been on and he said they had, but fortunately a band called The Flintstones had opened the night so we had not missed the Rolling Stones, who closed the first half. I don't know what happened to The Flintstones.

The Rolling Stones were great as usual, but somewhat overshadowed by Bo Diddley, Little Richard and the Everly Brothers, particularly the latter. We could not believe an act could sound so good live, with their fantastic close harmonies. I don't have the tickets for this gig, but we paid about 10/- (50p) each. Good value considering tickets for A-listers can now be nearly £100, and you have to pay £35 to see some of the same acts still doing the rounds and who were on the support bill with the Rolling Stones in the Sixties.

**I WAS THERE: BILL SHELTON**
They only had a 10-minute spot and sang 'Poison Ivy', 'Fortune Teller', 'Come On' and 'Money'.

## ODEON THEATRE
### 24 OCTOBER 1963, BIRMINGHAM, UK

**I WAS THERE: JOHN TANDY, AGE 16**
I bought tickets primarily to see the Everly Brothers. I went with Sandra, my girlfriend of the time – we were both sweet 16. Don Everly wasn't there because he was taken ill at Heathrow Airport when he arrived and had been sent back home. Phil Everly was terrific in performing without his brother and one of the band filled in on vocals. Ketty Lester was on the bill that night, promoting her latest record 'Love Letters'. The Stones came

out wearing those black and white tweed jackets. My lasting impression of Jagger was him shaking his maracas and the band wearing those tweedy jackets. They were promoting their record 'Come On'. I still have the single.

# GAUMONT THEATRE
## 26 OCTOBER 1963, BOURNEMOUTH, UK

**I WAS THERE: NORMAN SQUIBB**
My pal Gary was in a local group and I was sort of roadie to them. They had no gig that night so we went into town just in case we might get a look at the acts going in or out. There was an alley at the side of the cinema so we were by the side door when the Stones came along. The chap on the door let them in and Keith Richards - last in - saw us and, probably thinking we were one of the support acts, held the door open for us. Well, we are going in! Nobody questioned who we were. We did have the hair and fashion of pop stars after all.

Anyway, we watched the entire show from the wings, at one time sharing music thoughts with the singer Julie Grant, who was on next and watching with us. When the Stones came on it was absolute mayhem in the audience but we could hear fine, which was surprising as we were level with the speakers. Well, we never forgot that night as a non-performing support act and when we were doing gigs at pubs, etc., in Weymouth, Poole and other places we enjoyed milking that story. I doubt if it could happen now, with security and the safety of stars being what it is. Keith Richards is still my favourite assistant doorman.

**I WAS THERE: GEOFF COOPER, AGE 16**
I remember little of the Rolling Stones, the show being completely dominated by Little Richard, who closed the first half of the programme with an incredible set. Bo Diddley was also very well received which, alas, was not to be the fate of the Everlys, who were booed off stage by a crowd largely made up of motorcyclists. I loved those package tours and got to see and meet some great artists from that era. For me no-one ever came close to Little Richard in terms of generating atmosphere and energy. Brilliant!

### I WAS THERE: PAT SQUIBB (NÉE PEARSON), AGE 15

That era was a fabulous time to be a teenager. I used to go with my friend Carol Gibbons. On one occasion when seeing the Stones, one of the friends we were with managed to get on the stage and got me Charlie Watts' drumstick, which I still have.

### I WAS THERE: MARGARET GRAY, AGE 17

I went to the first concert they played there, and used to have the programme, plus a photo sold at that event. Unfortunately, I sold it when we moved in 2007 for £40. I also had a great A4-size black and white picture of the group which either came with the programme or I purchased as an extra.

I used to see the queues in the Winter Gardens of people waiting for tickets to go to see The Beatles and for some reason I didn't join them. I had seen the Rolling Stones on *Top of the Pops* and was immediately impressed - what a performance! I remember having a discussion about it in the Poole Wimpy bar with a young man who said, and I quote, 'They are scruffy long-haired oiks and they will never last.' I often wonder if he remembers that conversation.

It was the very first music show I had ever been to and was so exciting. I also bought their first LP and EP and used to play them over and over. I don't think I had to queue for tickets. Of course, the lovely Brian Jones was there as well. It did seem that most of the audience, and it was packed, were girls of my age. We had seats on the left and in the middle. We watched the show, the Stones coming on to deafening screams. At the time it was Keith who had my attention and I shouted 'Keith!' along with all the other screamers. We could not hear much of the music because the noise level was so very loud. We sat down for the Stones. How very civilised.

## GAUMONT THEATRE
## 27 OCTOBER 1963, SALISBURY, UK

### I WAS THERE: PETER WOOD, AGE 28

All the rage then were The Beatles, who were not my 'scene'. I was more into American Blues, Jazz, Bob Dylan, the Stones, and if I wanted something completely different, The Shadows. When the Stones came to the Gaumont Theatre (now the Odeon) in the New Canal, Salisbury, they had barely a following out of their London clubs circuit, or so it seemed. I went with Anne, who I had just married, my best mate Len Watts and his partner Eileen. The only real number I recall them performing was The Beatles' 'I Wanna Be Your Man'.

What I'll never forget though is that Len had an A35 van and was giving Anne and I a lift home. We lived at the bottom of Devizes Road. We were holding on in the back. There were no windows except the driver's and the passenger's. The windows were open and I was trying to gauge our whereabouts. I called out 'here it is' and he just braked. Behind us there was a squeal of brakes. We held our breaths, wondering if a crunch was coming. Then a heavy reversing, followed by a quick acceleration. We all sat in wonder and then more braking as a large motor pulled up alongside. A person's head literally leaned into the van and shouted, 'What fucking clown is driving this fucking van?' With that he drew his head back and their car roared off up the road. The silence was broken by Anne saying, 'That was Mick Jagger!'

---

*Mick Jagger leaned in and shouted, 'What fucking clown is driving this fucking van?'*

---

## GAUMONT THEATRE
### 29 OCTOBER 1963, SOUTHAMPTON, UK

**I WAS THERE: JOHN MARTIN**
There was a problem with the sound system during the Stones' set for maybe one or two numbers. I'm not sure they were appreciated by the majority of the crowd as it was a seated venue. My brother collected their autographs plus those of Bo Diddley and the Duchess on a black and white postcard picture of the group in a pub outside the station before they went on. I still have it somewhere.

THE ROLLING STONES IN THE SIXTIES: A PEOPLE'S HISTORY

# ODEON THEATRE
## 30 OCTOBER 1963, ST ALBANS, UK

### I WAS THERE: BRENDA PARKER, AGE 14

My friend Annette and I were both huge fans of the Everly Brothers, which is why we went, even though their glory days were behind them by then. My dad arranged for a friend of his to drive us there, then pick us up afterwards. We had great seats right in the centre, only a few rows from the front of the stage. I was really only interested in seeing the Everly Brothers, but it was clear things were changing when the show started and the Stones did their 20 minutes or so. This was when they were still wearing their matching outfits – houndstooth-checked jackets - and they weren't polished and slick like all the squeaky clean well-scrubbed pop stars on TV.

They were rough and raw and, in spite of the matching outfits, edgy and definitely different. They only played a few numbers, and such a brief appearance didn't give them time to make much of an impact. The applause was polite but not terribly enthusiastic. Mick didn't have his dance moves down yet so they just did their allotted few numbers and left - but I thought they were great. They were exciting and I'd never heard music like that before. I became a fan on the spot and credit the Stones with introducing me to what's turned out to be a lifelong love affair with the blues. That was the night it started.

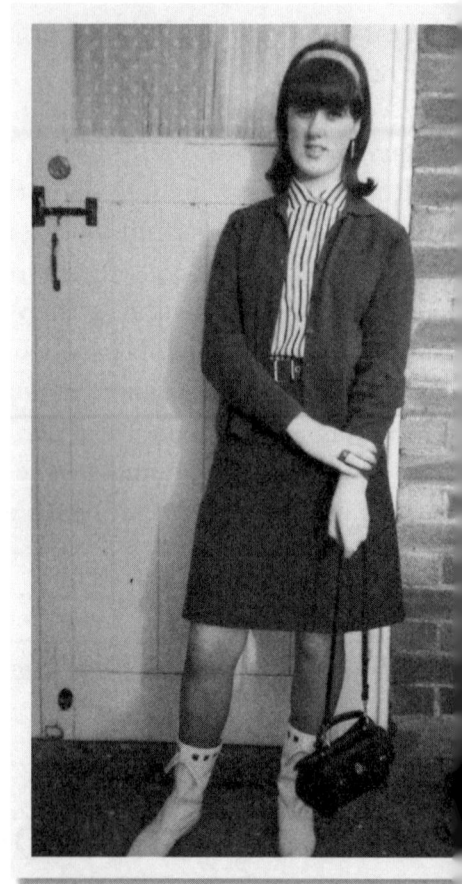

Brenda Parker recalls the Stones being rough and raw

THE ROLLING STONES IN THE SIXTIES: A PEOPLE'S HISTORY

# ODEON THEATRE
## 31 OCTOBER 1963, LEWISHAM, LONDON, UK

### I WAS THERE: SUSAN MCLAREN

The Stones were having a meal at Bettabar, near the Odeon. A few of us waited and chatted to them. It was very exciting for a 13-year-old.

---

*As the Stones' first British tour was concluding, they released 'I Wanna Be Your Man', written for them by John Lennon and Paul McCartney, as a single on 1 November 1963. It would reach No.12 in the UK charts.*

---

### I WAS THERE: ROBIN MAYHEW

They got that song from The Beatles – 'I Wanna Be Your Man' – and just whoosh!

# ODEON THEATRE
## 1 NOVEMBER 1963, ROCHESTER, UK

### I WAS THERE: TIM CROUCHER, AGE 6

I was only six years old. My babysitter screwed up her calendar and had to take me instead of her boyfriend. My only clear memory is of being frustrated that I couldn't hear the music for the noise of screaming girls.

### I WAS THERE: KAY HUNT, AGE 15

I went with my friend Jackie. I was very young and we tried but failed to climb into their dressing room via the window. The dressing room was on the second floor, so it was too high for us, even though we tried to bunk each other up to reach. We were too short. We did manage to pass our autograph books up though. I got Bill Wyman's autograph, which I still have. I really wanted Brian Jones' autograph because he was my favourite, so I wasn't that impressed with Bill's.

Kay Hunt went with her friend Jackie

### I WAS THERE: VALERIE GROVES

I went with my husband, not to see the Stones particularly, but to see the Everly Brothers. The Stones were in small print at the bottom of the bill. I wasn't impressed by the Stones – I wanted them to finish so we could see the Everly Brothers.

## GAUMONT THEATRE
### 2 NOVEMBER 1963, IPSWICH, UK

### I WAS THERE: GRAHAM DAY, AGE 13

I was 13 years old when my sister and eventual brother-in-law Michael started to take me to the package touring shows of the early 1960s. Michael had already loaned me some of his rock 'n' roll records, and I was eager to hear and see more. The Gaumont Theatre in Ipswich, with its larger-than-life manager David Lowe, was a frequent venue for these touring shows.

We started off with The Beatles and were disappointed not to hear any of the songs; the screaming of the girls was deafening. Later in the same year, we got tickets for the Everly Brothers tour, promoted by Don Arden (later Ozzy Osbourne's father-in-law). As well as the Everly Brothers with their country-influenced rock 'n' roll, there was Bo Diddley (sharply dressed in 'understated' red suit with black check pattern, playing his handmade guitars and producing rolling, rumbling rhythms), Mickie Most, who I had vaguely heard of, and The Flintstones and Julie Grant, neither of whom made much of an impression on me.

The third-place band on the bill were casually dressed and just ambled on stage and started to play. The Rolling Stones were on their first tour of the UK. The set only took around 10 to 15 minutes, comprising only half a dozen numbers, but included Chuck Berry's 'Memphis, Tennessee', which I grew to love, and - crucially – 'Route 66'. I was enthralled by the idea of an interstate highway covering thousands of miles between Chicago and California and visiting such evocative place names. I also recall Mick Jagger singing 'Come On', their first single. Unlike with The Beatles, we could hear what songs were being played.

All too soon their short set had finished, and they disappeared behind the stage curtains. But I was hooked. At secondary school we broke into two distinct camps - Beatles or Stones. The Stones always struck me a bit rebellious, anti-establishment, so being of the same ilk myself, they got my vote. That disappointed my late father as he always considered them scruffy and unkempt.

I can never forget my introduction to the Rolling Stones. Over many years since, they have formed an important, unshakeable part of the musical tapestry of my life.

### I WAS THERE: LINDA LEECH, AGE 17

Bo Diddley opened the first half and Little Richard closed it. The Stones opened the second half and The Everly Brothers closed it. What a line-up! The highlight for me was after the show when my boyfriend David - now my husband - and I popped into a pub nearly next door to the theatre and all the Stones were in there enjoying a drink and cigarette. How I wished I had got their autographs.

*After their first UK tour, the Rolling Stones returned to playing dance halls and ballrooms, attracting more interest as a result of 'I Wanna Be Your Man' having been released.*

## CAVERN CLUB
### 5 NOVEMBER 1963, LIVERPOOL, UK

### I WAS THERE: PAM PARADISE, AGE 16

The first time I saw the Stones live I had gone to see the support band. We had seen the Rolling Stones on TV and I wasn't impressed but my friend was, and she wanted to see them when they came to Liverpool to play The Cavern. We were Cavern members and my favourite band (or 'group' in 1963 language) was a blues band called The Roadrunners. I said I didn't want to go, but when my friend said the Roadies were the support act, I changed my mind.

The Roadrunners finished their set and when the Stones were part-way through theirs, I decided to go down to the front and see what the fuss

Pam Paradise (right) saw the Stones at the home of The Beatles

was about (I had been talking to friends at the back, more interesting than watching some 'Southerners'). Well, I clapped eyes on Mick Jagger in action and I've never looked back. I was 16 so Mick must have been 20. Of all the many bands I've seen since, absolutely no one has that almost animal magnetism. Yes, he's a very sexy man but it goes beyond that. People are drawn to him, both men and women. In later years watching the Stones in huge stadiums, that magnetism fills the huge space. He can hold massive audiences in the palm of his hand for every second he's on stage.

Even though it was a very long time ago, I clearly remember that first time, being so close and so overwhelmed. It was quite a month - 5th November discovering the Stones, 22nd November JFK killed. Neither event to ever be forgotten.

# QUEEN'S HALL
## 6 NOVEMBER 1963, LEEDS, UK

### I WAS THERE: GARTH CAWOOD
I started as a disc jockey. My parents had a ballroom - they were ballroom dancers. I started with a record player with a spindle where you put eight records on, but there were horrible pauses in between so

# THE ROLLING STONES IN THE SIXTIES: A PEOPLE'S HISTORY

I started to introduce the dances just to fill the pauses up. Then I met a skiffle group who came to rehearse in the ballroom one night called The Dingos - I started to manage them and eventually they went electric and went through their personnel changes and we got quite popular. Not to star status or anything like that but, locally, exceedingly popular.

Then we did a ballroom in Selby in North Yorkshire. The guys who owned it were two brothers called Christer who were doing promotions. They were going to do some promotions and one of the brothers said, 'Would you come to Leeds Town Hall? We've got a supporting band on, and we've read about them in the *New Musical Express* and *Melody Maker* but they've never been out of London. They always play at the Marquee Club. They're called the Rolling Stones. Is that alright?' We said yes, so we topped the bill, with the Rolling Stones as support.

# TOWN HALL
## 10 NOVEMBER 1963, CREWE, UK

**I WAS THERE: RAY HULME, AGE 16**

The Rolling Stones in Crewe? I was there. It was called The Sunday Star Club and it was 2/6 (13p) to get in. There were four of us - myself, Pete Hilditch, Terry Williams and Steve Buchan. We were all Rolls Royce apprentices.

We were there early as there was nothing to do on a Sunday between five and seven. We were outside the town hall when a van pulled up. It was something like an old Bedford van and out got Mick Jagger and Brian Jones. They asked if this was Crewe Town Hall. We couldn't understand them at first because of their London accents. Then we helped them

Ray Hulme saw the Stones at the Sunday Star Club

unload their gear to take it up the stairs. I'd never seen long hair like it, and Brian Jones was wearing a blue and white hooped tee shirt. They were casually dressed. We at that time were all in suits, shirts and ties. Mine was chocolate brown with bright red lining. We thought we were the bees' knees but seeing the Stones changed my outlook on how to dress. Of us four I was the only Rolling Stones fan and still am. It was a great night for me and one I'll never forget. I was devastated when Brian died.

**I WAS THERE: MICK HASSALL, AGE 16**
Me and my mate Chris Buckley went to that gig at the Town Hall. It was five shillings (25p) to get in. I was already a Stones fan. We had long straight hair, just like Brian Jones. At the halfway break me and my mate went for a pint in the other room. We were at the bar and Jones and Jagger came in and stood right beside me having a drink. A moment I will never forget.

**I WAS THERE: JOHN EDGLEY**
The event was promoted by Edgley Entertainments of which I was the founder and operated around the North West during the Sixties. We promoted dances at Crewe Town Hall on a weekly basis during this period, initially on Saturdays. We transferred from Saturdays to Sundays under the name The Sunday Star Club in November 1963. We booked the Rolling Stones to top the bill on the grand opening night, supported by the Cresters, and Frankenstein and the Monsters. I remember the event for a few reasons. The Rolling Stones' fee was very high for the time - £210. 'I Wanna Be Your Man' had only just been released and was their first big hit, 'Come On' not having been a major success. They did however have a big following in South East England. We had a whole series of major recording stars at this venue, the Stones being the second-highest earners, only surpassed by The Searchers in January 1964, having just released 'Needles and Pins'. The Rolling Stones' door attendance on the night was disappointing, only half of our house records with groups like Freddie and the Dreamers, the Tremeloes, Eden Kane, and The Searchers. In fairness, the Stones had competition on the night as The Beatles were on the Royal Variety Show on TV. And they committed the cardinal sin, blotting their copy book in arriving at the venue late.

# THE ROLLING STONES IN THE SIXTIES: A PEOPLE'S HISTORY

# PAVILION
## 11 NOVEMBER 1963, BATH, UK

### I WAS THERE: LYNN HARRINGTON, AGE 18

I grew up in Bath. I wasn't a regular Pavilion-goer but, because Brian Jones used to live near my auntie in Cheltenham and I used to visit her now and again, I liked to think I knew him. I remembered seeing something about Brian being in the Stones in the paper. My auntie said, 'That's the little boy who used to live just down the road from us.' He would have possibly been one or two years younger than me.

They were sometimes billed as Brian Jones and the Rolling Stones. There was a bit of screaming but not a lot. 'Come On' had just about charted. They had this strange instrument that looked like a kiddie's toy that they used, like a plastic kid's flute, and 'Come On' was the only thing they used it on. I remember being slightly bemused.

The support act was The Undertakers. They were also very good. Myself and a friend somehow managed to get backstage after the show and I spoke to Brian who said he could remember my auntie and her nephew – me - but he was probably just being polite. They weren't that famous then, so security wasn't very tight. I've read in some places Brian Jones wasn't a particularly friendly person but I found him very friendly that night. I got the impression he was just being polite when he said, 'I remember you from Cheltenham.' I think they were just quite pleased that a couple of people had come to the rear of the stage to see them.

### I WAS THERE: SHEENA HUNTER-HEDGES, AGE 13

I remember going to the Pav in 1963 to see the Rolling Stones. It was very difficult to get parental permission, particularly from my dad, as these events happened on Monday nights. I was at the girls' grammar school and homework took precedence over everything in those days. I didn't go with schoolfriends but with a girlfriend who lived just up the road and her schoolfriends. Her older brother was supposed to look after us. I don't recall him doing so.

Sheena Hunter-Hedges found parental permission problematic

The support band was the Colin Anthony Combo, and Colin Phillips lived two doors away from me, so that might have swung things in my favour with Dad. The support usually came on first, followed by the headline group, followed by the support, then a second appearance from the headline group.

We were able to get right up to the stage to watch these groups and one of the girls I was with feigned a faint and was lifted up on stage to recover just as the Stones were coming on for their second appearance. Mick Jagger was very concerned about her, stopped to ask if she was OK and autographed her arm or her hand. Brian K. Jones, a local promoter who always insisted on the 'K' so as not to be confused with *the* Brian Jones (as if anyone would have), was very firmly in charge and rushed us off the stage but not before this very enterprising young lady had stolen a kiss from Mick.

The Stones were very fledgling in 1963 and were good entertainment but not, in my opinion, anywhere near subsequent acts I saw there such as Johnny Kidd & the Pirates, Gene Vincent, Jerry Lee Lewis, Alan Price, and particularly Joe Brown and the Bruvvers, and Screaming Lord Sutch and the Savages. But the greatest of all had to be Little Richard. He was magnificent.

# CITY HALL
## 13 NOVEMBER 1963, SHEFFIELD, UK

### I WAS THERE: JULIA TAYLOR (NÉE BARRETT), AGE 16

I remember going to the Stones concert at the City Hall with my boyfriend at the time, Philip Battesby. They performed 'Come On' and I was impressed - they were different! I thought these lads are going to be big. They had a sound of their own. We were able

Joe Cocker was a second cousin of Julia Taylor

to listen to them OK. There was no screaming, as they were relatively unknown at the time. Joe Cocker was there. At that time he was part of Vance Arnold and the Avengers. I did not know until years later that he was my second cousin. When mum heard of Joe Cocker in the Seventies, she said it was her cousin's son, her cousin being Harold Cocker.

# MATRIX BALLROOM
## 16 NOVEMBER 1963, COVENTRY, UK

### I WAS THERE: BRIAN ROBINSON, AGE 18

The Rolling Stones were on at a place called the Matrix, in Fletchamstead Highway in Coventry. It's not there now. It was a fairly big crowd. I remember Mick Jagger walked rather gay, someone actually shouting up at him, 'Oh, what are you doing, you poof?' Charlie Watts stood up on his drums, threw the sticks down and came to the front of the stage and pointed at the bloke, and said, 'I'll have you outside, mate.' It was really funny.

### I WAS THERE: BOB DUNTHORNE, AGE 19

The Matrix was the local Saturday night dance. I went with my ex-wife. In those days you could see all the main groups for 10 bob (50p) or less. No screaming fans. In fact, sometimes group members would be at the bar, though I do not recall seeing the Stones off stage.

### I WAS THERE: MIKE RUSSELL, AGE 18

The Matrix Ballroom was really a canteen belonging to the Matrix factory. I was talked into going by a mate who had just bought their first record, 'Come On'. What a great night! Brian Jones had his lime-green guitar and Mick Jagger was on form. I can understand why the girls liked him. He had an aura about him and great stage presence.

There were more boys there than girls so no screaming I can remember. The local lads were trying to goad them, but they took no notice. No roadies then. What a great opportunity lost as it would have been so easy to have met them. They made an impression on me so much that I later went to the same venue to see the original Searchers, the Swinging Blue Jeans, Dave Berry, Cliff Bennett, and a young girl called Twinkle. There were only about 75 to 100 people there to see the Stones.

**I WAS THERE: GRAHAM BELLAMY**
I think it was six shillings and sixpence (33p) to get in. There weren't that many in the audience, maybe 100. This was a week or so before I was due to see The Beatles at Coventry Theatre. That was it for me - a Rolling Stones fan ever since.

**I WAS THERE: ARTHUR WARNER, AGE 18**
I remember going to the Matrix Ballroom to see Jerry Lee Lewis plus supporting group. The compere introduced the supporting group as a new group from London called the Rolling Stones. They opened with 'I Wanna Be Your Man'. They stood out to me due to their casual stage dress and their enthusiastic singer. Groups I remember in the early Sixties tended to be reasonable dressed on stage - booted and suited. The Stones were different on the night. The second half of the show they backed Jerry Lee all through his act.

## MCILROY'S BALLROOM
### 21 NOVEMBER 1963, SWINDON, UK

**I WAS THERE: MICHAEL NOLAN, AGE 16**
I went to all three Rolling Stones gigs at McIlroy's. At the first show the place was nearly empty and by the last show when they had become better known the place was heaving. I had actually bought the single 'Come On' before going to see them so was already a big fan. There was a story that after one of their shows their van had broken down and they were given a lift by a local taxi driver who took them to his house in Penhill to meet his mother and have a cup of tea.

**I WAS THERE: ADRIAN HEATH, AGE 18**
The Rolling Stones came on stage and with a 'one-two-three' from the lips of Mick Jagger the beat began with the number 'Come On'. When

the musicians started to strum their guitars, no sound came out and the house electrician had to quickly jump on stage to fix the fault. It took about 30 seconds for it to be all systems go. As a young bass guitarist, I loved every note.

### I WAS THERE: DAVID HYDE

I knew virtually nothing about them. After they had played a couple of numbers Mick Jagger announced they were one member short. As Jagger put it, 'The blond guy who stands here is on his way.' My friend and I didn't even know anybody was missing. The door at the back of the stage opened a bit later and Brian Jones walked on with his guitar. Magic! One number they did was 'Poison Ivy', the old Coasters' number.

### I WAS THERE: VIV FRANKLIN, AGE 17

My future wife Christine and I saw two of three Stones gigs at McIlroy's and remember them well. Christine was 16 at the time. One thing we vividly remember was that Mick Jagger told the audience that Brian Jones - the pin-up boy of the time - was delayed and might not make it to the gig, only for the crowd to see him peeping through the curtains at the back of the stage, at which everyone went wild.

Viv Franklin and wife-to-be Christine caught the Stones in Swindon

### I WAS THERE: JO POOLE, AGE 15

I went with my sister Helen in 1963. I was dreadfully upset when Brian Jones turned up late and was not on stage at the start of the show. My sister remembers me disappearing behind the curtain at the back of the stage and leaving her on her own. Afterwards I chatted to Mick and Keith, and Mick asked if I was French as my name was Josephine. Brian was leant up against

Mick Jagger asked Jo Poole if she was French

the wall and Bill and Charlie were at the back of the room. I had two promotional 'Come On' photos, signed by Mick and Keith. Luckily Helen still has hers as mine has been lost over time.

### I WAS THERE: BERNARD LINNEGAR, AGE 18

As a child my contemporaries and I were totally unaware of austerity Britain. It was just there and largely unrecognised apart from some rationing, which went on until the Fifties. Indeed, I can remember ration books. How things changed once we got to the Sixties.

I was 18 in 1963 when a new era in British pop music was emerging with the Stones and the Liverpool Sound. How fascinating it is looking back at all the fresh young acts that came to Swindon who went on to become household names. I saw a virtually unknown Cilla Black and a better-known Johnny Kidd & the Pirates at the Locarno Ballroom, which is now derelict, in another part of town.

At McIlroy's we were visited by the likes of Gerry and the Pacemakers, Freddie and the Dreamers, and a lesser-known group - as they were called then, not bands - also from Liverpool called the Big Three, one of whom I recall received an electric shock from his microphone. We of course, had to dress like our heroes, with fortnightly trips to London to buy the latest fashions in order to slay the local talent on the following Saturday night.

I was there on two of the occasions when the Stones played at McIlroy's. The attendance at the first show I saw was about the usual for a Thursday night – just a few hundred. McIlroy's Ballroom, a restaurant by day, was not huge, with a bar at one end and a tiny stage, and there crammed on said stage were the Rolling Stones. My first thoughts, I have to admit, were that they were not the most attractive people I had ever seen, perhaps not helped by the fact there was no smiling, even at each other. They seemed quite morose and made little or no attempt to communicate with the audience. But the music … wow, it was fabulous - all the old Bo Diddley stuff, which I loved. We called this R&B, but I think that means something else now.

### I WAS THERE: DAVID DAVIES

I was the drummer for the Soundcasters. It was the first time they played at McIlroy's. The Stones had only just got into the hit parade.

# THE ROLLING STONES IN THE SIXTIES: A PEOPLE'S HISTORY

McIlroy's had all the top names, as did the Locarno, so you could see anybody who was anybody for half a crown. Two and sixpence (13p). The promoter was a guy from London called Bill Chanel, and McIlroy's was a huge department store. It was a fairly big restaurant during the day and in the evenings for about three days a week they turned it into a bit of a dancehall for people. The stage was on the side, a fairly small stage, about three foot off the ground, not very deep and not that wide really. On the night we played with the Stones everybody had to set their equipment up, but the Stones' equipment was pushed to one side while we set up at the front and played our set.

There was a door at the back of the stage that went directly into the kitchens, so all the drum cases and the other cases were put down there in the kitchens and we had to change in the chefs' cubicles, where they changed out of their chefs' clothes.

We went on and did our spot and the place was beginning to fill up extremely well, and came off and obviously all the equipment had to be moved around. The Stones' amps and Charlie's drums had to be put up on the stage and we moved ours to the side. In the meantime, they were playing records as this was going on and the crowd by this time was absolutely heaving. It did break all the fire regulations because people got into trouble afterwards.

People at the back were standing on chairs and tables. They had fairly big windows at McIlroy's with big window ledges so people were stood on those as well so there was no room in the end. If it held 2,000 there would have been 2,000 in there.

Unbeknown to the crowd Charlie Watts hadn't turned up so there was a bit of a panic at the back. The promoter was getting irate about it, a lot of the crowd by this time, because they actually played a lot of records, getting a bit disgruntled. So, Mick Jagger said to me, 'Would you mind sitting in until Charlie Watts arrives?' And I said, 'No problem at all.' So I went on and sat on Charlie's kit. I used my own snare drum because drummers don't like people using their snare drum. I talked to Bill Wyman for about five minutes. He was going to give me the nod where there were certain breaks going on. He would tell me what the tempos were, where there was a shuffle or a straight-eight, and that was it. So it was decided I was going to sit in. We were going to play after the next record. We were going to start the set, the Rolling Stones' set. And then Charlie Watts turned up. So I never even got to play a song with them.

After they finished their set, we packed all the equipment up and I spent probably half an hour at least with Charlie Watts and Bill Wyman. Two lovely, lovely people. Charlie Watts' drum kit had a big burn mark on the floor tom-tom and I asked him where he'd got it from. He told me it was when they were on *Top of the Pops*. They were either on the night before or the week before and the lighting crew had put a stage lamp too close to his tom-tom and caught it on fire. And the TV appearance is why the crowd was so big, because they were just starting to get a name then. Yes, my claim to fame is that I nearly played drums with the Rolling Stones!

# THE BATHS
## 23 NOVEMBER 1963, LEYTON, LONDON, UK

### I WAS THERE: ELAINE SPINKS

I remember going with some school friends. There was a lot of excitement that we could go. There was a fair bit of screaming but nothing on the scale that came later, after a few hit records – we were still dancing round our handbags some of the time.

### I WAS THERE: ALAN MILES

The Leyton Baths was full to capacity and overflowing with people. Ronnie Kray was putting himself about, as he was in charge of the bouncers. I was in the very front row, about three feet from Brian Jones. He was playing his spearmint-green Gretsch guitar and had a silver band on his finger. I thought he had injured his finger but later came to know it was a silver band used for playing the slide guitar. As I admired Brian without actually knowing his name, I thought he may have been Mick Jagger and we argued amongst ourselves what the names were of each of the Stones, as we didn't really know who was who.

I had never seen anyone perform like Mick Jagger. He wriggled and twisted like an eel. They played 'Mona' and he played the maracas. Charlie looked bored and half asleep whilst Keith was hopping back and forwards with his Harmony guitar. Bill stood there with his bass guitar held vertically and chewed gum. As I was standing right in front of Bill's bass amp, I could hardly hear what songs were being played.

Many girls held up pictures of Brian Jones. I remember Brian studying one and his lips seemed to mockingly ask, 'Who's that?' I liked Brian and I still do. I had just begun to grow my hair long. Brian looked straight at me and gave me a couple of nods of approval. I knew the presenter at Leyton Baths, he was called Mick and he wore a nylon Beatles wig. Many girls were being carried up the stairs off the stage past Bill Wyman. Many of them had their blouses and skirts undone and they were being lifted out of the Leyton Baths for safety as they had fainted.

Some rockers to my right were yelling a few insults at the Stones, things like 'queers' and 'bum boys'. The Stones finished with 'Route 66'. Afterwards, Mick the presenter said to me, 'The rest have gone but Bill Wyman's still there' so I went in to see Bill with two of my friends. I sat next to Bill on the table and looked at Keith's Harmony and said to Bill, 'That cost £120, didn't it?' Bill replied 'No, he bought that second-hand for thirty quid.' Bill then offered me one of his cigarettes which I took, and I asked if he could autograph it for me. He said, 'No, I gave it to you to smoke, not to autograph.' He tore off a piece of his cigarette packet and autographed it. Meanwhile the two idiots who were with me had both got hold of Brian's Gretsch and were pulling it about, both wanting to strum it. I let loose a loud flurry of swear-words and told them to 'put the effing thing down.' I think Bill was a bit miffed by this and said it was time for him to go. So I saved Brian's Gretsch by my temper, but we had to say our goodnights to Bill, the nicest person in showbusiness I have met.

## I WAS THERE: BRIAN WILLIAMS, AGE 13

I live in Leyton in East London. My mother's friend Mick took a shine to me, because I had long hair. He was the compere at Leyton Baths and used to introduce the groups. I used to put the records on between the bands to help them out and get in free and see everything. So I used to be behind the stage.

I was taken into the dressing rooms and spoke to Keith Richards. The time I really remember is when they came straight from TV show, *Ready Steady Go*. I remember speaking to Brian, he was round the back of the stage, looking through the curtains at the band that was playing before them. I think it was Johnny Kidd & The Pirates. I was a 13-year-old kid and my hero was standing there. I couldn't think what to say. So I said, 'Is it true you haven't had a haircut for two years?' and he turned round to me and went, 'Don't be such a stupid little fucker. It'd be down my back if I hadn't!'

Everything just shattered. But I got over it. Then I was led into the dressing room by my mate Mick (the compere) and got to meet Keith. Mick Jagger asked if I could go over the pub and get some beers for them. I couldn't because I was too young.

I later helped Stu carrying all the gear, and got to hold that green guitar Brian played, that Gretsch.

They knocked Leyton Baths down and a Tesco stands on it now, which is terrible. The Beatles played on that stage, the Stones, Stevie Wonder. I watched them knock it down and thought, 'How can they do that?'

*The Stones played a second gig that day.*

# CHEZ DON CLUB
## 23 NOVEMBER 1963, DALSTON, LONDON, UK

### I WAS THERE: BRIAN WILLIAMS
The Stones played there. It was a small club run by a guy called Don White who also ran Leyton Baths in winter and the Coronation Gardens in summer. It was over the top of a big gents' outfitters. The stage was only two foot high. There wasn't room for more than 250 people.

### I WAS THERE: JOHN FOLLON
The Chez Don at that time was extremely popular with all Mods, and us gang of kids from Stepney were there every night of the week in those days, including my old Stepney mate Kenney Jones. On that particular night, the Stones were also appearing earlier in the evening at the Leyton Baths, a typical municipal building that doubled as a swimming pool by day and was covered over for dancing at night.

We said to the Chez Don bouncers we were off to see the Stones at Leyton. They said, 'If you leave now, you won't get back in.' We just said, 'Oh, OK. We'll see about that later.' So off we went to Leyton, and after the Stones finished their gig we hatched a plan to get back into the Chez Don. We hurried back to Dalston, waited for the Stones to turn up in their van then politely offered our services to the roadies and helped carry their gear in, mostly consisting of Charlie Watts' drum kit. The look on the faces of the bouncers, all of whom we knew well, was an absolute picture.

Whilst we were standing together listening to them and admiring them, Kenny turned to me and said, 'That's what I want to do.' The next time I saw Kenny was on *Ready Steady Go!* Yep, there before my very eyes was Kenny playing drums with the Small Faces. It was amazing.

## MAJESTIC BALLROOM
### 24 NOVEMBER 1963, LUTON, UK

**I WAS THERE: FRANK ABBOTT**

I do recall some of the Stones set list, which included 'Around and Around', 'Route 66', 'Mona', 'Off the Hook', 'Reelin' & Rockin', 'Walking the Dog', and 'Come On'.

**I WAS THERE: DAVID ARNOLD, AGE 17**

It sticks in my mind because I remember being in the queue and a girl behind us said Lee Harvey Oswald had just been shot by Jack Ruby. It was two days after JFK.

## PARR HALL
### 25 NOVEMBER 1963, WARRINGTON, UK

**I WAS THERE: CHRISTINE WOODS**

I was there with my friend Janet. We paid 7/6 (37p) in old money for the tickets. We loved the show – it was fab. Myself and Janet were upstairs chatting about the show before it started, about what it would be like and how good it would be, when a voice from behind said, 'It will be a good show.' We turned around. It was Charlie Watts!

Mick Jagger at Warrington Parr Hall

Photos: Martin Culleton

### I WAS THERE: SUSAN CLIVE, AGE 16

It was a Monday evening and I went with various friends from school. In those days it was a dance and the Stones played for quite some time as we all jived along. After they finished one of my friends knew someone backstage and we were ushered into their dressing room. Mick Jagger was so hot he took his shirt off and put on a clean one. His discarded blue shirt lay on the floor near where Brian Jones was standing, and I was pressured by my friends to ask Mick if I could have it. He said I could. I picked it up and pushed it underneath my coat and we were ushered out. We had to push our way out of the door as there were crowds of girls trying to get in. When I eventually arrived home and showed it to my mother, she wouldn't let me keep it. I don't know why. So I cut it into small pieces and gave it away to friends at school.

### I WAS THERE: MARION CASWELL, AGE 17

I went with my friend Patricia, who was 18. According to my mother I was being led astray - after all, they were long-haired louts. I think everything was moving too fast for our parents' generation then. It was a great night and we were at the front of the stage. It was quite a crush. We were able to meet them backstage. I don't know how we managed that,

# THE ROLLING STONES IN THE SIXTIES: A PEOPLE'S HISTORY

but security was not an issue then. I managed to get all their autographs – I've still got them - and shared a bottle of Coke with Mick Jagger. I was star-struck for months. I treasured the empty Coke bottle, then one day my mother threw it away. I was distraught.

## I WAS THERE: KEN MAGILL, AGE 15

I went with my older brother David. As I recall it was on a Monday night and I paid four shillings (20p) for the ticket. Four shillings represented half of my week's paper-round money. The hall wasn't jam-packed but was quite well attended. The Parr Hall on Monday nights had most of the popular groups/artists on at that time. I remember seeing Screaming Lord Sutch, the Walker Brothers, and The Hollies there. We knew a friendly bouncer who would sometimes let us in by the side door when the act had started.

Stones fan Ken Magill wasn't reliant on being let in at a side door this time

Because I really wanted to see the Stones, I paid for my ticket to ensure I got in. The Stones had just released the Lennon & McCartney song 'I Wanna Be Your Man'. I was transfixed by the length of Brian Jones' hair. He had the longest hair of all the guys. I've seen pictures now of that era and the hair looks quite tame. I was at secondary school then and wrote a piece about the concert and the rhythm and blues music scene for my English homework. To be fair it was well received by our English master, Mr Daniels. Mind you, he had long hair, but not in the rock sense. More the mad violinist.

## I WAS THERE: JOHN DOOLEY, AGE 23

It was great. I remember them playing 'Roll Over Beethoven', it was tremendous. A friend of mine had a brother who was a DJ at the time and my pal and myself were

Brian Jones with John Dooley at Warrington Parr Hall

invited to the dressing room, just a room at the back of stage. My friend was a keen photographer at the time and took a photo of Brian Jones and me chatting, which I still have. About four or five years ago I copied the photo and e-mailed it to Bill Wyman. He e-mailed me back, thanked me and told me the date. I'd forgotten that and had forgotten the name of the venue so we were both able to help each other.

# STAMFORD HALL
## 26 NOVEMBER 1963, ALTRINCHAM, UK

**I WAS THERE: STEVE WILLAMSON**
My dad was an ex-professional boxer known professionally as Frank Johnson. He was a British and Empire Lightweight Champion in the Fifties and used to work as a doorman at the Stamford Hall. My two brothers and I were young kids and every now and then Dad would take one of us with him to watch some of the bands who played there and we would usually stand in the stage side-wings and watch.

My brother, also called Frank, got to see the Stones that night. He said it was a fantastic gig despite the fact you could hardly hear anything over girls screaming. I was the unlucky one as it was my birthday. Dad took me to the Stamford Hall the following week and I saw The Merseybeats. No disrespect to them but I am now a big Stones fan.

I was talking to an older chap the other day called Shiny Shoes Tom. He said he remembered that day because he was in a pub called the Malt Shovels in Altrincham having a quiet pint when Mick Jagger and Bill Wyman walked in the side door and ordered a pint each at the short bar next to him. He knew their faces as they were at that time just breaking through in popularity after their first single 'Come On'. Tom had a chat with them and they said they were in town for a gig later that evening. Apparently the other band members were in the Barrington Hotel further down the road in Altrincham.

**I WAS THERE: CHRISTINE MURPHY, AGE 15**
I first saw them at my youth club. This was at the Stamford Hall in Altrincham and was set up by one of the teachers from the boys' school

opposite our girls' school in Timperley, Cheshire. The club was called the Young Ones Rock Club and it was run by Mr Bell, the gym teacher and an ex-boxer. There they were - slim, good looking and playing the blues. 'Walking the Dog', 'Not Fade Away' and so on. We just danced in front of the stage as they danced and played away. They were so cool and so good. Mick was so agile and moved about so much. Charlie was nonchalant on the drums. Bill was poker-faced and Keith was a different Keith then, quiet and just playing well. Brian was so cool, his long blond hair moving as he played. I was hooked and have been ever since.

# EMPRESS BALLROOM
## 27 NOVEMBER 1963, WIGAN, UK

### I WAS THERE: WILLIAM BLACKLEDGE

I was bassist and later band leader with the Wigan Empress Hall band from 1954 until 1969. There were hundreds of great acts that passed through in that time and the Rolling Stones was one of them. I'd like to say I was overawed but they were just another group passing through. I still vividly remember arriving at the Empress expecting a standard Wednesday night crowd. I was there as DJ, compere and general dogsbody. There were three groups on that night, two local groups and the Rolling Stones, who I hadn't heard of. But I had difficulty getting in. There must have been 1,500 people in Station Road, so I realised the Stones were popular.

Wigan poster

The evening went well and the Best Boys and the Cheetahs held their own as far as performances go. I'd like to say I was impressed but my feelings at the time were that groups like the Rolling Stones were threatening the livelihood of pro musicians. It was just another night at Wigan Emp.

## THE ROLLING STONES IN THE SIXTIES: A PEOPLE'S HISTORY

**I WAS THERE: RAY JONES**

I played lead guitar in a group called the Cheetahs from Widnes. We had an engagement at the Wigan Empress Ballroom, later called the Wigan Casino. I have a diary from that time and all I've got in my diary is Wigan Emp. So it looks like we didn't know when we got the booking we were actually playing on the same bill as the Stones.

The Stones were only just coming in then. They'd released one single and were maybe on their second. It was full. The ballroom hadn't seen anything like that, with queues outside. It was full to capacity, I think. There were two stages at the Wigan Emp. We didn't play on the main stage, The Stones did. We played on the stage at the other end of the ballroom and watched the Stones from a balcony looking down onto the stage. It was the first time any of us had seen hysterical girls in an audience (they were being hauled up by security guys from the Stones or from the theatre). They were pulling them up onto the stage and taking them backstage. They were getting crushed by the crowds rushing forward so it was quite novel. I'd seen The Beatles and it was a much more orderly organisation. The crowd applauded The Beatles. It went quiet when they spoke. Fellas in the audience were shouting out, 'John, can you play …' and they named a tune they knew. It was not like that with the Stones. It was squealing and screaming, hysterical really.

They'd been on the TV, therefore they were seen in the North as some of the big guys. Mick was a tremendous entertainer in those days so he would get them going.

# KING'S HALL
## 30 NOVEMBER 1963, STOKE-ON-TRENT, UK

**I WAS THERE: JUNE BROWN, AGE 13**

We went to see the Stones in the early Sixties at the King's Hall in Stoke. The fans screamed non-stop through the show so we could not hear them play. They piggy-backed on their boyfriends' shoulders so we could not see them either. The room was smoke-filled and jam-packed. We were glad to get out alive and go home.

THE ROLLING STONES IN THE SIXTIES: A PEOPLE'S HISTORY

# OASIS CLUB
## 1 DECEMBER 1963, MANCHESTER, UK

### I WAS THERE: BOB LEE, AGE 15

I couldn't get in. The Oasis was on Lloyd Street, off Albert Square, and the queue was from the club right round the block, right round the back, down Brazennose Street, where the Twisted Wheel was on the corner. So there was a queue for the Wheel and a queue for the Rolling Stones at Oasis. All these clubs had very primitive air conditioning, just like a fan blowing out, so if you ever wanted to hear any group at the Wheel or Oasis you had to stand outside near the fan and could hear them clear as day.

Bob Lee stood outside for the Stones at the Oasis

# ASSEMBLY ROOMS
## 2 DECEMBER 1963, TAMWORTH, UK

### I WAS THERE: WENDY BURTON, AGE 15

I attended this concert with my friend Paula - we were 15 years of age and are still good friends now. That night the Assembly Rooms rocked. The screaming nearly drowned out the Stones performance but nevertheless it was a fantastic evening and one I will never forget. I am almost sure their transport was a blue van. I remember it being parked at the side of the Assembly Rooms and also remember them leaving after the concert but can't

An autographed souvenir from the December '63 Assembly Rooms show

remember how many of them I managed to have a snog with. I don't know whether our parents knew where we were that evening, but it was certainly worth any trouble we may have been in when we got home.

### I WAS THERE: SANDRA HALE, AGE 16

My mates and I were there that night. It was brilliant and I have been a fan ever since. In the interval we went down to the bar and two of my mates were down there. One was with Mick Jagger and the other was with Keith Richards. What really sticks in my mind is Brian Jones and Charlie Watts were sitting down having a drink. Charlie had his legs stretched out and hadn't got any socks on. Everybody wore socks then.

### I WAS THERE: ALAN WOOD, AGE 16

My wife Carole and I were both 16 years old and both attended the concert, although we were not a couple then and didn't even know each other. I managed to get Mick Jagger to autograph a ticket. Carole went one better and managed to get a flyer for their latest release autographed by the whole band. The highlight of the night for Carole was snogging Brian Jones in the car park after the concert!

## GAUMONT THEATRE
### 5 DECEMBER 1963, WORCESTER, UK

### I WAS THERE: SANDRA LONGMIRE

After appearing in Worcester in October, they came to Worcester again in December and again played two shows. We didn't actually go to any of these shows - I suppose 12/6 (57p) was a lot of pocket money in those days. I certainly feel we picked up on the atmosphere though by waiting outside the stage door, and I feel very lucky to have grown up in those times.

In our youthful ignorance, we imagined they would remember us. Whether they did or not didn't really matter because they were again very friendly and more than willing to sign autographs - except Brian Jones, who always seemed quite aloof. Both Mick and Keith were friendly and natural young 19-year-old men. Charlie or Bill were more distant, being the older members of the band. This time I was very brave and got the autographs on my arms. In school the next day, I was asked to wash my arm and refused. I don't recall my mum being cross with me. I think she found it all quite amusing, although she preferred Gerry and the Pacemakers 'because you could sing along to his songs.' I seem to remember Gerry and the Pacemakers were top of the bill.

## OLYMPIA BALLROOM
### 8 DECEMBER 1963, READING, UK

**I WAS THERE: JULIE SUTTON, AGE 15**
Myself and some friends saw them at the Town Hall, then at the Olympia Ballroom which used to hold a Ricky Tick Club on a Sunday afternoon. The Ricky Tick Club was actually in Windsor but also staged Sunday afternoon shows in Reading for a while. We saw lots of Sixties bands, including The Animals, The Nashville Teens, the Walker Brothers, and The Kinks. In those pre-seven-day shopping days it was one of the few places open on Sundays. I don't have my membership card anymore but I do remember one particular Rolling Stones gig where a few of us managed to climb up on stage, and quickly got thrown off again. We were only about 15 and went into school the next day very proud of this adventure, only to find a couple of the other girls had actually had a lift back to Woodley with the band. Brian Jones had some family or a girlfriend living in Woodley, East Reading, and spent quite a bit of time there before the Stones really hit the big time.

**I WAS THERE: BEVERLEY CARRUTHERS, AGE 15**
My best friend loved Brian but I was for Mick, so no conflict of interests! The Stones were top of the bill and the support band was The Animals. We had never heard of The Animals. They came on dressed all in denim. Only the bin-men wore those clothes. Eric Burdon was chubby and spotty. Their songs were drowned out by all of us chanting 'we want the Stones!' until they played 'House of the Rising Sun' and suddenly they were more than okay. Then - bliss – the Stones. We didn't really listen. We were too busy shouting 'Mick!' and 'Brian!' at the top of our voices. Mick looked

wonderful - striped top and so skinny, and all that hair. Brian – such cute hair and looking sort of shy. The other three … well, they were just there. It cost us 7/6 (38p), which was worth every penny. Afterwards I bought a poster and photo and hung about. Mick signed the photo 'to Bev love Mick x'. I kept it for years and then I grew up, fell in love with David Bowie and threw the poster and photo in the bin.

## KINGS AND QUEENS HALL
### 11 DECEMBER 1963, BRADFORD, UK

### I WAS THERE: JUDITH YAXLEY (NÉE ACKROYD)

I was Student Union secretary at the Regional College of Art, Bradford. The Art College Union organised a number of social events each year and participated in planning and delivering the famous Rag Week events with other local student organisations. Our annual college highlight was the student dance, held in the Kings and Queens Hall. I was responsible for booking a band for this event in 1963.

From a list of options I chose one particular group, but they were unavailable so I chose an alternative at random as I quite liked the name - the Rolling Stones.

*Judith Yaxley booked the Stones at random*

Charging approximately £200 we thought we could afford to book this group. It was available so I confirmed the booking.

On the day the union officers worked hard setting up the hall and the band arrived in good time. We supplied them with basic refreshments in the Green Room after they set up their equipment, and the Treasurer and I manned the entrance - praying our publicity had done its work and we would take enough in ticket sales at the door to cover the band's fee. In the event we need not have worried, we were able to hand payment over to Bill Wyman who, even then, seemed to be the chap in charge of the group's finances.

The evening was a great and memorable success and the quality of the band shone through, with Mick Jagger performing as lead singer in the manner for which he was to become so famous very soon after. Only recently I met a man who said no one ever believed him when he told them of his presence at this historic event, so he was delighted when I was able to verify it had actually taken place.

### I WAS THERE: KEVIN HOLT

I saw them at a students' ball at the Queens Hall in Morley Street before they became so famous. I went with my girlfriend Carol (now my wife of 48 years) and friends Anne and Trevor. We got tickets from Anne's brother, a student at Bradford College. We were walking up the street before we went in and saw them unloading an old Commer van with their instruments in. They gave a great show considering they were an unknown band at the time. I can't remember what they sang but I remember Mick Jagger gave an announcement over the mic for a young lady to ring her mum.

Kevin Holt saw the Stones unloading their van

## HILLSIDE BALLROOM
### 13 DECEMBER 1963, HEREFORD, UK

### MY DAD WAS THERE: STEPHEN REID

My father (Bill Reid) and Jack Fallon, partners in JayBee Clubs, promoted the Rolling Stones' appearance at the Hillside Ballroom in Hereford. They called the night *Top of the Pops* - before the BBC TV show of the same name existed. The Stones made my dad a profit on the night of just under £330. They weren't as popular as Brian Poole, who drew a crowd of 1,200, or Screaming Lord Sutch (or plain Sutch, as my father noted him) who attracted 1,164 people. The Stones' attendance was 1,060. I now find out that two of my kids are going to the same schools Brian Jones went to in Cheltenham, and I see one of his former homes from my front windows.

Charlie Watts used to follow the Alex Welsh Band around, amongst others. My father, who played bass, told me this. Watts was a jazz head and loved Lennie Hastings' drumming. Lennie was on his uppers when he died in 1982 and Charlie paid for his funeral. A very cool guy and a decent thing to do.

# BATHS HALL
## 14 DECEMBER 1963, EPSOM, UK

### I WAS THERE: PAUL SONNEX, AGE 17
I was there and remember it well. The Sixties was a great time to be young and the Stones were one of several exciting new groups. I have a vivid recollection of standing in front of the stage watching Mick Jagger strut around and an expressionless Brian Jones strumming his guitar to 'You Better Move On'. The volume was tremendous and the atmosphere electric. The room was heaving with young people all having a good time. It was the first gig I attended and I remember my girlfriend and I being transfixed at the edge of the stage, totally stunned by the fabulous sound. Truly a night to remember.

### I WAS THERE: DAWN GOZDZ, AGE 16
I was accompanied by my boyfriend, later to become my husband, and also my big sister. We had a hard time persuading our dad to let us go but at the time my sister was recovering from a life-threatening illness and desperate to have some fun so dad eventually relented. The hall was so big and usually used for big brass band type of dances. It was brightly lit with normal high-watt bulbs. We went into a bare hall with a stage. The hall looked as if it was only about a third full as everyone crowded down by the stage, and some of the girls sat on their boyfriend's shoulders to get a better view, leaving loads of space at the back for the keen dancers.

# THE ROLLING STONES IN THE SIXTIES: A PEOPLE'S HISTORY

In later years it was nice to be able to say 'I saw the Rolling Stones live' but at the time it was just another weekend dance. My sister remembers people climbing in through the toilet windows see the Rolling Stones and to avoid paying an entrance fee. She enjoyed the evening and had a fantastic time, and it gave her the boost that life is for living and having fun. And luckily she is still enjoying good health and having fun today.

### I WAS THERE: KARIN STEVENS, AGE 15

I was at this performance albeit I should not have been. I was just 15 and a great Rolling Stones fan. My parents did not approve of my choice of band or their music. I was determined to see them but did not have enough money for a ticket. However, I knew the Baths very well, swimming there every day during the summer opening season for many years. On the evening of the performance myself and couple of others shimmied up one of the drainpipes and in through a small window. We thoroughly enjoyed the show. The Stones were still in their 'art school look' period and all wore black polo-neck jumpers. We did a lot of screaming. I also went to a party they held at the bungalow in Dorking Road that they rented for a while, but that's another story.

### I WAS THERE: EDDIE PATTERSON, THE PRESIDENTS

I was drummer with The Presidents at the time. For sentimental reasons I have hung on to my written record of payments received while playing with the group. My share for that gig in 1963 was the princely sum of £3. I have a vague memory that Ian Stewart played piano on a couple of our numbers, but that may have been in rehearsals.

### I WAS THERE: ROBIN MAYHEW

The Presidents were a big local draw around Sutton, Cheam and Epsom area. The guy who booked the Stones for Epsom Baths Hall knew if he booked us as well there was a good chance of getting an audience into what was quite a big venue. The Stones had just got their first chart success with 'I Wanna Be Your Man'. In those days we used to earn between three and five pounds for a gig each, which was really a basic wage, and we were doing probably four or five nights a week.

At the Epsom Baths Hall I think we went down better than the Stones actually. I know that sounds very glib, but we had such a following. We started our set with Chuck Berry's song 'Talking About You' and another friend of our band - none other than Jimmy Page - was in the wings playing harmonica. Jimmy Page knew our bass player Colin Golding and he knew me, and Stu was tinkling away on the piano. We were rather overwhelmed and I can't really remember much or anything about the Stones' performance. It didn't stick in my mind - let's put it that way.

## I WAS THERE: PETER CARDLE

In 1963 I lived in Epsom and with a group of friends we spent after-school hours swimming in the summer months in Surbiton Lagoon. In the inclement months, we frequented Epsom Baths, which we knew very well. When we heard the Rolling Stones were coming to the Baths, we polled our meagre resources and bought one ticket. Epsom Baths had a floor cover and rows of seats on either side above, with a walkway above with cinema-style crash exit doors that led onto outside gantries on either side. We knew that, so our designated ticket-holder went in and made his way to the last cinema door on the right side, just above the stage. We were in! Just below me was Brian Jones. He played that entire gig with his eyes closed.

At the same time, just off East Street, there was a pub which had a folk club. That is where I shook hands with Paul Simon when he played there.

## I WAS THERE: JANE TOMKINS (NÉE SHILLABEER), AGE 15

I was still at school near Epsom. There was a boy in my class called Robert who wanted to be my boyfriend and when he said he wanted to take me to see the Rolling Stones perform at Epsom Baths, I wasn't about to argue. The gig was, of course, fantastic and I decided to leave just before the end in order to find my way backstage to try and meet the boys and get their autographs. I was lucky to be the only fan there and they each walked past me separately, giving me enough time to ask each one to sign their autographs. I handed each

Jane Tomkins took up the offer of a special date at the Baths

of them a card which was available at the gig, with a black and white photograph of them on one side and the name of their early releases on the reverse. As the photo was predominantly black, two of them had to sign on the back. The breath-taking moment was when Brian Jones handed me his famous green Gretsch guitar to hold while he signed his autograph. Little did I realise at the time that his untimely death only a few years later would crystallise that very poignant memory.

I was so excited that I had met and spoken to the boys that I can honestly say I do not remember what happened afterwards. I can't remember how I got home or what happened to the poor boy who had so kindly taken me there - I must have brushed him aside when I next saw him in school.

## I WAS THERE: JOHN SHINGLETON, AGE 17

It was a cold night. Epsom Baths Hall was a rather tatty venue, the stage was small and what normally would have been the water was covered with a wooden floor and the audience stood there. I am pretty certain there were no seats. I was in my final year at Glyn Grammar School, Epsom at the time. Some of my mates said there was this fantastic group playing at a club in Richmond who were coming to play in Epsom and we should go to see them. Tickets were five shillings. My father, who was typical of the time, was outraged I was 'wasting my hard-earned newspaper-round money to go and see a stuffy bunch or rock 'n' roll singers.' But I went anyway.

I remember little about the music they played. I do remember Mick Jagger prancing across the stage as he still does, and he was wearing a pair of scruffy white tennis shoes and a pair of crumpled dark grey, what looked like Marks and Spencer slacks which finished with big turnups way short of his ankles. He was also wearing a white long-sleeved shirt, half tucked in. He would have confirmed my father's worst fears.

I have a vague recollection that it was far from a full house (perhaps five shillings was too much so close to Christmas) and I was very close to the stage on the right-hand side. The audience, including me, were very enthusiastic and there was a lot of cheering and yelling. At the time, this would have been a novelty, as we were all much more restrained back then.

# THE ROLLING STONES IN THE SIXTIES: A PEOPLE'S HISTORY

I am still a Rolling Stones fan but the ticket price was way too much for me the last time they visited Australia, where I now live. Sadly, the five-shilling tickets had suffered the ravages of inflation and were now 500 Australian dollars.

## I WAS THERE: BRIAN HOWARD

The Stones played the Baths Hall twice - in December 1963 and January 1964. The Fiore Coffee Bar in Bookham was one of a number of coffee bars I used in the Bookham, Leatherhead, Ashtead and Epsom areas to market some of the tickets. Epsom Baths Hall was licensed for music and dancing for 962 persons. Of course, that was for 'old fashioned' dancing and was certainly well below what our sort of event would happily accommodate. As a consequence, I ordered 1,250 unnumbered tickets for the first show, gave 850 to the box office and sold the remaining 112 (read 400!) via the coffee bars and youth clubs. Happily, no one picked up on the discrepancy.

When I ordered the posters and tickets the prices shown on them were five shillings and sixpence (28p) in advance and six shillings and sixpence (33p) on the door. By the time they arrived, I knew I had under-priced the tickets and I didn't need to offer the 'in advance' incentive. I planned to go through every poster and ticket and cross out the lower price, which would have made me over £60 extra. However, my dear mother, bless her, talked me out of it, saying, 'If you were to sell 1,250 tickets at 5s 6d each, would you be very pleased?' When I said yes, she told me not to be greedy, so I left them as they were.

When I arrived at the Baths Hall around 7pm for an 8pm start there were approximately 500 people on the steps, all without tickets. The manager, a dour Scotsman called John Smith, was very proper and couldn't be encouraged to 'look the other way' so we had to turn these additional punters away - most distressing. Whilst The Presidents were playing, the hall was very nicely full, with our uncounted 1,250 punters, but when the Stones came on the surge forward left the back third of the hall empty. Plenty of room for that extra 500.

Sadly, I don't still have the contract which, I guess, would be worth real money. However, I actually signed the contract in August before the Stones' first record 'Come On' was released. Whilst their normal

# THE ROLLING STONES IN THE SIXTIES: A PEOPLE'S HISTORY

Saturday night fee at that time was circa £60 the agent - hedging his bets - asked for 50% of the gate money. I thought about it for a few days, played around with the numbers and went back with an offer of £50 plus 20% of the gate money, which the agent accepted. My recollection is that the gate money (at least the declared level) was £300 so I ended up paying £110 for the Stones rather than the £150 I would have had to pay on the original offer from the agent. By the time The Presidents and the hall, posters and tickets were paid for I was left with something like £145. So for one night in my life, I earned considerably more than the Rolling Stones, who had to pay their agent and roadies and then share the remainder between five of them. To cap it all in December 2013, 50 years minus one day after the gig itself, I sold at auction a poster advertising the gig and an A4 signed photograph of the Stones from that night. I cleared £7,500, which I then blew on my 70th birthday party. What a great party, and we drank a toast to the Rolling Stones.

## I WAS THERE: MERVYN HARPER

Being four years older than Mick Jagger, I had already been through the skiffle and trad jazz phases by the time the Stones, The Beatles, etc. started making a name for themselves. My one indulgence in the early Sixties was Wednesday night at the Savoy Ballroom in Catford to hear Brian Poole and the Tremeloes, a band whose records never really came close to their stage act - probably the reason for Ted Lewis' error of judgment in signing them ahead of The Beatles. My contact with the Stones was second-hand, when I worked in a south-east London garage. I went to work for Car Mart Sales Limited at 163 Bromley Road, London SE6, opposite the Robertson's jam factory, in 1960 after National Service. These days it is a Turkish restaurant. Back then it was a 24-hour petrol service, and the regular night pump attendant was a strait-laced northerner, a Mr Mitchell who as far as I know never revealed his first name but who was always immaculate in pressed white overalls and a blue beret. When the Stones had been performing in London, they would frequently pull onto the forecourt late at night in their ramshackle Austin J2 van and Mr Mitchell would serve them with 10/- worth of petrol to get them home. To the surprise of those staff who had never met the Stones, and only heard scurrilous stories, Mr

Mitchell would never hear a word against them, got to know them by their first names and, when asked, would declare they were 'a really fine bunch of lads.'

# TOWN HALL
## 17 DECEMBER 1963, HIGH WYCOMBE, UK

### I WAS THERE: RUTH BOWLER (NÉE DAVY), AGE 17

I went with my 20-year-old boyfriend - now my husband. I lived in Marlow and there was nothing else of its type for miles except the Adelphi at Slough, where we saw many famous acts of the time. The hall was so packed with people that we were upstairs trying to get a good look. The sound was amazing as the acoustics were obviously very good. It was deafening and everyone was screaming and rocking to the beat. It was a wonderful evening, and they were electrifying. It was a wonderful time to be a teenager.

*The future Mr & Mrs Bowler headed off to High Wycombe for the Stones*

# LIDO
## 20 DECEMBER 1963, WINCHESTER, UK

### I WAS THERE: ELAINE HOWELLS (NÉE GILBERT), AGE 17

I wasn't actually at the Lido - my parents didn't allow me to go. However, I did see the members of the group at very close quarters when they went to the nearby Hyde Tavern during the evening.

I was at the youth club in the parish hall next door and word got around that the Rolling Stones were in the Tavern. I crept in and sat down with a friend. I was so much in awe of them that I didn't know what to say. They were of course very recognisable but there was no

# THE ROLLING STONES IN THE SIXTIES: A PEOPLE'S HISTORY

big fuss - they were just a group of lads having a much-needed drink amongst themselves and I got the feeling they wouldn't welcome attention. I remember thinking they looked distinctly unwashed. I did register at the time that this was a really big moment in my life, being within touching distance of such famous, notorious celebrities.

Elaine Howells saw the Stones at the Hyde Tavern

## I WAS THERE: BAZ MORT, AGE 18

I remember they put up the price for this show from the usual 5s (25p) to 7/6 (37p). Also, you needed to buy a ticket in advance when normally you could just turn up and get in. Maybe the 50% increase put off a few of my friends as it turned out I went by myself. In retrospect this was probably the most important gig I'd been to although I was a regular at the Lido and can also boast seeing Cliff Richard and the Shadows in Southampton at the tender age of 14. I vividly remember queuing up outside

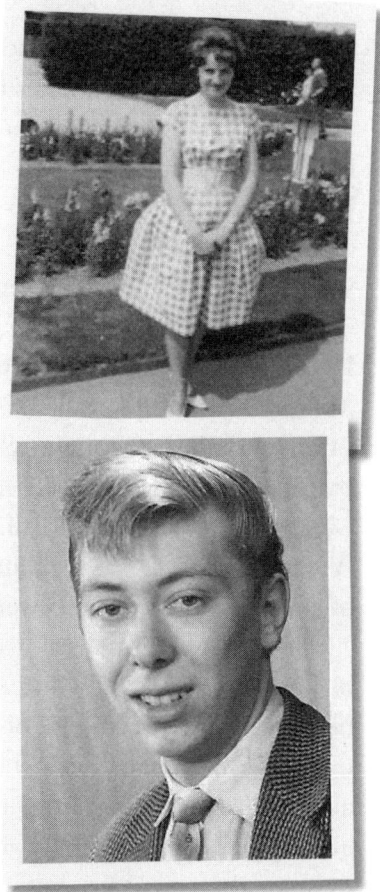

Baz Mort recalls the price increase

on a dry winter's night, having first had a couple of drinks at the Prince of Wales, now converted into flats. Inside the Lido was packed and, not being the tallest of kids, I made my way to the balcony. I managed to find a good spot in the centre with a great view of the stage. The stage wasn't very high and there were a few long-haired lads standing on the stage waiting for the Stones to appear. Down below it was packed, girls being hoisted onto shoulders so they could see. From then on it becomes a bit of blur.

I remember the Stones coming onto the stage but the only numbers I really remember are 'Come On' and 'I Wanna Be Your Man', introduced by Mick as 'our new single.' I guess they played maybe 30 to 40 minutes.

This has gone down as the legendary Winchester gig and when I tell youngsters I saw the Stones for about 35 pence in 1963 they are either in awe or disbelieving. My friend John Martin happened to be in another local pub, the Hyde Tavern, that night and in the back bar were Brian Jones, Keith Richard, Bill Wyman and Charlie Watts. He told me Mick came in and said, 'Right lads, we're on now' and off they went. I only wish I'd gone to the Hyde that night instead of the Prince.

**I WAS THERE: JOHN MARTIN**
My girlfriend and I walked into the Hyde Tavern public house on Hyde Street and all the Stones (except Mick) were lounging around in the back bar. I am sure Keith was lying on a settee. After 15 minutes or so Mick walked in wearing a scarf and a dark Crombie and just said to them all, 'We're on.' We left as well and followed them to the Lido, only a couple of minutes away. Tickets were 7/6 (37p).

They got a great reception and I remember lots of girls on the shoulders of boyfriends. After a while we went upstairs to the balcony for a much better view. They did a lot of Chuck Berry numbers plus 'Hide and Go Seek' by Bunker Hill, which I will never forget. I often wonder if any of the Stones even remember that song. Being a smaller venue, the atmosphere was brilliant and the sound was very good. It's also difficult to estimate the crowd size but it was a sell-out. There was a large following at that time in Winchester of R&B groups rather than the Liverpool/Manchester groups, which often appeared at the Lido, such as the Big Three, The Searchers, Billy J Kramer, The Hollies, and The Merseybeats. My big regret was missing the chance of seeing the Stones at the Station Hotel in Richmond early that year. I was living and working in Acton and often got invited over by work colleagues, but never made it.

# ST MARY'S HALL
## 22 DECEMBER 1963, PUTNEY, LONDON, UK

**I WAS THERE: PETE BROWN, AGE 16**
They lined up along the stage wearing leather waistcoats. Their hair was long and they looked grown up to me. I don't think there was a lot of

movement, and Mick and Brian shared the vocals and harp playing. The music was Chuck Berry and Bo Diddley plus other R&B of the time. It was very exciting. The whole evening is a bit of a blur now, as most bands at that time became relatively easy to see, but I remember it as one of the best gigs I ever saw.

# STUDIO 51, KEN COLYER'S JAZZ CLUB
## 30 DECEMBER 1963, LONDON, UK

### I WAS THERE: ADELE TINMAN

The crowds got bigger and bigger. It was a Monday night. I can remember when they did their last gig there. There were more people there by then. They sort of graduated to one evening performance there, because that was the time when they were going off to do a tour somewhere. And it was a farewell thing at the club. It wasn't a huge crowd because you wouldn't have been able to get in the club.

# DRILL HALL
## 31 DECEMBER 1963, LINCOLN, UK

### I WAS THERE: ROGER WILLIAMS, AGE 16

It was my first year at art college. There were three of us, my friend Max who was studying accountancy and a lady friend of ours - Tolly - also at the art college. It was Christmas break. None of us lived in Lincoln at the time - we were commuting students. I was living in a place called Horncastle. I don't know how we got in because I don't think we had any money. It was their first tour outside London.

The band started playing and it was the blue denim shirts and leather waistcoats because they were in Manchester a couple of days later and were on *Top of the Pops*.

After the show we were in Broadgate heading back to a flat where we were staying the night. Round about midnight we spied the Rolling Stones in a street in front of us - four of them. Not Brian Jones. We had a bottle of cider. So we caught up with them and cigarettes were exchanged. I remember Keith Richards offering us cigarettes and we had a bottle of cider and I think we shared that with them. We were 16-year-olds and they were 20/21, and a bit older in Bill Wyman's case. They were staying in the Grand Hotel - which no longer exists - on St Mary's Street. Somebody said Brian Jones stayed in the White Hart. That was it, a heady night for young teen. Tolly, wherever she is, will be able to tell her grandchildren she snogged Mick Jagger on New Year's Eve 1963. When we got back to college in January, nobody believed us.

# TOWN HALL
## 4 JANUARY 1964, OXFORD, UK

### I WAS THERE: DAVE BARDEN, AGE 18

Ann and I were courting. She was working at Morris Motors in the trim shop and I was an apprentice toolmaker at the Radiators on Woodstock Road. We travelled in that Saturday night on my motor bike. I remember parking in St Giles, me with my Beatles high-buttoned suit and Ann in her trendy Sixties mini-skirt and wearing a leather cap. What a fantastic venue. We paid at the door and walked up the grand staircase in the Town Hall, paying about a shilling to leave my suit coat and Ann's coat in the cloak room. When we got in, we were right down at the front of the stage. I remember them coming on stage via what seemed to be stairs coming up the middle of the stage. It was a great night but not a full house. They did numbers by Muddy Waters and Howling Wolf, a lot of blues numbers with Mick Jagger on mouth organ.

### I WAS THERE: NIGEL MOLDEN, AGE 15

I was a pupil at City of Oxford High School. My father worked for the company that supplied the bar at the Town Hall for Saturday night dances. They were organised by a lady called Mrs Osbourne for Bee's Catering. The perk for me was that my father could nearly always obtain two free tickets for me, hence I was able to be at the Rolling Stones appearance with a friend. By this time the popular music explosion had been generally accepted and I do not recall any scenes of hysteria or screaming. I do have a very clear memory of the band coming on stage, performing with an exotic mixture of equipment. Brian Jones was playing a green, wide-body electric guitar, and one set of speakers was a very large handmade unit. Interestingly the equipment was a problem almost from the outset. After a few minutes there was a short break as roadies ran around trying to repair something. Shortly after that a more serious problem developed and there was another break of something like 10 minutes whilst more repairs were under way. The band stayed on stage through all this and Mick Jagger, still playing maracas, mumbled a number of apologies in the almost dismissive style we have all come to recognise.

Nigel Molden had two free tickets, thanks to his dad

The Saturday night shows were about the best Oxford had to offer at the time. Everything had to be over before midnight as the Town Hall was a municipal facility. I still have my ticket, and another is framed and has been on display on the wall of the Town Hall for some years.

### I WAS THERE: BARBARA BOLDER, AGE 14

It was quite amazing. Oxford Town Hall was the place to see all the upcoming groups. My friend Freda and I had arrived early and stood by the stage, all made up in our highest heels and wearing all our latest clothes, as you did at 14. It was the first and only time everyone was so mesmerised by a group that no one danced - we all just stood and watched. They were so different and so exciting. And a bit scruffy, which was different. At some point Keith Richards' guitar string broke and he had to change it. He walked across the stage to us and handed his plectrum to Freda. She was thrilled – she still has it.

### I WAS THERE: ANDREW CRISP, AGE 26

Traditionally on New Year's Eve in Oxford Town Hall there was a large public dance. In 1964 the Rolling Stones were to be top of the bill and the main attraction. In those days there might be up to six groups performing in one evening, all doing a relatively short slot. The Stones were on last and opening the proceedings was my brother's band the Falling Leaves, popular in the Oxford area at the time. The drummer with the Leaves had rather too much to drink the day before so, being a drummer, I was asked to step into the breach. No matter that I was a trad jazz musician, I managed to make a fair fist of the blues numbers. With all the bands that were on there was much confusion on the stage with amplifiers, speakers, etc. all over the place. I asked Charlie Watts if I might move his kit so I had space to set up my meagre equipment. 'Don't bother,' he said, 'use mine.' So I played on Charlie Watts' Gretsch kit.

Andrew Crisp's brother was with the Falling Leaves

Mick Jagger apart, the Stones carried their stuff from the band's van up the Town Hall steps and set it all up themselves. There were very few roadies around then. Mick, however, made an entrance, forcing his way through screaming female admirers. I also spoke to Brian.

I went to Art College in Cheltenham in 1961, and us students used to frequent a café called the Black Tulip. It had a pin-board and on it was a notice asking for musicians to form an R&B band. I was interested in the American blues stuff (Howling Wolf, Muddy Waters, etc) coming into England at the time, so wrote to the name on the notice, a certain Brian Jones. He kindly replied, thanking me for my interest, but he wanted to go fully pro, which I couldn't do, having just started on my art course. When I talked to Brian about his Cheltenham notice he said, 'I remember. You are the guy with the italic handwriting.' What a fine fellow, with none of the big-time attitude that rock stars are supposed to have.

THE ROLLING STONES IN THE SIXTIES: A PEOPLE'S HISTORY

# ADELPHI THEATRE
## 7 JANUARY 1964, SLOUGH, UK

### I WAS THERE: RICHARD TUCK, AGE 19

I was chairman of the students' union at Slough College of Further Education and we had someone named Dave who knew the Rolling Stones. He acted as an intermediary for booking them. At that time there was inadequate space at the college, so we booked the Adelphi. The first time we pais the Rolling Stones £16 to play and that went so well we booked them to play another gig for £22. However, they didn't turn up for the second occasion as their first record had come out and they had other things to think about.

I like to think we gave them their first big break! It was not part of a tour but before it - a very informal arrangement, demonstrated by the fact that they were able to drop out of the second gig - with notice. Locally they were well known, particularly in Windsor and Eel Pie Island, but not nationally at that time. I remember it was very loud but they didn't have flashy amplifiers, rather DIY amplifiers and guitars. I think a small wardrobe featured as one of the loudspeakers. There were perhaps about 500 people, and I think they played for the whole evening with two sets of an hour each.

The audience all stayed on the dancefloor separated from the band, which was on an alcove-like low stage with a handrail and gates at the front. The audience was either students or serious fans of the Stones, so there was no hysteria but much appreciation.

---

*After starting 1964 with a handful of dance hall shows the Rolling Stones embarked on a second British tour, comprising entirely English towns and cities apart from two shows in Cardiff. This time they appeared second on the bill to all-girl group The Ronettes and ahead of the Swinging Blue Jeans, Marty Wilde & The Wildcats, and Johnny Kidd & The Pirates. The Ronettes would close the first half of the show, with the Stones closing the second half. But even on their nights off from the package tour, the band often played a club or dance hall.*

THE ROLLING STONES IN THE SIXTIES: A PEOPLE'S HISTORY

# GRANADA THEATRE
## 9 JANUARY 1964, KETTERING, UK

### I WAS THERE: LESLEY SMITH, AGE 19

The night the Stones were appearing at the Granada my husband was out with his band, so I went to watch them with my friend Janice Chapman. The Ronettes were top of the bill. At the end of the show, Rex Smith, who was the manager and knew us, asked if we would like to meet the Stones. This we did and got all their autographs. I kept them for years but sadly during a house move they were lost. I wonder how much they would have been worth today.

Lesley Smith went along with her friend Janice Chapman

### I WAS THERE: JEAN WALLACE, AGE 15

I had just started work when I attended the Rolling Stones' concert at Kettering Granada with my friend Chris. I was not impressed. They were falling about all over the stage. I felt I had wasted my money. It was the worst concert I went to, and I saw many in the Sixties at the Granada.

### I WAS THERE: DENA HUBBARD, AGE 16

I went with my friends, and we paid about five shillings (25p) in old money. My wage was £4 10s (£4.50) for a 42-hour week. We sat three rows from the stage. They were the best days. The Granada is now a bingo hall.

# GRANADA THEATRE
## 10 JANUARY 1964, WALTHAMSTOW, LONDON, UK

### I WAS THERE: ALAN MILES

I saw the Stones play with The Ronettes at the Walthamstow Granada. At the side of the Granada was an alleyway where the Stones' Volkswagen was slowly pulling out. Sitting in the front was Keith

# THE ROLLING STONES IN THE SIXTIES: A PEOPLE'S HISTORY

Richards. I had a large rolled-up photograph of the Stones with me. He beckoned to me through the window so he could have the photograph. He passed it round inside the van, gave it back to me with every Stones autograph on it, then they drove off to the right, towards the West End of London.

## I WAS THERE: FRANCES PYMONT (NÉE REDFORD), AGE 23

It's seared in my memory. I was a bit older than the Stones. It was just different – very, very different – from what things had been. These were bands that appealed to teenagers and previously there hadn't been things like teenagers. There weren't teenager-type clothes until the Sixties came in, then they had the short skirts, etc.

I remember when I was 14 or so, we just got something that our mums would have worn and would have cut a bit off the bottom. They used to have quite a lot of pop stars at the Granada. I'd seen Bill Haley and His Comets, and I'd seen Jerry Lee Lewis but I'd never come across such an atmosphere as for the Rolling Stones.

Those times you were either Stones or Beatles, and quite honestly I never really thought very much of The Beatles. I thought they were the sort your parents would have approved of if they met them and if you preferred something like that and if your dad approved of somebody like that coming home with you – well, that was no good. I think with the Stones the fact that they were 'a bunch of scruffy gits,' as my dad described them, with long hair - it was a bit of rebellion. I went to chaperone my sister Monica, who was 17. She didn't particularly like the Rolling Stones. Her thing was Marty Wilde. I went to a concert with her and suddenly there was this ear-splitting shriek and I looked and there was my sister standing on the seat. We were in the second row from the front for the Stones, so we had an extremely good view. Unfortunately, when they came on there was this terrible pandemonium that broke out. There was screaming,

Frances Pymont has the experience seared in her memory

screeching, stamping, thumping. I couldn't hear a word of what they were singing about. I couldn't tell you what they sang. I remember Mick wore a string vest and camouflage trousers. He was obviously singing because he was prancing up and down as he did, opening and closing his mouth, but you really couldn't hear a thing. The people in front of us – it was a family – in the front row got up and said it was disgusting and walked out. So the people behind just climbed over the seats to get a better view. And as it went on it got more and more noisy and then girls started to try and climb on the stage and the security men sort of chucked them back off and they kept trying to get on, and it was getting a little bit out of hand.

At the Granada on either side of the stage there were the ladies' and gents' toilets and out of these came policemen to assist in keeping some sort or order.

When you look at them, the way Mick Jagger sort of prances around now, it's the same as it was then. They seem to have remained – well, obviously his face has gone and the other members of the band look rather dodgy if you look at them – but they've got a certain style about them.

### I WAS THERE: MARILYN PAYNE

I was a big Ronettes fan so I probably originally bought the tickets to see them. But I know that when my friend and I were on our way we were very excited to be seeing the Stones. I remember us saying to each other, 'Shall we get up and dance?' And we did!

### I WAS THERE: PAUL BARRY

I climbed onto the stage at the end of the concert and slid through the curtains to see Charlie Watts disassembling his drum kit. Whilst he looked at and signed the poster, Mick came on stage, saw the poster and took me up to the dressing rooms where the rest of the band also signed. As I walked through the dressing room corridor, members of The Ronettes looked out to see who was there and also greeted me. I still have the poster.

# THE ROLLING STONES IN THE SIXTIES: A PEOPLE'S HISTORY

# BATHS HALL
## 11 JANUARY 1964, EPSOM, UK

### I WAS THERE: JOHN SUTHERLAND

Our next-door neighbour's son, Brian Howard from Bookham, was the promoter and booked them. My late father owned the Fiore Coffee Bar in Church Road, Bookham and sold some of the tickets. Needless to say, they sold out very quickly. In their early days the Stones did a lot of Chuck Berry numbers, and 'Oh Carol' has always been a favourite with me.

### I WAS THERE: BRIAN HOWARD

The January '64 date at the Baths Hall in Epsom was part of a week-long booking of the Stones by a professional promoter rather than me, the gifted amateur. Like the manager of the Baths Hall, he was called John Smith. I believe he came from Reigate and, having booked them for a week, he put them in different venues each night. John Smith the promoter came across John Smith the hall manager and learned that he couldn't be bought. As a consequence, he phoned me and asked, 'How on earth did you cope?' I was flattered that the professional was asking me - I wasn't yet 20 - and when he asked if I could market some tickets through the coffee bar network I was pleased to agree. He got tickets to me, and I did the rest.

Then a couple of days before the event he phoned again and said, 'Can you get the tickets back?' Naturally I said that would be impossible. Whereas I had bought my 1,250 tickets all at the same time he had ordered his in two batches and while the first batch were a browny green in colour the second batch were a greeny brown, ie. similar but different. One of the Epsom youth clubs was run by a policeman and, when he saw some of his kids had tickets of different colours, his copper's nose caused him to go and visit the hall and ask questions. That led to the promoter getting a call and the game was up. The outcome was that they had stewards on the door with counters and the first 962 ticket holders were admitted and the remainder received a refund but were then turned away. I've spent the last 51 years feeling ever so slightly smug that I managed to sell 1,250 tickets for the earlier concert.

# THE ROLLING STONES IN THE SIXTIES: A PEOPLE'S HISTORY

## I WAS THERE: BARRY DENMAN, AGE 17

I saw both Stones shows at the Baths Hall in Epsom. They were really exciting times. Half of my mates liked the Stones and half liked The Beatles. I had photographs of all the Stones inside my locker at work. And my dad, being a very old-fashioned dad, said, 'There must be something wrong with you, having photos of long-haired boys.' The funny thing is - looking back - their hair wasn't very long at all. But compared with the rest of us it seemed long at the time.

I was an apprentice compositor in the printing industry and, after watching the earlier show with a crowd of my mates, we liked it so much I went down there to get a ticket for the following one that a couple of mates and I copied. In the old days, the tickets were like business cards and the tickets for this show were a small card with a green edge fading into the white.

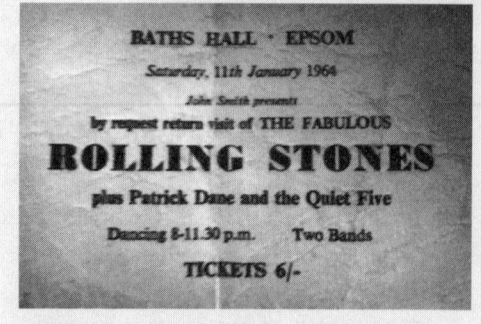

Barry Denman (top) and one of the tickets he forged

We reproduced tickets for the show, cutting the card to size, painting the edges and matching the various type faces. It took us a long, long time to get them exactly right. We had to get all the typefaces to match properly. And because it wasn't a sit-down concert there was just a number stamped on the back, so we stamped random numbers on the back. We just gave a few out to our mates. When we went back down there for the concert, we couldn't believe the amount of people queuing up outside without tickets. If I was a real forger, I could have made a fortune.

What properly annoyed me more than anything was that I gave my ticket to the guy at the door and he hardly looked at it. He just tore it in half and let me in. I was hoping he would scrutinise it, because they were perfect. They were exactly the same as the legitimate ones.

I never kept any of those tickets and assumed they had all been used until about a year ago when I was reminiscing with my oldest mate and he said he had a tatty one and was only too pleased to let me have it. I hadn't seen one since the day of the show.

I thought both shows were brilliant - it was a wonderful time to grow up during those times. The main thing I remember is how charismatic Brian Jones was. That concert is the best one I've ever been to.

## I WAS THERE: TRISH COLE, AGE 14

It was very strange to me as I used to swim at the Baths regularly. I lived in the village of Ashtead, about 15 minutes away by car. I went with a friend, whose name I can't remember now. I seem to remember the friend's father picked us up after. There weren't many people there, but the music was very exciting. Cathy McGowan from *Ready Steady Go!* was in the seated audience, whereas I was just on the floor. My older sister lent me a pair of Courrèges-style black boots. I felt like the bees' knees.

## I WAS THERE: COLIN SMITH

The Stones were not that well known then. I remember Brian Jones standing on the side of the stage looking quite spaced out, almost detached from the rest. I also remember a great performance. I'm sure our school rock band played that evening, and they were on immediately before the Stones. In December the supporting group was The Presidents, but they did not appear at the event I went to and this was not our school rock band. I have a feeling it was either in April or September, the floorboards covering up the swimming pool. I also think it was before I went to university (at the end of September 1963) and the price was around 2/6d. I also remember this because our School Group (from Glyn Grammar) played just before the Stones and one of the band members was Ray Booth, a friend of mine.

Colin Smith saw the Stones at Epsom Baths

# GRANADA THEATRE
## 12 JANUARY 1964, TOOTING, LONDON, UK

### I WAS THERE: CHRIS EVERETT

Although I liked the Stones, I was more interested in The Ronettes, because they were very sexy and 'Be My Baby' was a big hit at the time. It was obvious to people of my age that the times they were a-changing! Pop music was changing and so were attitudes. You could just feel it. They were heady days. There was a lot of optimism around. Bands like the Stones and The Beatles were quick to give credit to their heroes, who were all black – Marvin Gaye, Chuck Jackson, Howlin' Wolf, Muddy Waters, Chuck Berry, Bo Diddley, BB King. And those people were able to launch and re-launch their careers by coming to Britain and Europe thanks to them. The best thing about the Stones performance was Keith Richards charging around the stage like a maniac, really pushing things along.

# BARROWLAND BALLROOM
## 13 JANUARY 1964, GLASGOW, UK

### I WAS THERE: TONY LENAGHAN

I was still at school at St Gerard's in Govan. I had two milk-rounds before school and I was paid on Tuesday and a Thursday, 15 shillings (75p) for one, twelve shillings (60p) for the other. Across from the Barrowland, there were two pubs - the Saracen's Head and Hurrels Tavern. They both served scrumpy, which was I think a shilling a pint. The night the Rolling Stones were playing we were in Hurrells, and it was raided by the police looking for underage drinkers, which we were. Fortunately, a fight broke out further up the pub and we were able to escape (one of the reasons I remember the night so well).

We had never seen anything like it in Glasgow. They were brilliant. The audience was predominately female, and they were going ballistic, fainting, screaming and so on. We had girls on our shoulders - at one stage I had two! This is Glasgow in the conservative Sixties, remember, and girls were getting carried across the stage, having fainted and in various stages of dishevelment. One memory that sticks in my mind is of a young girl having fainted and being passed over the crowd and carried across the stage, her large breasts exposed, and Brian Jones following her, still playing his mouth organ. A great night.

### I WAS THERE: DANNY GILLAN

My dad's name is Mike Gillan. His band The Haloes supported the Stones at the Barrowlands and Brian Jones actually borrowed my dad's amp for the night. I don't think they had much interaction with them though, as my dad's band were hired by the venue, not the Stones themselves. The Haloes also supported The Hollies on one occasion, but they never really progressed beyond the club and wedding circuit.

## GRANADA THEATRE
### 14 JANUARY 1964, MANSFIELD, UK

### I WAS THERE: MARGARET AUDIN, AGE 15

Myself and a couple of friends were avid autograph hunters. We didn't purchase any tickets for the show, but we were hanging about the theatre with lots of others hoping to get a glimpse of the group. Someone got the back doors of the theatre open and we all ran in, up the stairs and onto the balcony. I remember Mick Jagger looking up, probably wondering what was going on. We were all soon rounded up and thrown out.

The three of us found the van the Stones were using and the door wasn't locked so we went in. It was full of all sorts of things. We took some clothing. But after about 10 minutes we felt guilty and decided to take the stuff back. When we got back to the van the roadie was inside and he wasn't too happy. We told him we'd brought the stuff back so he let us in. We persuaded him to get us the Stones autographs, so he took our autograph books into the Granada and got them for us. Unfortunately, many years later my mum and dad threw out my autograph book when moving house. I had some good autographs, including The Ronettes, The Searchers, and Billy Fury, but the best ones were the Stones.

# THE ROLLING STONES IN THE SIXTIES: A PEOPLE'S HISTORY

### I WAS THERE: ESTELLE FOWDEN

I went with my friend Angela. We went to the stage door and I asked Brian Jones for his autograph, which I still have. I can see his face now, very pale and drawn with big bags under his eyes. He didn't look at all healthy for a young bloke.

I thought the performance was rubbish (I also thought this at the concert in Hyde Park a few years later after Brian Jones died) but I remained a fan. I think to see them do a gig earlier in their career in a pub would have been great, as would their current high-tech concerts, but Mansfield Granada was not the right venue. I would never have said this at the time - I was a big Stones fan. Maybe it was the fact that we were screaming and not listening. Why did we do that? How stupid.

### I WAS THERE: DAVID EAMES, AGE 15

I was a spotty adolescent at the time, with an admission ticket to see the Rolling Stones. It cost 11/6 (57p), which swallowed up my paper-round money. This type of venue was very small compared to what is expected today. Everybody had a good seat and wasn't that far away from the stage. You felt the raw energy of the Dartford version of US rhythm and blues. The set-list from that night included 'Come On', 'Mona', 'You Better Move On', 'Roll Over Beethoven', and 'I Wanna Be Your Man'. I had to leave as the Stones set ended to make sure I caught the last bus home.

David Eames felt the raw energy at Mansfield's Granada Theatre

# GRANADA THEATRE
## 15 JANUARY 1964, BEDFORD, UK

### I WAS THERE: DAVID ARNOLD, AGE 18

I attended the second performance that evening, a few rows from the front in what I recall as being the eight and sixes (43p seats). The tour was called Group Scene 64 and featured amongst others The Ronettes. They weren't on for long. They played six or seven songs at most. They did 'Come On' as their first record, and 'I Wanna Be Your Man'. The Ronettes made a lasting impression - we were only 18 after all.

One of my friends recalls The Ronettes apparently had some sort of clothing malfunction - either a strap or a bra. After the show we made our way to the back of the venue. I remember the sight of the Stones all being in a Mini. These screaming girls had surrounded the Mini as they leapt into it, and off they went. The Ronettes were signing autographs at the stage door and the Stones were being ripped apart by several enthusiastic girls. One had a trophy of half a black knitted tie. We had a chat with Ian Stewart. He had the Commer van with all the gear and stuff. They'd left him to drive home with it. We said, 'Where have they gone?' thinking they might have gone to a pub in Bedford, but he said, 'No, no, they're on their way back to London.'

Bedford Poster

Bedford programme

### I WAS THERE: DAVE HOWARD, AGE 9

I was only nine. Which strikes me now as particularly young, not to be in the St John Ambulance, but to actually be allowed to attend something like this at that age. I don't think it would happen now. This was two gigs in a day, seven o'clock and 9.15. They only had short sets in those days.

I was at the seven o'clock showing as I had to be home from Bedford to where I lived in Stotfold before it got too late. Dave Berry and the Cruisers performed and Marty Wilde and the Wildcats were also on the gig. And I remember the Swinging

Blue Jeans because they were flavour of the month - I think 'Hippy

# THE ROLLING STONES IN THE SIXTIES: A PEOPLE'S HISTORY

Hippy Shake' was in the charts about then.

I remember one of The Ronettes had a wardrobe malfunction and her bra snapped in the back and one of the other Ronettes danced around the back, sorted her out and danced round again. But that might just be a very young boy's imagination. Girls were screaming so you could barely hear the Stones and what they were singing, girls fainting and asking for help and being carried out on stretchers. Some girls had collapsed. It was a form of hysteria.

### I WAS THERE: DEREK EDMUNDS, AGE 23

The Bedford Granada was a premier venue in those days, and we saw many new and established acts there. It was located in St Peter's Street and we used to form a queue in a passageway to the left of the building. When I saw the Rolling Stones I thought they were absolutely brilliant. My wife had a different opinion and as we left the Granada she said, 'Who were that scruffy bunch? They were awful.' To which I replied, 'I loved them. They will be big one day.'

*Derek Edmunds felt the Stones were absolutely brilliant*

## MCILROY'S BALLROOM
### 16 JANUARY 1964, SWINDON, UK

### I WAS THERE: RICKY PORTER

When I was boxing back in the Sixties, I was out of work as I couldn't get a job at my trade so to make ends meet I had a little club on the corner of Station Road and Bridge Street called the Blues Cellar Club. I also used to make ends meet by working on the door at McIlroy's. Several Americans from bases at Fairford, Brize Norton and Burdrop who were friends of mine used the club, and one used to sing in a group from Swindon called The Hummelflugs - John L. Watson.

One particular night the group asked if they could use my gear as they were supporting a band from London called the Rolling Stones. I was working up there that night, so it was not a problem. The night arrived, I took my gear and set it up, the Hummelflugs went on and when they finished their set there was an interval. Halfway through the interval the Stones arrived and had to go on almost immediately. I remember Mick Jagger clearly. He approached me, looking a bit dishevelled and wearing a powder-blue pullover with holes in the elbows. I remember him saying, 'The guys tell me this is your equipment, we are late, would you be kind enough to let me use it?' I told him it would be no problem and they quickly changed into their stage gear and did a set. However, my gear was

Ricky Porter leant Mick Jagger his equipment

nowhere near the quality of the equipment they used and after their first set they quickly set up their own gear. It was a lot of fun, and there were a lot of Americans there to see John L Watson, but they loved the Stones' bluesy kind of music too.

The girls were really screaming for the Stones, but I'm afraid it was not them that were drowning out the sound of the Stones. It was just that my equipment Jagger was singing on wasn't powerful enough to cut through the noise the crowd were making.

## CITY HALL
### 17 JANUARY 1964, SALISBURY, UK

**I WAS THERE: GEOFF COOPER, AGE 16**
I made an effort to get to a Stones gig in Salisbury Civic Centre. My first attempt was thwarted before I had even left Bournemouth. Having borrowed a friend's Vespa scooter, I was apprehended by a Police panda car. I was 16 at the time, no licence and carrying a passenger. I was escorted back to the police station.

The second time we all went in a pal's car on what turned out to be quite an exciting evening, Brian Jones kicking a very persistent girl in the face to prevent her from getting on stage. No security in those days.

## PIER BALLROOM
### 18 JANUARY 1964, HASTINGS, UK

**I WAS THERE: ANDRE PALFREY-MARTIN, AGE 16**

I saw the Stones three times on Hastings Pier. They did the three gigs, which were January, April and August '64. In January they were just beginning to cut their teeth in terms of bigger ballrooms. The Pier ballroom legally took about 1,400. But I don't think they ever came in that sort of numbers, not early in the day, because we were talking about 'Come On' having been released, possibly the first album.

The support would have been a group from a local coffee bar, the Pam Dor, and we would have been there because it was the only real place to go at that time. It was the Pier Ballroom, or the Happy Ballroom as it was known, featuring the longest bar in Hastings and at the end of the pier on the promenade end - the nose-end right at the end of the pier. We always used to say it was a sixpenny bus ride to get there in the winter. It was like a great big aircraft hangar, and you expected to see a couple of seaplanes parked

*Hastings Press press cuttings - Andre Palfrey-Martin*

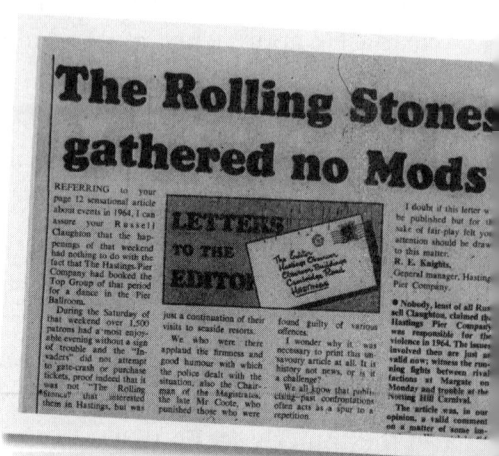

# THE ROLLING STONES IN THE SIXTIES: A PEOPLE'S HISTORY

**CROWDS** were waiting for the Rolling Stones for their session on Hastings Pier on Saturday night. The group were smuggled there in a really quiet way—by ambulance. And here they are inside it.

## SCREAMS GREET THE ROLLING STONES

Only a performance by The Beatles, one imagines, could have produced more enthusiastic scenes than those at Hastings Pier on Saturday. It was the day The Rolling Stones came to town!

The unappreciated heroes of the day were the Pier attendants, who stood on each side of the stage as The Stones did their best to make themselves heard above the shrill screams.

It was their unenviable task to haul a number of overexcited girls—in various states of collapse—from the front row of the audience and carry them bodily off the stage for a breath of reviving sea air. And they were kept hard at it, such was the effect of the five long-haired rhythm and blues specialists.

They also had to guard every conceivable entrance to the dressing-rooms, but a few fervent female fans, like the one who explained to an 'Observer' reporter that she had cut her leg in trying to climb through a window which she had just broken, were not so easily discouraged.

When the screaming subsided The Rolling Stones came through 'loud and clear' with their own distinctive harsh v

in there. That was I think when they wore the leather waistcoats as part of their outfit. They were just another band of the Sixties. It wasn't very full on that first gig. I think it would have been average numbers - five or six hundred, maybe a few more. They were supported by the Four Aces. Admission price was 6/6 (33p) in advance, 7/6 (37p) on the door.

THE ROLLING STONES IN THE SIXTIES: A PEOPLE'S HISTORY

# COVENTRY THEATRE, AKA HIPPODROME
## 19 JANUARY 1964, COVENTRY, UK

### I WAS THERE: LIZ LAURIE, AGE 13

Like many theatres in the early Sixties, Coventry Theatre hosted pop concerts, usually on Sunday evenings. These consisted of about six current pop acts, each performing five or six numbers. I was very excited to have a ticket for the upper circle for the Rolling Stones. It cost six shillings (30p) and was all I could afford from my pocket money. Also on the bill that night were The Ronettes.

I went with a school friend, Pam, and recall the electric atmosphere. The screaming of the girls in the audience meant that almost nothing, musically, could be heard and the upper circle could be felt moving slightly with all the audience's excitement. They sang 'Come On', 'It's All Over Now' and 'You Better Move On', still one of my all-time favourites. I attended quite a few Sunday pop concerts in those wonderful days, but it's the Rolling Stones concert I have always been happiest to have attended. I always remained very glad to have seen them when Brian Jones was in the group.

### I WAS THERE: PETER JONES, AGE 16

We went to see them at the Coventry Hippodrome, now the Coventry Museum of transport. The Stones were third on the bill. The headline act was either The Ronettes or Helen Shapiro. The Stones came on and they all looked incredibly sheepish because it was that period in their history when they wore those black and white houndstooth jackets, black trousers and Cuban heels.

Peter Jones reckoned the Stones looked 'incredibly sheepish'

# THE ROLLING STONES IN THE SIXTIES: A PEOPLE'S HISTORY

## I WAS THERE: GRAHAM BELLAMY

I saw the Rolling Stones at Coventry Theatre when they finished the first half and Freddie and the Dreamers were top of the bill. When the Stones came on, I remember some plonker shouting out, 'Get your hair cut!' To which Mick replied, 'What, and look like you?'

Graham Bellamy, second left, recalls Mick Jagger's retort to hecklers

## I WAS THERE: DAVE JONES

We saw Freddie and the Dreamers. It was when he managed to 'accidentally' drop his trousers as part of his act. Not the sort of thing you are likely to forget.

## I WAS THERE: JOHN CROFTS, AGE 16

I spent the night outside the box office with a bunch of girls from Lyng Hall to be first in the queue for tickets. Highly successful – I got a seat in the middle of the front row. Unfortunately, as I left the box office there was an *Evening Telegraph* cameraman in wait. My ecstatic expression made it onto the front page, seen that evening by the headmaster of Bablake School. An unpleasant interview followed, and a Saturday morning detention was the result.

However, it was well worth it to see one of the great rock 'n' roll bands early in their career, playing proper rhythm and blues. When the Stones played here again, I was in town with a friend of mine who bore an uncanny resemblance to Mick Jagger, and we had to take refuge in what I vaguely remember was the Golden Egg.

## I WAS THERE: DAVE JONES

My friend Bernie Spencer and I went to see The Rolling Stones twice at the Coventry Theatre in our teenage years. We were walking home after one of the shows when we reached a major crossroads about half a mile from the theatre at the junction of Holyhead Road and Queen Victoria Road. As we approached the traffic lights, a large black limousine pulled up alongside us. The window was wound down and Mick Jagger appeared and asked, 'Which way to London, mate?' We replied that they should turn left and left again at the next junction. 'Thanks, mate.' And off they drove. We caught a glimpse of Brian Jones on the back seat looking slightly out of it. We were both speechless and stood there for a while. The road layout has completely changed now, but I would always tell my daughters Rosie and Angie the story every time we passed the spot, so much so that whenever they are in the vicinity they repeat the tale to their friends.

## GRANADA THEATRE
### 20 JANUARY 1964, WOOLWICH, LONDON, UK

**I WAS THERE: KEITH DUNWOODY, AGE 19**

I was at art school in Gravesend. Prior to the Stones/Beatles era, Chuck Berry and Bo Diddley were the most popular artists in my circle, but that was a time when young people's music was everywhere, taking over from the BBC Palm Court Orchestra era, which was awful. Live music was available in all manner of venues - pubs, clubs and even youth clubs, usually identified by the day of the week they were open, e.g. Wednesday Club, Friday Club, etc. Most of them were run by local churches, but we did not have any interest in religion.

The most popular local music venue for us was the Black Prince at Bexley, next to the A2. This was also the era when Radio Luxembourg 208 was being replaced by the pirate radio stations just off the coast.

I saw the Stones at the Granada cinema by Woolwich Ferry. I remember it cost five bob (25p). I went with a couple of friends from art school, Ted Trott and Noela Waghorn, and another girl whose name escapes me. All I remember of the actual show was that they were scruffy. Jagger had a jumper and it looked like a moth had attacked it. However, their performance was well up to standard and they managed to produce enough volume to overcome the screaming girls, who were always an annoyance at concerts at that time. They played 'Not Fade

Away', their new record. Marty Wilde was also on the bill. I remember him not because I was a fan of his but because he played 'Orange Blossom Special' on the harmonica, which was absolutely brilliant. I remain a staunch Stones devotee, having chosen the Stones over The Beatles from the outset. The Beatles appealed to the old people and the Stones to us youngsters in those days. I remember my dad saying, 'This music will be forgotten in a couple of months.'

# GRANADA THEATRE
## 21 JANUARY 1964, AYLESBURY, UK

### I WAS THERE: LINDA HAILEY, AGE 15

I went with my mum, her friend, and a school friend of mine. I remember standing in the foyer and seeing Mick Jagger talking to one of the staff, then dashing back to my mum to tell her. The show was great – the first time I had been to any show like that. I stayed a fan of theirs for years after.

### I WAS THERE: BILL HANNAY, AGE 13

As a guitar-mad young adolescent, it was the first time I was allowed out on my own for such an event. I don't think my mother was too keen on them for some reason.

The evening was probably notable for the absence of Brian Jones. I remember the official announcement referred to prevailing foggy conditions and travel problems. What was the real reason? I've always wondered. As far as I was

*It was the first show Bill Hannay was allowed out on his own to*

concerned, it didn't seem to detract overly from the tight and punchy sound produced by the quartet of Mick, Keith, Bill and Charlie. Keith was playing his sunburst Harmony Meteor and Bill his usual Framus Star bass, with the band wearing black leather waistcoats and tab-collar shirts, their familiar stage uniform of the period. All exciting stuff, and to think I was part of a live audience witnessing in Aylesbury the early incarnation of a rock 'n' roll phenomenon! I still have the show programme, salted away somewhere.

### I WAS THERE: JILLY WILLIAMSON, AGE 15

It was very foggy and Brian Jones didn't make the show I went to. The *Bucks Herald* newspaper at the time featured a photograph on the front page of two girls kissing the door handle Mick Jagger had touched.

## GRANADA THEATRE
### 22 JANUARY 1964, SHREWSBURY, UK

### I WAS THERE: BARBARA ROBERTS

I went with my husband Keith and two friends. Before the show as I walked across the road, I found a ticket on the floor. It was a front seat and I handed it in at the box office. As soon as the Stones came on my husband and my friend Bette took hold of my arms - they were afraid I would run to the Stones. My husband was having a good laugh as girls were being half-carried, half-dragged back into the lobby.

When we came out, they were still screaming, 'Mick! Mick!' It was such a wonderful night and I still think about it. I can't believe I sat there screaming for them, but I did. It was a night I'll always remember.

### I WAS THERE: SYLVIA STARKEY, AGE 18

I was a junior in a fashion shop on Castle Street, Shrewsbury. The day after the concert I was out buying cakes for the staff tea break when I bumped into all the Stones. They had been into a coffee shop called Sidoli's. They stopped and spoke to me and then they all gave me their autographs. Unfortunately, over the years I have lost the autographs, but I still remember that day.

THE ROLLING STONES IN THE SIXTIES: A PEOPLE'S HISTORY

# THE PAVILION, ROYAL HOTEL
## 23 JANUARY 1964, LOWESTOFT, UK

### I WAS THERE: YVONNE ALMOND, AGE 19

At the time I was working at the Pye television factory so a crowd of us girls went along. What a night! Being teenagers then, we all went a bit mental as the Stones left the stage, wearing blue shirts, leather waistcoats and dark trousers. We along with many other girls chased them from the stage. As they reached the stairway to their upstairs rooms the girls grabbed them, tearing their clothes. My friend came away with a piece of shirt. We often laugh about it now, saying if she had kept it then it could have become a collector's item.

*Yvonne Almond went along with fellow Pye factory workers*

### I WAS THERE: SHEILA ROLL (NÉE KEABLE), AGE 13

I went with my friend Lynda. It wasn't a concert – we were dancing, and I remember being near the stage and noticing how muddy their boots were. They were on a stage about four feet high as we danced to their music. I think they had only had a couple of hits by then – 'Come On' and 'I Wanna Be Your Man'.

*Sheila Roll's prized autographed possessions*

After the performance my friend and I walked round the building and saw an iron fire escape leading to a window. Bill Wyman was leaning out of the window looking at the sea. He waved to us to come up and happily took our autograph books, passing them around the dressing room.

## CALIFORNIA BALLROOM
### 25 JANUARY 1964, DUNSTABLE, UK

**I WAS THERE: DAVID ARNOLD, AGE 18**
They did four gigs at the Cali and the fourth was just pandemonium. That last time the whole hall was packed to the rafters. When they did 'You Better Move On', Jagger said, 'We've got the heavenly choir in the background' - Brian Jones and Keith Richards.

They used to have to make their way from the stage to the dressing room through the crowd. I remember Brian Jones being held by this girl by his jumper and he just couldn't make any movement at all. He wasn't a big fella. He was just sort of laughing. Someone had to give him a helping hand to pull him along from the clutches of this girl.

## DE MONTFORT HALL
### 26 JANUARY 1964, LEICESTER, UK

**I WAS THERE: GISELA OAKES, AGE 15**
A friend called Penny Williams and I bought tickets for the concert at the de Montfort Hall because we were great fans of the Rolling Stones, who were supporting Freddie and the Dreamers. We were both nearly 16 and had chosen our clothes very carefully. In those days, most teenagers were either Mods or Rockers and we considered ourselves as Dolly Rocker Mods. I'd bought some bright green pumps with tartan on them so had made a bright green dress with tartan bib and collar to match, and one of those funny caps that were in vogue then.

We travelled to Leicester from Northampton by coach. I can't remember much about the actual performance but by this time we'd struck up

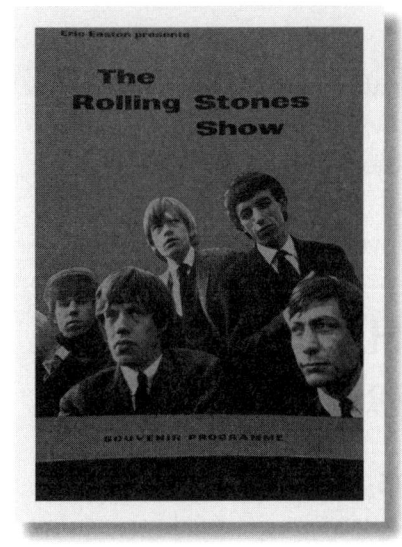

# THE ROLLING STONES IN THE SIXTIES: A PEOPLE'S HISTORY

Above: Fans flock after the show at De Montfort Hall

conversation with a boy, older than us, who wasn't a roadie but who seemed to know the Rolling Stones slightly. After the concert was over, he beckoned for us to follow him up the right side of the stage. All I can remember then is Brian Jones and Mick Jagger at a long table, clearing up. I really cannot remember what was said, only that they were both charming and friendly to us. Mick Jagger said 'goodbye' and went off to do whatever he was doing, and Brian Jones brought photos with autographs. I remember thinking how quiet, shy, calm and gentle he was. By this time, we were in such a panic because we'd missed the last coach back to Northampton. In those days, people used to hitchhike a lot, so we hitched a lift with a lorry driver who brought us back to Northampton. I'd missed the last red bus home so thought I'd try the green bus at the Derngate Bus Station, but that one had gone also. I got home somehow, and my parents were very relieved to see me.

## I WAS THERE: WENDY FROST, AGE 17

The hall was packed solid, all the teenagers shouting and singing Stones songs. The place was buzzing with excitement. I was there with my boyfriend, and we were both wet with sweat at the thought of the Stones music. The curtains opened and the crowd went wild, screaming. The band looked great and Brian Jones, the leader, always looked very smart and well groomed. When the show finished my boyfriend and I left there in a hypnotic haze and walked down London Road, where all the other Stones fans were talking and singing and very happy. A Stones fan for life!

### I WAS THERE: MARTIN OSBORN

We saw the Stones a number of times after the Station Hotel, mostly at the De Montfort Hall in Leicester, where they appeared with, amongst others, Phil Spector's very sexy girl group the Ronettes, Joe Brown and the Bruvvers, and the Spencer Davis Group. We stopped going to see them because we could not hear the band over the screaming girls.

## COLSTON HALL
### 27 JANUARY 1964, BRISTOL, UK

### I WAS THERE: JOHN WHELTON, AGE 15

Tickets for the two concerts went on sale at 9am on a Saturday morning and I was one of five school pals who after leaving school on the Friday afternoon went home and met up later that evening, spending that night on the steps of the Colston Hall queuing for tickets. We obtained front-row seats as it was all seated in those days, costing half a crown each (13p). Our parents thought we were crackers. But it was well worth it.

## PUBLIC HALL
### 31 JANUARY 1964, PRESTON, UK

### I WAS THERE: JAMES TUCKER, AGE 14

My Mum worked for Preston promoter, John Dell. She was reliable, needed the money and was pretty, so consequently got the box office job for every event Dell promoted. As a result, she took me to many varied gigs at the Public Hall. She was working the box office when the Rolling Stones played there. I was allowed to go with her and to bring my friend Tommy. We arrived at the venue around 3pm and Tommy and I just roamed around the hall, stage and balcony, and went to the dressing room and sat around with the lads. I got their autograph, but it was just scribble... I gave the book to my sister.

As well as trying out the stage for the soundcheck, Brian Jones and Bill Wyman went way over in the rear of the hall and up into the balcony over the front doors. Then Mick Jagger was shouting and screaming, and Brian and Bill were shouting and screaming back, saying how they liked the acoustics. There was no one else around. At one point, Keith Richards said to Mick Jagger, 'Whose are these kids?' and Jagger replied, 'They're with the promoter, mate.'

### I WAS THERE: SUSAN GRIERSON, AGE 15
My best friend Sandra and I attended the Rolling Stones concert at Preston's Public Hall, which was a fabulous building. I went to English Martyrs Girls School, we used to have our school reunion there, and I sang on the stage in the choir. When Sandra and I saw the Stones, we were very young. Our mothers didn't know we were going. We sneaked into the Stones dressing room, spoke with them, got all their autographs.

# WILLENHALL BATHS
## 5 FEBRUARY 1964, WILLENHALL, UK

### I WAS THERE: SANDRA LOWE, AGE 15
I saw the Rolling Stones at Willenhall Baths with my friend Joyce Kingston. It was a fantastic night and everyone was in awe of the Stones. Tickets were six shillings each. Willenhall Baths was a swimming pool in the summer and a dance hall in the winter as they covered the pool over. They had a lot of dances there, but this was the only time I went. Brian Jones was in a grey suit. What stood out for me was that when the Stones came on stage, there weren't many people in the audience. It wasn't full at all and there was room to dance. After each song we'd just stand and clap them. There was no histrionics or screaming or anything. It was very polite and very English. I often wonder what they thought of us as an audience. I remember staring up at them after they'd played a song and thinking, 'I'm looking at the Rolling Stones,' because it was a small venue and we couldn't believe they were playing there. I don't know why we as an audience didn't go wild and give them more encouragement.

I lost touch with Joyce, but she tracked me down via Facebook. When we spoke again after all those years she said, 'Didn't we go and see the Rolling Stones at Willenhall Baths?' I said, 'Indeed we did.'

*The Rolling Stones started their third UK tour on 8 February 1964. As with the first two package tours they had appeared on, they were part of a line-up that featured other artists. This time the programme was headed by John Leyton and Mike Sarne, and billed as All Stars 64.*

## GRANADA THEATRE
### 11 FEBRUARY 1964, RUGBY, UK

**I WAS THERE: JOHN PHILPOTT, AGE 15**
You couldn't hear a thing for all the screaming, but what struck me was Brian Jones' harmonica - I'd never heard blues harp before and it knocked me out so much that I went out the next day and bought a Hohner Vamper harmonica for 10 shillings and sixpence (53p). Half a century later, I have more than 50, in various states of playability.

John Philpott couldn't hear a thing at Rugby's Granada Theatre

**I WAS THERE: JANET SKINNER, AGE 15**
I went with my 14-year-old sister and a friend. The tickets were a Christmas present from my parents. We had never heard of the Stones before they came to Rugby, as they were not top of the bill. Mike Sarne was on the show as well. On the morning of the concert, we went up the Granada steps to look at the poster. There were two young men also looking. They turned out to be Mick Jagger and one other of the group. It was a great concert.

**I WAS THERE: CLAIRE GEISBERGER (NÉE CHADBURN)**
I went to their first concert when they appeared with John Leyton, then again in March 1965. I met them backstage and had two photos taken with them in their dressing room. One photo was published in the *Rugby Advertiser* together with an article.

# THE ROLLING STONES IN THE SIXTIES: A PEOPLE'S HISTORY

## I WAS THERE: SUE MCCABE, AGE 10

Believe it or not I went with my mother and my brother. I *think* the Swinging Blue Jeans wore blue jeans and pink shirts but that may or may not be accurate. Looking back, it's funny to think of my mother being at a Stones concert.

## I WAS THERE: RICHARD MORRIS, AGE 18

I joined the English Electric Company in Newbold Road as a graduate apprentice in September 1963. The first six months were at Rugby College of Engineering Technology. Some of the other students were from London and had seen the Stones at the Crawdaddy Club and Eel Pie Island. At the time they had only released a couple of singles.

I remember the performance at the Granada Cinema, although memories of the Swinging Blue Jeans, Billie Davis and Mike Sarne have gone. I do recall Jet Harris, who probably played 'Diamonds' and 'Scarlett O'Hara'. Most people, especially the girls, only really went to see the Stones, who got a rapturous reception and screaming from the girls.

John Leyton was the final act and he was booed harshly after he appeared following the Stones. Based on records to date and about to be released, the playlist was probably 'Come On', 'Poison Ivy', 'I Wanna Be Your Man', 'Mona', 'Walking the Dog', and 'You Better Move On'. Obscure blues numbers would not have gone down well with record-buying teenagers. The Sixties was a great time for lots of reasons but especially the live music scene.

## I WAS THERE: PETE SHILTON, AGE 10

I went to this concert as a treat for my tenth birthday. I went to the 6pm early show and my dad drove me and some mates from my class at Dunchurch School - Richard Harris, Robin Bartlett and Graham Evetts - in our old Standard Eight car.

I remember us standing up and shouting during the concert, which comprised of about

Pete Shilton had a rather special 10th birthday present

# THE ROLLING STONES IN THE SIXTIES: A PEOPLE'S HISTORY

10 acts that maybe did three or four songs each. The acts I remember particularly were the Stones, the Swinging Blue Jeans, and ex-Shadow Jet Harris. I remember a lot of screaming girls, particularly when the Stones came on. I'm sure the Stones did 'I Wanna Be Your Man' and 'Poison Ivy'. I'd not long bought *The Rolling Stones EP*, so I was looking forward to seeing them. I'm pretty sure both performances were sold out as I know my mum had to stand in a long queue a couple of weeks prior to it. I still have the programme. Sadly, they demolished our great theatre in 2011, and the land currently operates as an ugly interim car park. How short-sighted.

## I WAS THERE: DAVID CUMELLA, AGE 14

I must have gone to the first show because my parents would have been a bit dodgy about me going to the later one. I remember standing on the top step, slightly offset from the main queue, waiting to go in, when a black Daimler-type saloon swept onto the forecourt and the group, all in long black coats, piled out and ran straight up the steps at full speed and into the theatre. It's significant to me because, when I say, ran up the steps and into the theatre, the majority did, but Keith wasn't

*David Cumella, knocked for six by Keith Richards*

really in the moment and crashed right into my left shoulder, knocking me for six. He recovered in a second or two and scrambled to continue his journey on in. I was perfectly alright although very surprised, a bit bemused that they hadn't gone in through the back door where all the other performers normally went in.

The other thing I'll never forget was that after it finished, my mate and I just sat in our seats - ground floor centre - while all the audience made its way out. We then continued to just sit in our seats for another five or 10 minutes or so while Charlie Watts carried on tapping his high-hat and doing some unmemorable drum practice, totally oblivious to anyone else being in the place. I don't remember being asked to leave but we must've eventually just wandered out in the knowledge that the next lot were just about to come in. I wonder if we'd have been allowed to do that these days.

They were a very good group even then. I know that because I subsequently played in several groups as a drummer and occasional bad guitarist during the Eighties and never managed to do quite as well as they did. Quel dommage.

### I WAS THERE: SUE SMYLIE, AGE 15

I was still at school and having no money and no chance of getting any from my dad in order to see – in his view – the sons of the Devil 'gyrating' on stage, I had to find some other way to see my favourite group. They weren't known as boy bands in those days. I then discovered that a boy in my acquaintance had two tickets, so I set about charming him into taking me with him. Admittedly, it was not my finest hour, but needs must – I remember his name but not much more about him.

We queued outside before being let in. Everybody was highly excited and full of anticipation, including me – this being the first live concert by a famous group I had ever seen. They were great, especially Mick Jagger, his dancing thrilling to a very excited 15-year-old girl. They have remained my favourite group ever since.

## ODEON THEATRE
### 12 FEBRUARY 1964, GUILDFORD, UK

### I WAS THERE: VERONICA SEWELL, AGE 14

I was only three rows from the front and tried to get on the stage. I remember security got me and threw me through the air. I don't know who I landed on. But it didn't deter me. I nearly touched Mick's foot, and that was wonderful. It seems stupid now, doesn't it? At the time it was wonderful. I'll always love the Stones.

*I nearly touched Mick's foot, and that was wonderful*

THE ROLLING STONES IN THE SIXTIES: A PEOPLE'S HISTORY

# GAUMONT THEATRE
## 14 FEBRUARY 1964, WATFORD, UK

### I WAS THERE: ANNE WAINE, AGE 13

I went with three friends – Janice, Sheila and Vanessa. We all attended Francis Combe Secondary Modern in Garston, near Watford. We sat in the front row and one of my friends remembers the Stones were not top of the bill - that was Gerry and the Pacemakers. All I can remember is them singing 'Come On' and possibly 'I Wanna Be Your Man'.

*Anne Waine went with three pals*

### I WAS THERE: SUSAN FORD, AGE 11

I was there! I went with my cousin Alan, three years older. I was only allowed to go because his Dad took us and picked us up afterwards. Oddly, the only thing I really remember, apart from how the Stones looked, was standing on my seat. We were in the stalls, about six or eight rows from the front. In those days it was the height of anti-social behaviour to stand on seats and my cousin kept telling me to get down. I've seen the Stones twice since then but never quite so close.

### I WAS THERE: JOHN DEALEY

I saw the Stones twice in the old cinema as you go into Watford. They closed the first half of the bill which, and if my memory serves me correctly, included Jet Harris, Billie Davis, and The Swinging Blue Jeans. It was shortly after their second single, 'I Wanna Be Your Man', was released.

The Stones were fantastic young rebels and my main memory of the evening was the top of the bill, John Leyton, being totally drowned out by the audience chanting right through his act with 'we want the Stones!' - something I will never forget. At the same time, I remember feeling sorry for John Leyton. As far as I recall, the Stones became top of the bill following that night, for the rest of the tour.

## ODEON THEATRE
### 15 FEBRUARY 1964, ROCHESTER, UK

**I WAS THERE: JOAN SMITH (NÉE MORGAN), AGE 19**
All I remember is the screaming. We couldn't hear the music. I'm no fan of the Rolling Stones.

## REGAL THEATRE
### 18 FEBRUARY 1964, COLCHESTER, UK

**I WAS THERE: CATHY GRAHAM**
My family owned a garage and cafe at Gun Hill in Dedham, Colchester. It was known as Sampsons' Garage, Gun Hill at the time. This was on the main London to Ipswich road, before the A12 opened. The Stones visited the garage and ate at the cafe twice. My nan, Marjorie, wasn't impressed with them as she took a dislike to Marianne Faithfull who, she explained, was 'messing about with them all.' She reckoned they were all high. Marjorie didn't have time for 'rock stars or nonsense.' Her words!

**I WAS THERE: CYNTHIA ALLCOCK, AGE 16**
I remember attending all the Rolling Stones concerts at The Regal in February and September 1964. We screamed all the way through the performance, sang all the words and jumped up and down to the music. It was deafening and obviously better than performances now at the O2 and Wembley, because the audiences were so much smaller and you were much closer to our idols. Other groups also played there. Eden Kane was one person who performed. I remember him kissing my friend's hand. She didn't wash it for a week!

I recall that after going to these concerts I got my voice fully back in time to go to work on Monday, then we used to queue up again to re-book for the next concert for the following month.

I shared a Dansette record player with my younger sister and there was always a 45rpm record on it – my Rolling Stones or her favourites The Beatles. I used to buy my records from Mann's Music Shop in the High Street, because you could take them into the music booths and listen to them before you purchased … or not. Those were the good old days.

THE ROLLING STONES IN THE SIXTIES: A PEOPLE'S HISTORY

# ODEON THEATRE
## 19 FEBRUARY 1964, STOCKTON-ON-TEES, UK

**I WAS THERE: ANN WOODWARD, AGE 13**

I went to see them on my own. All my friends were Beatles fans (I was also) but I was captivated by the Stones' music. My friends thought them too frightening! I will never forget the sound and feeling of that night. The music was raw and undiluted. No backing musicians - just pure magic. My mother was waiting for me to come home. My father, who was a musician, wasn't told where I was going. He certainly wouldn't have approved.

**I WAS THERE: GEORGE MORLAND, AGE 15**

I was in my last six months at school and went with a group of schoolfriends to see them. The price of a ticket was 9/6 (47p) and John Leyton was top of the bill. I had seen The Beatles three months earlier at the ABC and could hardly hear them for all the screaming. The one thing that sticks in my mind about that Stones gig was that Mick Jagger was sat on a stool on stage backed by the other Stones, singing 'You Better Move On', and you could have heard a pin drop. Brilliant!

**I WAS THERE: DAVID DEGNAN, AGE 18**

During the Sixties I lived in Darlington and every time there was a show at Stockton we went by coach to see many stars, including Billy Fury, Eden Kane, and the Dave Clark Five, and 15 to 20 staff from the TSB bank where I worked went to each show, including the All Star 64 show featuring the Stones.

*David Degnan saw Bill Wyman struck in the eye by a snapped bass string*

The line-up was the Leroys, Billy Boyle, Don Spencer, Billie Davis, the Swinging Blue Jeans, Mike Sarne and, after the interval the Innocents, Jet Harris, the Rolling Stones, Bern Elliott and the Fenmen, Mike Berry and - topping the bill - John Leyton. According to the programme Mick and Keith and Brian were 19, Charlie was 21 and known as Beau Brummell, and Bill was 21. The programme cost two shillings (10p) so I must have had a bit of pocket money in those days. I remember Bill Wyman's guitar string snapped and hit him in the eye. He had a little blood on the side of his face.

### I WAS THERE: SHEILA SOLBERG (NEE EVENDEN)
Middlesbrough had a few clubs at the time, the Outlook and Scene being the two we went to most, and we saw so many acts. We saw the Stones at the Odeon and had a great night.

We left the theatre quickly and found ourselves at the stage door. The roadie had parked the Stones bus against the stage door, making sure no one could get to the group. Unfortunately, he hadn't closed the window properly. One of our gang put her hand through the window as the lads were getting - rather quickly - into the van and snatched Keith's cap off his head. He shouted, 'She's nicked me bleeding hat!' - she being Mary Harrison, the fastest runner in class, who took off with a horde of girls chasing her to get his cap. They didn't catch her.

Back on the coach taking us home, the lining of the cap was taken out and shared out. I ended up with the hat, a houndstooth cloth cap I kept long after I got married, much to the annoyance of my mother, who viewed it as something not quite clean. I eventually chucked it out when I was in my 30s.

## ODEON THEATRE
### 20 FEBRUARY 1964, SUNDERLAND, UK

### I WAS THERE: JOE WEST, AGE 19
I was blown away by the slide-guitar of Brian Jones and remember them playing 'Not Fade Away', as I had the original record of that by Buddy Holly.

After the concert they stayed at the Scots Corner Hotel and much to the disgust of the older generation they left papers all over the floor with telephone numbers on them and trod biscuits into the carpet. This publicity

Sunderland advert

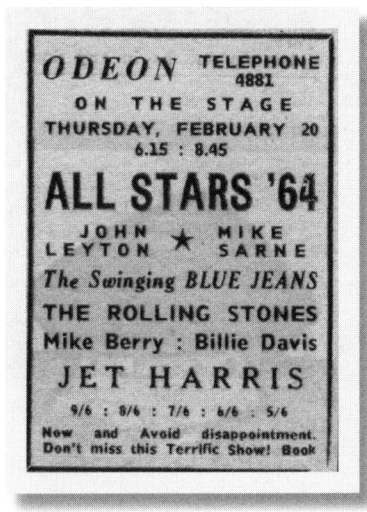

did them much good as did their later refusal to go on the revolving stage at the London Palladium, as they came across as bad boys. The first show had John Leyton and Mike Sarne top of the bill but by the end of the tour the Stones had the biggest following. They still remain one of the best bands I have ever seen.

# WINTER GARDENS
## 22 FEBRUARY 1964, BOURNEMOUTH, UK

### I WAS THERE: DICK IRISH, AGE 18

I went to all their early concerts in Bournemouth except the first one which the Everly Brothers headlined – at that time we didn't know who the Rolling Stones were. John Leyton, as the headliner, appeared on stage after the Stones. The audience wanted the Stones back, so you can imagine the atmosphere, screaming and yelling 'we want the Stones!' My mother was a great Stones fan. Of course, I discovered that the Stones were playing R&B and moved onto the blues which inspired them in the first place, so I got a guitar and learnt to play. I've been in several local bands and I'm now playing bass.

Bournemouth 1964 ticket and press cutting

Dick Irish was inspired by the Stones to learn guitar

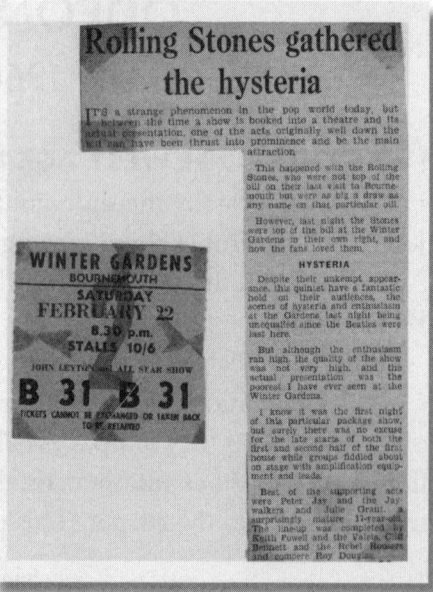

### I WAS THERE: RODNEY CURTIS, AGE 16

They came to my hometown of Bournemouth. They were not top of the bill; that was John Leyton. Also on the bill were Jet Harris (ex-Shadows), Mike Sarne, Billie Davis (Jet's girlfriend at the time), and the Swinging Blue Jeans. One of my mates brought a bag of jellybeans along for a laugh and we threw them at the Stones, just like girls were throwing jelly babies at The Beatles.

*The Stones played a second gig that day.*

## CLUB NORIEK
### 22 FEBRUARY 1964, TOTTENHAM, LONDON, UK

### I WAS THERE: FRANCES PYMONT

There used to be a place called the Club Noriek in Tottenham. It was on the corner of the High Road and Seven Sisters Road and used to be a converted cinema. It was only a very small sort of gig, because the place itself was very small. There were lots of narrow stairs and they were there one evening. It used to be frequented by Tottenham Hotspur players, which I was more interested in because I rather liked Dave Mackay at the time.

### I WAS THERE: DAVE COLYER, AGE 22

One day at work, one of the clients told me he was a security guard at the Club Noriek in Tottenham and there was a Stones concert on. So I invited Linda, a girl from work, along. We stood outside for about an hour in the queue until they started letting people in, and when I approached the security guard he pretended he didn't know me and wouldn't let us in as we didn't have the tickets he'd promised.

We went back in the queue again and as we surged forward I waved some blank pieces of paper at the doormen and we were allowed in, although I still paid for tickets inside. It was packed inside and we could hardly see the Stones, because a group of rockers crowded the stage area.

# HIPPODROME
## 23 FEBRUARY 1964, BIRMINGHAM, UK

**I WAS THERE: SUE MILNER**
We couldn't afford to go to all the shows. Instead, we would hang out at the stage door, at least as close as security would allow us to it. Freddie of Freddie and the Dreamers sang 'You Were Made for Me' to us from the toilet window of the Hippodrome. John Leyton was performing on the same bill as the Rolling Stones. At the time I preferred him to the Stones. When his car drew up at the car park gate at the back of the Hippodrome, my friends and I were squeezed against the barrier. The security guard opened the gate just enough for the car to pass through. I don't know what I was thinking but I squeezed through between the gate and the car. The door opened and John stepped out. I don't know who was more shocked - him or me. I was so close to him, so what could I do? I kissed him, much to the delight and envy of my mates. I became an instant hero and they all wanted to know what it was like. My big moment over, I was sternly escorted back behind the barrier.

**I WAS THERE: WENDY COTTRELL, AGE 11**
My mum took my seven-year old sister and me. Mum had managed to get tickets in the third row from the front, so we had an absolutely brilliant view of the show. The concert was a sell-out and the audience consisted mainly of teenage girls. There was a brilliant atmosphere - the Stones were strutting their stuff, but you couldn't hear anything of the music because the majority of girls, myself included, were screaming their heads off.

I had a huge crush on Brian Jones and in fact wrote to him several weeks before the show, asking if I could go backstage. Brian himself replied – a very nice letter, but no, I couldn't. The Stones must have performed for about an hour or so, and that whole period was utterly electrifying.

THE ROLLING STONES IN THE SIXTIES: A PEOPLE'S HISTORY

# ODEON THEATRE
## 25 FEBRUARY 1964, ROMFORD, UK

### I WAS THERE: RAY FRENSHAM

In 1963 I turned 11. I was an only child growing up in the East End of London, and an avid pop music fan. I never missed an edition of *Pick of the Pops* or *Saturday Club*. A few weeks before its release in June 1963, 'Come On' was played a few times on these shows, and I kinda liked it. I was fascinated trying to work out what words Mick was singing - he sang them so fast. But that was as far as it went.

Then a week or so before its actual release, I remember going through the *Daily Mirror* and looking at Donald Zec's *Pop Page* and stripped along the top of the column was a photo of five young lads leaning over a wall, looking into the camera. They weren't exactly unkempt but, for the times, they looked trouble. Then my father came up behind me and leaned over, looked at the photo and said, 'Who are they?' I replied, 'It's a new group called the Rolling Stones.' My father said, 'Eurgh! It looks like they haven't had a bath for weeks!'

That was the moment I knew I had to follow these boys. For my birthday present I joined the fan club (No.746) and, the following year, for my 12th birthday present my parents took me to see them at the Romford Odeon. Their third single, 'Not Fade Away', had just been released.

Queuing outside the venue, of course we bought one of the mini-poster sized photos of the group from an obvious 'tout'. Inside, I sat on the front row of the circle, my father on my left and my mother on my right. The Stones were top of the bill and their set was only about 15-20 minutes in length.

I have two abiding memories of that night. I recall my mother, whose first experience of teen hysteria this was, saying, 'But why are they screaming so much? You can't hear the music.' And I remember Brian Jones' famous teardrop guitar. I now know that it was white but with the reflection from the footlights it looked a beautiful subtle lime green. I looked at that guitar and I wanted one just like that.

I never got one, of course, and later learned that only about seven of them entered the country, although decades later I bought a guitar from a chap who told me about the then-current whereabouts of Brian's guitar.

## THE ROLLING STONES IN THE SIXTIES: A PEOPLE'S HISTORY

### I WAS THERE: JILL SNOWSELL (NÉE GOODALE), AGE 15

I was at Mulleys Commercial College and the Odeon Cinema was opposite. My friends and I at the college wanted to get tickets for the concert but they went on sale at the Odeon on a weekday morning. I was nominated to ask our very strict Head if we could pop out to the Odeon to get our tickets during our mid-morning free study hour. She was extremely cross at such a request, but we got permission.

Jill Goodale was nominated to ask the Head

There were five of us on the front row of the balcony and my abiding memory is looking to my left and seeing my four friends leaning forward shouting 'Briiiaaan!' He wouldn't have heard them above the deafening screaming. And I didn't know him then but Alan, who became my husband six years later, was also there.

# RIALTO THEATRE
## 26 FEBRUARY 1964, YORK, UK

### I WAS THERE: DUNCAN CURRY

I saw the Rolling Stones at the Rialto but they weren't top of the bill. A fellow called John Leyton who became an actor - he was in *The Great Escape* - was top of the charts with a thing called 'Johnny Remember Me'. The Rolling Stones closed the first half. They were doing 'Not Fade Away' and stuff like that.

### I WAS THERE: GILL THOMPSON

My parents owned the Edinburgh Arms, which was almost directly opposite the Rialto Theatre. It was the nearest hotel to the Rialto, and the Stones stayed with us. The reason I remember it is because we used to take cups of tea up in the morning. This was in the days before courtesy trays in bedrooms. In most places, like ours, it was just two or three rooms with bed and breakfast. What the landlord would do was take them up a cup of tea at, say, eight o'clock in the morning to wake them up for the day, and breakfast would be about half past eight or nine o'clock. My dad told me he had seen Keith Richards in bed with a hat on.

# HIPPODROME
## 29 FEBRUARY 1964, BRIGHTON, UK

### I WAS THERE: FRANK HINTON, AGE 20

I saw the Stones at one of their Hippodrome gigs in 1964. I emphasize 'saw' because in those days the girls screamed non-stop while their idols were on stage. I've seen the Stones, but I can't really say I've heard them.

Who did I go with? 18 months or so ago I would not have been able to tell you but, after not seeing her for about 45 years, I saw her in my local library. Her name was Shirley. She wasn't my girlfriend, just one of my near neighbours. She had hardly changed. I approached her and tentatively asked, 'Did I take you to see Gerry and the Pacemakers many years ago?' 'No,' she said. 'It was the Rolling Stones.' That cleared that up.

Top: Frank Hinton went to the Hippodrome with a near neighbour Above: Frank Hinton's ticket for Brighton Hippodrome

*The Rolling Stones were beginning to attract more of an audience reaction, with scenes of hysteria amongst their predominantly teenage female audience only previously seen at Beatles' concerts.*

# EMPIRE THEATRE
## 1 MARCH 1964, LIVERPOOL, UK

### I WAS THERE: TREFOR JONES

The package tour was billed as All Stars 64. My mates and I had bought tickets by post for the first performance and travelled by train from Prestatyn in Wales. Inside the theatre we sat near the front, and I remember there were many rows with empty seats so the first house was not a sell-out. Not all the artists advertised appeared, but I enjoyed Jet Harris and Bern Elliott and the Fenmen. People were shouting for the Stones and when they came on the place came alive. The songs that stick in my mind from that day were 'Walking the Dog' and 'Not Fade Away'. When I think back to that day, I can still picture each of the guys on stage and feel so glad to have been there.

### MY HUSBAND WAS THERE: GLADYS WOOD

There was a very narrow passageway leading to the stage door. My husband Chas, a police officer, was guarding the stage door while two of his colleagues were trying to clear the passage of a crowd of young ladies as there was a risk of injury to them. Police at the front had cleared the foyer and were trying to disperse them by saying that the group had already left. Suddenly the girls moving out turned back and they were falling over. Chas looked up to where the girls had their eyes on a window, which had Mick Jagger looking out and waving. Chas opened the door, bolting it behind him, rushed upstairs to the room where the band were sitting, pulled Mr Jagger away from the window and slammed it shut. He then took hold of Mick by his lapels and said, 'If you put your head out of that window again, I'll knock it off!' He then left to return to guard the stage door.

*PC Chas Wood preparing for stage-door duties in Liverpool*

THE ROLLING STONES IN THE SIXTIES: A PEOPLE'S HISTORY

# ALBERT HALL
## 2 MARCH 1964, NOTTINGHAM, UK

**I WAS THERE: SUE COVELL (NÉE BURBRIDGE)**

My friend Jill and I went to see the Stones at the Albert Hall. We sat on the second or third row. Jet Harris and Billie Davis were on the bill too, along with Mike Berry, who sang 'Sunshine of my Life'. At that time there was seating at the back of the stage and some fans that were sat at the back of the stage pulled Charlie Watts off his drum stool. It was a brilliant concert. We had seen The Beatles, but this was totally different.

**I WASN'T THERE: FRANK MORGAN, AGE 17**

I didn't go to the gig but remember the bus I was on stopping outside the Albert Hall, where a group of girls who had been to see the Stones got on, including a girl called Margaret who I quite often used to walk home with from the bus stop, as we lived quite close to each other.

What was uncanny that night was that Margaret's character completely changed. She appeared to be in a trance - she literally couldn't talk. The next time I saw her she had reverted back to her normal self. This showed me the excitement the Stones generated in their live shows – that they could affect a typical 'girl next door' so completely.

**I WAS THERE: PAULINE SILVESTER, AGE 15**

For many years my late mother was best friends with the mum of Sixties pop star Mike Berry, and whenever Mike was due to be performing anywhere near our home in Beeston, he came to stay with his Auntie Joan, as mum was affectionately known. Mike was due to appear at the Nottingham Albert Hall as part of a touring show which included Mike Sarne, the Paramounts (later to become Procol Harum), Jet Harris, Billie Davis, and, top of the bill, the Stones. A few days before he was due to arrive Mike contacted my mum and asked if he could bring 'a few friends' with him from the show. My mum was only too happy to agree but secretly doubted it would happen.

I subsequently went to the concert with a friend. It was absolutely electrifying. We returned home on the bus and, as we rounded the corner of where I lived, were astounded to see hordes of people everywhere trying to get into the house where I lived. Mike had brought his 'few friends' with him and had been followed from the concert hall. In fact, he brought most of the performers in the show plus three of the Stones - Brian Jones, Bill Wyman, and Charlie Watts. Somewhere I have some newspaper cuttings about the story that appeared in the local press the next day. Whilst they were there, Charlie took a phone call telling him that 'Not Fade Away' had just gone to No.1 in the hit parade. Needless to say, word got around very quickly, and I was certainly the most popular girl at school the next day.

# OPERA HOUSE
## 3 MARCH 1964, BLACKPOOL, UK

### I WAS THERE: SYD BLOOM, AGE 17
It was that strange tour where they started off almost bottom of the bill and finished up top of the bill. They'd just released the first album, so 'Walking the Dog' was a big track at the time. We were sort old enough to go into the bar and I spent my time ripping beer mats, getting Keith Richards to sign them and flogging them to girls outside. But Jagger was never anywhere to be seen, and nor was Brian Jones. But the others were. Richards was the most friendly.

### I WAS THERE: STEVE GOMERSALL, AGE 15
I had the pleasure of meeting the Rolling Stones in the little Spanish bar in the Winter Gardens during the interval of their first show at the Opera House early in 1964. About four of us from Blackpool had seen The Beatles at the Queens the year before and we were desperate to see how good the Stones were live. Even though we were only 15 at the time, nobody questioned you if you looked 18, so we decided to beat the rush and have a drink before the second half of the

*Mick Jagger gave young Steve Gomersall a knowing sigh*

concert, when to our astonishment in walked the Stones, without any minders or entourage. I couldn't resist such an opportunity so said, 'You are going to have fun and games escaping after the show.' To which Mick Jagger replied, 'Yeah, I think you are right.' I didn't wish to overstay my welcome, so just said, 'Great show, cheers!' To which he modestly replied, 'Well, thank you' whilst giving me the thumbs-up. As they were pushing their way through the throng, trying to make their getaway after the gig, he picked me out of the crowd and gestured a knowing sigh with a shrug of the shoulders and waved goodbye. That made my day and, yes, they were very good.

# ODEON THEATRE
## 5 MARCH 1964, BLACKBURN, UK

### I WAS THERE: JIM TAYLOR

I attended the first of their two shows at Blackburn's Odeon cinema theatre that evening. The place was only half full. I remember that most people were on their feet, grooving to the show. A female friend rushed to the front of the stage, calling out, 'Mick!' Obviously, she couldn't get close to him now. But there was no visible security with their show back then.

### I WAS THERE: DENIS NEALE

My mate said he had managed to get two tickets to see the evening show and I was impressed when he told me we were on the second row from the stage. They also did a matinee performance in the afternoon that my brother-in-law, a couple of years younger than me, attended.

On the night we took our seats looking forward to seeing, but more so to hearing, the songs we had listened to on record for the last year or so. There was an electric atmosphere in the air that night. As the Stones took the stage and launched into their first song, 'Come On', the screams from the many girls in the audience drowned it out completely. They could have been miming for all we knew. It was on a par with Beatlemania. The continuous screaming and hysteria escalated, and it wasn't long before there was a surge of girls from the back of the Odeon towards the stage, by any means available. Bouncers were throwing girls off the stage as the band was trying their best to play. We were into the music but couldn't hear a note being played. At some point during the performance, someone opened the emergency exit doors and dozens of screaming girls rushed in from outside the cinema and tried to storm the stage. It was total chaos. The band were fending off hysterical girls and gamely trying to play on. The security staff were working overtime, hauling people off the stage.

The concert ran its course, but I was left with an overwhelming feeling of disappointment at not being able to enjoy the music we had gone to hear.

## I WAS THERE: MICK MARKHAM, AGE 17

Myself and two mates got into the theatre via the coal chute to the boiler house and ended up in the wings on stage with them during the whole performance. Nobody questioned our presence there. I still can't believe it. We were there for the full gig. I think the Stones thought we were with the theatre, and the management thought we were with the Stones. My wife-to-be was in the audience and amazed to see me pop my head round the curtains. She thought she was seeing things. After the concert, with the fans screaming outside the stage door, Mick Jagger pushed me out first. I was quickly rejected by the fans when they realised I was a nobody. My one claim to fame.

Mick Markham, left, with fellow attendee Keith Mercer, entered via the coal chute

## I WAS THERE: PETER FORBES, AGE 12

Me and a mate had 25 bob (£1.25) front-row tickets at the Odeon on Penny Street. Our own nascent pop group The Rotaters had just been joint clapometer winners with a four-year-old 'Shirley Temple' on the Odeon Saturday morning club talent competition, playing Beatles and Stones numbers to 250 kids. On the same day, on the same stage, in the morning! The Yardbirds, with Eric Clapton, were the other support act that day and night.

When the Stones came on an avalanche of screaming girls invaded the space between us and the stage, in unprecedented Blackburn fashion. The usually gruff and aggressive bouncer, who barked the kids into withering submission at the Saturday morning club, was at a complete loss in the face of that torrent of teenage hormones. We were getting peeved too, having paid all that money only for our front-row privileges being usurped to the point where we could only see and hear jumping girls and their tumultuous cacophony mixed in with a distant rendering of 'Not Fade Away'. So we climbed on our expensive seats to restore some consumer justice and get our money's-worth of the bad boys. Thwarted by the tide of rampant female youth, the beefy bouncer approached us with refocused wrath and dragged us down from our improvised perches, to our mortified indignation. There was only one thing left to do - we threw ourselves in amongst all the girls and started jumping and screaming too. And two young lads began to learn some more about the cathartic pleasures of adolescence, courtesy of Mick, Brian, Keith, et al.

Peter Forbes with joint clapometer winners, the Rotaters

## GAUMONT THEATRE
### 6 MARCH 1964, WOLVERHAMPTON, UK

**I WAS THERE: DAVID COX, AGE 20**
I went with a pal named Keith Parkes. I don't know what happened to him but the funny thing about the show was Keith's granny threw our tickets away by mistake, so we had to speak to the manager, who led us to our seats after everyone was seated and the two spare seats were ours. I always liked the Stones more than The Beatles. That's why I went. It's too long ago for me to remember all the songs but I remember 'Little Red Rooster' and 'Walking the Dog' as they were favourites of mine, and I think they opened with 'It's All Over Now'.

THE ROLLING STONES IN THE SIXTIES: A PEOPLE'S HISTORY

# INVICTA BALLROOM
## 15 MARCH 1964, CHATHAM, UK

**I WAS THERE: SHEENA POPE**

I met the Rolling Stones in March 1964 as a guest of our local paper at the Invicta Chatham. It was the only time they played without Charlie on drums, as he missed his flight. Mick Waller played with them. A wonderful night, and they were so kind.

# ASSEMBLY HALL
## 17 MARCH 1964, TUNBRIDGE WELLS, UK

**I WAS THERE: COLLIE CULMER, AGE 15**

We just couldn't believe the Rolling Stones were coming to Tunbridge Wells. They were our idols. My friends and I were local Mods and worked in Woolworth's and Boots the Chemist. That night we got to the front of the queue so were able to be in front of the stage. When they came on the screaming was unbelievable. I remember leaning on the stage, grabbing Mick Jagger's leg, him saying, 'Calm down, girls.' After letting go of his leg I noticed my pink plastic handbag had

*Collie Culmer, with a friend, grabbed Mick Jagger's leg*

been melted by the stage lights - a great big hole appeared in it. When the show finished, we tried to get backstage for their autographs but they had already left.

**I WAS THERE: LORNA PARKER, AGE 16**

I must have gone with some girlfriends. Everybody - the whole gang of you – went every Tuesday, on the circuit for the Liverpool groups. It was at the Assembly Hall, which is still there. It was a no-alcohol affair. I'd just started work. For everybody you worked with or knew it was somewhere where you could go at 16.

They were scruffy. And they were somehow naughty. And we all thought 'Cor, this is the way to go.' Because it was so different to what we'd had before with the Liverpool sound. They got done for urinating up against some bloke's garage somewhere and all the rest of it. My favourite Stone was Brian Jones, he had a nice smile. He looked quite sweet compared to some of the others.

### I WAS THERE: DAVID WHEELER, AGE 17

We lived in a village three miles away and attended most of the gigs that were held there. I'm sure I'm correct in saying none of them were as packed out as that night. We were all around 17 and it was all so new to us, I think I'd be correct in saying we were overwhelmed. One thing that sticks in my mind was when Brian Jones' guitar string broke and he taunted the fans before he threw it into the middle. I remember the floor going up and down as the fans jumped up to try and catch it. I'm sure today's health and safety would put paid to that.

### I WAS THERE: RICK HODGE

My wife Sandy Morgan - as she was then - went to the Tunbridge Wells Concert. She was 19. She remembers the floor bouncing up and down as the audience were dancing. It struck her at the time how skinny and young they looked.

### I WAS THERE: JENNY GLADWISH (NÉE BRIDGER), AGE 15

Me and my pal Cecelia Bell bunked off school early in the afternoon to go to hers to get ready for the evening. We arrived at the Assembly Hall late afternoon with a couple of other friends and were right at the front of the queue. When the doors opened we rushed to the front, directly next to the stage, to get the best vantage position and stayed put all the way through the performance of the backing group. When they'd finished, the compere came on stage to announce, 'Here they are - the fabulous Rolling Stones!' And all hell broke loose.

There were so many people, mostly screaming girls, pressed so tightly together - a whole sea of bodies surging forward. The barrier broke and we, right at the front, were pushed forward. One of my friends had her blouse ripped and I had that in one hand to protect her modesty whilst I propped up another who I think was on the verge of fainting. There were bouncers and security everywhere. It was complete chaos.

### I WAS THERE: LINDA WALSHAW, AGE 17
My parents were horrified that I went to see the Stones and suggested it might not be the best idea. Mick Jagger did not endear himself to any parents and after The Beatles, who were less of a threat, he showed the face of something quite different. Interestingly, after all those years I went to see them again and it made me smile at the cost. They are the best showmen and in my opinion always have been.

### I WAS THERE: LYNDA PEARCE, AGE 17
Every week there was a dance at the Assembly Hall. We saw Freddie and the Dreamers, Gerry and the Pacemakers, The Animals and many more, and usually the bands played, and we danced. However, when the Stones played everyone just stood and listened, and it was a completely different atmosphere. I was lucky enough to see The Beatles in Brighton at much the same time, but while it was a brilliant concert they really couldn't match the Stones.

### I WAS THERE: NEIL ROWSWELL, AGE 15
I attended with a school friend, Mick Short, who was 14. We both lived nearby in Southborough. I blew an entire week's wages from my paper-round which amounted to 6/- (30p) for the admission. It was my first ever live event and the chance to see a rapidly rising group was too good to miss. I think my most vivid memory was of how pale Brian Jones was. My favourite song of the night was 'Poison Ivy'. It was an amazing night and with everything they have achieved since it has become one of my claims to fame - seeing the Stones twice for 30p, as I also saw them at the free concert in Hyde Park in 1969.

I have a friend who paid £250 for a pair of tickets to see them perform at one of their London gigs, and take great delight in reminding him of my expenditure and how he never got to see Brian Jones.

### I WAS THERE: ROD PADGHAM, AGE 19

It was obviously the early part of their career, so we were unaware of what the future held for them. The good thing about the Assembly Hall was it was a dance hall rather than a seated concert. The day after, I went into my local, the Foresters Arms in Tonbridge, and discovered the Stones had stopped off on the way from the gig but the landlord, Mr Les Barret, refused to serve them, much to the dismay of his young daughter. Last orders were 10.30pm and, while he was normally flexible with us locals, five long-haired teenagers were not welcome.

# CITY HALL
## 18 MARCH 1964, SALISBURY, UK

### I WAS THERE: WENDY LAWRENCE (NÉE CATLIN), AGE 17

I was due to attend the concert, but my father died on the 12th, and I was unsure whether to go. My mother said I should, so I agreed to meet friends in the bar at the Cathedral Hotel, including my closest friends, Sally Warner and Gordon Plumb. I was greeted warmly and handed a double vodka on the rocks - I was two months short of my 18th birthday.

We then walked to the City Hall, where I distinctly remember dancing to 'Get Off of My Cloud', doing all the actions to illustrate each line, i.e. pointing at someone - 'Hey you!' - then waving arms about suggesting coming down from a cloud. Sounds mad, I know, but we were very young. I only recently discovered this particular tune was not released until the following year, which almost made me doubt my memory.

### I WAS THERE: GEOFF COOPER

My first attempt to get to this gig was thwarted before I even left Bournemouth. Having 'borrowed' a friend's Vespa scooter, I was apprehended by a panda car and, not being in possession of any of the required paperwork – I was 16 at the time, no licence, and carrying a passenger – I was escorted back to the police station. The second time we all went in a pal's car on what turned out to be quite an exciting evening, with Brian Jones booting a very persistent girl in the face to prevent her from getting on stage. No security in those days.

# THE ROLLING STONES IN THE SIXTIES: A PEOPLE'S HISTORY

**I WAS THERE: JEAN DEVINE**
I had two handwritten letters from Brian Jones. After their first tour of the States, I wrote to him as a fan through the post and he replied, and it was his own handwriting. I used to carry this letter with me everywhere and had it in my bag when I went to the City Hall.

I got up on the stage to grab hold of Phil May, the singer of the Pretty Things, and I left my bag at the foot of the stage, and it got nicked, along with my letter from Brian. I wrote to Brian and told him my letter had been nicked and he wrote me another one. That one I just lost over the years. It was such a shame. I had such a crush on Brian.

# THE WHITEHALL
## 21 MARCH 1964, EAST GRINSTEAD, UK

**I WAS THERE: KAREN TYRELL**
My grandmother's friend lived next door to Bill Wyman in Penge. I have a photo of them, probably one of their first press photos, signed by each of them on the back. This was just after they recorded 'Come On'. I also have quite a lot of newspaper and magazine memorabilia too, and books, tickets, etc. The first time I saw the Stones live was at a little hall in East Grinstead, in the middle of the High Street, The Whitehall, later turned into a nightclub and since closed. It was so packed that you couldn't even lift your hands up to clap.

Then I noticed various girls fainting and thought, 'Well, that looks like a good idea!' Consequently, I was lifted up over the audience, skirt round my backside and taken to a little room offstage where I 'recovered'. I spent the rest of the gig standing next to Keith Richards on the side of the stage.

I saw the Stones a few times after, at the Hippodrome in Brighton and Fairfield Halls in Croydon where – and I don't know how we did it – we managed to get front-row seats. The most recent occasion was at Hyde Park in 2013. They were fantastic.

**I WAS THERE: RICK HODGE, AGE 15**
They kicked off with 'Walking the Dog' and the place erupted. I remember being pressed against the stage by screaming girls, one of

whom gave Bill Wyman a box with scissors in. He promptly cut off a lock of hair, placed it in the box and threw it back to her. No gig I have since been to has equalled that evening. I've been a fan ever since. When I got home my parents were appalled I'd been to see 'that dreadful group'.

# THE PAVILION
## 22 MARCH 1964, RYDE, ISLE OF WIGHT, UK

### I WAS THERE: PAUL WAVELL, AGE 16
The concert was organised by my science teacher, Mr Sparks, of Ryde School. It was a private fee-paying school which was always thought to be a bit posh. The thought of a master acting as impresario for a rock band did not go down too well with the headmaster and board of governors. The band started with 'Route 66' and played 'You Can't Judge a Book by the Cover', 'Mona' - with tambourine and maracas - and 'Come On'. There was only one policewoman to control a crowd of hundreds.

### I WAS THERE: ANNE GRANT, AGE 15
I was there at the 4pm performance with my friend Jeanette Butt. I had to run from Ryde County Secondary School in Belvedere Street to the Pavilion.

We didn't have time to change from our compulsory school uniform into civvies, but I recall we removed our school ties and stuffed them into our school bags. The Cherokees were a well-known local group, considered the best of all the Isle of Wight bands. They got the show off to a great start, then the Rolling Stones came on. This was amazing for the island, at the time was very staid to say the least. We could hardly believe the Stones were appearing on our little island. It was a great performance and something I've never forgotten.

### I WAS THERE: LORIS VALVONA, AGE 14
The Beatles and the Mersey Sound had swept all before them for a year or so but already there was an emerging new wave of wild rhythm and blues groups with longer hair and a harder image. In the forefront of this new sound, with two hit singles already, were the Rolling Stones, fast

becoming the biggest group around, sending audiences wild throughout the land.

The concert was announced and the tickets went on sale. There were going to be two performances - at 4pm and 7pm. I was determined to see them and although the box office queue was big I managed to get a seat for the afternoon show.

As the date approached the fame of the Stones seemed to grow daily. It was hard to believe they were actually coming to the Isle of Wight. On the day I caught the bus to Ryde Esplanade and the sight as I arrived is something I will never forget. It seemed as if every teenager on the island had gathered around the Pavilion Theatre. The Stones were staying at the Ryde Castle Hotel just across the road. A number of fans got into the hotel and were running around the place amongst the suits of armour, stuffed animal heads and African artifacts, the hotel décor at the time. The Stones' transport, a Ford Thames van or similar, was parked nearby and was covered in messages of love from all over England, some in lipstick and others scratched into the paintwork. There were no spray cans in those days.

Inside the atmosphere was electric. The Shamrocks then the Cherokees were the support bands. The highlight of the latter's set was when they announced, 'One we wrote this afternoon' and launched into a perfect version of The Beatles' 'Can't Buy Me Love', which had only just been released. The crowd went mad, and the excitement went up another notch or two.

The crowd started chanting 'we want the Stones!' as we watched equipment being moved around on stage and, as time dragged on, 'Why are we waiting?' Suddenly there was the biggest collective scream I've ever heard and there they were. A group we had only seen on black and white televisions was now standing on stage in front of us – the Rolling Stones! What happened next is a bit of a blur. I seemed to be carried forward in the mass hysteria of it all as the crowd rushed the stage. The Stones seemed to be used to this and hardly reacted as order was restored and they could get on with their performance. I hardly recall any details of the set or anything else, but the excitement and newness of it all is something that has never left me. The concert was a talking point for weeks. It was great to think the Stones had been to our neck of the woods. One girl at school had a button from Brian Jones' coat, which she had torn off during the chaos in the hotel. Some months later it was rumoured that another young lady had a rather different souvenir of the Stones visit. The Swinging Sixties had definitely arrived on the Isle of Wight.

### I WAS THERE: ANGELA HAMILTON, AGE 1

This concert was organised by my dad. My sister and I have a lot of paperwork from the concert, including the original contract agreement signed by Brian Jones, a ticket for the event, a flyer with all five signatures, and Charlie Watts' drumstick. My sister, then aged seven, sat on Mick Jagger's lap to watch the support band. I was a baby in a pram backstage, so have no memory of the event - only what my parents told me.

# TOWN HALL
## 25 MARCH 1964, BIRMINGHAM, UK

### I WAS THERE: DIANE TUBB

As a teenager still at school I couldn't afford to go and see the event. I stood outside the door by the fountain. All of a sudden, the door opened and out came Brian Jones. He was amazing. He looked so cool smoking his cigarette - I just took hold of his arm and wouldn't let it go. Then a white van arrived which ran over my foot. Brian got into the van and it drove away. It all happened so quickly but it was an unforgettable memory.

Signed programme

# THE ROLLING STONES IN THE SIXTIES: A PEOPLE'S HISTORY

## I WAS THERE: NEIL REYNOLDS, AGE 16

I was still in the Sixth Form at Saltley Grammar School at the time and was also a big fan of Wayne Fontana and the Mindbenders, who were on the same bill. When I saw Wayne Fontana perform at other gigs he always referred to them as the Bricks or Rolling Bricks. My abiding memory of the Stones when I saw them is that they were all dressed the same, in black and white dogtooth jackets and black trousers. They never dressed like ever again. I went backstage after the Town Hall show and got their autographs. I've kept it all these years. I thought all five of them had signed it, but it looks like there's only four. I'm not sure whether it's Mick or Keith who's missing but Brian Jones' signature is clear, so I guess it must be worth a few bob.

Neil Reynolds, in sixth form then, remembers how the Stones were dressed

## I WAS THERE: SALLY MYNOTT, AGE 15

I paid five shillings (25p) and sat behind the stage with schoolfriends Lorna Smith and Jennifer Mellings. We all went to George Dixon Grammar School. I must have been 15 - I can't see my parents letting me go at 14, which is why I missed out on The Beatles. I would have had to pay for myself, and had a Saturday job when I was 15.

I can only admit to seeing them, as we could not hear them due to us all screaming very, very loudly! When we left the Town Hall, it was a bit of a shock as there were loads of rockers waiting to have a go at us in Chamberlain Square. We all scarpered as fast as we could. One girl from school caught her bus home and, when she got off, a rocker had followed her bus, spat at her and drove off on a motorbike. We managed to get some autographs and I kept the book.

THE ROLLING STONES IN THE SIXTIES: A PEOPLE'S HISTORY

# TOWN HALL
## 26 MARCH 1964, KIDDERMINSTER, UK

**I WAS THERE: PAT DAVIES (NÉE SUCH), AGE 16**

I lived on the Comberton estate. I was a Mod then, very much in love with Mick Jagger. I remember it was eight shillings and sixpence (43p) entrance fee and they were fantastic. They played 'Little Red Rooster' and 'It's All Over Now'. I've always been a massive fan. I still think Mick's fantastic.

Kidderminster Stones flyer

Pat Such, as she was in her Mod days, thought the Stones were fantastic

# WINDSOR EX-SERVICEMEN'S CLUB
## 27 MARCH 1964, WINDSOR, UK

**I WAS THERE: STEVE TURNER**

The last time the Stones played Windsor was March '64, back in Peascod Street, this time at the Ex-Servicemen's Club. It was very different from the nights at the Star.

THE ROLLING STONES IN THE SIXTIES: A PEOPLE'S HISTORY

# WILTON HALL
## 28 MARCH 1964, BLETCHLEY, UK

### I WAS THERE: MIKE HOLMAN, AGE 16

The queue for the gig stretched all the way down Church Green Road and around onto Buckingham Road. I also remember being squashed like a sardine in the hall. I'm sure there were many girls sitting on blokes' shoulders to get a better view. The Stones had to stop about halfway through their act because it was totally manic in there, but they continued after a short while. Anything else about that evening is a bit vague, but like most blokes in those days I always wore a suit on Saturday evenings, and my hair hung over my collar.

*Mike Holman was squashed like a sardine at Wilton Ha[ll]*

### I WAS THERE: TED ELDRED, AGE 13

The first picture I ever got of them was out of a newspaper. A black and white picture, probably only three inches by three. Me and my brother had bunk beds and I had the top bunk and started collecting pictures of the Rolling Stones there. My brother wasn't into them. He was more Beatles. They were kind of rebels in their way in the beginning. They'd only just brought out their first record.

I was the first person at the front door and remember somebody coming up, trying to offer me two or three quid for my ticket. I said 'no way!' I wasn't giving my ticket away. I was probably there about half past one in the afternoon. I'm pretty sure a mate of mine - Johnny Carroll - was with me. All I remember is getting right up in front of the stage on the left-hand side and the piano being there. I'll always remember Mick Jagger got up on top of the piano, and Bill Wyman wearing his black waistcoat. I even got to the stage where me and my friend Johnny were going to start our own group. Because it inspired me a little bit. I bought a set of drums and he had a guitar and I remember cleaning out my dad's coal shed at the side of the house, making it all tidy so we could try and do some music in there. It didn't come to anything.

### I WAS THERE: VIVIEN WHITE (NÉE WHEELER), AGE 16

I was an apprentice hairdresser in Bletchley. I was so excited. I made a large scrapbook with every picture and newspaper cutting I could lay my hands on. The protocol at the time was to leave autograph books and other stuff at the desk and collect them all, duly signed, at the end of the evening. I handed my scrapbook over and had a great time. The band was fantastic. At the end I went to the desk to collect my signed masterpiece. What a disappointment! All the autograph books had been signed but my scrapbook had been put on a different shelf because it was bigger and had been missed. Unfortunately, the Stones had already left. I was so upset but it hasn't stopped me from going to several Stones concerts since. We had some good times at Wilton Hall in the Sixties, and I have very fond memories of my time dancing and watching bands there.

### I WAS THERE: STEVE FUNNELL, AGE 17

We would visit Wilton Hall once or twice a week. When the Rolling Stones came they arrived in a Dormobile covered in lipstick where girls had written all over it. I think the Stones were wearing blue shirts with black waistcoats. Outside the hall there were lots of Mod scooters. I was wearing a Beatle jacket with white jeans and shoes that had fur on them. I remember having a girl on my shoulders so she could see them. Later in life I found out my boss was at school with Andrew Loog Oldham. He said all he thought about was pop music.

### I WAS THERE: LIBBY CULSHAW, AGE 14

I went with my friend, also 14. We lived in a village 11 miles from Bletchley and an older boy from the village had a green van in which he was ferrying half the village youngsters to Wilton Hall. My mum came out and quizzed him on his safe driving before we all set off. We all rolled around in the back like a litter of puppies. He could only just have passed his test and in hindsight the grown-ups were worried. There weren't so many cars on the road, but it was all new world, exciting stuff.

We were in high spirits at the prospect of such an adventure.

The Stones were beginning to be heard in our community and across the UK. We walked into Wilton Hall and looked up in amazement at the balcony. We wandered around and looked down from the balcony. We thought we were the bees' knees being in such a grand place, compared to our village hall. We ascertained where the loos were, then went into the main hall to watch everybody else and join in. Everything was so easy then. You simply walked up the steps at either side of the stage and had a wander and a gander round the back. We spoke to the artists. Basically, they were just kids like us but a little older - mainly curious and innocent.

At the break everyone ambled down to the Eight Belles pub, had a few beers and then came back for the second half. I sat in the pub with a half of bitter, terrified every time the door opened in case it was a policeman coming to check my age.

After that Wilton Hall hosted great groups. I remember traipsing down to the Eight Belles at half time when The Hollies played there. It was funny sitting in the pub with Alan Clark and co. Just as if we were out with our mates and supporting their music, which we were.

## I WAS THERE: KEITH WHEELER, AGE 17

I consider myself one of the lucky ones to have been a teenager in the Swinging Sixties. You wouldn't believe it, but Bletchley was a good place to be if you were into live music. There were two live bands at Wilton Hall every Saturday night and a disco dance midweek. There was also a weekly disco dance at the Labour Hall in Buckingham Road. We also had the option of going to the California ballroom in Dunstable, where you were guaranteed at least two good bands. The only problem was the lack of transport. There were no buses or trains, so you had to have your own transport or hitch a lift.

We saw most of the well-known artists at these venues and sometimes travelled to surrounding towns if they featured someone we hadn't seen. I remember cycling to Luton to see the Everly Brothers and also managed to get a ticket through Rodex Coats to see The Beatles at Northampton, which turned out to be a complete waste of time as you couldn't hear a thing for girls screaming.

When we heard the Stones were coming to Wilton Hall we said it doesn't matter who is on elsewhere, we must see the Stones. Just after this I was hit with bad news - my parents had booked a holiday in Great Yarmouth, which meant I would miss the Stones. I spent the next few weeks pleading to get out of the holiday but there was no way I would be left at home. I must have spent most of the holiday moaning about missing the Stones, when my father eventually gave in and said he would drive me back to Bletchley on Saturday afternoon and we would return to Yarmouth the next day. You can imagine how long it took in an old Standard 10, with no main roads as there are now.

I got to Wilton Hall just before the Stones came on. The hall was packed to the rafters, the atmosphere was electric, and it's a night I will never forget.

## I WAS THERE: JACKIE STEVENS (NÉE LANE), AGE 16

I was a Saturday girl at Woolworth's and because I lived in New Bradwell I had no time to leave work, get a bath and dressed up. I went to another girl's house in Eaton Avenue, where we got ready. I wore a royal blue satin dress, which my mother had made for me some weeks earlier when I had gone to see another band there, which may have been Johnny Kidd & the Pirates.

My father had been killed in a road accident in 1962, and this was my mother's first little holiday since then. She was going to Butlin's somewhere and said she would have been very worried about me getting home because we used to thumb a lift if we missed the train to Wolverton. She insisted that my grandma came to stay for the weekend to make sure I got home safely. I don't know what she would have done if I hadn't. We had no phone and no transport of our own. I remember it being 2/6 (13p) to get in. I earned 17/10 (89p) for a Saturday at Woolworth's and had

Woolworth's Saturday girl Jackie Lane, as she was, got changed at a friend's house

# THE ROLLING STONES IN THE SIXTIES: A PEOPLE'S HISTORY

15/4 (77p) left for a drink at Wilton Hall and my 1/6 (7p) train fare home. The remainder was my pocket money for the rest of the week.

I was, after that gig, a massive Mick Jagger fan, and still am. However, I loved their early things best, especially 'Not Fade Away', 'It's All Over Now', 'The Last Time', and most of all 'Little Red Rooster' and other bluesy numbers.

### I WAS THERE: BRENDA POLLARD, AGE 17

I was at Northampton School of Art at the time and the group had a big following there. We especially loved 'Come On'. We were so thrilled the Stones were coming to Bletchley and told our friends from London, one of whom lived next door to Bill Wyman's brother Paul Perks in Penge. At the time my sister and I had a Saturday job on Bletchley market on a jeans stall. We were paid the grand sum of £1 a week. The 10 shillings (50p) to see the Stones was a vast sum of money to pay for the dance on a Saturday night. We didn't call it a concert or a gig then.

I bought a pair of jeans from the stall and rushed home to undo the hems and fray the bottoms so I could wear them to the dance. This was very 'in' at the time and perfect to wear to college and get covered in paint. I can't remember much about the queue but I do remember that once inside we could not move. It was one big crush, shoulder to shoulder, but nobody minded. There was no room to move let alone dance. There was also no alcohol sold at all, but you didn't need it.

It was a fantastic experience and all these years later I cannot believe that we actually saw them in Bletchley and that they still command great audiences today.

Our dad couldn't stand the Stones and couldn't understand why on earth we would want to spend all that money to see them and wear our 'bloody overalls' to go in. He called them long-haired louts.

### I WAS THERE: PC PAT KENNY, AGE 36

I was in the old Bucks Constabulary – now Thames Valley – at the time based in Bletchley. I was on duty there and before proceedings started all the cars were parked on the car park. Towards the back was a car covered in lipstick – 'love you, Brian.' It was Brian Jones' car. His car doors were not locked, the windows were wound down, and there was a lot of expensive gear on the back seat. There were two special constables there and I said to them, 'Has anybody gone in to tell Brian Jones about it?' They said, 'No.'

I went to the dressing room and there they were - with the girl fans all around them. I told Brian what I'd come for, he thanked me and off he went off to make the car secure. Mick Jagger then called out to one of the roadies, 'Give the officer one of our photos, and we'll sign it for him.' Back comes one of these postcard-sized photos and he says, 'No, not one of them - those we got yesterday' and when he came back with it, it was a large photo about 22 inches wide and about 10 inches in depth. It was like a panoramic photo, there were big pictures of them on there, and he said we will sign it for you.

By this time Brian had come back and each one of them signed it. I couldn't believe my luck. I was in there about 10 minutes chatting with them. Although they looked scruffy, I found them very polite. When they were prepared to start their performance, I was in the ballroom at the back of the hall. The hall was packed. You couldn't move. And all round the stage were these bodyguards. I could see why they were there. As soon as they started playing there was a surge forward of those trying to get onto the stage.

Afterwards I got several offers of five pounds for the photo. We put it up for auction some years afterwards. It raised £420. One of my daughters said, 'Oh, you've got rid of our inheritance!'

## WEST CLIFF HALL
### 31 MARCH 1964, RAMSGATE, UK

**I WAS THERE: LINDA PLANT, AGE 15**
My dad got the Stones and The Kinks and all these other top groups down to Ramsgate. I used to go down to West Cliff Hall to see all the groups and go backstage. Dad was involved with Ramsgate Football Club. He wanted to get some funds. The best way of getting funds for a football club was to hold a dance. The promoter was a chap called

# THE ROLLING STONES IN THE SIXTIES: A PEOPLE'S HISTORY

Gordon Eddy. He managed to get all the acts to come down from London. They managed to book the Stones before they rocketed. They weren't as popular at that time as The Beatles.

We didn't need to advertise the Stones. It just went round the town, word of mouth. It sold out just like that. The Stones had their photo taken with my dad. I was there when the picture was taken, but was behind the door. It was quite amazing how different each member of the group was. You got Charlie Watts dressed up in a suit, sat on the drums, quite withdrawn; you got Bill Wyman, clearly the eldest, but he made more sense if you spoke to him than any of them; Brian Jones never made a lot of sense because I think he was on one substance or another; Mick Jagger just stood around grinning; and Keith Richards looked 90 when he was in his 20s.

*That night I was stood in the wings when they were playing and girls were fainting in the front*

That night I was stood in the wings when they were playing, and girls were fainting in the front. They'd got a barrier up and the bodyguards, such as they were in those days, were handing over the girls because they were passing out. We thought there was going to be a riot at one stage. But it all went off very well. We had a good time. It was innocent, but we had a good time.

*April 1964 saw the Rolling Stones fulfil a number of ballroom and dance hall commitments entered into before the success of 'Not Fade Away', released in Britain on 21 February 1964 by their record label Decca and peaking at No.3 in the UK charts. 17 April 1964 also saw the release of the Stones' debut album.*

THE ROLLING STONES IN THE SIXTIES: A PEOPLE'S HISTORY

# LOCARNO BALLROOM
## 1 APRIL 1964, STEVENAGE, UK

*Photos: Brenda Parker*

The Stones in action at Stevenage's Locarno Ballroom

### I WAS THERE: LYNNE WALTERS, AGE 16

The Locarno Ballroom, or the Mecca as we all called it, was an old-fashioned ballroom with a mirrored glitter ball, even though it was quite a new building. There was a proper wooden dancefloor with a low semi-circular stage at one side for the band. The dancefloor was surrounded by a carpeted area with tables and chairs and a bar. There was also a balcony upstairs with tables and chairs. On Saturday nights they had proper dances but for teenagers the important night was Wednesday - that was when there were live bands.

# THE ROLLING STONES IN THE SIXTIES: A PEOPLE'S HISTORY

Looking back, it was quite incredible that we saw all the important bands of the Sixties there – I remember seeing The Searchers, The Swinging Blue Jeans, The Dave Clark Five, The Who (or The High Numbers as they were then), Geno Washington and the Ram Jam Band, Small Faces, Spencer Davis, Georgie Fame, Them, and many others.

*Lynne Walters recalled a shocked bouncer with his shirt buttons ripped off*

Image: Lynne Walters

Stevenage was very much a Mod town and mostly kids who went on Wednesday nights were Mods who liked to dance and show off their latest outfits. I guess the Stones had been booked before they had become as big as they were by the time they played. I was a Mod and with my boyfriend all the usual crowd of Mods were there but there were also a lot of girls desperate to get as close to the stage as possible.

As the stage was only just about a couple of feet high, the Stones were quite vulnerable to being grabbed so the management got all the bouncers usually on the door and patrolling the dancefloor to surround the stage and link their arms to form a barrier between the screaming girls and the band. I had seen The Beatles a few months before at Hammersmith so had heard that sort of screaming before, but it was quite unusual at the Mecca because we were mostly Mods and therefore super-cool! I don't really remember much about the music as I probably couldn't hear very much of it. My most vivid memory is afterwards when I saw one of the bouncers – they all had to wear a sort of uniform of white shirt, black jacket and bow tie - looking totally shocked as all the buttons had been ripped off his shirt. That night stands out in my memory as it was quite wild. I hasten to add I was not one of the screaming girls.

### I WAS THERE: PENNY SCOOT (NÉE RACHER), AGE 17

My late dad Stanley was publicity and advertising manager at Geo. W. King, Argyle Way, Stevenage until 1966. He told me that my favourite group the Rolling Stones was going to perform at the All Fools Charity Beat Ball on 1 April 1964, being organised by the Geo. W. King Apprentice Association. He asked if I would I like to sell raffle tickets at the Locarno Ballroom that night and as a reward would probably be able to meet the Stones backstage.

Penny Racher and Jacky Jenkins, as they were, saw the Stones at the All Fools Charity Beat Ball

My oldest friend and next-door neighbour Jacky More (née Jenkins), also 17, was invited to come with me. We were both very excited and I remember selling a lot of raffle tickets as well as being able to watch the Stones and accompanying bands. Both Jacky and I were privileged enough to go backstage and meet the group. They all signed my autograph book, which I still have. Afterwards my dad picked us up and took us back to Hitchin. Both Jacky and I remember them as being very polite and courteous.

### I WAS THERE: ROGER GLAZEBROOK, AGE 18

I went with my mate Mick. Tickets cost 21 shillings (£1.05). It was perhaps the Mecca's greatest moment. It was packed, but as 18-year-olds we thought, 'What a great night - it would be all girls.' Big mistake. Yes, there were girls, but no one was dancing. They were all screaming around the stage, so we ended up just going to the bar. The day the Stones turned up in Stevenage was a great talking point in town. About two years later my old firm booked Cream at the Hermitage in Hitchin - Eric Clapton, etc. We also had The Who, Geno Washington, Manfred Mann. But nobody topped the Stones.

### I WAS THERE: PAT KINGSLAND, AGE 17

We weren't supposed to be there because Wednesday nights were for over-18s as they had a bar. But Monday nights was a disco night – called a DJ night in those days - and it was for the younger ones really. I don't think my mother would have let me go if I was 16.

The girl I worked with had been a schoolfriend and lived opposite us. She and I went together. We worked in the local hairdressers' and neither of us at the beginning of the day had a penny to our names but we obviously did well with our customers because as apprentices you didn't get much pay but we'd had good tips so had enough money to actually have a drink that evening.

The ticket price was six shillings (30p) and there were loads of other groups there. I don't remember any of the others. I think it was just that the Stones were so good. It was a great night. My brother was a King's apprentice and said the Stones were only paid £50 that night because when they booked them they hadn't had a hit record. They got them really cheap. My boyfriend Terry – my husband now - decided that night he didn't want to go. I had a ticket for him and I kept the ticket. When I came home my brother said, 'You're stupid - you should have sold it on the door for 10/6.' (53p). I think the ticket price at the time was only six or seven shillings (30p - 35p). A few years ago we sold it because it had Rolling Stones autographs on the back, and we got nearly £800 for it.

## I WAS THERE: ANNA ASKEW, AGE 15

I was in the Red Cross in Stevenage. As a cadet I used to come to the Mecca for emergency aid and saw all these stars who visited the town. I used to stand on the side of the stage and was there when the Stones played. There's a photograph of me on the night with a girl who collapsed after screaming too much, trying to get at Mick Jagger. I went with my mother and later had a drink with all the members from the group.

## I WAS THERE: PEEWEE COCHLAN, AGE 17

I went with my mate Mitch – John Mitchell. We were both No.1 fans of the Stones. I can't remember if we pulled that night or not. I do remember that we paid 7/6 (37p) and they were dressed in smart casual clothes.

*Peewee Cochlan (right, with John Mitchell) can't recall if he scored that night*

# THE ROLLING STONES IN THE SIXTIES: A PEOPLE'S HISTORY

## I WAS THERE: ROGER COMLEY, AGE 19

I was one of the 115 apprentices that year at Geo. W. King. Another apprentice named Tom Clitheroe managed a band in Stevenage and we were members of the G.W. King Apprentice Association, which organised visits to many shows, like the Stones, Freddie and the Dreamers, The Beatles' Christmas Show, and others at the Empire, Finsbury Park.

Tom Clitheroe booked the Stones for £500, and we sold tickets for the Locarno show at 15 shillings (75p) each for apprentices to buy. I had about 20 apprentices to
contact at work to advertise events and sell tickets. I was given a job to help marshal the balcony and clear up the chairs after. It was mostly a boys' night out, with some girls as guests of the boys.

## I WAS THERE: MIKE PEG, AGE 14

I was there with my first girlfriend - Susan Gunning from the Chells. She went to Heathcote School. I lived in Shephalbury. Stevenage was great in those days. The Stones were my favourites and that day lives in my memory. We were young Mods and the Mecca was our regular. That night was special and the place was packed. We stood in the middle of the dance floor, not far from the stage and just jumped up and down and joined in the noise - as you do. It was crazy. We saw The Who at the Mecca around then, in equipment-smashing mode, but the Stones were the best.

## I WAS THERE: DEREK TURNER

I was on the committee that organised the dance at the then Mecca ballroom. I remember the night, turning up in my best suit as you did in those days, to help administer the event. We formed a cordon completely around the stage to keep the frenzied mass of teenage girls from overrunning the stage. As it was, there were many girls fainting and being passed over the top of the crowd to safety.

I remember wondering whether we could hold the crowd back from the stage as the pressure of the masses was huge. We had to brace ourselves against the stage to keep the cordon together. The Stones were a scruffy bunch compared to us teenagers at the time. I thought, with all the tugging and pulling, 'Will my best – and only – suit survive the night?' and 'What the hell are we doing protecting such an outfit?'

# THE ROLLING STONES IN THE SIXTIES: A PEOPLE'S HISTORY

## I WAS THERE: MARY ABRA, AGE 15

None of my friends wanted to go but I was determined, so went alone. I remember there was a line of bouncers with arms linked at the front of the dancefloor before the stage. I was right at the front, quite small, and the crowds were pushing forward. The bouncers were worried I would get squashed so they let me and a few other girls who were also in danger of getting squashed go through and onto the stage and to the back of the stage to safety. However, when I got onto the stage I took the opportunity of sitting next to Charlie Watts and his drum kit. I was soon hauled off and taken to the back of the revolving stage. My idol at the time was Brian Jones. I loved his floppy hair.

*Mary Abra (left, with sister Margaret) found the Stones friendly and polite over breakfast*

My next encounter with the Stones was in the summer of 1976 when they appeared at Knebworth. I was working as a waitress at the Blakemore Hotel, Little Wymondley, which was where the Stones stayed. I was on duty on Sunday morning when they turned up. Mick Jagger came bounding into the foyer, where there was only myself and the receptionist. I stood at the reception and signed in the casual waitress book whilst Mick Jagger booked in. The receptionist said to him, 'Name please.' He replied 'Jagger.' Then she said, 'Initial' - as if she didn't know - and he said, 'M' and disappeared up to his room. I thought 'gosh, he's quite short!' I seemed to remember him being tall all those years ago when I'd seen him at the Locarno.

The other Stones all came into the dining room, where I served them breakfast. They were friendly, polite and no trouble at all. I didn't ask any of them for their autographs, I don't know why - I wish I had. 1976 was a very hot summer. I was living in Bude Crescent in Symonds Green, not far from Knebworth as the crow flies. That evening, standing in my garden, I could hear their music from Knebworth. It was pure magic.

# THE ROLLING STONES IN THE SIXTIES: A PEOPLE'S HISTORY

## I WAS THERE: MARGARET SENIOR, AGE 19

They were well on their way when they appeared there. At the Locarno, on the Saturday nights when different bands use to play, us girls were usually eyeing up the talent as were the boys.

I recall several bands that went on to become really famous who played the Locarno - The Beatles and the Rolling Stones being the most popular. The Locarno had a half-circle shaped stage and not much room, but a huge dancefloor that had a balcony all around it where some just stayed up there watching the dancers. The memory I have of the Stones was skinny, hippie-looking boys who looked scruffy compared to other bands.

## I WAS THERE: FRANCIS CROUCHER, AGE 14

It was every other Wednesday night that they would have a top Sixties group. We would go to the Black and White café in the High Street before. That's where the groups would go before the show. One night whilst walking to the town to see Manfred Mann there was a van parked about 200 yards from my house in South Road and as I walked past one of the group got out and asked the way to the Kayser Bondor - what a shock. We saw the Swinging Blue Jeans, Johnny Kidd & the Pirates, and others. But the top group was the Rolling Stones. The place was packed - you couldn't move in there. l remember their van, because the girls there had written all over it. It was an old Bedford.

## I WAS THERE: DON MAXWELL

I had a band called the League of Gentlemen, named after one of my favourite films at that time. I had a good relationship with the then manager of the Locarno – Mr Dijon. He liked the League of Gentlemen very much and always gave us the opportunity to support up and coming acts, so when he phoned and asked if we would be interested in supporting the Stones I accepted straight away.

I rolled up early evening to set up and walked into the dressing room backstage, where I met Charlie Watts. He had arrived on his own and was sitting by himself drinking from a large bottle. He looked up and I said 'hello' and he acknowledged me. He didn't seem to have much to say so I didn't indulge in conversation.

The rest of the Stones turned up later that evening and by the time they went on the whole place was buzzing. The Locarno had a revolving stage and as it began to turn, they were introduced. At this point the whole crowd surged forward. Safety barriers were unheard of in those days – there was just a row of bouncers trying to keep the girls off the stage. During the show many girls were fainting and being transferred to the back of the stage by the bouncers. The crush was really heavy and my soon to be wife and her friend had to force their way to the side of the room. I had climbed onto a photo booth on the left of the stage and had a perfect view of their show. It was a very electric atmosphere, and their performance was excellent.

I went backstage afterwards and got them to sign my future wife's autograph book. They didn't hang around for very long and were not the most talkative, but it was obvious that their career was beginning to take off rapidly and they were living life at a very fast pace. All in all it was a great night, and at that time no one really knew just how big rock 'n' roll would become.

## I WAS THERE: COLIN STANDRING, AGE 17

The Stones were the first band to sell out the Locarno - over 2,000 tickets. They were also the first band I saw that ignored the 'revolving stage' procedure. The stage was built on a large revolving disk format with a backdrop in the middle. When the support band finished the stage would revolve with the band playing out and the new band would come around already playing their first number. Not the Stones. The stage revolved around to reveal just the equipment. Jagger and co then walked on nonchalantly, picked up their instruments, tuned up at leisure and started to play. In those conservative days that was a sensation.

## I WAS THERE: BRENDA PARKER

I saw them when they played the Locarno Ballroom in Stevenage. By then they'd had a hit with 'I Wanna Be Your Man' and had released 'Not Fade Away'. The show was organised by a company called George W. King, where my dad worked, and when he heard that they were looking for someone to sell raffle tickets at the show and that the reward for doing so would be actually getting to meet the Stones, he volunteered me immediately. Mums and dads may have hated the Stones at that time,

# THE ROLLING STONES IN THE SIXTIES: A PEOPLE'S HISTORY

but my dad was cool and knew I was a huge fan and how excited I'd be.

Annette and I dutifully sold our fair share of raffle tickets, but no one told us when and where we were supposed to go to meet the Stones, and by the time we found out how to get backstage there was no one there to introduce us, so it was a bit of an anti-climax. I was very shy back then so just stammered something about how much I liked their records and they just smiled politely. Apparently, there was a photographer from the local paper and although I didn't see him take it, a picture appeared in the next edition showing Annette, another girl I didn't know, and me with Keith, who was reading the *NME* when I approached him and in the picture he's reaching out to sign a photo of the Stones that I'm holding out to him.

One thing I remember very clearly and which I thought was very odd at the time was that Brian wasn't with the others. He was all by himself in a very small space not much bigger than a closet. Now that all the animosity they felt towards him because of him originally negotiating more money for himself has come out it makes sense that he wasn't with them, but I had no idea they'd started to isolate him and freeze him out as early as that. He was very sweet, but I remember feeling sorry for him because he was just being ignored. It's really quite shocking how Brian's been relegated to the dustbin of history when he was so talented and played such an integral part in the Stones' story. He was my favourite Stone.

Unfortunately, we had to leave a few minutes later so they could do the

Brian Jones was Brenda Parker's favourite Stone

Keith Richards is kept busy with signing duties, with Brenda Parker among his customers

show. And the show was great. By now they'd given up on the matching outfits and I remember Brian was wearing a striped waistcoat. I've no idea why that stuck in my mind. The stage was pretty small, and there was a huge crush of people pushing and shoving and trying to get as close as possible.

Mick had learned how to strut his stuff by now and was vigorously shaking a pair of maracas, and Brian had a tambourine and kept coming dangerously close to the edge of the stage to shake it in people's faces. He may have been persona non grata backstage, but he really came alive during the show and seemed to be having a great time, taunting people with that tambourine. People kept reaching up to grab him and Mick, but at the last seconds they'd both somehow skip back just in time.

At this time, Brian was very much in the forefront of the group and people were screaming and reaching out to him just as much, if not more so, than Mick. Bill never moved but just stood there like a statue, holding his bass almost vertical to the ground, pretty much ignoring all the chaos going on all around him. It was really an exciting show - the best one of all the times I saw them.

In April '64 the Stones weren't the huge superstars they went on to become, so although there was a massive crush of bodies pressing forward to try to get to them and some girls calling out the names of their favourite Stone, you could still hear the music and feel the raw energy they were generating from it. A lot of that got lost, as they became genuine pop stars and started appearing regularly on TV and headlining their own tours. Don't get me wrong - they were still wonderful. But when Mick stopped singing 'I Just Wanna Make Love To You' with a salacious sneer on his face and switched to lamenting about 19th nervous breakdowns, a lot of the danger and the edginess that had set them apart was gone.

# PALAIS
## 3 APRIL 1964, WIMBLEDON, UK

**I WAS THERE: JANE TOMKINS**
By the time I went to see the Stones again, at Wimbledon Palais, they had become much more famous and I found the whole experience quite an eye-opener. Girls were going crazy and it was extremely crowded and

hot. With a great degree of determination I managed to force myself quite near to the stage and was so excited to see the group up close. Some girls were fainting and being hauled across our heads and onto the stage by security. Nearer the end of the show, we were all soaking wet because it was so hot. I remember laughing as one girl said her brand-new outfit had shrunk as she had been sweating so much.

I smile when I remember having to explain to my bemused mother the following morning why my brand-new white shoes had become completely black and wrecked by the stampeding fans. I saw quite a lot of other famous groups back then, as they even appeared at local village halls. I remember seeing The Animals, The Yardbirds and The Who in Wallington Public - it all seems so improbable now.

## MCILROY'S BALLROOM
### 9 APRIL 1964, SWINDON, UK

**I WAS THERE: MALCOLM CLARE**

I was in a group called Rob and the Rockettes. I remember queuing up Regent Street to get in and was overjoyed to see the bad boys of rock, as this was my first time at any rock concert and I would not have missed it for the world. I was extremely lucky to have a spot right up against the left side of the stage and could touch Brian Jones. I was that close. He was playing his lime green f-hole Gretsch guitar. Charlie Watts was a joy to watch, as he was an excellent jazz drummer, playing my instrument of choice. The supporting group on the night was a local band called the Whispers who had Justin Hayward in their line-up, pre-Moody Blues, being a Swindon lad in those days.

Malcolm Clare, with Rob and the Rockettes, behind his kit, and posing for the camera

# THE ROLLING STONES IN THE SIXTIES: A PEOPLE'S HISTORY

## I WAS THERE: BERNARD LINNEGAR, AGE 18

The second Stones gig I went to at McIlroy's was a completely different kettle of fish from the first. Some hit records had been produced in the interim and the situation had changed somewhat. The place was heaving. There were a record number of people in that room. There was talk at the time of there being 2,000, which would never be allowed now. I remember just about getting through the door but no further and because of the lack of floor space people were standing on windowsills. I followed suit. There was a large single sheet of glass – there was no double-glazing then - between me and the street below. Imagine what the health and safety police would have to say about that these days.

At some point I had a pass out to get a drink at a nearby pub, it being impossible to get to McIlroy's bar. It was then that I witnessed what was to become my most enduring memory of the whole evening. In the street outside was a fleet of vehicles from Leighfields, a now defunct local building company, who had a team of workmen inside the department store busily propping up the ballroom floor above them with Acrow props. Can you imagine?

## I WAS THERE: VIVIEN EDWARDS (NÉE CROXON), AGE 17

When the Rolling Stones came to town, that was a big event. They played three shows at McIlroy's. I went to the last one. I remember queuing for a long, long time outside and when we actually got in McIlroy's you had to go up this lovely staircase to the ballroom, then there was more queuing upstairs for the cloakroom to put your coats. I remember we thought 'no, blow that, we're not gonna wait that long!' So we put our coats on the floor in the corner. But everyone else had the same idea. So when we came back to get our coats everyone else had done the same and there was a great big pile of coats on top and ours were at the bottom. It took us ages to find them and then we had to get the last bus home. I suspect we

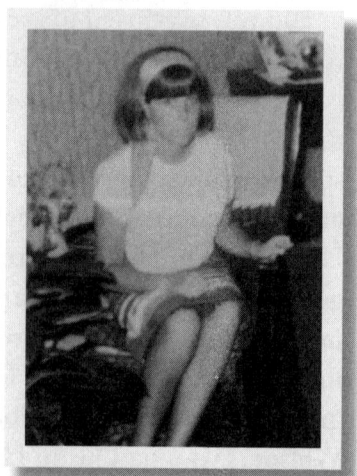

Vivien Croxon, as she was then, saw the last of three Stones shows at McIlroy's

missed it and probably had to walk home that day.

I think it was about five shillings to get in. I went with friends. I can even remember what I was wearing, a brown suede dress with lace up the front, with criss-cross, and then it was fashionable to put your cardigan on back to front so the buttons were at the back. I remember sitting on someone's lap. I was right at the front. I remember being so close I could touch them and screaming maybe at one stage. My picture was in the *Adver*, the local newspaper. Looking at the picture now I can see that I'm mesmerised by them, and some of the audience are really screaming.

## PIER BALLROOM
### 11 APRIL 1964, HASTINGS, UK

**I WAS THERE: CHRISTINE TOMS, AGE 16**
They arrived late and my boyfriend at the time helped to run the speedboat, so they were brought in on that from the beach as all the fans were packing the pier. I helped them up the steps and took them into the dressing rooms at the back of stage. I managed to get their autographs of course. Then a lot of girls broke in and it was chaos for a while. They were very tired, having already done a few gigs down the coast, possibly Brighton, and I seem to remember they only stayed for about 20 minutes as they were headlining that evening.

## CUBI KLUB
### 16 APRIL 1964, ROCHDALE, UK

*The Stones were scheduled to appear at the Cubi Klub but, with the venue full and the band backstage, the decision was taken to cancel the concert for health and safety reasons due to the huge numbers of people in the audience.*

# THE ROLLING STONES IN THE SIXTIES: A PEOPLE'S HISTORY

## I WAS THERE: PETER OLDHAM, AGE 18

I remember going into this basement of this factory or warehouse, thinking it was a disaster waiting to happen. I cannot remember the size of the room, although I feel it was not that high and had pillars, but it was hot with body heat so I can only presume there was limited ventilation. I was at the front, right up to the stage, and the barrier was made out of church pews, where the backs can be moved over to sit either way. There was no security staff or bouncers. The stage entrance was to my right, little more than 10 feet away. I could not see what was happening behind the curtain, but I recall at one point a cheer and messages passed down the line that the group was there and had been seen by those who could see behind the curtain. I cannot remember how long I was there until a guy came on stage and said the Rolling Stones would not appear. I seem to think we exited peacefully. In retrospect any sort of stampede, crowd rush or maybe a fire and the loss of life would have been substantial.

## I WAS THERE: MIKE DUNKERLEY

The club was opposite the Yelloway bus garage. I was there with hundreds of others milling around outside. Police were trying to maintain some sort of order when word came that the show had been cancelled due to 'safety reasons'. Later stories appeared to indicate a car carrying two of them from Leeds had broken down and they would not be able to make it.

## I WAS THERE: BOB LEE

There was the famous club appearance that wasn't at Rochdale. I went to that. My take on it is that there was almost a riot. Thousands of us turned up there. You could book in advance but when we got there, they said they couldn't go on because it was our fault – they'd sold too many tickets. The police had stopped them because of the fire regulations. They couldn't have that many people in.

  I just thought, like everybody did at the time, it was just a con to get people there. It had been done before in Manchester with other groups. Some years after, a club in Oldham advertised the Cream at the Stax Club, and I've got the ticket for that. That was another club where everyone turned up and the group didn't. It was only afterwards that I found out that the Stones did turn up - but they were advised it wasn't safe for them to perform.

# LOCARNO BALLROOM
## 17 APRIL 1964, COVENTRY, UK

### I WAS THERE: SUSAN BROWN, AGE 17

I bought myself a blue mini-dress with see-through nylon sleeves and eight buttons at the cuffs. It was so in fashion at the time and cost me three weeks' wages to buy from C&A. Plus I put on my silver charm bracelet. I'd collected loads of charms. I was really proud of it. With my long red hair, back-combed into a beehive, I was, I must say, looking great.

When we got to the concert, I'd never seen so many girls in one place. The music started, on the stage came the Stones. It was so magical. Everyone was screaming, including myself. All I wanted to do was to get nearer the front. We pushed and shoved until we were right on the front row. As I looked up, Mick Jagger was just picking up his tambourine from the floor. I lent in to touch his leg, pulling myself onto the stage, when my charm bracelet got stuck on his trouser leg. He had started his song running across the stage, with me at the bottom of his trouser leg, and they started to slip down at one side. The next moment a gang of men were there with fire extinguishers trying to control us.

Once outside the venue, I was like a drowned rat. We tried to get on the last bus but missed it, so with stiletto shoes in hand we walked home. Luckily Mum and Dad were in bed. I had a job the next day explaining about my dress, which was never the same again. It was one of the greatest times ever.

### I WAS THERE: TED GARRATT

By the time I went to see them again, the following April, 'Not Fade Away' was out. I went with one other friend, again on the bus, to see them at the Locarno, which is now Coventry Library. That night was complete carnage. There was a riot. There were people jumping up and down on the balcony. The building seemed to be swaying and they revolved the revolving stage and the fire brigade came round from the other side and began hosing down the audience. The Stones disappeared round the back because of the revolving stage. That got a lot of media attention locally.

Because we'd gone on the bus, we found out they were staying at the Leofric Hotel and went and stood outside there. I'm quite a freckly, ginger-haired, big lips sort of character and got asked for my autograph because one of the girls standing outside the hotel thought I was Mick Jagger! The girls all sloped off and this minivan came up with two or three characters in it and said, 'What are you doing?' We said, 'The last bus has gone so we're just going to kill the night in Coventry,' and they said, 'Come with us.' So we went up to this café and it was Charlie Watts. And we sat in this café for two or three hours with Charlie. Then they went back to their hotel and we went back with them, got dropped off, and slept in Burton's shop doorway. We caught the 6.30am local 658 back to Hinckley in the morning.

## I WAS THERE: TONY CAMPBELL

I ran a band called the Mighty Avengers. We started up in about 1961. We were working for a guy called Reg Talbot. Reg ran a load of venues all around the Midlands. We played with the Stones at the Locarno in Coventry. Around this time we were taken on by a Manchester agency, Kennedy Street Artists, who got us a recording contract with Decca. This led us to record three Jagger and Richards songs, one of which did very well for us, called 'So Much in Love'.

*The Mighty Avengers recorded three Jagger and Richards songs*

Our recording manager was Stones manager Andrew Oldham, and that's when we got to know Mick and Keith quite well, and actually recorded with them. In fact, on 'So Much in Love', the session men were John Paul Jones and Jimmy Page.

We met them personally more than worked with them, because we used to go down to Andrew Oldham's flat in north London when we were rehearsing songs. Mick and Keith were there and went through the songs with us. Also, Marianne Faithfull was there one weekend.

THE ROLLING STONES IN THE SIXTIES: A PEOPLE'S HISTORY

# GAUMONT THEATRE
## 24 APRIL 1964, NORWICH, UK

### I WAS THERE: MARGARET LEE-CASTON, AGE 15

At the time I lived 20 miles out of Norwich, so we went to the gig on an organised coach trip with lots of other Stones fans. I can't believe my parents allowed me to go - my father was a Church of England vicar and rural dean, and I was a day-pupil at the Convent of the Sacred Heart in Swaffham, Norfolk.

In our class we had two camps. You were either in the Stones or the Beatles camps. We were not allowed to like or support both bands. I went with my then best friend Linda and the main thing I remember about the concert was you couldn't hear the Stones performance very well, because of all the screaming girls in the audience. It was all extremely exciting. I mainly wanted to see Brian Jones, who I thought was amazing, talented and very attractive.

After the gig everyone hung around outside the building hoping for a glimpse of the band as they left. Unfortunately, we were disappointed. The next day I had a sore throat but all my classmates were very envious. From the day I first saw the Rolling Stones on *Top of the Pops* I was hooked.

### I WAS THERE: ROSEMARY BRUCE, AGE 10

It was against my mother's wishes. I saved up all my pocket money to go. I was in the very back row. I went with my best friend and there was a lot of screaming going on. Of course, there were no big screens then, so they looked very small figures on the stage.

### I WAS THERE: MERVYN BLAKEWAY, AGE 18

At the time I lived in Beccles and my girlfriend was a lovely 17-year-old named Jeanne Salluyts, who lived in Shipmeadow. We travelled to the city on my trusty BSA Gold Flash. The Stones were amazing. We were about two rows from the front. Obviously, Brian Jones was still with then. Performing with the Stones were several other artists – Mike Berry, the Leroys, ex-Shadow Jet Harris, Billie Davis, and Heinz, who usually did Eddie Cochran material. I recall the audience were well behaved, although a few girls who ventured too close to the stage were stopped by security guards. It was a great evening. My diary reads I finally reached indoors at 2.30am.

# GAUMONT THEATRE
## 25 APRIL 1964, NORWICH, UK

**I WAS THERE: TIM CLAXTON**
I lived halfway between Norwich and Great Yarmouth and hitchhiked to both the Gaumont in Norwich and the Regal in Great Yarmouth to see the Stones. The noise from the girls screaming is my biggest memory. 'Walking the Dog' with Mick whistling resonates, but with the small amps and screaming it was really all about the atmosphere.

**I WAS THERE: RAY COSSEY**
I was the manager of the Gaumont that night, and it was some experience. We had to secret the lads into the theatre inside an inconspicuous-looking van, which we were able to back up right to the stage door. The problem we had at the Gaumont was that it had no orchestra pit, only an apron stage, which meant you could step up from the auditorium seating directly onto the stage. This meant me having to hire maybe 20 security guys to form a linked line across the front of the stage to keep the screaming girls from getting onto the stage. The noise was the loudest I ever experienced in any theatre I managed; so much so that, quite frankly, you really could not hear the Stones.

At the end of the show, the same van was deployed to whisk them away from the theatre to their hotel. They were amongst the best-behaved artistes I have had to host and were, unlike many of their then contemporaries, very well behaved and with none of the artistic temperaments so often displayed by some performers. My most vivid memory is that the lads asked me to arrange for fish and chips to brought into the dressing rooms. They offered to pay, as one did in those days, but had quite a heated discussion on whose turn it was to cough up the money.

## PUBLIC HALL
### 28 APRIL 1964, WALLINGTON, UK

#### I WAS THERE: JOHN FLETCHER, AGE 17

They had released their first LP and were amazing. I was right up front and have an abiding memory of Bill chewing gum, holding his bass vertically. When they did 'Mona', we had never heard anything like it – brilliant!

## MAJESTIC THEATRE
### 30 APRIL 1964, BIRKENHEAD, UK

#### I WAS THERE: JENNY WILSON, AGE 17

We used to go every Thursday and Sunday and danced most of the night to all the local groups, including The Beatles. It was a fantastic night, until the stage was besieged by fans and the Stones went off. They were singing 'Time Is on My Side' - one of my favourites. I have never forgotten this event and was so upset when they went off.

#### I WAS THERE: SUE HAMMOND, AGE 17

It turned out to be a non-event. The stage was very near the audience and not very high. They came on stage, sang a couple of numbers, the crowd moved forward, they went off, and that was it. I don't know the reason why they went off. We were not very concerned about the reason, just disappointed. We had seen The Beatles there on several occasions with no problems.

#### I WAS THERE: MARJ KURTHAUSEN (NÉE CROSS), AGE 14

My friends and I had gone to see what we thought would be The Beatles, with the Stones as the supporting act. I had it in my mind to marry one of The Beatles. In fact we dyed our hair in the hope they would see us, and fall madly in love. We also changed our names so they would sound more exciting. I was to be called Sherie. Imagine my surprise when another group of boys arrived on stage like a thunderbolt. I was horrified - it was so sexy! The lead singer Mick Jagger had makeup on. It was called pan-stick in those days. He was so scary, but mesmerising, and the music was fantastic. Raunchy was only a word I would know later, but I still think dangerous was the word that came to my mind then. I knew then that they were the bad boys of rock. I would always be in love with The Beatles, because they were my first crush, but the music of the Stones makes me want to move, and I love it. I still dance around the kitchen to 'Brown Sugar' with my air guitar.

### I WAS THERE: BARBARA PALMER

They were fantastic, as they still are to this day. I remember it as if it were yesterday. Mick with his fabulous dancing, Brian Jones as cool as a cucumber, and the lovely Keith, my favourite Stone. Bill and Charlie were fab as well of course.

What a view I had. My friend and I saw them from a side door. We were on the street and in our school uniforms. You can imagine how full of ourselves we were when we told all our friends about it next day at school. Yes, we were on a real high until one of the teachers gave us a real good telling off. Would you believe we had been seen by one of the other teachers coming away from the Majestic after the show had finished. We were told we should have been at home doing our homework instead of watching pop groups.

# BRIDLINGTON SPA
## 2 MAY 1964, BRIDLINGTON, UK

### I WAS THERE: HELEN SMALLEY, AGE 12

I remember it well, or rather... not. I was besotted by Brian Jones, with pictures from *Jackie* magazine on my bedroom wall. I nagged my dad for weeks to let me go to the concert only to be told I was too young, which I suppose I was. However, he did relent and take me down to the Spa on the night, and in those days you could walk to the back entrance and watch the acts go in. Of course, I was not the only one to have that idea but being there early was one of the ones near the front of the barrier. In due course the Stones arrived and alighted from their transport inside the barrier. Well, all hell broke loose, and I remember being crushed against the barrier. The next thing I remember was being lifted up and plonked down by one of the bouncers - right next to Brian Jones. He said, and I remember it well, 'You alright, love?' My one moment of fame, only I was tongue-tied and just nodded. I've regretted it ever since. But the highlight was that he touched my hand - imagine how many weeks that tale was retold at school.

## I WAS THERE: BRUCE GEE, AGE 14

I went to see the Stones with a friend. I remember buying a couple of tickets for the concert as soon as it was announced. It was 7s/6d (37p) instead of the five shillings (25p) we paid for lesser-known groups. I would have been wearing jeans, t-shirt and Cuban heel boots. We met up in the Spa with some schoolmates, the big lads all of 16. We arrived at the Spa about two hours before the doors were open to savour the atmosphere. Nearly opposite the Spa we saw a couple of lads climbing up the drainpipe of a four-storey B&B to get to one or two of the Stones, who were waving from the top-floor window. The police stopped any further progress up the drainpipe when the girls tried to join in. We walked round to the back of the Spa near the stage door and spotted a dark blue Mk. I transit van covered with graffiti – Mick, Keith and Brian in lipstick or scratched on the van. Unbeknown to us at the time, it was Ian Stewart unloading amps, guitars, etc. 'Dinnae go near the van, lads,' he said. We didn't.

When the Stones appeared on stage, it seemed strange to me when Mick raised his arm to wave to the crowd. His jumper had a bloody great hole under the arm, which was not usual with the trendy clothes they were seen with in magazines, unless he got ragged by the fans before he got on stage. I don't think the Stones were on stage for more than 45 minutes and we only heard the opening bars of the songs they played, such was the noise of the girls packed at the stage front.

## I WAS THERE: ELAINE WILSON, AGE 17

When I was in the sixth form at Scarborough Girls' High School, for one winter season only the Bridlington Spa ran monthly all-night dances. We saw the Rolling Stones, The Hollies and The Animals twice. It cost 12/6 (63p). I hired a coach from Scarborough and collected the money beforehand to pay for the coach. We did not need to book beforehand - we just turned up and paid at the door. When I saw The Beatles in concert at the Futurist in Scarborough they all wore pale grey mohair suits with Chanel-style high-necks without collars, white shirts and narrow black bootlace ties. In contrast, the Stones wore casual clothing. Charlie Watts alone wore a suit. Mick Jagger wore a pale grey marl crew-necked sweater and danced around on stage wearing bell-bottom jeans. We all wore them, but girls then did not wear jeans in the evening. Large posters of them in black and white sold for five shillings (25p) and I had one.

# PALACE THEATRE
## 3 MAY 1964, MANCHESTER, UK

### I WAS THERE: CHRISTINE MCDERMOTT, AGE 12
I was a massive fan of the Stones back then and lived in Ardwick, Manchester. Memories I have of all the concerts I went to are of queuing up for nights on end to get tickets. Hence, I got seats near the front, in this case seat F28 in the stalls. This was always a fabulous social thing to do. I managed to climb and jump on to the stage and grab hold of Mick's ankles. Eventually two big blokes came on stage and extrapolated me from Mick's legs and took me off stage, and out through the stage door I went. It was worth it to be able to touch Mick.

I waited outside the front and at the end of the concert the staff let me back in to get my bag from under my seat. Amazingly, it was still there. When I jumped I landed in the footlights on my knees. As I was wearing fishnet tights, I had diamond-shaped scabs on my knees for weeks afterwards.

### I WAS THERE: PETER ALTON GREEN
My band Tony Martin and the Mods were booked onto the Stones show to back both the McKinley sisters and the Overlanders. The journey from Hull to Manchester in those days was not an easy one. There was no M62. We arrived at the theatre in the early afternoon and began setting up our equipment around the other band's gear and the Stones'

## THE ROLLING STONES IN THE SIXTIES: A PEOPLE'S HISTORY

Vox set-ups. Our amps were one Vox 30 on a stand, one blonde Fender bass amp, and a kit of Trixon drums.

The Stones had a full set of new Vox 30 amps and a bass stack. As we were setting up, Bill Wyman approached Pete, our bass player, admiring his amp. Bill said, 'I love these amps.' Pete's reply was, 'Well, you're earning good money - buy one.' Bill said, 'I would, but we have to use Vox as they give it us free.' I was just setting up my amp when I was approached by Brian Jones. ''Ere mate, got a plectrum?' I showed him my spares and he chose one.

As the afternoon wore on, we went to the Stones' dressing room to find out what songs they were going to do. We played a similar set and didn't want to clash. The smell of those 'French cigarettes' was very strong. I noticed that the Stones were all taller than I thought, then noticed the Cuban-heeled boots they were wearing.

It was nearly time for the show to start, and Mick was in the stage wings near the emergency doors. Screaming girls were peering through the crack. One shouted, 'Oh Mick, you promised,' to which he laughingly shouted back, 'Fuck off!'

Tony Martin and the Mods opened the show. For some reason the McKinley sisters didn't turn up, so we had to fill the spot. Next on were the Overlanders (pre-'Michelle'). We'd backed them before, and just bass and drums were required here, so I watched from the wings. Now we played in dropped tuning. When I fingered an E-chord, I was in fact playing a D. With this in mind, our bass man had two basses, one in dropped D and the other on concert. He passed the bass to the Overlanders to tune - which they didn't. Their entire set was played in the wrong keys by our bass player, who explained, 'If they can't be bothered to tune up, I can't be bothered either.' No matter ... the crowd noise was so loud hardly anyone noticed. (One guy, Jerry Page, did and we made a record with him in 1967.)

Next on the list were The Sundowners, who played a couple of things before backing vocalist Julie Grant, who was chaperoned by her mother. Compere on the night was broadcaster 'Diddy' David Hamilton. Just before the Stones, Manchester's own Four Just Men performed, a terrific band previously known as Pete Maclaine and the Clan.

THE ROLLING STONES IN THE SIXTIES: A PEOPLE'S HISTORY

# SAVOY BALLROOM
## 9 MAY 1964, CATFORD, LONDON, UK

### I WAS THERE: LYNNE PHILLIPS

I went with a boyfriend (I forget his name) who played guitar in a local group in the Bromley area and had a scooter, much to my parents' dismay. I often went to the Savoy to dance with various friends. This time we went to see what the fuss was about, not expecting very much. There were lots of groups around - some good, some awful – but we were smitten and came out dedicated fans.

*Lynne Phillips went to see what the fuss was all about*

### I WAS THERE: CLIVE CHASE

The group I was with was called Bobby King and the Sabres. We played covers of just about everything that was in the hit parade. As such many Saturday and Friday evening gigs saw us playing second fiddle to a chart group. Although we seemed to play alongside groups like The Hollies, The Merseybeats and Tony Rivers and the Castaways quite a number of times, we only played with the Stones once, and that was a first-floor dance club or ballroom in Catford, South London – one of our regular Saturday night places.

*Clive Chase caught the Stones in Catford*

It generally held about 700 to 800 on a good night. The night the Stones played we were told by the bouncers 'they've let 1,200 kids in' - probably true because it was shoulder to shoulder pushing. Anyone who wanted to go to the loo would have had a half-hour shove through the throng to get there. Dancing? No chance! In fact, a number fainted with the heat. The bouncers said there were twelve ambulances in attendance outside taking the unconscious and minor wounded away.

# THE ROLLING STONES IN THE SIXTIES: A PEOPLE'S HISTORY

It was a fairly usual evening's schedule in that the DJ would kick off around 7.15pm or so, then we would come on around 8pm to 9pm. The Stones were then due to appear at 9pm for an hour, then the DJ and then us, finishing with the DJ again. But it didn't happen like that. Equipment had been set up by around 5.30 to 6pm. Nothing seemed too out of the ordinary as there were occasions when top groups would make their entrance just a few minutes before they were due to start, their roadies having set everything up. That said, in that era many top groups would be there and want to soundcheck things themselves and certainly not act the celebrity.

But no Stones! We played our first set from 8pm till 9pm. It was hot. Still no Stones. The management got a message to us - play on, play on! So we did. 9.30pm. Nothing. 10pm. Nothing. Having played for two hours and with the steam rising almost literally, we were told the DJ would do a stint.

The management must have been having kittens. No mobile phones back then. We retired to the only dressing room - that's a polite word for it. It was a sizeable area backstage. I can't be sure of the time but at some juncture in burst the five of them. They had arrived. They seemed a mix of out of breath and giggly. They were late - very late. They had clearly been hurrying on foot across an area behind the venue and then up into the rear as they would have been totally unable to enter through the throng of 1,200 or so kids. Remember this hall was on the first floor, so I'm not sure how they got up from the ground floor. There was a long concrete staircase at the rear from the road behind, where groups brought their stuff in, but that staircase led to the main auditorium.

One of the management was asking – telling - them they had to get on. I recall both Jagger and Jones saying in a very nonchalant way he should - well the equivalent of - 'keep your hair on.' But they did then get into gear a bit. They had a small attaché case each, which seemed to hold odd clothes that would be worn on stage. Not all of them changed. Some decorative bits were pulled out - a scarf, for example - and thrust around the neck. For Jagger I seem to recall there was a pair of very, very sparkly tight trousers. But the thing that made me smile the most was that in these small bags, as well as the clothes, there were also the remains of old food. In one, I can't recall whose it was, was the best part of a cold fish and chip meal still trying to closet itself partially inside the newspaper wrapping it had been bought in at some earlier date.

There we were, five kids of around 18, each driving our own almost new car and each fairly impeccably dressed in our matching mohair suits and ties. Maybe that's where we were going wrong. The Stones finished what they were doing and were gone - onto the stage. I remember the sheer vibe of their music as it hit. It was good - very good. Bill Wyman had two Vox Foundation speakers with 18-inch units in each and had one either side of the stage. As a bass player I was amazed how good the sound was. That said you could not actually hear the individual notes that he was playing, but the sheer depth made such a tremendous impact. We never did see them again. When they finished, they were escorted off by bouncers to the concrete steps which exited from the hall itself and not that far from the stage and they were gone - job done. I later learned the reason that were late was because, rather than come to the gig they were booked for, they made the decision to go and see Chuck Berry at the Finsbury Park Astoria.

## I WAS THERE: MEL MAY, AGE 16

The Savoy was a purpose-built ballroom back in the very early days with a sprung floor. The Dave Clark 5 song 'Bits 'n' Pieces' was banned because people used to mimic their stomping, which wasn't good for the floor.

I remember the gig vividly as I played in the first support band on that night, Brian Lee & The MJs, and we were followed by Bobby King and The Sabres. The Stones were late, delayed in London, and when they did eventually appear, the hall was so packed we couldn't get off the stage and had to sit on Charlie's drum cases right next to him. What a night! Girls passing out and us pulling the girls out of the crowd.

The stage had two tiers and the top one was for drummers. Just behind the drummer was a very small door that led to the manager's office and an extremely small dressing room. The Stones roadies had to manhandle their Vox amps and drum kit through this small door along with their own PA. Back then, house PA's were awful. On top of one of the Vox AC30s they lined up Brian Jones's harmonicas in key sequence, along with Mick's maracas and tambourine. There was then a quick tune up of the guitars and they put them on their stands.

# THE ROLLING STONES IN THE SIXTIES: A PEOPLE'S HISTORY

All of a sudden, the small door opened and one by one the Stones appeared through the door and clambered down to the stage, the crowd now going crazy. They started with no soundcheck of any kind or apology for their lateness.

My overwhelming memory is the smell of their hair shampoo and how long their hair was compared with The Beatles. There I was, sitting an arm's length away from Charlie on one of his drum cases. Can you imagine that being allowed these days?

After they'd finished their performance, they vanished through that small door as quickly as they arrived. No encores back then. Their roadies appeared and, scratching their heads, started getting their gear out, the crowd still going nuts and girls still fainting. One of the roadies gave us Brian's harmonicas. I wish I knew where they are now.

We also played downstairs in the nightclub, Mr Smith's, at times famous for the Kray/Richardson gang murder. I know all this crazy Savoy info because our drummer's mum was the manager. An even crazier thing is that I've started playing lead guitar in a band again, after many years not playing guitar at all. My wife thinks I'm nuts.

## I WAS THERE: JOHN RICHARDSON, AGE 18

I lived in Greenwich at the time. It was like the Savoy was the best place around at the time. Saturday night they used to have Johnny Gray and his Band of the Day. That was fun because he was a boozer and we used to enjoy boozing with him. I got involved only because I used to go up there regularly. I went up there with a friend of mine, Dave Harris, who now lives in Australia. We only used to go up there for the birds, you know, like you did.

Brian Poole and the Tremeloes were the resident band. We had all sorts. Freddie and the Dreamers were there. The Undertakers. They used to have some good groups there during the week. We used to go down in the bar afterwards and chat to them. When the Stones eventually came on they did about half an hour or three quarters of an hour. They weren't on all night. The Stones were very professional even then. I remember Mick looking down at these people, just glaring at them. The Stones were great, but the gig was chaos.

THE ROLLING STONES IN THE SIXTIES: A PEOPLE'S HISTORY

# COLSTON HALL
## 10 MAY 1964, BRISTOL, UK

### I WAS THERE: KEITH GWINNELL, AGE 15

The original plan was to see The Beatles, but the tickets had sold out. The friend who had been given the task of buying the tickets used his initiative and purchased tickets for the Stones instead. It turned out to be a good move. The show by the Stones was the first live show I had attended ... and what a first.

It was a most exciting experience - the noise, the music and the energy was mind-blowing. The Colston Hall is not the largest of venues so even though I was in the balcony I felt very close to the action on stage. I still have the ticket stub for the concert - 7.45pm for the second house. I paid 10 shillings and sixpence (53p) for the ticket, a fair amount as my only income was as a Saturday boy at Woolworth's, which paid the grand sum of £1 for eight hours work. An hourly rate of 2/6 (13p). But 50 years on I am still able to recall those energetic performances, especially of Jagger and Richards and the accompanying hysteria of the audience.

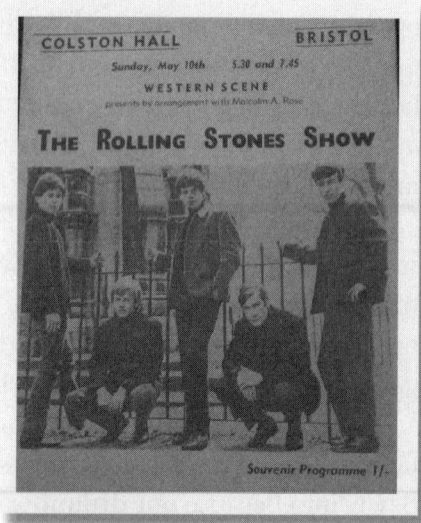

*Bristol programme*

### I WAS THERE: MARY KING, AGE 16

I went with my friend, Gaynor. We were both 15. The support acts included Gene Vincent. He was clad in black leather. He'd had a car accident and played extensively on his bad leg, striking convulsive poses during his act. He was brilliant, but a lot of the very young audience such as I didn't really know who he was. I wasn't really interested in seeing him but his performance was something else.

Next came Millie of 'My Boy Lollipop' fame. We all expected her to be good, but she sang sharp and to our unsophisticated ears it really jarred. Knowing what I do today about West Indian music, it is the trend to sing slightly sharp. If you listen to Susan Cadogan singing 'Hurt So Good', and in many other renditions of West Indian music, you will hear it again. It has become acceptable to my ears now, as I am a bit of a music geek. But everybody chatted throughout her performance, which was quite rude I thought.

Then came the Stones. The stage went dark and somebody came on. Everybody started screaming but it was only a roadie or one of the stage crew. They certainly kept us waiting. Someone else came on and we thought it was Bill Wyman, but he went off again. Sometime later the lights went up and Bill Wyman was on stage. I went ballistic as he

Mary King also recalls Gene Vincent and Millie's sets

was my favourite. Everybody was screaming and me, and my friend looked at each other and burst out laughing as we were both screaming. We ended up laughing throughout most of the performance but were delighted to be there.

Then the other three came on - I don't remember in which order - then last of all Mick. They played a set lasting about 40 minutes. I was a bit fed up because there was so much screaming, I couldn't hear them properly. I really enjoy music of all sorts and I was studying music and theory at the time, and I wanted to hear how they performed live. I was hoping for them to play 'Little Red Rooster', which was my favourite. I don't remember what they played - it was impossible to hear.

I have little recollection of events after the concert. It took so long to get out of the hall that there was no chance of getting autographs. I expect they were whisked away.

## WINTER GARDENS
### 11 MAY 1964, BOURNEMOUTH, UK

**I WAS THERE: ANDREW PHILPOTT, AGE 19**
It seems incredible now but the lead act on the poster was Heinz Burt, formerly of the Tornados, and the name Heinz occupied most of the

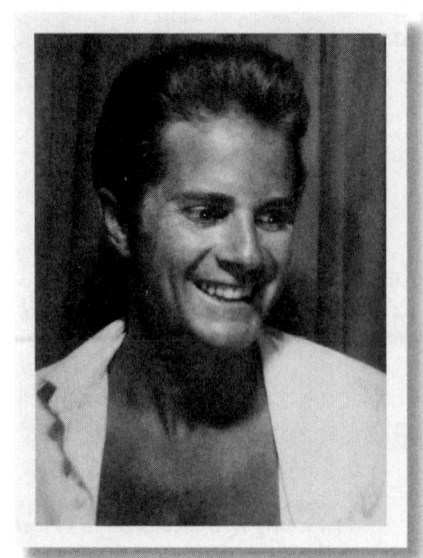

# THE ROLLING STONES IN THE SIXTIES: A PEOPLE'S HISTORY

Andrew Philpott recalls Mick Jagger prancing around in tight trousers

Bournemouth mementoes from the night

left side of the poster. Jerry Lee Lewis was on the same bill and was the most exciting performer I ever saw. Gene Vincent and the Outlaws were also on the bill - what an incredible line-up!

The Rolling Stones' name was in small print halfway down the right side of the poster and when my mates and I saw Mick Jagger prancing around in tight trousers I have to say we had a job not to laugh. It seemed so over the top even to us, but we enjoyed them and one of my mates from those days - who I saw recently - reminded me I was told to get back in my seat by the manager when dancing in the aisle. I never told my parents when I went to pop concerts. They strongly disapproved of pop music. If they had seen the Rolling Stones perform, they would have been horrified.

### I WAS THERE: ROGER GIBBINS, AGE 16

I worked in the camera shop in Brights, a big store in Bournemouth. I remember it being a beautiful summer's day. I went with my friends Margaret Stockley, Maureen Felsed and John Elliott, who was really mad on the Stones. I admit I was more into The Beatles but the first Stones

LP still remains one of my all-time favourite albums, as do their first half-dozen singles. As usual with most parents, mine thought they were dirty and unwashed. We didn't hear a thing – just screaming.

# CITY HALL
## 13 MAY 1964, NEWCASTLE-UPON-TYNE, UK

**I WAS THERE: ROBIN ALDRICH**
I was approaching my 16th birthday. I was already an avid Stones fan. We kids hung out at a small local record store in Blyth. The Stones' first LP had recently been released. I couldn't afford to buy it, but we listened to the tracks incessantly in the store's sound booths. My mum asked what I wanted for my birthday and the answer was simple - a ticket for the Stones' upcoming appearance at Newcastle City Hall. I took the bus to Newcastle and secured a ticket as near to the front as possible, a few weeks in advance.

It was my birthday on the day of the concert and when I arrived, I rushed to my seat next to the aisle, quite near to the front. It was my very first rock concert and I was nearly deafened by the roar of high-pitched screams as the band came out one by one to perform their set. I can't remember who the supporting acts were, or much more of the evening, except that Jagger wiggled his rear end in the direction of the audience, which produced even more pandemonium.

**I WAS THERE: ROZ SLATER (NÉE GIBBONS), AGE 23**
At the time I was a youth worker at the Borough Road Hall youth club, initiated by St Paul's Church, Jarrow, and which met every Friday night. Some 98 members expressed an interest in this concert, for which they paid 5/6 (27p), 6/6 (33p) and 8/- (40p) each. I remember going to pay and collect the tickets with a bag full of cash. I organised three coaches to take us from York Avenue to Newcastle. The air of expectation was great – as was the crowd.

The presenter did all in his power to build up the atmosphere for the Stones. When they finally appeared on stage the whole audience stood up, and being small I had to move around to see the event. It was for me one of noise, noise and more noise. It was impossible for hear the words.

When they left the stage - they didn't come back for an encore - the silence was punctuated by the click of the seats as people sat down again.

Many of the girls were sobbing from sheer exhaustion and exuberance. Then the task began for me of collecting my 98 members, who were all over the venue due to the different ticket prices. Finally, we located our three coaches. It was the first concert I had ever been to. The members were aged 16 to 20 and, even a week later, were still reeling as a result of the event they had been a part of. The gig changed the running of the club. It used to be 7pm to 10pm, 6d (3p) to get in and free tea, coffee, juice and biscuits with games like table tennis, darts, etc., closing with a barn dance until everyone had paired off and left for home. As a result of seeing the Stones we started to arrange a monthly dance with people paying 2/- (10p) admission and local groups playing.

# ST GEORGE'S HALL
## 14 MAY 1964, BRADFORD, UK

**I WAS THERE: ANN HOLMES, AGE 14**
I went to the concert with a group of school friends from Belle Vue Girls' Grammar - heaven knows how we persuaded our parents to let us go. We sat up on the first tier of the balcony and it all just seemed so unbelievable that we were actually seeing the Stones. As usual in those days we just screamed through the performance.

My real memory though is after the concert, when we went round to the stage door to see if we could catch a glimpse of them. I don't know how, but Brian Jones got separated from the rest and to get away started running up Bridge Street past the Victoria Hotel. It must have been awful to have a load of hysterical, screaming teenagers chasing you. Unfortunately for him, he fell on the pavement in front of us. At this point those screaming teenagers turned into an embarrassed group of schoolgirls, all looking at each other, as if to say, 'Oh dear, what do we do now?' Luckily his security men soon caught up with him and got him back to the rest of the group. As you can imagine, this was the talking point for a long time to come at school - how we had touched Brian Jones! It just seems so unreal now to think and tell people that the Rolling Stones came to Bradford, of all places. And I was there!

# THE ROLLING STONES IN THE SIXTIES: A PEOPLE'S HISTORY

## I WAS THERE: BOB MILLER, AGE 16

Myself and my girlfriend Jenny Holmes went to this one too. We were both still 16 and I was at Carlton Grammar School. Again, the Stones looked great and their performance was fantastic, what we could hear of it! Jenny remained focused on Brian Jones, although we went on to get married in October 1967, remaining together all these years on.

## I WAS THERE: CHRISTINE MCCABE

People of our generation were so lucky to have been part of the music scene of those days. I got the Rolling Stones' autographs at the stage door of St George's Hall. My friend and I left early to go up to Chester Street to catch a bus to Bingley so we weren't late home. En route we just went to the stage door. Everyone else was in the hall clapping away to try and get them to come back on stage. Luckily for us they were sneaking out of the stage door and stopped to sign the first bit of paper we could lay hands on.

I remember those nights as being great fun with girlfriends and to a point we were lucky as our parents let us go and make memories. So many of my friends' parents didn't let them go. We were 16 or 17. My husband never saw the Stones - his parents didn't allow him to go, and coming of age was 21 in those days.

## I WAS THERE: LESLIE SMITH

I was a serving police officer in the Traffic Division and was on night duty. Whilst most officers were out on patrol, it was procedure for two or three to be kept in reserve in the police garage only to be turned out in emergencies. On the night of one of their concerts I was on reserve, and after the show the Stones were escorted back to the police garage. After alighting from their car, I went to speak to them and asked for their autographs, which they duly gave me. Mick Jagger was not amongst them and I was told he was still recovering in the back of the car. I went and sat in the car with him and he asked for two or three minutes to come round. After a short while he signed for me. I must say he was exhausted, and sweat was all over him.

## ODEON THEATRE
### 17 MAY 1964, FOLKESTONE, UK

**I WAS THERE: JEAN GATEHOUSE (NÉE SAUNDERS), AGE 15**
My mum bought me, and my friend Sandra Perry tickets for my 16th birthday on 24 May. It was amazing. We were Mods in those days but got very friendly with a group of Rockers and all enjoyed the night and met up again on the Sunday down the harbour. The Pretty Things were a support band for them.

**I WAS THERE: DANUTA PIERCE (NÉE KRAWCZYK)**
My best friend Julia Tappenden and her older sisters Marion and Gloria and I attended. We were both still at the Girls' Grammar School and talked Julia's mother into queuing for tickets. We found a way in through a fire door round the back of the Odeon and met some of the other acts and – still, my beating heart - some of the Stones. Not, unfortunately, Bill - my favourite. Mick was carrying some wrapped parcels of fish and chips in a bucket. He said, 'You wanna chip, mate?' My claim to fame.

## CHANTINGHALL HOTEL
### 18 MAY 1964, HAMILTON, UK

**I WAS THERE: MICHAEL PRATER, AGE 10**
I stood outside, unable to get in. There was a riot at the show due to forged tickets, and the place was packed solid. There was chicken-wire around the stage and the Stones played stripped to the waist due to the heat. Cars were damaged and there was a lot of unruly behaviour. I have seen the Stones 17 times now and remain a huge fan.

**I WAS THERE: PATRICK MCCUE, AGE 15**
What a night it was. Though an ardent Beatles fan at that time, two of my friends who were into the Stones managed to get three tickets and persuaded me to accompany them. There we were, three Mods, all decked out in black plastic coats and trilby hats to match. We thought we were the bees' knees. On arriving at the hotel, it was obvious the crowd

was way in excess of what the hotel could cope with, so we made it our aim to get in as quick as possible. As we entered it was obvious this night was going to be somewhat hot, so we duly checked our coats into the cloakroom. Though it was May it was still a bit chilly and many people who had coats on did likewise.

My enduring memory of that evening after what can only be described as the best gig I've ever been to, is the chaos following it. Yes, before it there was a lot of disruption due to the word going around that there had been a lot of forged tickets being shown at the entry points, and this caused a degree of mayhem, but there was more to come. At the end, when the crowd including myself and my two friends were heading for the cloakroom, it was announced that the cloakroom staff had lost the ticket stubs and it was to be 50 people at one time to go into the cloakroom and pick up their coats. I was lucky enough to be in the first 50 and I duly picked out my black plastic coat and headed on outside to the cold night. After about 20 minutes or so my two friends hadn't appeared, and I began to worry if they were okay. Needless to say, about 30 minutes after I had got myself out, they arrived, both sporting what could only be described as expensive Crombie coats. When they noted I had chosen my cheap plastic coat they both fell about laughing, saying 'Pat, what an opportunity you missed. You must be freezing.' So much for honesty, eh?

## I WAS THERE: HUGH PHILLIPS, AGE 21

I was in a five-piece band called Beat Unlimited. We'd been playing in the Hamilton area for a few years, so we were quite well known in central Scotland. It was quite a remarkable night. We opened the show that night, quite an honour. When our van drove into the Chantinghall Hall Hotel we were mistaken for the Stones, so we were quite chuffed with ourselves at that point. The queue was over a mile long down into Hamilton. The cloakroom just became a room where people were piling their coats on top of everything else. My wife's sister had a new coat which disappeared. Afterwards, people were taking other coats because they couldn't find their own.

The crowd was double what was supposed to be there because of fraudulent ticket sales. It was pandemonium, and something that would never happen nowadays. The temperature was way up over 100, I'm sure. The band were stripped to the waist. The Stones were on a big scaffolding and there was actually chicken-wire up in front of it to keep the crowd off. Dave Berry and the Cruisers had just had a hit with 'The Crying Game'. He was also on the bill but by the time the Stones finished, by the time the whole show finished, I don't think Dave Berry even made the stage. We managed to get hold of their tambourine with their five names signed on it. It was the tambourine they used on the recording of 'Not Fade Away'. Unfortunately, we played the following Monday in a hall in Bathgate – the Bathgate Palais - in the east of Scotland and we raffled the tambourine for charity. We got 30 bob (£1.50) for it, which is probably the worst financial transaction I've ever made.

### MY BROTHER WAS THERE: MARGARET MCGOWAN
My brother was there when the Stones played in Hamilton. He often spoke about how mad it was and how he lost his coat. After the concert, the Stones came back with him and his pal to a flat in Shettleston. At one time I had a picture of them all sitting on a couch in the flat. If I could find it now, it would probably be worth a fortune.

## CAPITOL CINEMA
### 19 MAY 1964, ABERDEEN, UK

### I WAS THERE: DAVID MIDDLETON
In the mid- to late-Sixties many big groups came to Aberdeen, in particular either the Beach or the Capitol Cinema. I saw the Stones from four rows from the front for 15 shillings (75p), as well as seeing Small Faces, The Who, and many more.

## UNIVERSITY STUDENTS' UNION BAR
### 23 MAY 1964, LEICESTER, UK

### I WAS THERE: DAVID SNEATH, AGE 19
The Stones' university booking had been agreed before the Stones made it big, which their management honoured. Girls I knew in the audience found themselves onstage in the wings, and when Mick Jagger stubbed

out a cigarette and put his heel on it, girls raced to pick up what was left of it. For some reason there was unimportant heckling from the audience, to which Mick replied that the barracker should, 'Get on down to your Palais de Dance, where you'll find things ain't no different.'

### I WAS THERE: DAWN YOUNG

They all seemed fatigued, worn out from their tour. But once the curtain went up it was as if everything else in the world was erased. The boys became their alter-ego, the Rolling Stones. Mick owned the stage, strutting clapping and gazing into the audience with his bedroom eyes. Bill, Keith and Brian backed him up on guitars, while Charlie kept the beat moving on the drums.

## GRANADA THEATRE
### 25 MAY 1964, EAST HAM, LONDON, UK

### I WAS THERE: MIKE BYRON, AGE 16

The ticket cost 10 shillings and I had to choose whether to see The Beatles or the Stones. I couldn't afford both. There were girls jumping up and down and screaming. Oh, the screaming! I saw and heard hardly anything of the Stones. When they were announced, after the support acts, someone in front of me stood up and left. Obviously not a fan.

## TOWN HALL
### 26 MAY 1964, BIRMINGHAM, UK

### I WAS THERE: DIANE CAREY, AGE 26

It was a fantastic show and full of energy, but every number they played was completely drowned by girls screaming. I was with my Mum, who was always a fan of popular music, and my two younger brothers, who at that time were in their

*Diane Carey and her younger brothers*

early teens. We were surprised to find that Mick Jagger - always a snazzy dresser, we believed - was wearing what we described at the time as a tweed sports jacket. When we got back home our dad said, 'Were they good?' to which we replied, 'Yes.' 'What did they sing?' Well, we hadn't a clue because we couldn't hear a word. Even so, we had a wonderful night out and, yes, we enjoyed the show.

**I WAS THERE: ELIZABETH KNAPP**
All I can remember is screaming my head off with all the others.

## ESSOLDO THEATRE
### 28 MAY 1964, STOCKPORT, UK

**I WAS THERE: DAVID MASSEY, AGE 15**
I saw the Stones at the Essoldo with my mate Wilf. One thing that sticks in my mind was the electric atmosphere. The girls were screaming and gave it all they had but, because of the size of the speakers on stage and our position about four rows from the front, we could hear OK.

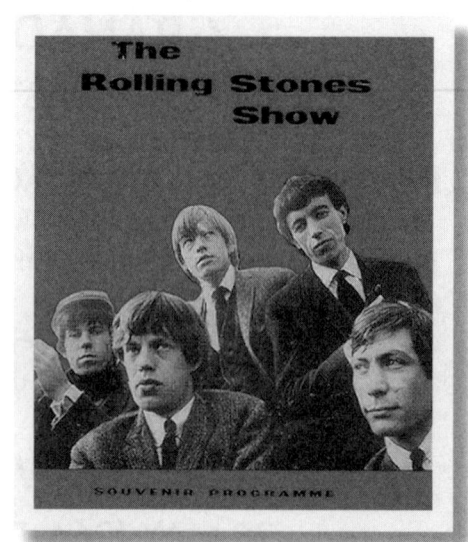

**I WAS THERE: SHIRLEY BROOM, AGE 17**

Stockport programme

I went to that concert with my boyfriend, who later became my husband. I have a souvenir programme of the show. Peter and Gordon were also on the bill, along with the Barron Knights, Julie Grant, The Overlanders, and David John and the Mood. But I don't remember the other groups as I only went to see the Stones.

We were dressed in our Mod gear. I also remember Rockers being outside as the concert finished and the Fire Brigade coming and turning the hose-pipes on us all.

# THE ROLLING STONES IN THE SIXTIES: A PEOPLE'S HISTORY

## I WAS THERE: JEAN WALKER

My boyfriend and I were the first in the queue for those tickets at the Essoldo for the Stones concert and got into trouble for being late for work. However, did we care? Not back then. What great days they were - absolute magic. We were advised to get on the third row from the front so we could see better, and we did. And even though the screaming was deafening - who cared? I caught the attention of Bill Wyman, who waved at me, and then Mick Jagger did too!

## I WAS THERE: SANDRA STRONGE, AGE 14

My dad was the commissionaire at the Essoldo. I had seen lots of stars there, like The Shadows and Gene Vincent, to name but two. Well, when my dad said the Rolling Stones were coming and he had two tickets for me and a friend, I could hardly believe it. I took my best mate at the time, Sylvia.

Our seats were fantastic – just a couple of rows from the stage. I remember the excitement when the Stones came out. Mick was about 19, I think, and on seeing him screaming just seemed to happen. I remember it being a fabulous show and I have been a fan ever since. We bought posters of the group – they did not sell merchandise like these days. My dad had taken my autograph book backstage and got all the group's autographs, including Brian Jones'. I must have impressed my mates at school when I took it to show them. I have kept the book all these years.

## I WAS THERE: JENNY BENTLEY, AGE 13

A few months before they came, I was walking down Wellington Road South towards Mersey Square when I saw a poster outside the Essoldo advertising the concert. I stopped in my tracks, unable to believe they were actually going to come to Stockport. Very bravely, I crossed over to the cinema and went into the foyer and asked if they had any leaflets on it, and they gave me one. I couldn't wait to get home so I could write a letter and send it along with the leaflet to their fan club, requesting their autographs.

A few weeks later my self-addressed envelope was returned. I almost screamed the house down with excitement when I saw the leaflet returned to me with all their signatures on. Next day I took it to school to show my friends and was very put out when one of them asked me to cut up the leaflet so I could share the autographs with them. I didn't, of course - I told them to send off for their own.

I went to see them at the Essoldo with two other girls from school. We were all 13. I wouldn't be 14 until September. When we arrived on St Petersgate, the queue to get in was right round the block about three or four deep – mainly girls. We saw several girls pass out with excitement, being tended to by St John Ambulance staff.

We had tickets for the stalls and were on the right side facing the stage. It was the first concert any of us had ever been to and we were all keyed up and wished the other acts would hurry up so it would be time for who we had gone to see to be on the stage. I can't remember who else was on except Peter and Gordon, who sang 'World Without Love'. The roar that went up when Mick came onto the stage was deafening. Everyone was standing on their seats screaming, calling out the names of their favourites. I loved Brian Jones too, but it was Mick whose name I screamed, like almost all the other girls. Although we could see the boys on stage, it was impossible to hear them because of all the noise we were making. Mick's moves got all of us in a frenzy.

When we came out, I had to walk all the way home by myself and was in such turmoil that I cried all the way home. My mum couldn't get any sense out of me and said, 'That's the last time you ever go to see them.' But it wasn't. I saw them at least another three times in Manchester. I was so upset after that first concert that I had to have the next day off school and spent the day alternately sobbing and reliving the night before.

## I WAS THERE: COLIN JOY, AGE 8

We had heard about the Stones but seen very little of them as we only had two TV channels - ITV and BBC. There was no *Top of the Pops* then, or Radio 1, but the BBC did have *Juke Box Jury*, which played some of the latest tunes, plus some artists would manage to get a slot on children's TV shows like *Blue Peter* and *Crackerjack*. Granada TV catered for the Mersey Beat and Manchester scenes, with The Beatles and Gerry and the Pacemakers getting maximum exposure on local news programmes. But the London Scene received very little coverage unless you lived in those areas. Our next-door neighbour Geoff was chief projectionist for the cinema and wangled his son David, my brother Brian, and me, through the back door of the Essoldo, and we were allowed to watch the show from the comfort of the projector slots on the rear walls.

I say 'watch' as, once The Rolling Stones came on, we couldn't hear a bloody thing as all the girls started screaming non-stop throughout. All the Stones were smartly dressed in casual pants and shirts – no jeans in those days – and very clean cut. The audience were the same. Dress code was observed at all times. The Stones were on stage for just over 30 minutes. Keith Richards, Brian Jones, and Bill Wyman mainly stood posing and strutting without moving, with Charlie Watts looking bored drumming. It was Mick Jagger with his weird hand-clapping strutting routine dancing around the stage who was the main attraction, but he was timid then compared to the showman we know nowadays.

*We couldn't hear a bloody thing as all the girls started screaming*

As the night came to a close and the curtain came down after the Stones had finished, I remember there was an incident which caused the audience to suddenly surge towards the stage, trapping those at the front.

It was a fully-seated venue. The safety curtain went up again and the Stones reappeared on stage and started pulling those trapped at the front on to the stage and filtering them away to safety towards the back. We were asked to vacate the theatre as quickly as possible. We later found out a load of Mods had turned up on scooters and were fighting Rockers, or Greasers as we used to call them, outside the Essoldo, and police had been called to join in the battle. The riot started outside the cinema as the Mods tried to force their way into the venue, hence the surge, but police moved both parties back toward Mersey Square as the bikers continued knocking hell out of each other.

THE ROLLING STONES IN THE SIXTIES: A PEOPLE'S HISTORY

# CITY HALL
## 29 MAY 1964, SHEFFIELD, UK

### I WAS THERE: ANDY THOMPSON, AGE 15

Mates of mine from school were postering for Pete Stringfellow's brother, who was a promoter, and I remember being in the schoolyard one day and he brought out a flyer - a picture of the Rolling Stones - and they'd got the black leather waistcoats on and he said, 'Pete's on about booking them.' That was the first time I heard of them.

Then they had a couple of showings on *Ready Steady Go!* I don't think I heard them on the radio. There used to be the Light Programme and the Third Programme, and you'd get up to go to school in the morning and you'd have orchestras playing light songs and music. There were no pop channels at all. They did have something

Andy Thompson saw the Stones at Sheffield City Hall

on a Saturday morning called Uncle Mack. It used to be on between 9 and 10 and he used to play requests for pop music like Anthony Newley and stuff that was popular at that time. Then you had commercial radio stations like Caroline. Luxembourg you could tune into on your little transistor radio under the bedclothes. They were no bigger than an old mobile phone. Everyone used to do it. They used to have the top 20 on a Sunday night so you could listen to it on that.

I saw them in '64 at the second house. As we were going in some of my mates were going out and they said Gordon Waller from the support band Peter and Gordon had got hit in the eye with a jelly baby - because they used to throw jelly babies at The Beatles when they were on stage. We were up in the balcony, and you couldn't really hear the Stones because of the screaming. To be honest, Sheffield City Hall doesn't lend itself particularly to bands.

They were doing a lot of stuff off the first album. 'It's All Over Now', 'Not Fade Away' ... I remember them doing 'I Wanna Be Your Man'. There's a lot of good stuff on that first album.

THE ROLLING STONES IN THE SIXTIES: A PEOPLE'S HISTORY

# ADELPHI THEATRE
## 30 MAY 1964, SLOUGH, UK

**I WAS THERE: PAM MORGAN-BROWN, AGE 12**

I haven't a lot of memories of the actual performance, but I remember that the support act was the Barron Knights. In the audience were quite a number of uniformed armed forces. They listened to the Barron Knights and when the Stones came on, they made a lot of noise, getting out of their seats and leaving the theatre. The Stones waited until they'd left, then Mick thanked the armed forces for 'their support.'

My sister was also at the concert but recalls even less than me – and she was 15. I can only presume she was screaming so much she didn›t notice much else. I lived in Burnham in Buckinghamshire, where Mick's then girlfriend Chrissie Shrimpton lived. We were driving down the High Street one Saturday on the way to the hairdresser's and I suddenly spotted Mick and shrieked! My dad wouldn't stop and took me to hairdressers for my appointment. However, while I was there, he searched the High Street and found Mick delving into a freezer in a shop. He said to Mick, 'Mr Jagger, I have two young daughters at home who would love your autograph.' You can imagine my delight when he presented me with the piece of paper with the autograph on.

*June 1964 saw the Rolling Stones undertake their inaugural tour of the United States, and the release of their fourth UK single, 'It's All Over Now'.*

# SWING AUDITORIUM
## 5 JUNE 1964, SAN BERNADINO, CALIFORNIA

**I WAS THERE: SANDRA CARVER**

In 1964 I was a 17-year-old high school senior. The British Invasion had taken over the surf music my friends and I were listening to. We liked all the British bands but The Beatles and the Rolling Stones were our favourites. Imagine our surprise when my best friend Susan and I heard the Rolling Stones were going to play a concert at Swing Auditorium at the San Bernardino County Fairgrounds in June, just prior to our graduation from school.

Susan and I showed up early and immediately scoped out the back of the building, where we knew the greatest rock 'n' roll band would soon arrive. Sure enough, a black four-door car pulled up.

Sandra Carver was at the Swing Auditorium

The back door opened and Susan spotted Charlie. By then there was a small crowd of teenage girls behind us. All of a sudden Susan let out a gasp and pulled Charlie by the arm saying, 'Out, Charlie … out!' The crowd behind us surged forward, knocking me into the back of the car. I sat up and saw what had made Susan act in this unusual way. I was now sat next to Mick Jagger.

I was just 17, and very naïve. I couldn't get a word out, and I'm sure the look on my face was pure panic. All Mick said was, 'No worries, bird.' Wow. Mick Jagger talked to me! Almost immediately, the car door opened and I was unceremoniously yanked out of the car. As the five lads were making their way up the ramp to the back door, they had girls all over them. I remember yelling at one to stop pulling Brian's hair. The bandmates looked a bit afraid, but did escape through the backdoor to safety.

Susan and I walked up the ramp to the back door and slowly opened it. We were both rather shy so this behaviour was not in our normal comfort zone. Brian spotted us and quickly lifted his hand to stop us, pointed to a policeman that was backstage, then waved us forward when the policeman looked away. Unfortunately, the policeman was rather diligent in his duty of protecting the Stones from the crazies. We were spotted.

When the back door was opened so we could be ushered out, the girls outside went crazy. A San Bernardino police officer stopped us and threatened to arrest us for inciting a riot. Susan looked him right in the face and told him her father was the mayor of Riverside, a nearby city.

He asked her father's name and she told him. He let us go. I should note here that Susan's father had been deceased for many years. I asked how she knew the Riverside mayor's name and she said she didn't - she'd just made up a name. Whew. That was a close one. My mom thought I was babysitting, not in another town at a Rolling Stones concert.

We enjoyed the concert immensely. Bill Wyman wrote a book about the Stones and lists all their shows. There's a photo of the 1964 San Bernardino concert, and there I am, close to the stage, admiring Mick. That photo brought back a lot of memories. The sound equipment wasn't then what it is today, but the Stones sounded great. It's hard to imagine Mick Jagger standing at the microphone, singing with just a little in-place footwork. The Jagger 'moves' were pretty simple then, but still enough to stir awakening sexuality in us young naïve girls. Remember, this was a couple years prior to the hippie/love movement in the US. I believe they sang 'It's All Over Now', 'Time is on My Side', 'Around and Around', and several others, but I could be confusing these songs with other Stones shows I've attended.

## BIG REGGIE'S DANCELAND
### 12 JUNE 1964, EXCELSIOR AMUSEMENT PARK, MINNEAPOLIS, MINNESOTA

**I WAS THERE: BOB ROEPKE, AGE 17**
We were just out of high school. There were three or four of us. I don't remember if it was a Friday or Saturday night but it was a weekend night and we were just going out. And part of that amusement park had what was called Big Reggie's Danceland. Local and other bands would perform there so you'd run into other young folks - young girls - it was a popular place to go. We were out on the fringe of Minneapolis and pretty rural - still cornfields and small towns. The population of Excelsior was less than 10,000. The Excelsior amusement park was just that – an amusement park with all kinds of rides and a big wooden rollercoaster and circus rides. Back in the Fifties and Sixties dance halls were pretty popular. You'd find dance halls in a lot of small towns, and they were the popular gathering place. So the Excelsior dance hall, close

to a big lake – Lake Minnetonka, always an attraction with a big boating area - was a gathering place, a magnet for younger people. And Big Reggie – I don't even know the guy's last name – he'd bring the young bands in there, and that was good for us. There were local bands we'd follow and they'd play in those places and in those little towns, and that's where we'd go.

That night, about nine o'clock we went over there because one of the guys heard there was a band playing. We didn't know much about it. We hung around and talked with others and asked the question, 'Who's this band?' 'It's a band from England.' 'What's their name?' 'Oh, it's the Rolling Stones.' Then we asked, 'What is it to get in there?' I think it was $6. We said, 'Are you crazy? We're not paying $6 for a band we've never heard of.' We had some curiosity about them because they were a band from England coming over here - now that was something we hadn't seen or experienced, so there was curiosity … but not for $6.

Because nobody really knew the Stones back then, they just didn't have that early draw. Others have reported that at one point there were maybe a couple hundred people in there, but it was a big dance hall so maybe there was more than that. But it was a small number regardless. So we said, 'Oh, let's take off' and went some other places and hangouts.

We came back at around 11.45pm that night. It was not a big crowd outside but there were still people milling around. We said, 'Are they still goin'?' 'Yes, they're still goin'. 'Many people in there?' 'Not too many.' 'How much to get in?' And they said, '50 cents.' So we went in. I said, 'I'm gonna go in there for 50 cents.' So we went in there and - I'm not kidding - there were I think 35 or 45 people. There was nobody dancing, nobody out in front of them. I actually walked over there in front of them to take a look because there was nobody on the dancefloor. Now they were not very happy. They weren't the happiest of campers, that was pretty obvious, but they continued to play. We were standing off to the side, talking to some other folks. We probably stayed 15 minutes then said 'let's go' and left. And the only thing we ever experienced was watching their success after that.

I would have loved to have taken a selfie. Can you imagine what it would have been like to take a picture with them in that empty hall back then? I'm sure if they'd come back a year or two later the place would have been booked full. But not that night. Mick Jagger signed autographs at the University of Minnesota recently. How cool would it have been to just wait in line and go up to him and say, 'Do you remember the Excelsior amusement park in 1964?' He had to remember Excelsior. It would have been just a fun conversation to have because I could have said, 'I was there! I was one of those handful of people that was there.'

# DANCELAND
## 17 JUNE 1964, WEST VIEW PARK, PITTSBURGH, PENNSYLVANIA

### I WAS THERE: PHILIP LANDO, AGE 21

I attended with a friend from school - Duquesne University in Pittsburgh – whose name was Tony Gentilcore. We went because we were already fans of British Invasion bands, even though this was before the popularity of the Liverpool and other bands in the United States. The two of us were deejaying dances following basketball games at the school, and had been supplied demo records by a local radio station called KDKA. These were usually records that were not then on the station's playlist, including records by Freddie and the Dreamers ('I'm Telling You Now'), Gerry and the Pacemakers, and other British bands. We liked what we heard and read all we could about The Beatles and other British bands.

When The Rolling Stones came out with their first album, *England's Newest Hitmakers*, I bought it and liked it. So we knew who the Stones were well before anybody else we knew had heard of them. Their initial concert tour was not accompanied with the kind of publicity that greeted The Beatles. I don't recall how we got the tickets exactly but there was no great competition to buy them. I remember that we enjoyed the show. The Stones had already assumed their bad boy image, and Mick Jagger had already mastered some of his moves. A highlight was the performance of 'Not Fade Away'. The venue was actually a dance hall, and there were no seats that I recall. We stood within 20 feet of the stage. There were no more than 200 in attendance, generally our age or thereabouts. The crowd was attentive and appeared to enjoy the performance.

---

*The Stones interrupted their US tour to fly back to England to honour a booking made many months before to play at Oxford University, which the group was unable to get out of. It cost them £1,500 in air fares to pick up a £100 fee.*

---

# MAGDALEN COLLEGE COMMEMORATIVE BALL
## 22 JUNE 1964, OXFORD, UK

### I WAS THERE: VIV BOORMAN

The band was booked before they hit the big time. The Commem. organisers were guided by a guy called Churchill (real name? nickname? I never knew), the Magdalen guru of pop. His ambition in life was to be Phil Spector. He shared a flat on the Woodstock Road with some mates, whose quarters were all classical texts, beer bottles and decaying socks. Churchill, however, was established in elegant style in the old breakfast room, with a coal fire, armchairs and the biggest collection of LPs I have ever to this day seen. Just before the ball, the Stones' agent let it be known they wouldn't be able to perform for the agreed fee: indeed, they might well all turn out to have colds. Churchill left his lair and went with the dance committee to the then Professor of Jurisprudence, Prof H.L.A. Hart. Nothing like getting good advice. Heaven alone knows what he suggested they threatened the Stones with, but it worked. They did their stuff.

### I WAS THERE: IAN LEWTY

We had a phone call from their manager, Andrew Loog Oldham, asking if we can boost the fee a little, but we told him there was nothing doing. It's the year's bargain.

### THE ROLLING STONES IN THE SIXTIES: A PEOPLE'S HISTORY

**I WAS THERE: NEIL ROBINSON**

My group The Falling Leaves supported the Stones on two occasions. One was the infamous Magdalen College Commemorative Ball, when they were flown back from the States for a £300 payment, and the other was at McIlroy's Ballroom in Swindon.

---

*After a few days off in early July to recover from their American trip, they were gigging again in Britain, as 'It's All Over Now' became their first UK No. 1.*

---

## QUEENS HALL
### 12 JULY 1964, LEEDS, UK

**I WAS THERE: CLIFF WATSON, AGE 16**

I saw the Stones at Queens Hall, an ex-tram shed in Leeds. It had a stage which was in the centre of the large room with no tiers and turned at 90 degrees after each song. We were lucky to be sat on the second row from the stage. I went with my then girlfriend for her 16th birthday. I remember my parents being a bit miffed about me going to see a 'long-haired group of

Leeds poster

layabouts' and taking a girl with me. Their attitude was similar for The Beatles. It was the end of music as my parents had known it and they never took to any of the 'new' groups at all. A couple of the support acts were Lulu and the Luvvers, who had just recorded 'Shout', and a Liverpool group whose name was the Rustics. The seats were all loose and girls were still seated as they shook their coats or

217

cardigans as they screamed at the Stones. They had just recorded 'It's All Over Now' and finished the show with it. I went and bought their first LP the following week. At that time most young people were either Beatles or Stones, although anyone with sense appreciated them both.

### I WAS THERE: PAULINE HAYDOCK, AGE 21

I became an avid fan when the group emerged, soon knowing all the lyrics of their early hits. I still do! So when they appeared at a large venue in Leeds I eagerly arranged for a group of us, aged 21 to 23, to go from York – a big deal for us in those days. We were sitting about halfway back but still had a good view. However, immediately they came on stage all the surrounding fans – mainly young teenage girls – jumped onto their seats and started screaming and shouting. We all remained seated for a while, looking stupefied, then realised it was a case of 'if you can't beat them, join them.' So we got up there for the whole performance. We barely caught a glimpse of the band or heard much either, but I wouldn't have missed this early, exciting experience of those heady times.

# BEAT CITY
## 18 JULY 1964, OXFORD STREET, LONDON, UK

### I WAS THERE: RICHARD LUETCHFORD

I had seen the first Stones appearance at the 3rd National Jazz Festival the year before. They were ending the festival on Sunday evening after a day of various British trad jazz bands, most of which I missed. Long John Baldry and Cyril Davies did good sets, but the Stones were superb and had the crowd shouting for more at the end of their short festival-closing set. At the time I was working at a music shop in the West End and during my lunch break would often have lunch in an Italian café called La Gioconda in Denmark Street, or Tin Pan Alley. It's still there, but it's now an upmarket restaurant. Back then it was full of musicians recording at Regent Sounds Studios (now a music shop). In the booth next to mine were the Stones, smoking and drinking coffee and taking a break from recording their first LP. That was the closest I got – I was too shy to speak to them – but another time I got to see Jimi Hendrix in the same street.

# THE ROLLING STONES IN THE SIXTIES: A PEOPLE'S HISTORY

A year after the festival, a friend and I got tickets for the Stones' 'only London appearance' at Beat City, a club we were not familiar with. It was a very warm day and Beat City turned out to be an unventilated basement. The promoter crammed it with Stones fans eager to see the group close up. The walls were already running with condensation when Alexis Korner's Blues Inc. kicked off the show. We were curious to see Alexis and his band given his reputation and early support for the Stones. Charlie, Brian, Mick, Keith and Ian Stewart had all played at the Ealing Blues Club, which he founded, but living in South London we had never ventured out that far.

Alexis was followed by Tom Jones and The Squires, then newly arrived in London and virtually unknown. This was a year before Tom's big hit single, 'It's Not Unusual', and the crowd - impatient to see the Stones - gave him a hard time. His provincial rock 'n' roll act did not go down well with this cool London crowd. Tom seemed a bit older and his music, though well performed, was not the blues and R&B that we craved.

By the time the Stones finally arrived on stage, the heat and lack of ventilation had started to affect the audience. Girls at the front were fainting and being passed over the crowd to the back of the club and the exits to get some air. I don't remember there being any drinks available - or toilets - but there must have been some facilities provided.

The Stones finally arrived in a riot of colour and sound. The stage was quite high and close, so we had a good view. And they were loud too. Brian Jones seemed to delight in taunting the audience, waving and bashing his tambourine on 'It's Alright'. Brian was often the focus of attention, stage right, stealing the limelight from Mick, who did not have much room to move around at the front of the small stage.

They played their hits and ended with their latest, 'It's All Over Now'. It had been a great show, but it was a relief to emerge into the London evening air and head to the nearest pub for a long cool drink.

## I WAS THERE: SHIRLEY RAWSTORNE

My older brother, at this time political journalist for *The Guardian*, had bought his first house in Nazeing, Essex, on the outskirts of North London. My friend Alice and I went for a week's holiday and were taken to see the sights of London by my sister-in-law. Initially we spent our free time at a local swimming pool, listening to the small radio we had brought along with us. The Rolling Stones were a particular favourite. We loved the rebellious blues sound of the Stones.

Somehow, we noticed the Stones were playing at a club in London and after some deliberation my brother agreed to get us tickets if he could. Philip is much older than me and a very responsible person - not at all rock 'n' roll - but during a break from work he queued up to get us tickets. It is still one of his many stories over dinner. Alice and I went on the train to the concert. We managed to get right at the front. The stage was very close and low, and we were in easy reach of the group. We were just amazed with the music and the atmosphere. I remember hearing 'I'm a King Bee' for the first time, being totally bowled over by it. The club was crowded, hot and sweaty, and a young bloke came along the front with a bucket of water and sponge. He wiped all the faces of the group and wiped ours also. What we looked like was insignificant - we had been wiped with the same sponge as the Stones. When we left the club and caught the train back to Nazeing, we vowed never to wash our faces again.

# HIPPODROME
## 19 JULY 1964, BRIGHTON, UK

**I WAS THERE: KEITH TAPSCOTT, AGE 14**
Things were easy and uncomplicated then. No call centres. I simply wrote to the Brighton Hippodrome enclosing a postal order, asking for the best seats possible for me and my girlfriend. It was about 10/6 (53p) for centre seats in about the seventh row. We arrived at the venue and it was swarming with teenagers outside, a fairly even mix of boys and girls. I endeavoured to copy the appearance of Mick Jagger – crew-neck lambswool sweater, light grey slacks and long hairstyle. I was very

Keith Tapscott was mistaken for Mick Jagger

pleased when several people said I looked like Mick. My girlfriend was chuffed too.

Vendors were selling large black and white photos of the band. I bought a large one of Brian, a slightly smaller one of Mick, and one of the entire band. Once inside I also bought a programme, which I still have to this day. We entered the theatre and everyone sat down and remained so throughout. There were lots of attendants to keep control and St John Ambulance volunteers to carry out the girls who fainted during the Stones' performance. Each act was politely applauded, and there was a few screams for Marty Wilde, but at the age of 24 he was a bit old in comparison. As the show progressed the tension, anticipation, and excitement built up and up.

There were no fancy light shows or dramatic music played through the PA, but there were curtains, which were lowered between each act. The roadie at the time, Spike Thompson, had long hair like the band and occasionally lowered his head, poked it through the gap in the curtains and shook it, to tumultuous screams.

When the time came you could feel it in the pit of your stomach - the compere's introduction was lost in a cacophony of screaming and shouting and the place erupted. The first thing that struck me was just how ghostly white they all were, presumably a result of their lifestyle of playing and partying at night and sleeping by day. For most of the time the screaming was louder than the music, but that only added to an electrifying performance. They opened with 'Walking the Dog' and ended with 'It's All Over Now'. Mick shook the maracas on 'Not Fade Away' while Brian played harmonica on that and on 'I Just Want to Make Love to You'. Between songs Mick would check the set-list, written on a scrap of paper. Mick very much played to the audience while Brian teased it, Bill appeared aloof, and Keith grinned and moved with the music. Mick and Brian were wearing sports jackets, Bill a waistcoat, Keith a casual jacket, and Charlie a sweater. Sadly, too soon it was all over. In those days they played for around 25 minutes and there was no encore. As we left some were animated, others dazed. My ears were ringing and then hissing from the screaming. It somehow felt a little unreal as it was all over so quickly. There were crowds of people outside, queuing for the second performance, eagerly enquiring what it had been like and, in a lot of cases, what the Stones were wearing.

### I WAS THERE: NORMAN SCOTT

I did a bit of writing for a girls' magazine called *Valentine*. I deejayed at a youth club and the husband of the lady who worked in the canteen worked for *Valentine*. Most of the people who worked for these magazines were middle-aged men. They didn't know anything about pop music. So I got to know him and he invited me to concerts with him. He said, 'You tell me who's who, what's what, and everything.' So I used to do a bit of writing. And he'd put it in under his name and he'd pay me. That's how I used to meet a lot of people like the Rolling Stones. I've got a lovely picture of The Rolling Stones, with Keith Richards missing. I don't know where he buggered off to. We were waiting and waiting and waiting. Mick Jagger in the end said, 'Can't wait any longer' so I've got this nice picture with the other four.

## EMPRESS BALLROOM
### 24 JULY 1964, BLACKPOOL, UK

*The Stones' concert at the Empress Ballroom, Blackpool was held during Glasgow Fair, the seaside resort seeing a seasonal influx of factory workers and their families travelling down from Scotland to take their two-week summer holiday, with many Glasgow businesses closed. The events that unfolded at the concert led to Blackpool Council imposing a ban on the Stones performing in their town, a ban not lifted until 2008.*

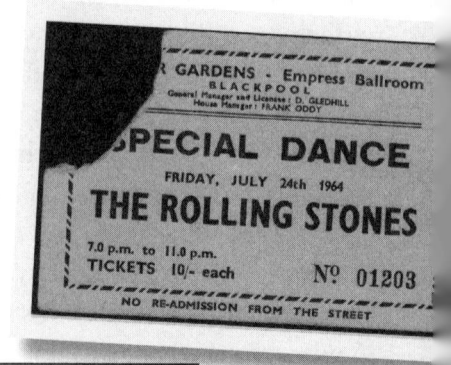

Blackpool ticket

### I WAS THERE: EILEEN CORNES, AGE 16

I was on holiday in Blackpool with my parents from Shropshire. I attended with my cousin Jean and an older Scottish girl we befriended at

# THE ROLLING STONES IN THE SIXTIES: A PEOPLE'S HISTORY

the hotel. The waiters at the hotel obtained the tickets for us as well as tickets for a Beatles concert held in a different theatre during the same week, for which we had seats.

Approximately three-quarters of the way through the Stones' concert the venue seemed to get rowdy. Our Scottish friend advised us to take off our shoes and run to the back of the venue as she feared that there was going to be trouble ahead. I hesitated at first, not really sensing danger, and she screamed at me to move. Without more ado I did what I was told, and we all went back to the hotel. The following day we found out the Stones' piano had been thrown off the stage into the crowd. I don't know who did it and don't know if there were any serious injuries.

## I WAS THERE: PETER FIELDING

The band I was with when the Stones came to the Empress Ballroom at Blackpool was called The Executives, and we were the support band for the concert. It was the night when the crowd wrecked the ballroom, getting on the stage, pulling all their stuff off and kicking it to pieces, the band running off for their lives.

They didn't get much playing done, to be quite honest. One of the audience tried to spit at Keith Richards, and I think he tried to push him off with his foot or something on the front of the stage. There was a bit of a fracas that went on and it erupted into them throwing bottles and all sorts, then we ran on to get our gear off, and it just went bananas. The only number I saw them do if I remember rightly was an early rhythm and blues song called 'Mona'. We sort of heard one and a half numbers off in the wings, you know, after we'd been on.

The Executives supported the Stones at Blackpool's Empress Ballroom

We were on stage and the crowd were throwing pennies at us - coins - and shouting, 'We want the Stones! We want the Stones!' They weren't interested in what we were doing at all. So we did our first set and came off and ... well, we didn't quite do a full set because they were throwing coins and we thought we'd cut it short. We never saw anything else. They'd gone and we got most of our gear off the stage. I don't know whether Charlie got his drum kit. He possibly did because it was right at the back of the Empress Ballroom. It was the amps really that got jumped on and stamped on. There was a grand piano on the corner of the stage, a big one and a very valuable one. They ended up pulling that onto the floor and smashing that. It just went mental.

They were wrecking anything they could find. There were so many of them. The attendants and bouncers were overwhelmed. Our bass player got his amp smashed.

We went back the next day. The debris was all over the place. They ripped the ballroom apart, it was unbelievable. It was the only scary experience of my career. It was menacing. You could have been killed, trampled to death or something.

## I WAS THERE: SYD BLOOM

I've been to thousands of gigs in my life and I've never been to one like that. It was Glasgow weekend. I've never ever been in a worse situation in my life. The place was beyond belief, just absolutely ridiculous. I knew Pete Fielding, who was in the Executives. They were local and opened and did a spot, then the Stones came on. Unusually they went off after their first spot. The Executives came back on, then the Stones were coming on for a second spot.

Allegedly what happened was there was two or three Scots guys who got their way to the front right by the stage and one threw a fork at Keith Richards, who promptly went forward and kicked his teeth out with his Cuban heel. It kicked off from there. So the Stones ran for it. Then the police came, and it was suddenly mayhem. Guys were lobbing bloody bottles at the chandeliers, which were about 35ft up. Girls had lost their shoes, they were running around cutting their feet to shreds on broken glass. It was just absolutely ridiculous. The police came first of all, and sort of occupied the stage. But under a hail of missiles they all buggered off.

The Winter Gardens is connected to the Tower, and they brought all the bouncers from the Winter Gardens and the Tower onto the stage because the police had cleared off. There were a lot of locals there and a lot of the locals had had a load of grief with these guys, a history of being given a good hiding. One guy jumped on the stage, grabbed hold of a ginger-haired bouncer and pulled him off, and the guy just got kicked to shreds. A lot of the bouncers for the Tower company were just absolute nutters. And they got what they deserved.

Then the grand piano got thrown off the stage. Anything that was there got trashed, absolutely completely trashed. The cymbals were being thrown around - if you can imagine a more deadly weapon than a cymbal. It was a dance hall, like an open ballroom. Around the edge of the room was the equivalent of cinema seating. Rows of seating and they ripped those up and used them as a battering ram.

I shudder to think how many people were in that ballroom. The people were like sardines. All the way back and all the way up the sides. And it's quite a wide, large ballroom. People were lobbing glasses and bottles all over the place. They were actually aiming to see if they could get the chandeliers, and they did. I just wanted to get the hell out of the place.

It was reported in a way that it became front page of the papers. And the Stones almost immediately did a gig in Paris and there was another riot there. And one wondered whether this was because it had been reported that way. I was pretty bloody scared at the time. I got a bus home later and I'd got a jacket that was a purple colour that I'd worn quite a few times. My shirt was still wringing wet and my white shirt was purple from the dye off the jacket because I'd sweated that much. It was absolutely beyond belief. The Tower Company was clearly to blame. They just let anybody and everybody in for the equivalent now of 50p apiece. There was no such thing as booking, because there were no seats. Hence it was their second and last appearance in Blackpool.

### I WAS THERE: KEVIN WHITTAKER, AGE 17

I was waiting to go into the Army. I was at the front, near the stage on the left. I remember one of the girls trying to grab Brian Jones' leg. He kicked her hand, which caused her to scream in pain. Her boyfriend then mounted the stage with his mates. Seconds later we were all on the stage as the Stones legged it. I helped to push the grand piano off the stage. I picked up the tremolo arm off Brian Jones' guitar and had it for many years. I remember walking out of the foyer and a lad in front of me was carrying one of the big red stage curtains over his shoulder … none of the security guards stopped us as we got outside. We then started to chant, 'We want the Stones!' A few windows got smashed too. It was a really mad night. We heard that the Stones had gone across the rooftops to safety. I'll never forget that night.

## I WAS THERE: PAT SMITH, AGE 18

I was going out with my husband-to-be. It was certainly a night to remember. We were both just a couple of people away from the very front of the stage, so had a great view of what happened. A lad in the audience started it, spitting on stage. Then the trouble started, and very soon all hell broke loose.

## I WAS THERE: DAVID CLARK, AGE 21

It's one concert I will never forget. I took my sister Joyce, who was 16, and her friend Sheena Gow. We managed to get to the very front of the stage, to the right of Mick Jagger, and it was a seething mass of a crowd with not much elbow room at all.

Jagger was wearing a green striped blazer of the type you imagine Oxbridge students would be wearing at that time. The others were not smartly dressed. We had seen The Beatles at Kings George's Hall, Blackburn and they were much more uniform and smart, but I guess that was part of the Stones' attraction. Whilst we were at the front, I became aware of hostility towards the band from many of the crowd around us, who seemed to have Scottish accents.

*David Clark recalls an Oxbridge look*

When the interval came, I told my sister and her friend it wasn't safe to remain there for the second half. I could feel trouble brewing. So they reluctantly followed me to the upstairs balcony, looking down on the stage. Not long into the second half the people at the front appeared to start spitting at Keith Richards and Mick Jagger. I next saw Keith Richards take a swing at one the offenders with his guitar. I couldn't tell if he connected with his target from where we were, but from that moment on all hell broke loose. One minute the band were on stage, the next second they were gone.

# THE ROLLING STONES IN THE SIXTIES: A PEOPLE'S HISTORY

The people at the front then stormed the stage. Some security men who were far too old to be in the job were dragged from the stage. The amplifiers and mics became the first targets and these were smashed into the smallest pieces they could break them into in their rage. They then dragged the curtains of the walls, and even the Empress Ballroom clock above the stage became a target. There was pandemonium on the dance floor as there was no seating except on the balcony and at the sides, and normal fans began to flee.

Then a long row of policemen appeared, and baton-charged the offenders. They can't have been far away as it seemed such a short time from trouble starting to them appearing on the scene. I suspect they were expecting trouble and had received a tip-off about what was going to happen. We watched the dance floor clearance and baton-bashing for a while then said we had better go home as there would obviously be no further performance that night. Everybody leaving the building was stopped and searched by the police, including us. The following day I was driving my travelling shop around Penwortham outside Preston when I saw a crowd gathered round a bungalow off Marshalls Brow and I discovered it was the house of the Stones' northern agent, John Dell. He had an indoor swimming pool tagged onto his house, and the band were swimming in it, thus attracting local fans.

### I WAS THERE: MARGARET JOHNSON, AGE 12

I have never been to a Stones concert, but I do recall them coming to Park Lane in Penwortham just outside Preston. At the time it was said that their manager lived there, and he had an indoor swimming pool. I was living just up the road in the council houses in Studholme Crescent. Park Lane was considered very posh and there was a great crowd of us outside, screaming our heads off.

### I WAS THERE: DAVID BENSON

I joined Preston Borough Police in 1963 and started real policing in 1964. There was an infamous concert in Blackpool that year, on a Friday night. I was on an early shift in Preston on the Saturday. The Stones were whisked away from Blackpool and taken to the Bull and Royal Hotel, Preston. I remember seeing Mick leave in a minibus on the Saturday around lunchtime. I was detailed to patrol outside the Bull and Royal, but there weren't many people there and there were no incidents.

# IMPERIAL BALLROOM
## 25 JULY 1964, NELSON, UK

### I WAS THERE: FIONA COOMBES, AGE 16
I was determined to see them live but my friends all thought they were dreadful. My father, a local GP, took me and sat at the bar in the Imperial drinking brandy while I screamed at the front of the stage. My father found the whole evening ear-splitting and never wanted to experience such a night again. I remember them singing 'Come On'. Mick was fantastic but I was mesmerised by Charlie too.

### I WAS THERE: MEL HIGHMORE
I was a police constable on patrol. In the early hours of the morning, I was instructed by radio to drive the police Land Rover to the back of the Imp and take four males to the police station. On arriving at the rear door, four very scruffy-looking young men were ushered in through the back door of my vehicle. I thought they had been arrested and drove straight to the prisoners' entry door at the back of the police station, where the custody sergeant admitted them. It was my supper time, so I parked up and went up to the dining room on the first floor. Two or three of the group were playing snooker on the table in that room. I started to eat my sandwiches, then two of the group sat down. The remaining player stayed at the table and asked if anyone would like a game. I went to the table and started to play. I don't remember how long the game lasted - probably no more than ten minutes. Nor do I recall much in the way of conversation with him. I wasn't very clued up about pop music. It was only afterwards that my sergeant told me who the lads were – the Rolling Stones – and who I had played snooker with - Mick Jagger.

# ULSTER HALL
## 31 JULY 1964, BELFAST, UK

### I WAS THERE: LYN MORRISON, AGE 16
My friend Christine and I queued all day to be sure of getting in. It was great fun. We grouped together with strangers and elected someone to go to a shop to get sandwiches. We were eventually admitted into the

hall. There was no seating in the hall. Christine and I were thrust forward in a tidal surge to a position right at the front, close to the stage, which spanned the full width of the hall, about shoulder-height. The moment the Stones ran on there was another surge forward and we got squashed.

Christine passed out and the next thing I saw was St John Ambulancemen heaving her onto the stage before carting her off into the wings, where my brother Peter found her. It is as well he was there, but I was sickened he had been able to walk in at the last minute without having to queue. I'm told the concert was abandoned after three songs. I don't remember that. I just recall the crowd noise was deafening and drowned out the band. Christine heard nothing of course. I still see her every week. We play bridge together.

Lyn Morrison gave a helping hand to a very tired Stones fan

## I WAS THERE: JIM SHAW, AGE 16

On that particular day I was working in Bangor, County Down. I was serving an apprenticeship as a sheet metal worker and helping to erect ventilation in Bangor Dairies. I had no transport of my own, but at around 11 in the morning I asked could I go home early as I was going to the doctor's ... not.

My request was granted and I got on the bus to Belfast and joined the queue outside the Ulster Hall along with a few of my friends - Ed Lindop from Holywood, Brian Irvine from Denmark Street, Billy Barnes from West Circular Road, Ann Denver from Crumlin Road, Veronica Jackson from Creagh, and a few others. Long hair was the order of the day. Well, we thought it was long then – oh, I wish I had it now! We wore coloured shirts and some of us had roll-neck sweaters. Bell-bottom jeans had made their way in the fashion scene and boots with heels. That was just us males!

It was a standing concert, and I was fortunate that we were near the top of queue, so as soon as the doors opened we made a mad dash to just in front of stage. The next few hours were bedlam, mainly due to the crowd pushing and shoving and trying to get in front of others. I cannot remember if there was a supporting group because the anticipation of seeing Mick and company close up meant I was oblivious to what was happening prior to their appearance.

When they appeared it was just a mad push from the rear of hall and you just about could hear them going through their set. People were attempting to get on stage and a few girls did manage to get close to Mick, but the next thing they knew, they were being led away by the bouncers. I remember one of the girls who was with us fainted, as did lots of others because of the heat. I lifted her over my shoulders and carried her through the crowd to the back of the hall, a St John Ambulanceman helping to bring her round. Believe it or not, as soon as she was up, she headed straight back into the crowd.

When the concert was over there were lots of people lying around the hall, exhausted by the heat. I made my way home that night by walking the whole way from Bedford Street to Dunmurry, where I lived. I was one of the fortunate ones as both my father and mother were quite liberal in their way with me. All they asked was, 'Did you enjoy the concert?' Enjoy was perhaps not how I would have described the experience. To this day I can remember the total joy I got from going.

*To this day I can remember the total joy I got from going to the show*

### I WAS THERE: GRAINGER ALLEN, AGE 16

We had to camp outside the ticket office all night to be able to buy our tickets. They cost 12/6 (38p). Even though the show was short it was worth the wait. They opened with 'Not Fade Away'.

One clear memory is of the police having to clear the stage after only four or five numbers as girl fans were going frantic and were in danger of getting crushed.

*After performing in Belfast, the Stones made the 28-mile journey to Ballymena to play a ballroom show the same evening.*

# THE ROLLING STONES IN THE SIXTIES: A PEOPLE'S HISTORY

## FLAMINGO BALLROOM
### 31 JULY 1964, BALLYMENA, UK

**I WAS THERE: MARTIN STEWART, AGE 18**

In the Sixties, many famous or up and coming singers or groups came over here. A phenomenon of Northern Ireland in the period before the Troubles was the ballroom. Ireland north and south was covered in them. Most weekends saw dancing taking place to showbands, but once a month or so promoters would bring in a big act from the UK or US.

My local haunt was the Flamingo Ballroom, Ballymena, owned and run by the late Sammy Barr. In 1964, the Rolling Stones came to Northern Ireland. They appeared at the Ulster Hall in Belfast but also at the Flamingo, playing for about an hour.

Ballymena's Flamingo Ballroom

They arrived late from the Belfast venue and as usual, a showband was playing for the bulk of the evening. The ballroom was packed to capacity that night and we had paid the princely sum of less than £1 to see them.

Martin Stewart with The Vampires

They came in through the back door behind the stage. They used the amps and mics belonging to the showband, bringing only their own guitars. I think Charlie Watts brought his own snare drum. They were playing on the stage at the front of the ballroom, about three feet above floor level, with no barriers, to keep the crowds back. I was less than 10ft from Mick Jagger as he Brian, Keith, Bill and Charlie belted out their set.

# THE ROLLING STONES IN THE SIXTIES: A PEOPLE'S HISTORY

It was all very restrained on the floor. A few girls fainted, more from the heat than the music. At the end the Stones went out through the back door, and that was that. The supporting showband resumed the stage for the remainder of the night. I had seen the Rolling Stones at first hand. I was to play on that same stage many times as a member of a local supporting group, for both show bands and headline acts from the UK and the US. Great times.

## I WAS THERE: JAMES BROWN, AGE 19

Sammy Barr owned the Flamingo Ballroom. He used to run a little coffee shop and then built the Flamingo. He would put on shows at the Town Hall - Marty Wilde and the Wildcats, Adam Faith, those kind of people. Then he built the Flamingo and brought over top stars like Tom Jones, the Stones, Roy Orbison, The Merseybeats, Gerry and the Pacemakers, and all the famous showbands of Ireland. Every weekend, Friday or Saturday, there was always a top showband. These people were stars. There was a big gateway, and they would drive down the back and close the gate, unload all their equipment, and go onto the stage.

Sammy would let me go in and I would help set up the amplifiers. I remember that night very well. Ballymoney Street was all cordoned off. Sammy let me stand at the front door. At the front door you'd go up the stairs to the ballroom. 'It's All Over Now' was the top record at the time. Instead of the tour manager bringing the big van with all their gear, two large Mark X Jags drew up and stopped in the street. Mick Jagger got out, then Keith Richards, Brian Jones, and Bill Wyman. They all jumped out of the Jags and ran in through the front door, past me. They were all carrying their guitars. I could never understand it, because the roadies brought their AC30 amps up that way. They ran past me carrying their guitars. Bill Wyman was carrying his bass and Brian Jones his teardrop guitar. Maybe because the street was closed and everything was barricaded off, and they knew no one was going to get near them to tear them apart. I think Sammy squeezed in two or three thousand that night. No way you could get moving. Not in a million years. They were just terrific.

THE ROLLING STONES IN THE SIXTIES: A PEOPLE'S HISTORY

# PIER BALLROOM
## 1 AUGUST 1964, HASTINGS, UK

### I WAS THERE: ANDRE PALFREY-MARTIN, AGE 16

'It's All Over Now' had just been No 1. It was branded the second Battle of Hastings - Mods and Rockers were just about to kick off. The Stones were escorted on and off the pier in an old ambulance by the police as a security measure. We originally thought someone had tried to get them off the pier on a fishing boat or speedboat. The police report from that time gives details of when they appeared on stage, time-wise, and when they were taken off and subsequently dispersed.

They went on and did something like a 35-to-40-minute set. The police report said, 'The Rolling Stones beat group was scheduled to give a performance at Hastings Pier Ballroom from 9pm to 9.30pm.' This was extensively advertised. The manager arranged for the rendezvous at the Central Police Station in Hastings at 8pm. Several thousand people were congregating on or in the vicinity of the pier. So there were a lot of people outside as well as on the pier itself. By 10pm the Stones were transported off the pier in the ambulance, conveyed to the central police station and subsequently escorted out of the borough in their private cars.

### I WAS THERE: MAURICE VINEY, AGE 35

The boys on the stage were very young but their music was excellent. The main point I remember was that a very nice young lady removed her pants and threw them at Mick in the centre of the stage.

# LONGLEAT HOUSE
## 2 AUGUST 1964, WARMINSTER, UK

### I WAS THERE: JOHN LEIGHTON, AGE 14

Three friends and I cycled from Bath to go and see them in Longleat. That was 20 or 25 miles on these tatty old bikes. It was chaos, absolute pandemonium. You couldn't see and you couldn't hear them. I remember the Marquis of Bath looking totally bemused on the steps, with it all going on. He'd obviously never seen anything like it before. It was a good day out but for 14- and 15-year-olds cycling there and getting pushed around it was a little scary.

### I WAS THERE: DAVID HYDE, AGE 16

I remember the concert being in front of the house. With everybody waiting with great anticipation for the start, a figure ran out of the house with long hair and people at the front went mad until they realised it was not a Stone but somebody with a wig on, who we were led to believe was Lord Bath.

When I got back to Swindon that night my parents were concerned that I was okay, because the news on TV reported disturbances and people being thrown into ponds outside the house. I can honestly say I saw none of this, but it was always good to report anything bad to do with the Stones. My parents didn't like The Beatles until the Stones came on the scene. Then they thought The Beatles were okay.

### I WAS THERE: JEAN GOODLAND

The Rolling Stones' first television appearance was on *Thank Your Lucky Stars*, promoting first single 'Come On'. As soon as I saw them on the screen my life changed. In a flash, I knew there was 'another way' and I didn't have to stay in a small town thinking or living or following the traditional route of engagement at 18, marriage at 21, and motherhood thereafter. This image told me I could be free and live how I wanted to live. And I did, so it's their fault. They were wild. Newspapers

Jean Goodland saw girls fainting and being lifted over the wire

around the country in the following days reflected the horror of parents and all things establishment at this piece of terrible and threatening audacity. Suddenly The Beatles were bordering on acceptability. We saw them live when they played as part of various package concerts touring the UK after that. But my most vivid memory is when they played Longleat House in 1964, 20 or 30 miles away, deep in the Wiltshire countryside.

We hitchhiked everywhere in those days, so myself and two intrepid friends set off in total excitement. Thinking back on this hitchhiking malarkey, we took lots of risks, but we were fearless. I was wearing denim jeans, striped T-shirt and a denim waistcoat. We had duffel coats and what were called duffel bags with us.

Tension was rife, as with all Stones concerts in those days. Excitement was growing and the crowds were gathering. It was an outside event - one of the first rock concerts. There were no seats. The band was going to play on a sort of patio at the grand entrance to the stately home. There was a chickenwire fence about six feet high around the house. Within the wire were St John Ambulance and officials, and outside were the fans. The crowd pressed up closer and closer to the wire.

The band came from nowhere onto the porch and started playing. Everyone went mental. Girls were fainting and being lifted over the wire to the safety of the first aiders' arms. Hmm – I noted that these girls were getting to be on the inside of the wire, near the band, so got a little plan going. We were right at the front and one by one the three of us all pretended to faint. People moved back and allowed us to be carried over the fence. Soon as we were on the other side we got up and ran up the steps. Suddenly we were on stage, to the bemusement of uniformed ambulance staff.

There were a lot of people up there – sound people, security, Longleat staff, but only one or two other fans. Not many had managed to slip past the officials as slickly as we did. It was breathtaking, looking out at thousands in the crowd screaming, waving, shouting, pushing and shaking their hair in a Jaggeresque mime. But we also noticed more and more people were being carried over the fence in waves and taken to the emergency unit at the back of the house.

We were silently standing at the side of the stage, totally stunned at our closeness to them. Brian's tambourine was sitting on an amp right next to me. Wow - what treasure! It seemed sacrilege to even touch it. We didn't have long to wallow in our good fortune. The organisers came out in front of the stage and announced that the concert would have to end prematurely. The pressure of the crowd was increasing, fans were in danger of being crushed, no one having anticipated this level of excitement and frenzy.

For some reason, we were ordered to go inside the hallway of the house. There seemed to be an air of chaos. Bodyguards were surrounding the boys. There was pushing and shoving, and they looked genuinely puzzled. Then I saw Mick Jagger coming towards me. He walked past me. I remember having a fleeting thought that I should at least touch him as he was so close - not an opportunity to be missed. I stroked his back as he was marched past. To my surprise he grabbed my hand from behind and pulled me along, but I pulled away as Brian Jones was coming next. He had his eyes closed. Another fan mobbed him and without opening his eyes he said, 'Please don't.' He looked in a bad way. He passed by. Next came a lolloping, grinning Keith. He grabbed both myself and one of my friends, pulled us down the corridor, then proceeded to kiss - like, properly kiss - both of us, one at a time. I don't think we responded very well, to be honest. I think we were both in a state of shock. Then, in a millisecond, he had disappeared behind closed doors and a guard of security. My friend and me just looked at each other – what just happened?

We rushed back out to the front of the stage. The crowd were quiet, completely emptied, trying to recover from a short but brilliant live Rolling Stones concert and its abrupt end. It was a blend of despondency, disturbance, confusion, and total disbelief.

It was there at all their early concerts after they went off stage - a sort of vacuum of some minutes where people were really trying to process what they had seen. Could anybody sound that good, that sexy, that connected with something so deeply primordial within us all? It was an unwitting release from what would turn out to be outmoded conventions, traditions, sensible clothes and haircuts. These were defining moments.

We waved to the crowd. 'We kissed Keith,' we shouted. We screamed. The faces pressed up against the chickenwire were disappointed and envious and spent. We were eventually escorted down the steps to the now dispersing crowd. Exhaustion set in. It had probably been not much more than an hour, but what emotion for us young teenagers. The world was definitely changing, both within us and without. We felt on the edge of a precipice. And, of course, we were. The sunshine started fading and dusk was not far away – we had to get home.

I grabbed a teddy bear that someone had tried to throw at Mick, discarded on the grass. We started down the road and thumbed a lift. Someone stopped, picked us up and we got in, but there was something sinister about him. Suffice to say, there was a scuffle and I asked him to stop so we could get out. I literally tore my friend away from him and we ran and ran. He seemed to give up eventually and drove off, leaving us in pitch-black darkness.

We had no idea where we were. Cars were in short supply in those country lanes. Eventually we did get another lift, from some parents who were looking for their daughter who had also gone to the concert but had not returned. They dropped us off somewhere in a village near Bristol. A young man was our next driving host. He took us to his flat, parked outside and said we could sleep in the car overnight, which we did. We talked all night about the Rolling Stones, their music, their hair, their clothes, their attitude. We finally realised we really loved them. In the morning we found other lifts to our small town in Somerset, got home on a Sunday afternoon and boasted to our friends. I left the teddy bear on the dashboard of our overnight accommodation with a thank you note for the young man. Our parents believed we had had a sleep-over at each other's houses.

*On 8 August 1964, the Stones flew to The Netherlands for a one-off show.*

# KURHAUS
## 8 AUGUST 1964, DEN HAAG, THE NETHERLANDS

### I WAS THERE: AART BOESER, AGE 15
I already owned all the Rolling Stones records that had been released. When I got wind that they were coming to perform in the Netherlands (the Dutch newspaper *De Telegraaf* announced the news with the headline 'Import of Ugly People'), I made an appointment to go with my friend

Wim, an avid Beatles fan. I was 15 years old, Wim 16. We both had mopeds, and although I was not allowed to ride one yet, off we went, me on my Tomos, Wim on his Puch, to Scheveningen in The Hague.

When I saw how many youths had gathered around outside the Kurhaus, I knew things would not go well. We entered the Kurhaus – and don't ask me how I got in, as you couldn't pre-order tickets. Our entry into the room went smoothly, without any pushing or pulling. The Kurhaus was a small hall with a neat stage, including a curtain that was pulled open when the artists came on. It went wrong after that. In my opinion, the support act lasted far too long. Booing soon broke out and the first seat backs flew around. There were perhaps five police officers trying to restore order.

The Stones got pushed on stage and started playing something. I don't remember what it was, but their performance at the Kurhaus lasted no longer than 10 minutes, after which the genteel Kurhaus was a garbage dump. All hell broke out and Wim and I were in the middle of a crowd of crazy young people, all kinds of things flying around. Policemen on horseback came into the hall and onto the stage. The Stones tried to continue playing, albeit without vocals, because the PA installation was apparently already broken. Then they were pulled behind a curtain by the police and chaos ensued. The performance made the international press. Memories may be exaggerated as to exactly what happened, but it was an unforgettable performance that remains etched in my memory.

## TOWER BALLROOM
### 10 AUGUST 1964, NEW BRIGHTON, UK

**I WAS THERE: GORDON VALENTINE**
In the Sixties I played bass and sang with Teesside group The Johnny Taylor Five. Along with a lot of other stuff we played the Liverpool Cavern a couple of times and beat the Liverpool groups in a competition. We ended up having to appear in the finals at the Tower Ballroom, New Brighton. The compere was Jimmy Savile and top of the bill were the Rolling Stones. What a night.

# THE ROLLING STONES IN THE SIXTIES: A PEOPLE'S HISTORY

## I WAS THERE: JENNY WILSON

My boyfriend, Terry Wilson and I remember being crushed on the balcony. It was very dangerous by today's standards, but another fantastic night. There were huge crowds queuing to get in, but we managed to jump the queue with our tickets.

## I WAS THERE: NADIA DAVIES, AGE 16

I saw a poster advertising the show. I didn't have much money, but it was the Sixties and I loved pop. I had no one to go with so I went and queued up outside the hall and only had enough cash to get in and didn't want to lose my place in the queue, so I stood all day - no food or drink.

At the gig, I was at the front, Mick was jumping about all over the stage. I was hot and my arms were crossed to stop me from being crushed. I then fainted and remember being picked up and carried over the heads of others to the side of the hall, where the first aiders were. My arms were stuck, crossed over my chest. They gave me a drink and I relaxed. They were surprised to hear I'd had no food or drink. I then went back into the hall and the show finished. I had to run home along the seafront. It was dark and late, and I didn't hang about.

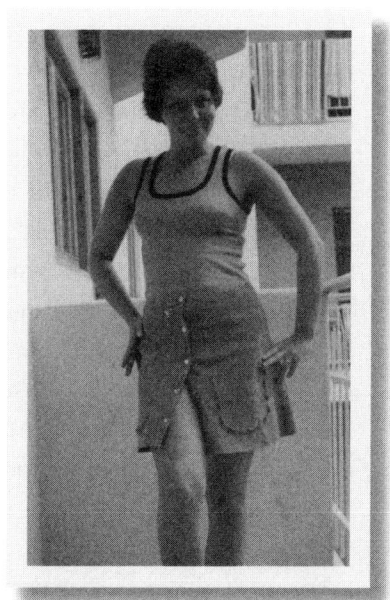

Nadia Davies went to the show on her own

## I WAS THERE: DAVE PRICE, AGE 15

I was a Beatles fan first. To me everything in the world started with 'Love Me Do'. I loved The Beatles and they got more and more successful. Then the Stones came along. I bought 'Come On' when it first came out and everything subsequently. The Beatles versus the Stones was only really a thing used by teenage magazines like *Rave* and that sort of thing.

The more middle of the road fans didn't like the Stones. It was just too much for them, whereas you could take The Beatles home with you. It was a little outrageous when it first started but gradually everybody

# THE ROLLING STONES IN THE SIXTIES: A PEOPLE'S HISTORY

came to love The Beatles. With the Royal Variety Performance with John Lennon and the rattling jewellery joke, everyone's mum and grandma could say, 'Oh well, they're quite nice lads really. It's not my sort of thing but I can see why you like them.' But they were never going to say that about the Stones. It was a much more generational thing. The Stones had appeared at The Cavern in Liverpool the November prior to that. The queue went all the way around the block and people camped out overnight. Everybody that came up from London to play The Cavern was raved about and the Stones were the No.1 band.

New Brighton Tower Ballroom was a huge Victorian ballroom and had a balcony, which went round, but for this Stones show it was purely ground floor, standing only.

I went with a friend of mine and our then girlfriends. The preliminary was a thing that had been going on for some weeks in conjunction with The Cavern, a competition of twelve local bands playing 10 minutes each. The prize was supposedly a recording contract, and it was done by a company called Rael Brook, famous for making drip-dry shirts, which was quite a thing at the time. Part of the reward if you won was that your group would be renamed The Toplins, the name of the material that was used.

We were about two or three rows back standing when it started, but by the time the Stones were starting we were about 20 rows back. It was a maelstrom of people, absolute havoc. I've got the *Liverpool Echo* press cuttings, which praised the fans for their behaviour and said there were only a few arrests. But when you were in it, it was more or less a riot.

There were girls being passed over heads who fainted. There were people on the stage pointing in the spotlights. There were police dogs behind. You couldn't see what was going on but it was pretty much a riot. You would hear little wafts of songs but basically you couldn't hear anything.

The whole thing was liquid. The whole crowd was moving. You had to fight to keep your feet because if you'd gone down under that you'd probably have been trampled to death. There were 4,000 people there apparently. It was a huge venue. They were probably relieved they were so far from the crowd. There was no chance of anybody getting at them. There were bouncers everywhere, and uniformed stewards.

THE ROLLING STONES IN THE SIXTIES: A PEOPLE'S HISTORY

# PALACE BALLROOM
## 13 AUGUST 1964, DOUGLAS, ISLE OF MAN, UK

### I WASN'T THERE: SUSAN SMITH, AGE 10
I was nearly 11 years old, but because of the Stones' bad boy reputation my mother wouldn't let me go. She said it would be too violent. I was heartbroken.

### I WAS THERE: SANDRA LORD, AGE 18
I went with my friends Pam and Jane. My late father was Bob Wilkinson, managing director of the Palace Derby & Castle Company, and he did all the bookings for the summer shows and cinemas on the island. I remember that night, people saying, 'Is that your father at the corner of the stage?' as the girls were being thrown out. Of course, I denied it. I have a great photo of Dad at the Fairy Bridge with a very bored looking Stones and also a postcard they autographed. Dad kept notes from those times and the following is an extract:

*After the 'Big Band' era in the Palace Ballroom came the groups. One of the biggest attractions was the Rolling Stones. That night we had 6,500 paid admissions and what a night it was!*

*I had to have a 'cage-like' barrier built in front of the stage to keep the fans from climbing onto it. The police dog with its handler was there along with many extra security staff for the night. However, the girls still managed to fight their way onto the stage, but as fast as they got on, they were thrown out through the stage door.*

*That night when I arrived in the Palace Ballroom there was nearly a riot starting. The crowd was chanting, 'We want the Stones!' I asked my manager what had happened as the Stones should have been on by then. It transpired that Mick Jagger had decided they wouldn't go on until they had been paid. I soon got them on, giving Mick my personal cheque for the group's guaranteed share of the gate money!*

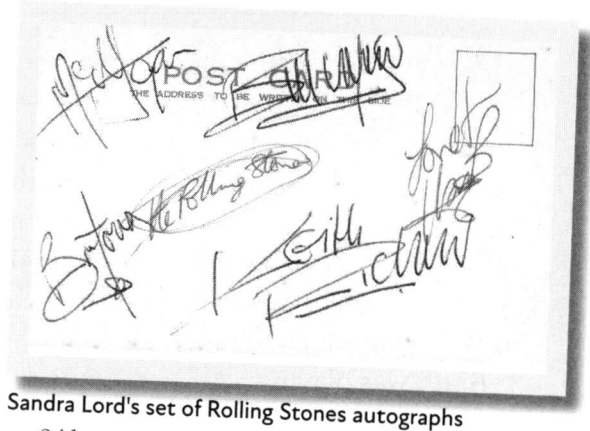

Sandra Lord's set of Rolling Stones autographs

# NEW THEATRE BALLROOM
## 19 AUGUST 1964, ST PETER PORT, GUERNSEY, CHANNEL ISLANDS

**I WAS THERE: KEITH TAPSCOTT, AGE 15**

My uncle was a flower grower and one of his staff was married to a man who worked for British European Airways. After several days badgering her for information she told me the Stones were flying in from Heathrow on the afternoon flight. I spent the whole afternoon at the airport waiting. At that time you could sit at ground level and look out from huge windows on to the runway close to where the planes parked.

There were not too many fans around so I had a great view when they arrived, rather like looking at a vast television screen in 3D. They were greeted by a relatively large number of people, some of whom lucky enough to have been allowed to join the welcoming party. The band sauntered down the steps, signed a few autograph books and were whisked away via one of the airport perimeter gates. I got the bus back, looking forward to seeing them the following two evenings.

I didn't go to the first evening as I originally planned to go to the second of their three concerts owing to a lack of money. Tickets were in the region of 12/- (63p). I'm not sure what this equates to today, but it represented about 6% of a weekly wage.

## *Keith was playing a Gibson Les Paul*

My uncle, however, came to the rescue and bought extra tickets for my cousin and me, so we saw them twice. The Westcoasters warmed up the audience and very good they were too, but the excitement started to build the nearer we got to the Stones taking the stage. There were more males than females and there was no seating. As a result, it all seemed more intense, rhythmic and louder, and the band seemed closer. There was no pushing and shoving - everyone was there to have a good time.

Keith was playing a Gibson Les Paul guitar which he acquired during their June tour of the US. Brian was playing a blonde Fender Telecaster and there was no sign of the Vox Teardrop. Soon as I saw that guitar I knew it was the guitar for me. Many years later I now have three of them. The set-list was more or less the same as when I'd seen them in Brighton – from 'Walking the Dog' to 'It's All Over Now'. Shortly before this performance the band had released 'Five by Five' and I think they played 'Around and Around' from that EP. It was over far too soon. When they left Guernsey for Jersey there was trouble. They got into an argument with an air hostess on the 15-minute flight which resulted in them being banned from flying British United. Great publicity but rather tame compared with subsequent years.

## SPRINGFIELD HALL
### 22 AUGUST 1964, ST HELIER, JERSEY, CHANNEL ISLANDS

**I WAS THERE: GERALDINE LAWRIE, AGE 16**
I was spending a month in Jersey and staying with relatives, having just taken my 'O' levels in Bude, Cornwall. I got a summer job in a shop called Macey's in La Colomberie, St Helier. It was a tourist gift shop selling drinks, cigarettes and souvenirs. Just before 1pm one day the manager rushed in, closed the shop, and in came the Rolling Stones. I served Charlie Watts and got all their autographs. I was so excited, as you can imagine. That evening I went to their concert at Springfield Stadium. I will never forget that day.

**I WAS THERE: BOB LAMB**
I was in the Army and on leave waiting to be posted to Malaya. The concert was at Springfield, in those days the main venue on the island. The main auditorium was packed so we sneaked up onto the balcony to get away from the screaming girls. There were only a couple of others up there, but no security guards. About 10ft away from me to my right was a guy in a brown leather jacket. Suddenly he took a brown paper bag from his jacket and started throwing

tomatoes at the Stones, at the same time shouting something about Buddy Holly. Everyone was taken by surprise, but he very quickly disappeared. The few security guards who were there ran up to us and ask what happened. We told them and they went away. The *Jersey Evening Post* later carried an article about the tomato throwing - apparently the guy didn't like their versions of Buddy Holly numbers.

### I WAS THERE: BILL DU HEAUME, AGE 20

My real memories of that night are of the tomato-throwing incident. The person responsible was Peter Smith, known to everyone as Biffo, somewhat a character in those days. For Biffo and myself the music had died after the death of Buddy Holly and Eddie Cochran. In Peter's case he remained locked in the Fifties era. Unfortunately, with the rise of the groups in the Sixties, Peter could not come to terms with cover versions of the legends' songs.

After the Stones recording of 'Come On' we heard their next record release was to be Buddy Holly's 'Not Fade Away'. I knew Peter would get up to something when they came to Jersey, such as stand at the front and heckle the group. So although we were very close friends I avoided him. As soon as the intro to 'Not Fade Away' started, the tomatoes followed.

Peter should have stayed at home that night. He couldn't of course – he had to make a statement. That was probably his 15 minutes of fame, as he was interviewed on our local television channel.

# GAUMONT THEATRE
## 23 AUGUST 1964, BOURNEMOUTH, UK

### I WAS THERE: TRICIA FOWLER, AGE 16

I went with my friend June Cole. I touched Mick Jagger's shoe and was taken back to my front-row seat by security. We were both 16 years old - I don't think my parents were very keen on me going, but I went anyway.

# GAUMONT THEATRE
## 24 AUGUST 1964, WEYMOUTH, UK

**I WASN'T THERE: RICHARD ARROWSMITH**

I was 18 when the Rolling Stones were gigging in Weymouth, Dorset. I unfortunately couldn't go as I was working a bar in a small nightclub. To my delight, late that evening in rolled the Stones - Brian Jones effing and blinding out loud regardless of who was within earshot. This in itself was unusual at that time 'in the sticks'. I was thrilled but my mischievous side kicked in later and I got up to dance quite expressively to the B-side of Manfred Mann's '5-4-3-2-1', which was called 'Without You'. I then put it on the juke box at least three further times. 30 years later, during a team-building getaway, I used this story as my claim to fame. Needless to say, dancing was not repeated.

# ODEON THEATRE,
## 26 AUGUST 1964, EXETER, UK

**I WAS THERE: PAUL WALTERS, AGE 14**

I went into the dressing room to meet the Stones. My father did security at the Odeon for a long time. I was beginning to be an old hand at wandering in and pretending I was supposed to be in places that perhaps I wasn't. I went into the dressing room, got the Rolling Stones' autographs, and Mick was upside down. He used to have a session, before he sang, of actually going upside down. He said, 'The blood rushes to my head and it's a good way to get invigorated before I go on.' He actually signed the autograph upside down. And he said, 'When we're really famous, this autograph will be worth much more than all the rest of the band's autographs, because this is signed upside down.'

**I WAS THERE: TIM TREE**

I saw the Rolling Stones in Exeter twice. The first time they played the ABC they did all the songs off their LP, 'Route 66' and all that sort of stuff, and were not terribly good. Keith Richards' guitar was constantly out of tune. But I still enjoyed it. The second time I heard them was up at the Odeon and they were really polished. It was really good. They played their

# THE ROLLING STONES IN THE SIXTIES: A PEOPLE'S HISTORY

No.1 hit at that time, 'It's All Over Now'. There was screaming at all the Stones shows, exactly the same as I heard at The Beatles' shows I attended. But not quite as loud – you could actually hear what they were playing.

### I WAS THERE: MAUREEN METHERELL (NÉE GORMLEY), AGE 14
I went with my friend Geraldine Balac. It was great. We screamed so much that an usherette came over and put her hands on our foreheads and asked if we were OK. What a laugh.

### I WAS THERE: CHRIS GALE, AGE 17
Despite all the media tosh at the time about rivalry between Mods and Rockers and the Stones and The Beatles, I was a great fan of both. I attended the Stones concert on my own. As soon as the music hit us everyone shot out of their seats and surged forward. It was our music and, because my dad did not like it, I did.

*Chris Gale felt the Beatles and Stones plus Mods and Rockers rivalry was a sham*

## ABC THEATRE
### 27 AUGUST 1964, PLYMOUTH, UK

### I WAS THERE: JACKI DOWNING, AGE 17
I went with my friend Carol Staverdes, her boyfriend Jim, Pat Jones, Francesca Dadela, Pat Hooper, and Jeanette. Jim and Carole called for me in the morning and we had lunch in Littlewoods. We wandered over to the theatre, where we found the Overlanders unpacking their gear. We also met Millie's backing group, the Five Embers, and the Barron Knights.

When they came on stage the place erupted. It was electric, the atmosphere fab. The Stones belted out 'Not Fade Away', 'I'm A King Bee', 'It's All Over Now' and 'I Just Want to Make Love to You'. Some girls tried to climb on the stage and policemen prevented them. St John Ambulance were also in attendance. Mick was all over the stage singing and Brian was good looking. Charlie, on the drums, did not smile and Bill stood stock still. his guitar upwards. Keith looked like a little boy - so young. It was a wonderful show.

## THE ROLLING STONES IN THE SIXTIES: A PEOPLE'S HISTORY

# TOWN HALL
## 29 AUGUST 1964, TORQUAY, UK

### I WAS THERE: LIONEL DIGBY

John Smith was the promoter for this show. He worked with his son. They organised dances and John contacted me and said he had got three dates on the Stones tour – Exeter, Torquay and Plymouth – and could I help out? I only got paid a percentage for handling it as it wasn't my particular promotion. I don't think the Stones had done any big halls before.

They used the Grand Hotel in Torquay as their base because Exeter is 20 miles away and Plymouth 30 miles. Their last night was at Torquay Town Hall, which is a 2,000 capacity venue, and they did two shows, both fully seated. They did two shows and neither one sold out. If they'd played just one house, they'd have filled it. And the PA system wasn't really powerful enough. It was just an ordinary Vox PA system that they brought with them – a pair of AC30s – not a big stack of Marshalls. The Town Hall's acoustics aren't too good to start with if it's half empty. But they went down alright. There wasn't a lot of movement on stage - it was just Mick Jagger shaking his hips, and Keith moving around a bit.

The other nights they went back to the hotel and more or less went to bed. But because it was the last night, we had a little party at the hotel afterwards on the Saturday. There were no fans in - it was just the group, myself and one or two other people, although John Smith didn't stay long.

---

*Because it was the last night we had a little party*

---

The bar in the big lounge was shut but the night porter could serve drinks all night. There was a small stage in the lounge with an organ and a set of drums. It was around 3am when somebody said something and they went and got their guitars, and with Ian Stewart on the organ and Charlie Watts on the drums, they started playing this boogie-woogie jazz stuff. It wasn't the same kind of material they had recorded, which rather surprised me. Then, all of a sudden, the hotel manager appeared in the lounge wearing a long night shirt, said, 'What the bloody hell is going on?' and stopped it all.

*With Ian Stewart on the organ and Charlie Watts on the drums, they starting playing this boogie-woogie jazz stuff*

On another night some girls found out that the Stones were staying at the Grand and climbed onto a flat roof to look in the windows. Mick Jagger came to the window and had a chat with them. Charlie Watts was the quiet one. He didn't say much at all really. There was none of the aggravation that supposedly happened later on between Keith and Mick.

*Torquay's a great town. But I shouldn't think there's much to do in the winter*
**Mick Jagger**

Torquay's Grand Hotel was the Stones' base for their south west tour dates in 1964

THE ROLLING STONES IN THE SIXTIES: A PEOPLE'S HISTORY

# ODEON THEATRE
## 6 SEPTEMBER 1964, LEICESTER, UK

### I WAS THERE: ELAINE GIBBINS

I'd first heard the Stones on Radio Luxembourg. As a teenager I used to listen to it in my bedroom at night. They played great music. The Rolling Stones at the Odeon in Queen Street, Leicester in 1964 was my first live gig. I queued for hours in pouring rain for my ticket. The ticket price was eight shillings and sixpence (43p) and my seat number was G64. I used all my saved pocket money for the ticket, and it was well worth it because they were amazing. The Odeon was full of young people getting up from their seats. Many of them were screaming and swaying to the music. I also saw the Stones at the Il Rondo in Leicester and at the University Rag Ball.

Elaine Gibbins was at Leicester's Odeon

# ODEON THEATRE
## 8 SEPTEMBER 1964, COLCHESTER, UK

### I WAS THERE: DEREK BROADBENT, AGE 13

I went with a friend at the time, Paul Blomefield. I can't remember who else was on the bill but I remember some of them being out the front on the pavement having a smoke while we were waiting to get in. I was upstairs in the circle and when the Stones came on we were pushed to the front of the balcony. It was very scary, with lots of screaming. You could hardly hear the group. It must have been an afternoon performance if that is possible, as it was still day-light when we went in. The one song that sticks in my mind was 'Little Red Rooster'.

### I WAS THERE: PENNY STONE (NÉE PHILLIPS), AGE 16

I started work at Alexis, a hairdressing salon in Colchester High Street, in August and all the girls went to see the Rolling Stones. It was a magical evening. The Stones were fantastic and have stayed in my mind ever since. I was going out with my boyfriend, Colin Stone, who was 18. I thought his name and the Rolling Stones' name being the same were great. And we remain together after 50-plus years of courting and marriage.

## I WAS THERE: SUSAN TUNSTALL (NÉE BONNER), AGE 17

I was with my best friend at the time, Diane Reeve. We were thrilled to be there on the day the Rolling Stones were voted the No.1 group in the UK. The atmosphere was electric and the young female audience was manic, with screaming and weeping girls. It was our first pop concert, and we were rather overwhelmed by the experience. We tried to get out to the front of the Odeon to see them leave, but we were too late - they had been whisked away in their car.

*We tried to get out to the front of the Odeon to see them leave but they had been whisked away*

## I WAS THERE: HEATHER WICKENDEN, AGE 13

It was the evening I met my future husband and the evening which set the path our lives would take. Me and my best friend Brenda, both 13, decided to go along. We were very excited to see the Rolling Stones but when we got there were also just as excited to see three boys sat behind us. They were Michael, Des and Ian - all aged 15, and school friends. They started to chat to us and shared not only their thoughts about the show but also their sweets. We carried on chatting after the show and arranged to meet them later that week. Michael and I got engaged four years later and married in 1971. They don't know it, but the Rolling Stones have a lot to answer for - we thank them very much.

*We were very excited to see the Rolling Stones but when we got there were also just as excited to see three boys sat behind us*

# THE ROLLING STONES IN THE SIXTIES: A PEOPLE'S HISTORY

## I WAS THERE: SUSAN LARNER, AGE 16

I met my boyfriend John - now my husband - while at St Helena School in May 1964. John was 15 and a school year below me when we met. I left school in July and started work the following week, having had a choice of three jobs. The Rolling Stones' gig was the first one we went to as a couple and it seemed to cost a lot out of our wages. An elderly work colleague said I would catch fleas from them as they were not clean. I didn't catch anything, but I couldn't hear the show very well because of the fans screaming.

## I WAS THERE: PENNY GILL, AGE 13

I went with my best friend Pat. We were both 13. Lulu was the support act and we had to queue for hours in the cold and pouring rain to get in.

## I WAS THERE: TERESA WILKINS, AGE 20

The Stones were my favourite group of the Sixties - much to my father's disgust. I wasn't a fan of The Beatles. For me the Sixties was much more about Bob Dylan, Joan Baez and Peter, Paul and Mary. I saw the Stones play at Colchester Odeon.

We had front row seats, which I was very excited about but - alas - we couldn't hear a single word they sang as the mainly female audience screamed loudly throughout the whole concert. It takes a lot to drown out Mick Jagger, but I assure you they did. Jagger oozed sex appeal. I can still see him as clear as anything in my mind as he looked that night. He wore a sloppy sweater and cord jeans. Due to the screaming of the girls, I just have a quaint memory and can boast I once had front-row seats for the Rolling Stones and didn't hear a word. I went with my boyfriend. He became my husband the following year … and still is!

Teresa Wilkins saw the Stones in Colchester

THE ROLLING STONES IN THE SIXTIES: A PEOPLE'S HISTORY

# ODEON CINEMA
## 9 SEPTEMBER 1964, LUTON, UK

**I WAS THERE: MARK TOLMAN, AGE 13**
It was exactly a week before my 14th birthday. I went on my own. It remains a puzzle how my parents allowed me to go unaccompanied. The most expensive tickets were 12/6 (63p) which were, naturally, for front-row seats. I managed to buy a ticket for 10/6 (53p), which secured a seat two or three rows from the front, so I had a good view. There were cheaper prices, which allowed a fellow grammar school mate of mine and his elder brother positions some way behind mine. I remember feeling smug that this friend and his sibling didn't have as good a view as yours truly, and I would occasionally look over my shoulder and give him a wave.

I recall a couple of the supporting acts, namely the Mojos from Liverpool and Charlie and Inez Foxx from the States, the latter of whom provided some transatlantic excitement. Needless to say, when the stars of the show appeared the noise level from the audience rose appreciably. I felt quite grown up for having attended such an occasion without any adult supervision.

**I WAS THERE: DAVID ARNOLD, AGE 18**
We saw them at the Odeon in Luton. My mate shouted out for 'I'm Moving On'. Jagger's response was, 'No, it's 'You Better Move On'.'

**I WAS THERE: BRENDA PARKER**
These were the years when people rushed the stage at every opportunity and big, burly bouncers struggled mightily to hold them back, people often hurt in the process. I was never a screamer or a stage rusher. You couldn't hear a thing except for everyone screaming their heads off. Just knowing you were in the same room as the Stones was enough to join everyone together in one big communal bout of near-hysteria.

When they toured with Charlie and Inez Foxx, I saw them with my friend Pat, who had a huge crush on Keith. By this time they'd become big stars and we were lucky to get tickets and were really excited and talked about nothing else for weeks before. A man who worked with my dad took us. He was probably in his mid-20s but seemed ancient to us and how or why he volunteered to take two teenage girls to what turned out to be a scream-fest is a mystery to this day, but I was always grateful he did. Pat and I had a great time. Not so sure he did though.

There already seemed a big difference from the April '64 show at Stevenage Locarno. The dynamic had changed and Mick was definitely becoming the main focus of attention. I remember he was wearing a long fluffy white cardigan and at some point someone threw bright green confetti - it went all over him and stuck to his sweater so he did the rest of the show covered with green splotches. Apart from the noise and the atmosphere, that's all I really remember about the show. I suppose, as he was the singer, it was easy to see why people would pay more attention to Mick. He was always prancing about. It was hard to take your eyes off him. He perfected a truly great stage persona and was totally unlike anyone else I ever saw. Sadly, there was never any sign again of the ecstatic tambourine-waving Brian dancing around at the edge of the stage with such a big smile on his face, or wailing away on his blues harmonica.

**I WAS THERE: JOHN SMAIL**
I saw the Stones at the Odeon Cinema on Dunstable Road, in Luton. All I really remember is that the Stones' music was in serious competition with the female screaming within the audience.

## ODEON THEATRE
### 10 SEPTEMBER 1964, CHELTENHAM, UK

**I WAS THERE: ORVILLE MATTHEWS**
I was at all four gigs they did in Cheltenham on package tours that toured the country's Odeon cinemas. I always did the second show. The Stones were top of the bill with Inez Foxx, who wore a green suit and was a mix of Little Richard and Prince in looks. Brian

Orville Matthews saw four Cheltenham package shows featuring the Stones

Jones was certainly the foundation of what the Stones became and was a couple of years older than me, and a Cheltenham boy. It was a long time ago but to me they were electric and exciting and are still in my mind.

## CAPITOL THEATRE
### 11 SEPTEMBER 1964, CARDIFF, UK

**I WAS THERE: JOHN RICHARDS, AGE 14**
We were about 15 rows back, just to the right of the stage. We'd not seen anything like it before. It was pure excitement. I have followed the Stones since 'Come On' and The Beatles since 'Please Please Me.' It was the decade of change in so many ways. Looking back, we had the music and bands the whole world was following, the weather, plentiful work. What a shame we didn't have digital cameras back then. Can you imagine what we could have captured?

## TWISTED WHEEL
### 14 SEPTEMBER 1964, MANCHESTER, UK

**I WAS THERE: BOB LEE**
It was my birthday, and I went to the Twisted Wheel. The Stones walked in and Roger Eagle, the club DJ, saw them and proceeded to play all the tracks off their first album, the originals, in the order they were on the LP. He was having a dig in some ways because he really was a purist, but they took it in good faith.

## ODEON THEATRE
### 15 SEPTEMBER 1964, MANCHESTER, UK

**I WAS THERE: CHRISTINE MCDERMOTT, AGE 12**
I was on the front row in the stalls – seat A22. I had such a good seat because I queued with friends from school, one being Chris Lee, a great friend of mine from the High School of Art in Cheetham Hill and also a

great Bob Dylan fan. When we were queuing, a Bob Dylan LP had been released, and Chris and I saved each other's place in the queue to each go and buy it.

### I WAS THERE: PENNY WHITNEY, AGE 15

My father was very anti-Stones, a good reason to be a fan. 'Get them in the army and get their hair cut' was his response whenever they were on *Top of the Pops*. I went with a friend, Mel, and two boys who were friends of our younger brothers. Mel would have been in her 'O' level year, and I was a year younger. Dick and Lewis were in the third year and were mad keen Stones fans. We went by train from Knutsford to Manchester. My biggest memory was that, when the doors of the theatre opened, the four of us rushed up the stairs, overtaking everyone, and got seats in the front row of the circle - the tickets weren't numbered and we'd paid six shillings for them. I still have my ticket and my programme from the show.

### I WAS THERE: BOB LEE

I'd booked to go and see them and decided I'd go to both shows. So I'd already bought one ticket and went and bought another. When I got the second ticket I asked to speak to the manager and told him what I was doing, because it was quite unusual to do that at the time and I said, 'Would it be possible for me, instead of going out and queuing up again, to just move upstairs?' Because I was in the stalls for the first show and on the balcony for the second. He said, 'Certainly you can.'

So the great day came and I saw them from the stalls. It was absolutely fantastic. I was buzzing. It was incredible. I started making my way up the stairs. I was about halfway up the stairs and in front of me was a policeman and an inspector. They used to carry a stick in those days. They were walking in front of me with arms behind their backs. One of them said to the other, 'Funny that, I could have sworn I saw a customer still in the auditorium' and the other one said, 'Yes, I think I did.' I was walking behind them and before I could get a chance to explain, they turned around and said, 'Out!' I said, 'No, it's okay' and tried to explain, but it wasn't happening. They said, 'You're not staying in here while we're on duty' or words to that effect. I tried to argue with them and they got physical and started pushing me. Then one of them got me by the scruff of the neck, marched me down the flight of carpeted stairs, pushed the fire door, and proceeded to throw me down the stone steps down to the ground floor.

I was down these steps and he followed me down. I was a bit battered and bruised and he just kicked me against the push bar, pushed the thing open, and pushed me out into the street. It had been raining and the pavement was wet. The queue was past the point at which I came hurtling out. People saw me and said, 'What's happened?' I explained it to them, word passed down the queue, and I ended up at the front of the queue so got in again. Soon as I got in, I complained to the manager who apologised and said there wasn't much he could do about it. Police in those days were a law unto themselves.

So I saw the second show in the balcony and, as on their previous two visits, I went to the Queen's Hotel. The Stones always stayed there on Piccadilly Gardens in Manchester so I went up just to see if I could get a glimpse. Another reason for going was there were always lots of young ladies hanging around the hotel as well, which is always good.

If they ever were in Liverpool or Sheffield, invariably they used to make their way and stay in the Queen's Hotel in Manchester. One of the reasons the Stones used to like going there was because the security was crap, and girls could get into the rooms. So I went up and was talking to people and saw Ian Stewart and said 'hello' to him. That was it and I thought nothing of it. About half an hour later he came out looking for me and said, 'Did you have trouble at the concert?' I said 'yes' and the Stones had heard about it. I was invited in and got to talk to Mick, Keith and Brian in one of their rooms. I can't remember whose room it was. I got talking to them, told them I was in the fan club, and they were really good, really nice and pleasant about it, and I told them I worked at the AA.

The following year, 1965, they were playing Manchester again and they'd just been given some sort of sponsorship and given cars. Two of them could drive and they were going to pick these cars up in Manchester and were going to drive to Sheffield. So they did no more than call into the AA offices on York Street, Manchester and ask for me, because they wanted a road map. Well, I tell you, my street credibility leapt! I could do no wrong with the girls in there for months afterwards.

THE ROLLING STONES IN THE SIXTIES: A PEOPLE'S HISTORY

# ABC LONSDALE THEATRE
## 17 SEPTEMBER 1964, CARLISLE, UK

### I WAS THERE: DAVID HANABURY, AGE 15

I was still at school, starting GCEs and the engineering exam G1. My elder brother worked at the BATA shoe factory in Maryport and some of the girls there got together and organised a bus to see the Stones. My brother Michael was no fan of the Stones but to me they were the best thing to have happened since Tommy Steele and his 'Little White Bull'. Well, I was six at the time.

The 25 miles or so between Maryport and Carlisle seemed like they would never end. The son of a face-working miner, we always travelled to Carlisle by train - buses were for the working class! However, we did finally arrive and by then the journey had become very tolerable. There was an aroma and an atmosphere on the bus I had never experienced at this intensity – excited women and rock 'n' roll.

We were booked to see the first of two shows. It was one of those rock 'n' roll tours of the day with a compere. I remember Mike Berry with his Buddy Holly tribute. There may have been other support acts but I can't remember - my mind was just about to be blown away by Charlie and Inez Foxx.

I was a fledgling Mod and the Stones were my band, but this brother and sister act were the best thing I had ever heard or seen … and their dancing. Their soul opened up another world of music and my side of the theatre just could not get enough and would not let them go. The other side of the ABC were shouting, 'We want the Stones!' but we drowned them out - we wanted Inez and Charlie!

Guitars and drums were tuned. The female throng around me were on their feet with excitement, anticipation, screams and - yes - some wet seats. The curtain opened - my heroes – 'going round and round.' A girl who travelled with us from Maryport stood up and with the athleticism of an Olympian and with no thought to her own safety took off over the seats. She covered the distance to the stage in the blink of an eye, shouting 'Keithhhhhhhhhhh!' and vaulted impressively onto the stage. Her flight was halted by security, and she was escorted straight out of the theatre.

# THE ROLLING STONES IN THE SIXTIES: A PEOPLE'S HISTORY

The Stones were fab. The following day my feeling of euphoria was somewhat dented when a games teacher found out I was at the concert and sought me out. I thought I was in trouble when he finally found me. What did I think of the bloody Rolling Stones? 'Fab sir,' was my reply. He informed me he was there. 'What?' He then informed me he had taken his daughter and lectured me on these degenerates and particularly the moron on the drums who, he said, 'could not drum his way out of a paper bag.'

## I WAS THERE: MARJ BIRBECK, AGE 17

I worked at Sekers Silk Mills at Hensingham, near Whitehaven, and someone said about getting a coach to go and see the Stones. We filled it easily and away we went. It was wonderful. The place was packed and there was that much screaming and shouting that some of the plaster fell from the ceiling, but everything just carried on. The plaster fell in the aisle, so no one was hurt.

A couple of days later one of my friends came to see me and gave me a photo she had taken of Mick and Keith sitting in the back of a car after they had finished and were leaving. A truly amazing night and one I will always remember. That time in Carlisle when we were all so young was something else.

## I WAS THERE: LINDA NICHOLSON, AGE 13

I was a schoolgirl and a massive Stones fan. My friend, Janice Raphael, was a Beatles fan but we went to both Stones concerts at the ABC. I seem to remember they turned up late for the second gig and the MC had to fill in as the other acts had done their stints, getting us to shout, 'We want the Stones!'

There was a coffee bar opposite the stage door in Cecil Street called the Fresco. We got wind that some of the other stars of that first Stones concert would be in there before the show, so we arranged to get down early, autograph books at the ready. Alas we weren't lucky but at some point I acquired Charlie Watts' signature and remember the torn piece of paper stuck in my little blue book - where did that go? He was always my favourite.

It was big news in a small city to have big stars appearing, and we went to many more concerts where many stars were on the bill with one headline act. The Stones were the biggest in my book.

### I WAS THERE: ELLEN KNIGHT, AGE 14

I went with my friend Carol, three years older than me. One of the local guys had organised a bus from Penrith along with two tickets for the show. I was so excited when my mother said I could go with Carol and her friends. When we went into the ABC the place was buzzing, other people as excited as me. We took our seats to the right of the stage.

Appearing with the Stones were the Mojos and Inez & Charlie Foxx, who sang 'Mockingbird'. There was an interval before the Stones came on. One of Carol's friends was so excited. The Stones were ready for the second half of the concert. The curtains opened. The stage was quite dark. Mick had his back to the audience. Everyone was screaming. He clapped his hands and wiggled his bum, and with that Carol's friend fainted! She was carried out by St John Ambulancemen and taken to the foyer with lots of other girls who were overcome by it all. She never got to see the Stones. We just took a quick glance at her before she was taken out - we weren't going to miss the Stones.

We screamed and shouted as the Stones sang songs like 'Around and Around', 'Not Fade Away' and 'Time Is on My Side'. It was one of the best times of my life. All very affordable - not like concerts today - and very special memories.

### I WAS THERE: DENNIS HODGSON

My mother would organise a minibus, and 12 of us used to go to Carlisle from Maryport. What I remember of the gig was quite a lot of screaming ladies.

## ODEON THEATRE
## 18 SEPTEMBER 1964, NEWCASTLE-UPON-TYNE, UK

### I WAS THERE: THOMAS MANN

My aunt and uncle used to manage the Percy Arms in the Haymarket, Newcastle. The Rolling Stones were appearing at the Odeon. That night in the Percy there was a bit of a commotion. A group of young men, the worse for wear, were insulting and arguing with the pub regulars. My uncle, ex-Royal Navy, asked them to leave. One in particular took offence at this, saying, 'Do you not know who I am?' As my uncle grabbed him and was ejecting him from the pub, he was shouting and screaming, 'I AM MICK JAGGER! YOU CAN'T DO THIS!' My uncle then went back into the pub and asked the rest of the band members if they wanted the same or were going to leave quietly. They left by themselves, without any help.

# ABC THEATRE
## 21 SEPTEMBER 1964, KINGSTON-UPON-HULL, UK

### I WAS THERE: CHRISTINE PINDER, AGE 14

I went with my schoolfriend Jean Baldwin. Her mum queued overnight to get us tickets. The Stones did two performances. We went to the second house, as it was called then.

The cinema had an orchestra pit in front of the stage with a velvet covered wooden balustrade around it. Whilst we were queuing outside to get into the cinema, word went round that during the first performance Mick Jagger had decided to strut along the top of this balustrade. This caused the audience in the stalls to surge forward, and Mick was knocked off the balustrade and into the orchestra pit! Because this caused such a riot, he wasn't allowed to do it in the second performance, much to our disappointment.

Christine Pinder saw Mick knocked into the orchestra pit

We sat in the circle, about three rows from the front. I remember the Stones coming onstage. I screamed, burst into tears, and came to with my head between my knees, having missed quite a lot of their performance. I was still crying on the top of the double-decker bus on the way home, but had to come to in order to properly face Mum and Dad at home.

## THE ROLLING STONES IN THE SIXTIES: A PEOPLE'S HISTORY

### I WAS THERE: JOHN BRANT, AGE 15

My mother wouldn't let me queue all night for tickets. However, my girlfriend Carol did, and followed them around the area. The performance in Hull was the first of their concerts to be filmed. Mick Jagger caused a near-riot by strutting his stuff around the orchestra pit instead of staying on stage. I fell out with Carol after I found out she had gone backstage into the dressing room. I had suspicions that Jagger had had his wicked way with her. I still can't fathom out why she preferred a millionaire rock star to a £5 a week shipping clerk.

# GAUMONT THEATRE
## 26 SEPTEMBER 1964, BRADFORD, UK

### I WAS THERE: MIKE ROBERTS, AGE 17

I went with my girlfriend, Maureen – now my wife for more than 50 years. The package included Mike Berry, and Inez & Charlie Foxx. The particular memory I have is of watching Bill Wyman who, throughout the entire Stones performance, kept turning to chat to a stagehand standing in the wings. He progressively sidled towards him to such an extent that he became obscured from the audience's view, leaving only the fingerboard of his bass guitar in sight.

*Mike Roberts with Maureen, his wife of more than 50 years*

### I WAS THERE: MARGARET MARSHALL (NÉE WHITE), AGE 14

My friend Glynis Mallows (née Jones) and I were both 14 and have vivid memories of seeing the Stones. We remember our excitement at purchasing the tickets and waiting for the date. We still talk about it these days when we meet up. After the show the police turned up as there were so many fans in the roads around the theatre.

### I WAS THERE: JOHN HEFFRON, AGE 20

My wife Pat and I remember it well as our daughter was born two weeks after. The night of the concert we were returning home by bus. We lived in Manningham, two or three miles from the centre of Bradford. We noticed crowds of teenagers screaming and running about outside the Gaumont, and the bus slowed down and eventually stopped as the kids were running across the road. Whether they had spotted one of their idols we did not know. As we stopped, I noticed a big poster advertising the Rolling Stones and supporting artists in concert that night.

Pat and I were both staunch Stones fans and I said to her, 'We have to have our tea and come back down and see if we can get tickets and go to the concert.' Pat, despite being eight and a half months' pregnant, agreed straightaway.

We got back about 7pm and went to the ticket office and said, 'Have you got two tickets for tonight as near the front as possible?' The lady said, 'Oh, I'm sorry but all those tickets have gone.' She gave Pat a look over and said, 'These are the best I can do. There will be nobody sat next to you. Your wife will have a bit of extra room.' How nice. We had a brilliant seat about halfway back, bang in the middle with a superb view.

There were four supporting artists. I remember Charlie and Inez Foxx, and The Mojos. And, obviously, the fabulous Rolling Stones. Their first No.1, 'It's All Over Now' was still rocking the charts. One of the music papers must have done an article about the Stones' likes and dislikes, and one of them liking jelly babies. When they started playing, they got bombarded with jelly babies. The fans brought bags of these in with them. Charlie Watts' drum kit was covered with them, and the Stones were laughing their heads off. What a fabulous night. The Stones were at their raw, hungry best. Simply the tops!

## ODEON THEATRE
### 29 SEPTEMBER 1964, GUILDFORD, UK

### I WAS THERE: WILLIAM MARTIN

I saw the second show at the Odeon Theatre. It was a brilliant concert - complete mayhem and non-stop screaming, with people rushing the stage. We tried to gate-crash the doors for the first performance, but soon got thrown out!

THE ROLLING STONES IN THE SIXTIES: A PEOPLE'S HISTORY

# COLSTON HALL
## 1 OCTOBER 1964, BRISTOL, UK

### I WAS THERE: DIANE KENYON, AGE 15

I went with my two best friends at the time - Valerie Evans and Valerie Coombes. It was the first time I had ever queued for hours to get tickets. The other acts were The Innocents, Mike Berry, The Mojos, The Le Roys, Simon Scott, and Charlie & Inez Foxx. Don Spencer was the compere.

I would probably have enjoyed most of these another time, but just wanted to see the Stones. I remember the review in the paper the next day saying the audience were all cheering Inez and Charlie Foxx, when everyone was really trying to hurry them off as we knew the Stones were on next. They didn't disappoint. I remember screaming along with everyone else. It was the best concert I'd ever been to.

### I WAS THERE: LESLEY WELLS, AGE 12

My father had the Webbington Hotel and Country Club. Some of the famous people of that time stayed there if they were playing in the area. One lunchtime my mother came and got me from school and said she was taking me to the Webbington. I thought something was wrong. We got there and Dad said the Stones had booked in overnight. They were at the Colston Hall.

They came down for breakfast at 1pm, unheard of in those days. After they had eaten, they asked my dad if we had any tennis rackets. We had an old tennis court. Dad said 'no.' Mick said, 'It's ok, we will use frying pans!' So that is what they did. It was so funny to watch them. The chef was not laughing though.

# GAUMONT THEATRE
## 4 OCTOBER 1964, SOUTHAMPTON, UK

### I WAS THERE: GRAHAM KESBY, AGE 14

It was just one mass of noise. Not just for the Stones but everybody else that was on the bill also. It did reach a crescendo when the Stones came on. It was, from a 14-year-old's perspective, something I'd never experienced before. It was quite something else.

### I WAS THERE: GILL HORN

My husband Bruce saw the Rolling Stones in Southampton with some mates. He recalls they couldn't hear them for the girls screaming. His mate Alan tapped a girl on the head with his shoe to quieten her. She and her friend moved to other seats.

# GAUMONT THEATRE
## 6 OCTOBER 1964, WATFORD, UK

### I WAS THERE: DAVID BUCKLAND

I went to both shows with my girlfriend Wendy, whom I later married. We have been together ever since. At that time it was fashionable to say you preferred the Rolling Stones to The Beatles, as it made you feel a bit of a rebel, although in all honesty both groups were terrific.

### I WAS THERE: MARY GALVIN, AGE 14

I wasn't allowed to go to the gig in Watford, but my friend Madeleine went and brought me back an autograph from Mick Jagger, which said 'to Mary quite contrary' - now a treasured possession. She also had an autograph from Mick on her stomach. She didn't wash it for weeks. We were all so envious.

### I WAS THERE: CHRIS DAY

I still remember that fantastic night in Watford. Four of us went - myself, Jim Halpin, my girlfriend Carol Jordan, and Sue Theobald. Carol and Sue camped out all night in the freezing cold to be first in the queue for tickets. We were in the front row. What an atmosphere. There were hordes of girls screaming and running down the aisles trying to get on the stage. I still remember a very young Mick Jagger gyrating right in front of us.

### I WAS THERE: CAROLE SAUNDERS, AGE 17

My husband, 19 at the time, and I were at the second performance. It was a Sunday, and the Nashville Teens were on the same bill. My husband says it was great. I cannot remember it, but hubby still lives in the Sixties.

## THE ROLLING STONES IN THE SIXTIES: A PEOPLE'S HISTORY

**I WAS THERE: JAN HOLDING**

Dad was in the RAF, and we were stationed at RAF Northolt. The scenes featuring Pussy Galore's Flying Circus in *Goldfinger* were filmed there, and we saw the filming. I was a Lancastrian, living in London, loving the Rolling Stones when all the other girls in my class loved The Beatles. I still remember those concerts - the raw energy and the screaming girls. I couldn't speak for days after. I still have my tickets and a flyer for the Watford concert, framed and hung on the wall. Wonderful times!

# GAUMONT THEATRE
## 9 OCTOBER 1964, IPSWICH, UK

**I WAS THERE: GLORIA ROODES (NÉE WILSON), AGE 16**

My friend Carol and I were chambermaids at the Crown and Anchor Hotel, Ipswich. We made sure we booked our tickets for all the shows at the Gaumont Theatre. The first time was in October 1964 to see the Rolling Stones, where suddenly we were caught up in the crowd pushing all the seats forward and rushing the stage. I lost my shoe, finding myself with my fingers getting electric shocks from the footlights as I hung on to the edge of the stage. Men were trying to sweep us off with those big stage brooms. They called it 'mayhem' in the local paper.

# HIPPODROME
## 11 OCTOBER 1964, BRIGHTON, UK

**I WAS THERE: HAZEL SMITH, AGE 14**

Growing up in Brighton in the Sixties was an amazing time, and we saw many groups in the town. My memories of the concert were that we couldn't hear a thing. The screaming was so loud, but I remember being excited to see Mick Jagger clapping and dancing his way around the stage. My other memory was

Hazel Smith was excited to see Mick making his moves

a man behind me starting to rub my back. I was a little alarmed, but it turned out he had dropped ash all down my back from his cigarette. We thoroughly enjoyed our experience of seeing the Stones - it's just a shame we couldn't hear much.

## I WAS THERE: BARBARA AWCOCK, AGE 15

Like Hazel, I remember the screaming and really enjoying seeing the Stones. My brother Jeff was in the Brighton police. Hazel and I went around the back after the show to try and get to the stage door for autographs and my big brother was there on crowd control duty. When he saw us amongst the scrum, he told us to go home. Being a bit afraid we scuttled out of there.

## I WAS THERE: DON MCBETH

I went with Lynda, my wife to be. We sat in the stalls, close to the stage. My lasting memory of the show was not of the Stones, who were good, but one of the supporting groups called The Mojos. They sang their hit, 'Everything's Alright', a No.9 record that they had written. During the performance the lead singer accompanied himself with a pair of maracas and at the end of the session he tossed the maracas into the audience. My wife caught one of them and politely passed it to the front, where a girl now had the pair. We assumed the maracas were given away at every performance… we were wrong.

During the interval the lead singer of The Mojos came into the audience and apologised for throwing the maracas away and politely asked for them back. It seems he had only borrowed them. They belonged to Mick Jagger, who had told him to go and retrieve them.

*In mid-October 1964 the Stones made a quick foray into Europe, playing one show in Paris and making appearances on French and Belgian TV shows.*

THE ROLLING STONES IN THE SIXTIES: A PEOPLE'S HISTORY

# L'OLYMPIA
## 20 OCTOBER 1964, PARIS, FRANCE

### I WAS THERE: DOMINIC LAMBLIN, AGE 19

I love the Rolling Stones. I spent a lot of time with them. Not as a fan. I was not chasing them. I was with them, being chased. I was a kid. I think they were 20 or 21.

The first time the Stones came to France I was Decca Records' company representative. I think France was the only country where they sent a guy who was the same generation as them to look after them. In England all the guys who worked with the Rolling Stones were much older than them. The only guy who was the same generation as them was Andrew. Most of the places they went, it was usually people much older. Even the guy in America - Bob Bonis, who took those incredible photographs of The Beatles and the Stones - was much older than them.

Dominic Lamblin with the Stones

They played the Olympia in '64. In fact, in the Sixties they only played the Olympia. They came back for three dates in '65 and again in '66 and '67. Then they played there in 1995 and 2003. I was at all those concerts.

We used to ride in paddy wagons. I ran from the fans all the time. We'd be riding in paddy wagons to get to the Olympia, although they would stay in a hotel which doesn't exist anymore, the Hotel de Paris. Some stupid guy thought, 'Oh, it's near. We're gonna put them in the hotel so they'd be able to walk from the hotel to the theatre.' Totally crazy because there's no way we could walk or anything. Even in 1964 they were already big stars. So that was pretty exciting when you think about it. For me it was a very exciting time, really amazing. They would be in Paris for two days, then they'd be gone, and it would get back to normal. And to them it was like that every day. It was constant excitement. I

# THE ROLLING STONES IN THE SIXTIES: A PEOPLE'S HISTORY

took some photos of the Stones on about four or five occasions and gave one photo that I took to Charlie and said, 'Do you remember where that took place?' He said 'no' because it was just another gig or another rehearsal. It was just one instance amongst many, many other similar events. He told me he loved the photo though.

The same thing with Keith. I gave one to Keith, but he didn't remember when the actual concert was. In fact, it was not a concert. It was when they were filming a TV show in Montreux, Switzerland. That's when I took a lot of photos.

Dominic Lamblin with Brian Jones

From a record company angle it was very exciting, and very fast. Very much of a rush. They were very professional. We didn't have any problems with them. Brian was the leader, no doubt about it, in my mind in 1964 and also in 1965 as well. Then by 1966 he had started slipping a bit and was no longer in charge. The band had been taken over by Mick and Keith. But in '64 he was definitely leader of the band and making all the decisions.

I remember, for instance, the first time they arrived in Paris, they went to the Locomotive, a club, and they were not supposed to play. They were just supposed to show up on stage, wave and say 'hi' to the fans, then leave. And the fans were really almost rioting, so when they arrived the owner of the club came up to them and said, 'Oh, you've got to play, you've got to play.' We translated this to them and said, 'Well, he wants you to play' and Brian said, 'No fucking way, we're not playing.' And that was it.

We rode around Paris. We showed them the billboard we had paid for, then we went to the Golf Drouot for another appearance. They did a TV show where they did 'Carol' and 'It's All Over Now' without their gear, because their gear had not arrived (it got held up with all the equipment). If you look at the show - which you can find on YouTube - they don't even have straps on their guitars. Keith's got this funny leather cap on his head. It's a French TV show and it's totally mimed.

*After their European visit, the Stones headed off on their second US tour in support of their album, Out of Our Heads.*

# ACADEMY OF MUSIC
## 24 OCTOBER 1964, NEW YORK, NEW YORK

### I WAS THERE: GERRIANNE BIZAN, AGE 14

My friends and I found out they were appearing in Manhattan at the Academy of Music. We went down and waited in a long line. At the concert the Stones were great. This was before good sound systems. My friends and I climbed over the backs of the seats and balanced on our seats to get a better view. After the concert my friend insisted on going backstage stating that, in her excitement, she had thrown her wallet on stage. Of course, this was a lie.

### I WAS THERE: BARBARA NEUMANNN BEALS, AGE 14

My sister Lynne and I were in the record store and saw this album, *The Rolling Stones (England's Newest Hitmakers)*. We knew nothing about them, but the album cover was enough. We bought it, took it home, listened to it 10 times, and she said, 'I've got to meet the group. I've got to see them.'

We were absolutely intrigued, loved them, and started to like them more than The Beatles. Back in those days before the mega-concerts and the stadiums, it was so much more innocent and funny. There was nothing groupie-ish. The name hadn't come up yet. There wasn't sex and drugs and rock 'n' roll. It was just, 'We want to meet them.' That's all.

At that time, she was doing a little modelling and PR work for a small magazine and was just a word of mouth kind of person. She found out they were coming to the city - the Academy of Music in Brooklyn - a very small venue. So before they came she found out what hotel they were staying at. It was the Astor Hotel, no longer there.

We dressed up as models, pretended we were from Sweden, and knew nothing about what was going on because we walked in the Astor Hotel and they said, 'Excuse me, girls, are you here to see the Stones?' 'No, no, we're from Sweden. We're doing modelling here.' And the guy believed us for some reason, and we got a room, actually got a room, and later that day my father found out and made me go home.

The next day Lynne and her friends, one of whom was called Sandy, dressed up as maids. They went into the closet in the hallway and found maids' uniforms and pushed the whole trolley thing down the hall and found out what room the Stones were in. Once they found out what room they were in, they took off the maids' clothes, put regular clothes on and just knocked on the door. And that was it. Lynne said, 'I just want to introduce myself. You know, I work at blah–blah–blah magazine and you know we're models, and we just want to say hello.' It was all very simple and very sweet, not, 'Oh, you want to go to bed?' It wasn't like that.

## *It was a different world then and it was wonderful while it lasted*

Lynne was 23. She was quite stunning. She was welcomed in. They talked and the next thing you know they're like old buddies. They're like, 'Do you think people like us in New York?' 'Oh my gosh, yes. My sister's dying to see you.' This was before they were hugely famous. Out of that my sister got me front-row centre tickets in that little Academy of Music Theater. And my sister and I used to look back and say, 'Can you believe we ever did that? That we could do that?' 'I can't believe I dressed up as a maid and found their room with my friend Sandy, knocked on the door and walked in.' It was that simple. She had a lot of nerve. They could have just said, 'Oh, leave us alone and stop bothering us,' but they didn't. She just made up some story, she was good at double-speak. She made it sound like she had a reason to be here. She was quite a character. Everything was like that back then. It was a different world. It was wonderful while it lasted.

THE ROLLING STONES IN THE SIXTIES: A PEOPLE'S HISTORY

# THE ED SULLIVAN SHOW
## 25 OCTOBER 1964, NEW YORK, NEW YORK

### I WAS THERE: LYNDA WILLARD

I saw the Stones the very first time they were on *Ed Sullivan*, and concerts in New York, Philadelphia, and New Jersey. I also met them twice. The Stones came along on the back of the '64 Beatles revolution thing. I must have heard them on AM radio. My girlfriend Wendy's mother was able to get tickets for their first appearance on *The Ed Sullivan Show*. We sat about 20 rows from stage. After the show we drove back to Jersey and stopped off at a Howard Johnson's to get something to eat. As we walked into the place, we saw the Stones sat at the counter eating. We were very polite in asking for their autographs and they were kind enough to sign them. We told them about how we loved them, but I don't recall what they said. When they left, Wendy and I proceeded to eat their leftovers.

I saw them another time on *Ed Sullivan*, but can't remember the date - they played *Ed Sullivan* six times in all. We were 16 or maybe 17. This time, Wendy and I had found out what hotel they were staying in. There was no security then like there is now. I recall walking up a bunch of stairs, looking in the hallways. Wendy said there would be a lot of security guys hanging around their room. We approached this one guy and begged him to get their autographs for us. Well, he knocked on the door and Mick answered. We were in shock - giddy, stupid - and asked for their autographs. Keith was laying in the bed, smoking. They gave us their autographs. We left, found Wendy's mom, and she couldn't believe what we did.

I went to just about every concert they had in New Jersey, New York, and Philadelphia. In '69 I went to Los Angeles, lived there about six months, and did the flower child thing. I saw the Jefferson Airplane at a 'love-in' at Griffith Park. Rumours were going around that the Stones were going to perform. It never happened.

I'm still a loyal fan.

---

*The Rolling Stones appeared at the Civic Auditorium in Santa Monica as part of the Teenage Awards Music International (TAMI) show, which was filmed and gained a theatrical release in the US.*

# THE ROLLING STONES IN THE SIXTIES: A PEOPLE'S HISTORY
# TAMI SHOW, CIVIC AUDITORIUM
## 29 OCTOBER 1964, SANTA MONICA, CALIFORNIA

### I WAS THERE: STEVEN RADILOFF, AGE 16

My parents had to drop me off because I wasn't driving yet. This was my first live concert and it was all kids in the stands. It had a strange line-up, from the Stones to Leslie Gore, the Beach Boys, Billy Kramer, Marvin Gaye, Chuck Berry, James Brown, etc. My favourite performer was Marvin Gaye. I loved his voice and style. It was cool seeing the Stones, and seeing James Brown tearing the house down. I enjoyed all of it since it was my first show and I was getting to see live musicians whose music I had heard on the radio. It's the show about which Keith Richards said it was the biggest mistake they ever made, following James Brown.

### I WAS THERE: DEEDEE KEEL, AGE 14

In October 1964 I was eagerly awaiting the arrival and performances of my favourite band, the Rolling Stones. Being a rebellious 14-year-old, I had switched allegiance from the clean-cut Beatles to the ruffian look and sound of the Stones. I secured free tickets to the filming of the TAMI show at Santa Monica Civic Auditorium, just one mile from my home. There was also a concert coming to the Long Beach Auditorium a couple of days later, and I was so excited. Advance tickets for Long Beach were going on sale at Wallich's Music City on Sunset and Vine in Hollywood, about 20 miles from my hometown, Venice Beach.

On the morning of the ticket sales, I took an early bus, firmly believing the line would be enormous. When I arrived, there was only one girl waiting to buy tickets! That was it - I paid $3 and went back home. The anticipation of seeing the band live was the only thing on my mind.

The *TAMI* show seating was on a first-come basis and I was able to get dropped off by my parents early, and got up close to the stage. My father was driving me crazy calling the band the Rotating Rocks and making fun of the songs he had heard. The more he disliked them, the more I loved them!

It seemed like an eternity waiting through the other performances, and the filming made for a few delays as they stopped to re-shoot a few of the bits between the music portions. We had to watch Jan and Dean roll onto the stage on skateboards a few times, which made the anxiety level even higher waiting for the Stones. I remember being so impatient as James Brown, in his flamboyant purple cape, kept leaving the stage only to return, screaming, 'Baby, Please, Please, Please!' Looking back, that one song by Brown was extraordinary to witness. I did not appreciate it as I do now.

Finally, the Rolling Stones appeared, and the feeling was surreal. I was so close to them it was hard to believe they were really there in the flesh. Mick Jagger's moves were hypnotizing, and his voice sent me into a trance, which made me feel as though every word from his lips was just for me. Being a young teen, I was not even aware of the sound as much as I was fixated on the way they looked, and felt like a statue just staring foolishly at them.

After the performance, I made my way to a side area hoping to slip into the backstage area. Each time a door opened I could see just a glimpse of the action and knew that was the place to be. I heard the Stones were staying across the street at the Surf Rider Inn and decided that was where I needed to be so headed out, only to be stopped by my father. Not a chance I was getting near a hotel with those bad boys. I could not wait to see them again in Long Beach.

## I WAS THERE: PEGGY JONES

I heard this was their first time in the US and they agreed to do the TAMI show to get their airfare costs back to England. Free tickets were distributed to local high school students, so my best friend Marsha Mankiller and I went. We noticed there was a 6ft partition wall between the audience and backstage, where we saw some of the performers enter. I managed to climb over that partition, and you can imagine my delight and surprise to see all the Stones plus

Peggy Jones caught the TAMI show in Santa Monica

# THE ROLLING STONES IN THE SIXTIES: A PEOPLE'S HISTORY

Marvin Gaye, James Brown, Gerry and the Pacemakers, and others hanging out, milling around waiting for their turn on stage. I went and got everyone's autograph and asked Mick when they were going on stage. It was the only thing I could think of to say.

*Debbi Letot discovered a whole new experience*

## I WAS THERE: DEBBI LETOT, AGE 12

My very first concert was on the Stones' first US tour. I went, along with my two best friends. I was living in LA, so we had to go see them at Santa Monica Civic Auditorium. I don't remember how we got our tickets; maybe at the door. I remember the excitement and anticipation. Our parents were all cool with it. It was 1964 and things were so different then. We didn't sit down through the whole show – we were up dancing. It was a whole new experience for me and now, I'm so glad it was the Stones. I was instantly captivated by them. Sometime during the show, some girl managed to get to the stage curtains and shimmied her way down to the stage. She was able to get to Mick, and security had to drag her away. I wish I had recorded it but back then you couldn't take a camera or anything else in.

That's where my fanaticism with the Stones started. I saw them a few more times at small venues, but that didn't last long. Then they started performing at larger venues. My family moved to Dallas, and I hated it. I still do! I remember seeing them in 1981 in Dallas. By that time, I had every album they made. By then, life happened. I was divorced with two children, so it was a long time until I saw them again, in 2015. Same magic. Same excitement. I will see them again if they ever come back to Dallas. I'm a fan for life.

THE ROLLING STONES IN THE SIXTIES: A PEOPLE'S HISTORY

# CIVIC AUDITORIUM
## 1 NOVEMBER 1964, LONG BEACH, CALIFORNIA

**I WAS THERE: STUART NARAMORE, AGE 19**

In November 1964, my girlfriend and I attended a concert by one of the so-called British Invasion bands, the Rolling Stones. I was a 19-year-old college sophomore, and the concert was an afternoon matinee held at the old Long Beach Auditorium. I am not certain how many attendees, but it was probably in the neighbourhood of 2,000. When we got to our seats, I took a look around and remember noticing two things. We were seated on the main floor and all the seats were folding chairs not attached to the floor. This fact becomes very relevant later. There was a balcony above us skirting about three-quarters of the arena and it was jam-packed with teenage girls and a few parents. One father had an expression on his face that clearly indicated he would rather be having a root canal than be here.

As was the norm for concerts back in the days before rock gods ruled stadiums, there were several warm-up acts before the headliners appeared. I can only remember the name of one, Dick and Dee Dee, who had a recent hit 'The Mountain's High'. These acts were received enthusiastically but politely by the crowd. In those days, concertgoers rarely stood to dance and were told to sit down if they attempted to. Finally, after about an hour and a half, several local radio DJs announced the Rolling Stones. There was instantaneous, pure bedlam! The high-pitched female screaming hit my eardrums with a force that actually hurt. I had to cover my ears. The artificial aisles disappeared within a minute. All those folding chairs started collapsing as hundreds of girls stood on them for a better view. My girlfriend and I climbed onto our chairs, but the girl behind me climbed onto the back of my chair and practically choked me while screaming directly into my ear.

The screaming was so intense, bouncing off the walls and ceiling, that I could not hear the music, except for the few opening notes. I could barely make out Charlie Watt's drums and could only feel the bass. The guitars and Mick Jagger's voice were totally overwhelmed. I looked up at that dad in the balcony and saw him bent over, holding his head in his hands, wondering why God had sent him to hell.

After only two or three songs, a fire marshal (I think) halted the show and had everyone sit down before allowing the concert to continue. The main floor was a mess, chairs lying helter-skelter, clothing scattered about. My girlfriend asked if we should get out before we got hurt, but I could not see an easy exit. The marshal then allowed the show to start again, but the crowd instantly reverted to its previous insanity. I was loving every second. After just a few more minutes, the officials stopped the show for good. The Stones rushed to get out after performing for perhaps only 20 minutes. For me it was absolutely worth the $3 ticket.

But the 'entertainment' was not yet over. As we left the auditorium, we looked below into the parking lot and saw the Stones' limousine make a wrong turn, accidentally returning into the lot rather than exiting. Within seconds the limo was surrounded by dozens of crazy teenage girls pounding on the vehicle, climbing all over it. The limo driver made the decision that the band was in real danger and slowly ploughed ahead in order to escape. This led to the Stones getting out of the lot, but a number of girls were hurt in the process. We saw several lying on the ground. I never learned if any suffered serious injury, and I hope everyone was OK.

As the years went by, I got to see the Rolling Stones several more times, but this first concert still stands out as the loudest and wildest show I ever attended.

## I WAS THERE: KERRY ROWLEY

Because I had a British penpal, I had heard the Stones' music early on so really wanted to attend a concert on their first US tour. My best friend and I went together. Our parents had no idea who the Stones were. My main memory of the event is of watching Mick take off his jacket and swing it around, teasing the audience. It made everybody scream like mad.

## I WAS THERE: STEVE HOCKEL, AGE 16

This was my first concert. I climbed through an open window with five other guys from our neighbourhood. Luckily, it was a men's bathroom window. We walked up some steps and were on the balcony level. The stage had huge velvet curtains drawn back at each side of the stage. At one point a girl stood up on the balcony near the curtains. Everyone was watching her, including the Stones, and wondering what she would do. After a minute or two she reached out, grabbed the curtain and slid down to the stage. I can't remember if she ran over to Mick or Keith but she wasn't there long before they got her off the stage. It was pretty wild. Lots of girls were throwing bras and panties on the stage. What a great first concert!

### I WAS THERE: PEGGY JONES, AGE 16

I went with my best friend. I was one of the fans who saw there was an empty mezzanine level behind the stage, with a curtain hanging from it that went all the way to the stage. I decided I would get up there and slide down to the curtain so I could hug Mick Jagger. I was able to do it, although I did fall about halfway down and sprained my ankle. I was about two feet from Mick when the security guys jumped me and carried me off stage, kicking and fighting to get loose. All my high school friends who were there saw me and couldn't believe what they just saw. I also went to the 1965 Stones concert in LA. I was a complete Rolling Stones fan!

### I WAS THERE: ANDREA TARR, AGE 14

I went with my friend. Because Long Beach was known to be an unsafe area at that time and because we were rather young her mother - who loved The Beatles and Rolling Stones as much as we did - decided to accompany us.

This was a wild concert. A girl from the audience climbed up near the stage and was climbing the drapes in order to get closer to the Stones. Billy Preston and the Soul Brothers opened the show. We couldn't see because a lot of the audience were standing on their seats, so we did the same. There was lots of screaming, but we all enjoyed this concert and actually thought the songs seemed like what we'd heard on the album and the radio.

### I WAS THERE: KENT E FISHER, AGE 16

The Stones performed at Santa Monica Civic Center three days before, closing the Teenage Awards Music International (TAMI) concert after a show-stopping performance by James Brown. The show was filmed then aired nationally on 14 November 1964. Locally, it played at the Strand Theatre in Long Beach, a stone's throw from the Civic Auditorium.

I chose to go and see the Long Beach Auditorium concert rather than sit in a movie theatre to view a film of the much larger TAMI concert or buy a ticket for the much smaller Bob Dylan concert at the local Wilson High School in December. I couldn't afford to go to all three, let alone arrange for transportation. No one but me wanted to go to the TAMI show, but a few of my surf and car turf friends were willing to see the Stones and what 'that scene' was all about. The tour was in support of *The Rolling Stones, Now!* album but the set-list leaned heavily on the first LP, *England's Newest Hitmakers*. I was in the nosebleed section and the girls in the crowd just got louder and louder the longer the band played. I remember them playing 'Not Fade Away', 'Walking the Dog', 'Time Is on My Side' and some Chuck Berry strutting before they began to close it down with 'I'm A King Bee' and wind up with 'I'm Alright'.

I also recall Otis Redding opening the show, giving an outstanding performance. He got a good response, but the Stones gave a performance that no one could hear. They were drowned out by the crowd from the opening lines of 'Not Fade Away'.

### I WAS THERE: TINA MCKINEY, AGE 13

I took my little sister, who was 10. We had to take the bus. I remember them trying to escape in their car, and my sister was smashed up against one of the car windows. She got the best view. We laugh about it now, but at the time it was scary. It was sheer pandemonium and chaos. We were lucky we didn't get injured. It was absolutely crazy. I wish I had a picture. I can still see her little face squished against the glass of the car window.

### I WAS THERE: KATHLEEN ROBB, AGE 15

I sat in the front row at the 1964 concert. I was a sophomore in high school – tenth grade. One of my close friends, Cecilia and I snuck out of her house in the middle of the night and walked to downtown Long Beach to camp out to buy tickets for their concert at the Long Beach Auditorium. She lived two to three miles away.

I think they may have started off with 'Not Fade Away', because we were screaming our heads off. Mick used maracas. I remember him dancing from one side of the stage to the other. Brian Jones and Bill Wyman were right before our eyes and Charlie Watts was in the back on the drums. I had on white go-go boots. I took off one white boot and threw it on the stage, and Brian held it up. We went crazy. Next thing I knew, my friend Cecilia was on the stage, hiding behind the curtain, peeking out. She was only ten feet from me. We got separated and after the concert she followed the Stones to the Long Beach airport, and they signed my boot.

Later, my mom threw the boot out. It would probably be of value if I had it now. My brother, Kevin Gannon, was also at the concert and sat in the balcony level six rows back. He saw my boot go on the stage and saw Cecilia on the stage. He said the opening act was Dick and Dee Dee.

Kathleen Robb snuck out of the house with her friend Cecilia

# PUBLIC HALL
## 3 NOVEMBER 1964, CLEVELAND, OHIO

### I WAS THERE: GEORGE SHUBA, 21

I was a freelance journalist in Cleveland. I worked for the newspapers and the radio stations. I'd just gotten out of the air force and my first gig was The Beatles. They said, 'Are you good?' I said, 'I'm the greatest thing that ever happened to Cleveland, Ohio.' And they said 'OK, prove it to us, we want you to shoot The Beatles.'

My partner and I were in the air force together and I said to my partner Don, 'Why the hell are we shooting bugs?' I didn't know who the hell The Beatles were. I was listening to Perry Como, the Four Lads, the Four Aces, people like that. I didn't know who they were and had to watch television in order to find out.

When the Stones came in for their concert, we were supposed to meet with them up in their room, but we went up there with the disc jockey from the radio station, WHK, and they were too busy entertaining some young ladies, so we never got the interview. But I did some shots with Mick and some with the group. I got maybe 30, 40 shots. I had the chance to be as close as a couple of feet. I didn't have any problems with them. And no negativity. They were very co-operative.

Sometimes I didn't understand what they were saying. Mick would say something and I would have him repeat something because I couldn't understand. I wasn't used to the language. The dialect, I should say, not the language. They were at the Public Hall, the same venue as The Beatles played. The Beatles said, 'Do not throw jelly beans at us, because they could hurt us.' So what the kids did was they got very inventive and took marshmallows. Now you cannot throw a marshmallow more than four feet, maybe five at the most. But if you put four or five jellybeans inside – now you've got a projectile! Anyhow, there was a balcony, so that's what they did at the Stones show. What a good waste of marshmallows.

## I WAS THERE: SHELLEY HUSSEY, AGE 13

I was at the show along with my mom, who would have been 35, and my 12-year-old friend Flora. We had missed The Beatles' first appearance in Cleveland that year, which in our minds was a horrendous and unforgiveable tragedy, but thought, 'Hey, the Stones are the next best thing.' So I convinced my mother to take us. Tickets were $4.

During the concert a teenage girl had fallen from the balcony with minor injuries. I was stunned to be part of what looked like just a handful of mostly pubescent girls in that 13,000-14,000 seat auditorium. There were

Shelley Hussey went with her mom

roughly 800 of us there that night. I remember the DJ, Bob Friend of WHK Radio, inviting all of us to move up close to the stage. We were in Row 59 or 61. My girlfriend Flora and I cried, moaned, shrieked, and screamed at the top of our lungs throughout the entire concert, especially when Mick Jagger began singing 'Time Is on My Side'. He was about 20 years old and I tell you there was nothing better than seeing Mick Jagger at age 20.

THE ROLLING STONES IN THE SIXTIES: A PEOPLE'S HISTORY

# MILWAUKEE AUDITORIUM
## 11 NOVEMBER 1964, MILWAUKEE, WISCONSIN

### I WAS THERE: BILL CLARK

In 1964, when I was a senior in high school, the Stones came to Milwaukee to play at the old Milwaukee Auditorium. They gave a press conference at which Brian was asked how he got his biting sound on the harmonica. 'Bite it,' was his reply. I was already deeply into the first album, and hungry for more. A magazine dedicated to the Stones included a list of their recorded works. There was an EP that was not available in the States. I didn't know about mail order then, but apparently Mick did. On the night of the show, only four Stones showed up. Mick announced, 'Brian is ill.' It was the first of four consecutive shows he missed. The crowd was small; 1,200 people showed up in an 8,000-capacity building. The band gave it their all anyway. I bought a fine souvenir booklet, which I still have.

Bill Clark saw the Stones in Milwaukee

*Returning to the UK, the Rolling Stones' fifth single, 'Little Red Rooster', was released on 19 November 1964. It would spend three weeks at No. 1.*

# FAIRFIELD HALLS
## 4 DECEMBER 1964, CROYDON, LONDON, UK

### I WAS THERE: KEITH TAPSCOTT

Just before Christmas I saw them at Fairfield Halls, Croydon. By then my hair was even longer and I felt very proud when once again I was told I looked like Mick Jagger. I got there early in the afternoon and had to go the box office to collect my ticket. As I walked in, I could hear them doing a soundcheck, without Mick singing. It sounded strange to hear them live, crystal clear but without being dominated by screaming.

I was never particularly over-confident and didn't have the courage to try sneaking up the stairs to the theatre to watch them. I was frightened I'd be caught and thrown out and not allowed to see them in the evening. I was seated quite close to the front and became a little unnerved as Mick stared at me several times in a disparaging way. Presumably he thought imitation was not the best form of flattery. Whilst they gave yet another excellent performance, they were clearly tired and worn out.

*After gigging extensively around Britain in 1963 and 1964, performing over 300 times each year, 1965 was to be a slightly quieter year for the Rolling Stones, but no less hectic for all that. The year was to see them perform more than 240 shows, of which barely 100 were in Britain. Australia, the USA, and continental Europe were the focus of much of their live activity. Part of the reason for this was the success of 'I Can't Get No' Satisfaction', which was released in the USA in June 1965 and reached No.1 there in July, enjoying a 14-week run in the charts. It was to top the charts around the world. The Stones were undergoing their transformation into global stars.*

## SAVOY THEATRE
### 8 JANUARY 1965, CORK, IRELAND

**I WAS THERE: SEAN GLEESON, AGE 15**
I was working as a helper on a lorry, so I wasn't in Cork when the tickets went on sale at the Savoy during the week. When I did get a chance to buy a ticket, the 8pm show was sold out, so I got one for the 5pm show. At the time I was disappointed as I really wanted to see the 8pm show. However, things turned out better than I could have hoped.

# THE ROLLING STONES IN THE SIXTIES: A PEOPLE'S HISTORY

When I took my seat for the 5pm show only half the tickets had been sold - the Savoy was only about half full. When I was shown to my seat it was an aisle seat in the front-row right side, so I was directly centre-stage. There were about three people in the front row on the left side, the rest of the audience seated throughout the theatre.

I remember the supporting acts – The Checkmates, Twinkle, who had a big hit at the time called 'Terry', and The Chessmen, one of the best Irish showbands. When the Stones came on, the curtains opened to a smattering of applause and went straight into their act. I remember Mick Jagger using a pair of maracas and Brian Jones playing his Vox teardrop guitar and Vox amp. He also used two harmonicas during the show and played slide-guitar. Charlie Watts sat behind them as if it was so easy playing drums, and Bill Wyman stood there playing bass. It was then that I realised the audience could hear the music and instruments very clearly. There wasn't the usual screaming mayhem which accompanied a Stones concert at the time, or indeed any concert by any of the top groups at the time. Anytime I had seen the Stones on news clips, all you could hear was screaming.

They played for 30 minutes. I remember some of the songs – 'Little Red Rooster', 'It's All Over Now', 'Around and Around', 'Off the Hook'. They were very, very good – Keith Richards and Brian swapping guitar parts on songs, Brian playing slide and letting his guitar hang from his shoulders when he played harmonica, Mick swapping the maracas for a tambourine, Bill holding his bass in an upright position, and behind it all Charlie keeping that incredible beat on the drums. They gave a great show. You could hear every instrument and song very clearly. It was amazing.

## I WAS THERE: OLIVE O'SULLIVAN

I attended both performances. I even sat in the same seat in the front row for both shows. During the interval between shows I went backstage and obtained all their autographs. A boy from the grammar school did an interview with them for his school magazine. I remember my mother was in hospital waiting to have her gall stones removed – I found it funny that we were both concerned with 'our Stones'.

The Stones were very nice to speak to - Mick offered me a Coke, when it came in a bottle. It was Elvis' birthday and they played a tribute to him. The crowd were respectful and appreciated the music. I was on my own but enjoyed the evening as everyone was there for the same reason – to see their idols.

### I WAS THERE: JOE O'CALLAGHAN, AGE 16
I was at the later concert. The Stones really knocked me out. I was in a band so I was very impressed by the harp playing of Brian and also his pear-shaped guitar. In those days Mick was just throwing shapes - the running around came later. Keith crouching over his guitar licks was great. This was all new to us. Girls were screaming and one guy got up on the house organ in front of the stage. We left our seats and went up to get a better view. Twinkle, also on the bill, had a song called 'Terry'. She was a one-hit wonder. She got mobbed after the show outside the Savoy. We had to run for the last bus home. We had school the next day.

### I WAS THERE: JEAN KEARNEY (NÉE MCCLEMENT), AGE 12
I was there with my friend Daphne. We were in for the 6pm show – given that we were only 12, I suppose that explains why. Certainly they were more trusting times if our respective mothers had no issue allowing us to go. The support acts included a young girl called Twinkle. My memory is that there weren't many at the 6pm gig, not more than 300. Daphne and I hid under the seats during the break, then stayed to enjoy the second show too – which had a big crowd, maybe even a capacity one.

### I WAS THERE: OONAGH O'HARE, AGE 15
Cork was a great venue because the Savoy was a 2,000 or so seater. It was one of the big old art deco cinemas and could take big crowds. A lot of great bands came to Cork. The Kinks, Pink Floyd, Tom Jones, The Bee Gees. We weren't the little backwater that people thought we were. The changes that came at the time were very big. Ireland previous to that was showband music, with boys on one side of the room and girls on the other. This was quite a thing for these long-haired guys to come to Cork.

My parents were quite liberal and were okay about me going to see the Rolling Stones, but I had to be home for nine o'clock. I saw the matinee, the afternoon show. There was no screaming and no shouting. There was some screaming but not like The Beatles' thing where they couldn't be heard. It got treated like a movie because the ushers and usherettes in the cinema couldn't even stand up. We were very near the front downstairs. My friend Jill Aitken bought a box of Milk Tray to throw at Mick Jagger, and when she did we were almost thrown out. Jill said if we got this box of chocolates on stage, they would see us and they would want to marry us because we were the coolest girls in the place. We were absolutely, totally convinced that if they saw us and if we got the box of chocolates onto the stage they'd think, 'Oh, my God, look at those girls' and want to marry us. But the chocolates went into the orchestra pit and we were almost thrown out. Not because we were being aggressive or anything, but because we did actually stand up.

I'll always remember Charlie Watts came out from behind his kit up to the front of the stage and announced a number. He was a big hit with the ladies. The drummers always are. My husband was there, and I didn't even know him. I remember I asked my mother if she would lend me some money for the ticket. I can't remember what I paid. I think it was possibly five shillings (25p). When we made our confirmations as young girls in Ireland, our long hair was cut to make us more frown up, and our plaits were kept and I sold mine for the money. I sold my plaits to see the Stones.

### I WAS THERE: PAUL GIBBONS, AGE 24

I still have vivid memories of a fantastic concert. Cork's Savoy Theatre was really rocking on the night. The Stones gave a thrilling performance with their driving raucous sounds. The concert was a sit-down one and I was seated in the top area of the theatre, an area known as the gods because of the amount of steps to climb up to that area. I remember as well having to leave the concert before the end as I had arranged to meet my girlfriend Eileen (now my wife) as she finished her evening shift at 10.45pm in Dunlop's factory, so I missed the finale of the show.

### I WAS THERE: MÍCHEÁL Ó GEALLABHÁIN, AGE 19

My ticket cost 12/6 (63p), the dearest in the house. The cheapest was five shillings (25p). The second house was full, but it seems the first house had a lot of empty seats. One of the support acts was a group called The Gonks. At the end of the second house, I saw Stones manager Andrew

# THE ROLLING STONES IN THE SIXTIES: A PEOPLE'S HISTORY

Loog Oldham carrying the young singer in his arms and saying he would never come back to Cork again. And he never did. Did he lose money on the concert? What screaming there was wasn't spontaneous – it seemed it was what you were supposed to do at a Stones concert. They sang all their hits but at the beginning of the eighth song some people rushed down towards the stage, at which point the Stones disappeared and the concert ended. I felt a bit cheated at only hearing eight songs. I felt that those who rushed the stage were not acting spontaneously but had read in the papers that was what was happening in England. The one who impressed me the most was Brian Jones. I thought his guitar playing was exquisite, while the bass player was very strong.

Mícheál Ó Geallabháin heard Andrew Loog Oldham vow never to return

## I WAS THERE: GREG AHERN, AGE 15

The Rolling Stones played in Cork on a school night. In the Cork of 1965 at 15 years of age you were obliged to obey your parents – 'no going out on a school night' – so it was permission denied. I really wanted to go, and was trying to figure a way out, when the sound of a Volkswagen engine starting brought a glimmer of hope. A quick check out the window revealed both parents were on board as it reversed out the drive. Whether it was good fortune or fate, within 15 minutes I was outside the Savoy where a friend was waiting with a ticket, bless her. We joined the expectant throng and made our way inside. Rolling Stones here we come - I would deal with the domestic consequences later.

Sitting in the front row with all thoughts of homework forgotten, the anticipation was building. Then the MC introduced a singer from England, Twinkle. The big red curtain went up and we beheld a vision - blonde hair, big eyelashes, dressed all in white. She sang of motorbikes and young love and as she called his name into the darkness 'Terry... Terry...' the excitement of the night was taking hold and my sense of amazement at having transitioned from homework to biker angel in such a short time continued to grow. Are such things possible?

The evening was building. The MC was doing his thing. The big red curtain went up and came down. We waited for the main event. Then there was noise and commotion from the stage behind the curtain. We felt the excitement. The music started. Rock 'n' roll! 'I'm gonna tell you how it's gonna be, you're gonna give your love to me.' No MC, no introduction, no curtain, no rules. The curtain was hastily raised and there they were, the Rolling Stones, Mick Jagger at the microphone, maracas in hand. This was amazing.

The songs, the electric sound, the energy, and the newness entranced us. The 'we don't give a shit how you judge us' attitude was palpable. The songs merged one into the other. The electric guitars, the electricity of the band, the long hair, the wildness of the drums, the energy, movement and the face of Jagger as he ponced, gyrated and strutted the stage, alert, sensuous and edgy. It captivated us.

As the music filled the auditorium I looked up and around at the huge dark space and at the crowd, pumping and carried by the beat of this thumping rock band. I became uneasy with a vague sense of fear and guilt, which I could not explain. I sensed, or imagined, something moving in the dark cavernous space, generated or invited in by the band - something dangerous, uncontrollable and unknown but known about. Then I became calmer when logic told me 'they' could not see what was going on inside the building.

When it was over and we spilled out onto Patrick's Street, we were buzzing and filled with the event. We were elated. We had never been at anything like it before. I bade goodbye to friends and headed home to face the (other) music. My run of good luck continued. The Beetle was not back home yet. What a night.

---

*After a short Irish tour, the Stones headed off on their first Australian tour, which saw the group playing 36 shows with Roy Orbison, The Newbeats, and Ray Columbus & the Invaders. Parts of the Sydney leg of the tour were filmed by Movietone News and screened in cinemas.*

# MANUFACTURER'S AUDITORIUM AGRICULTURAL HALL HORDERN PAVILION
## 22, 23, 26, 27 JANUARY 1965, SYDNEY, AUSTRALIA

**I WAS THERE: PETER BANKS**

I saw them in Sydney at the Hordern Pavilion. They put on a good performance, but Roy Orbison was the other act and stole the show.

**I WAS THERE: MARGARET VINCENT, AGE 17**

I fell in love with them as a student nurse. Whilst The Beatles were fabulous, my parents approved of them. But they considered the Stones 'dirty, scruffy and just plain criminal-looking.' So, in defiance of my parents, I decided they were just the group for me. On their first tour here, they played a very small, very downmarket venue on a Saturday afternoon and were back-up to Roy Orbison. Most people went to see Orbison, and the Stones were not well received. I think my sister and I were in the minority in just wanting to see the Stones.

The venue was not really designed for this type of show, the acoustics were terrible and the artists very difficult to hear, but we loved it. Being a very poor student nurse, I could only afford to buy very cheap seats. There was no graduated seating, so even the view of the Stones was like looking in the wrong end of a telescope. I fell in love with Brian, and was devastated when he passed away.

# CITY HALL
## 25 JANUARY 1965, BRISBANE, AUSTRALIA

**I WAS THERE: BARBARA BAKER, AGE 16**

I remember Mick singing 'Heart of Stone' and him lifting the microphone up when he sang, 'Never break, never break, never break - this heart of stone.' It drove all of us girls into an absolute frenzy. I stood on my seat screaming my head off. I don't remember there being a hand-held microphone, so Mick just took the microphone stand along with him.

THE ROLLING STONES IN THE SIXTIES: A PEOPLE'S HISTORY

# PALAIS THEATRE
## 28 JANUARY 1965, MELBOURNE, AUSTRALIA

### I WAS THERE: DAVID N PEPPERELL

It was a strange pairing for a start. Roy Orbison opening for the Rolling Stones? Were the promoters afraid the Stones didn't have the pulling power to fill a 3,000-seat theatre in Melbourne?

I felt sorry when Roy came on after The Newbeats, New Zealand's Ray Columbus and the Invaders, and Melbourne's own(ly) long-haired band, The Flies. It seemed such a comedown from his golden years when he headlined shows at the 7,000-seat Festival Hall, tearing fans apart with his orgasmic ballads. Still, he went down all right and a few girls screamed at him when he gargled in his throat during 'Pretty Woman', but it still seemed a major fall from grace to me.

You could feel the excitement rising as local DJ Stan Rofe told a few off-colour jokes then finally announced, 'And here they are, from England, THE ROLLING STONES!' The curtain went up slowly, revealing Mick Jagger's legs dancing from side to side. From that moment, the screaming never stopped. Opener 'Not Fade Away' had been a minor hit here, but from the reception you would have thought it had topped the charts for months. Melbourne always loved the Stones.

They were not greeted on their arrival in town by a 250,000 crowd, as The Beatles had been a year before in 1964, but the undercurrent of excitement at them being here built to a crescendo, climaxing with them appearing on stage at the Palais Theatre in downtown beach resort St Kilda.

Mick had the maracas going, Keith was spinning around like a dervish, and Brian was ice cool in dandy clothes and attitude. Great cover versions of R&B classics - The Drifters' 'Under the Boardwalk', Howlin' Wolf's 'Little Red Rooster', and the ubiquitous Chuck Berry's 'Around and Around' - were followed by early Stones compositions, 'Heart of Stone' and 'Time is on My Side'. The girls never stopped screaming. Where did all that energy come from?

They were still a young band on their way up, trying to compete with The Beatles - a near impossible task - so they put all their heart and soul into the show. At one stage Mick threw his microphone up in the air and spun around four times before catching it on the beat and continuing with the song. Unlike The Beatles, who stood at the front of the stage and sang, the Stones used every inch of floor space in a never-ending kinetic dance of ecstasy and swept all of us up into it with them. They were the first rock 'n' roll group I ever saw that didn't wear matching clothes, thus beginning a tradition for pop groups that continues to this day, but at the time that was such a rebellion.

Last song - they only played for a half-hour due to security concerns - was their biggest hit in Australia so far, Bobby Womack's 'It's All Over Now', and if I thought the screaming could get no louder, I was wrong.

Then they were gone and I found myself sitting in my seat with tears in my eyes. I loved The Beatles but I worshipped the Stones because they were, I believed, a harbinger of a New World to come. I still think I was right about that.

# TOWN HALL
## 8 FEBRUARY 1965, WELLINGTON, NEW ZEALAND

### I WAS THERE: DOUG HAYWARD

Perhaps surprising, considering the odd substance indulgence, I recall two occasions of hearing the Stones which established my lifelong love and fascination with them. I was a 17-year-old teacher's college student in Wellington when someone played their first album at a party. Wow, what a revelation! It was played over and over again, with 'Walking the Dog', 'Can I Get a Witness' and 'Route 66' the most memorable songs. A year later, I was at a student party in an old run-down two-storey house in central Wellington (no banister on the stairs and every second step missing) when someone played their recently purchased copy of 'Satisfaction'. For most of us, it was the first time we had heard it. It blew us all away and we played it all night long.

Doug Hayward saw the Stones in Wellington, New Zealand

# THE ROLLING STONES IN THE SIXTIES: A PEOPLE'S HISTORY

This period in the mid-Sixties was a most exciting time to be alive, with the amazing music that just kept on coming from so many quarters, the wonderful fashions and the changes in so many aspects of our lives. I can't believe there will ever be another time when so much will change in such a short time. At the centre of this, of course, was the music and the British Invasion in particular. I first saw the Stones in concert when they played two concerts in Wellington Town Hall in February 1965. This tour did not generate the hysteria or positive press The Beatles enjoyed when they were here six months earlier (I also saw one of their concerts). The Stones were billed as the 'bad boys of rock' but the fans all turned out and the concerts were full of good vibes and expectations, and despite sound problems at some of the venues and the Stones being less than enamoured with some aspects of New Zealand in 1965, those of us who saw them won't forget it. From memory they played only about eight numbers, including 'Walking the Dog', 'Little Red Rooster', 'Heart of Stone' and 'Time is on My Side'. Roy Orbison made a corny joke when he came on stage, waving his arms and saying how tired he was as he had 'just flown in.' However, his voice was great, and he sang all his biggest hits. The other support groups were The Newbeats, an American group who had a hit called 'Bread and Butter', and one of New Zealand's top groups of the time, Ray Columbus and the Invaders. They topped our local charts with 'She's a Mod' and were prominent on our music scene for many years.

During the Stones set, there were a couple of attempts by young ladies to get to the stage and some usual screaming, but nothing like at The Beatles' concert. From memory, the band were fairly static and staid compared to later concerts. I guess that partly reflected both the times and the fact that they weren't greatly enjoying the New Zealand experience.

## I WAS THERE: JIM MOBBS

On the bill were the Newbeats and Roy Orbison. I was 12 years old and it was my first concert. I've been a fan ever since. I saw them again a year later, at the same venue. A riot broke out and they stopped the show. As soon as Mick Jagger arrived on stage things got out of hand. These are by far my best musical memories. I also saw them arrive at the airport in 1966. I've seen the Stones several times since.

## PALAIS THEATRE
### 10 FEBRUARY 1965, ST KILDA, MELBOURNE, AUSTRALIA

**I WAS THERE: TREVOR SEARLE, AGE 15**

I saw the Stones in '65 and '66 at the Palais in Melbourne. Great shows and, with the exception of Roy Orbison, they blew everyone off stage. Shows were short by later standards but for a 15-year-old they were great. In '65 I had never heard 'She Said Yeah'. It hadn't yet been released in Australia. Why can't they do this number again? I have seen every tour since and thought the sound quality for the *14 On Fire* tour was fantastic. Pity they played the same old warhorses though.

## CENTENNIAL HALL
### 11 FEBRUARY 1965, ADELAIDE, AUSTRALIA

**I WAS THERE: GUS HOWARD, AGE 17**

I saw the Stones in a barn-like place called Centennial Hall, where most visiting rock acts played. Brian played a white Vox Phantom lute-shaped guitar, a lovely looking thing. The Stones' arrangements depended as much on hearing Brian's guitar voice as Keith's. They played 'Not Fade Away', 'Walking the Dog', 'Under the Boardwalk', 'Around and Around', 'Heart of Stone', 'Time Is on My Side' and 'It's All Over Now'. I think the lead guitar break on 'Heart of Stone' was played by Brian. All these songs had strong airplay in Australian cities.

*Gus Howard felt the band's clothes were more California than London*

Everybody had the singles, and the same Chicago and delta blues material was being mined by many Australian bands. The sound of the Stones was at that time not a lot different to many good generic bands of the time, but the charisma and attitude was very powerfully delivered, and that was it. Brian wore the 'look Ma' expression he often seemed to display, but concentrated when he stepped up. In the whistle-stop circumstances, they played really well. The large crowd included the usual proportion of screaming young girls, but there were also a lot of decidedly cool people there as well as many eagle-eyed fretboard watchers. It was summer in Australia and the Stones wore clothes that were more California than London. The crowd was dressed pretty much the same.

# CAPITOL THEATRE
## 13 FEBRUARY 1965, PERTH, AUSTRALIA

### I WAS THERE: ROBERT MCGOWAN, AGE 34

It was a Saturday. I was the head machinist at the theatre so I worked the three shows they played there that day. The first started about 2.30pm, then 6pm and 9pm. I had to start work at 8am and did not finish until after midnight. The theatre held 2,300 people and was sold out for all three shows. This was the biggest theatre in Perth at the time.

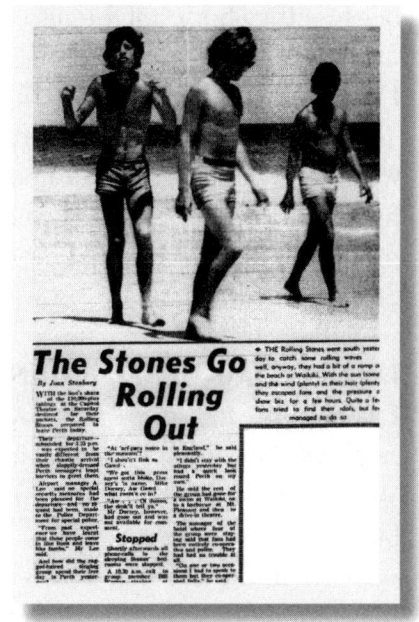

### I WAS THERE: CHRIS ANTILL, AGE 14

I went with my sister and brother. I was already very much into R&B and rock 'n' roll. The Stones shared the bill with Roy Orbison and the Honeycombs. Roy sat on his stool wearing his dark glasses and sang and was very cool, and received a huge ovation. The female drummer for the Honeycombs had been to the beach that day and had a very sunburnt bum. She had trouble sitting. The Stones were, as they say, not at their best that night and received a lukewarm reception. The word was that they were stoned. A lot of people booed.

# THE ROLLING STONES IN THE SIXTIES: A PEOPLE'S HISTORY

## I WAS THERE: CHRIS LALOR, AGE 21

There were six of us. We all married the girls we took to the show, and we are all still close friends, although one is now deceased. I still have the ticket butt. Sadly the Capitol theatre is long gone. There were seats but most of the girls just went down to the front area and danced away. No drugs, no booze - just the music. The Stones were in full flight and Ray Columbus and the Invaders from New Zealand were the support act. But I have to tell you my gang went to the theatre primarily to see the Big O, who stole the show. Fancy that, the Stones and Orbison on the same bill in little old Perth in '65.

It was a fantastic time for my generation's music - Elvis, Buddy Holly, Beatles, et al. I tell my own boys, now they have pinched our music because they both still listen to all of the above.

## I WAS THERE: DAVE PERRIE, AGE 18

They played second to Roy Orbison. A few days after Christmas 1999 we and 38 other families lost our homes in a fierce bushfire. I lost a huge collection of vinyl LPs and a lot of memorabilia including tickets, programmes, etc. collected over many years, including that from the '65 Stones concert.

## I WAS THERE: DEREK BRUINS

I went to the first show, a Saturday afternoon matinee, with my first real girlfriend, Lyn. I was playing in a band at the time called The Wanderers, so to go and see these superstars was the ultimate for a budding muso.

We sat in the nosebleed seats up the top, but that didn't matter much. If my memory serves me well, the show was opened by the original Troubadours (Rick Selby, Peter Bull, et al), followed by Ray Columbus and the Invaders. The Big O then came out. His stage presentation was uninspiring, but when he sang that was forgotten. He did all the favourites and then just left the stage.

Due to the fact they had just got off the plane and pretty much came straight to the theatre, the Stones seemed to go through the motions, but at the time we didn't really care. As an aspiring guitarist, I wanted to see Keith Richards close up, and he didn't disappoint. It was a great time in our lives in Perth, as not too may international acts came here, because of the tyranny of distance.

### I WAS THERE: CHARLES BRADER, AGE 19
I went with the company's social club. My memories of the gig are that the Rolling Stones were the warmup act for the main artist, Roy Orbison. I vividly remember Mick Jagger prancing about the stage doing 'Little Red Rooster'. It was such a contrast to Roy Orbison, who just stood centre-stage with his black suit and sunglasses, guitar in hand, singing 'Pretty Woman'. Looking back, it seems amazing that I saw Roy the Boy and the Stones on the same bill.

*Charles Brader recalls the Stones warming up for Roy Orbison*

### I WAS THERE: MARLENE MAYFIELD, AGE 18
My girlfriend and I went along to see the Stones as the lead-up act to the star of the show, Roy Orbison. I recall they got a great ovation, with fans wanting more. My friend and I sussed out the girls around us. The two in front who looked the wildest were in fact reasonably quiet during the show while the two behind us who looked so quiet just about blew out our eardrums with their constant screaming, proving one can't judge a book by its cover. It's quite incredible to think now that that we could see two fantastic entertainers on the one billing, and that the Stones would actually be just the warmup to Roy Orbison.

### I WAS THERE: PETER ROPER, AGE 16
I was there as a young Mod with my high-neck, button-down collar purple shirt, about 20 rows from the front. Everyone was 16 through to 20 years old. At the time I was with two girlfriends and together we formed the main officers of the Gene Pitney Fan Club (Perth branch).

The Capitol Theatre was a beautiful old building, the venue for many of the Sixties acts

*Peter Roper recalls a great night for young teens*

of the time. The Rolling Stones and Roy Orbison on the same bill was an unusual combination. Two contrasting acts you couldn't believe would go together. Roy was supposedly the headline act. It couldn't have cost much as I was only earning seven pounds a week.

Roy came on first, dressed in black and with the sunglasses of course, and was brilliant. The audience didn't move from their seats or make a sound as Roy sang. Everyone clapped each individual song, 'Crying' being the standout. There was an interval and then, with everyone back in their seats and the theatre in darkness, the Stones got into their positions and opened with 'Around and Around'. The teenagers swarmed the stage and lost control - a complete contrast to Roy. It was mayhem with all the noise. We got the sound of the songs and the riffs, but couldn't really hear the songs for the screaming.

We all congregated in the back alley after the show and pressed up against the windows of the limo transporting the group away to their hotel. A great night for young teenagers. No drugs around, and no violence.

### I WAS THERE: RAE PORTER, AGE 15

I attended with my 20-year-old sister. There were several Australian bands playing for the first half of the show, then there was an interval. I remember coming back after the interval and Roy Orbison was already singing as people returned to their seats. I remember how small he looked. The thing I remember most about the Stones was how blond Brian Jones' hair was. He was always my favourite.

Rae Porter recalls how blond Brian's hair was

### I WAS THERE: VICKI BROWN, AGE 15

It was the first pop concert I had ever been to, and a group of school friends went together - all girls. We didn't dress in anything special, just our goodish clothes. We probably were not too trendy at all. I was surprised everyone screamed as soon as the Stones came on stage. That was certainly something I hadn't expected. Also, girls started to cry. I found that a surprise too. I was also amazed everyone stood on their seats and proceeded to jump up and down and break the seats, throughout the whole show. I had never seen anything like that in my sheltered life.

We had to stand on the seats too, so we could see, but I hasten to add we didn't break ours. It was a really good show, with all the favourite songs from those days, and we were all picked up by our parents afterwards.

### I WAS THERE: CHRISTINE WANSBOROUGH, AGE 29

I was seven months' pregnant with my daughter. I went with my husband Philip. We sat up in the gods, the third level of the Capitol Theatre. I walked up all those stairs - it's a wonder I didn't have my daughter that night! I still remember Mick Jagger singing 'Walking the Dog'.

### I WAS THERE: KEVIN CURNOW

I lived in a country town and it was while visiting my fiancée in Perth that I heard 'I Wanna Be Your Man' on the radio. I was blown away. This was totally new to me. I was shell-shocked. My girlfriend at the time said, 'Oh, that is the Rolling Stones?' like it didn't have any importance. We broke up later. I, like others, was swept up in the fervour that was in the capital of Perth at that time.

Kevin Curnow, the only one there in a suit

It seemed like every young man wanted to be a Brian Jones lookalike. Clubs in Perth for all things R&B and just plain blues were springing up everywhere. Perth was becoming an exciting place. Then came the news that the Stones were coming

to Perth. There was no way I was going to miss this concert. Tickets were going to be sold to country areas first. I wanted to buy two, but my girlfriend's mother would not allow me to take her away for the weekend. I have no idea why she didn't trust me!

The local radio station started playing more Stones and Beatles and other Sixties music than ever before. I knew I could not afford to be late, so I was dressed in my suit before I left. Sure enough, I was the only one there in a suit. If you know what it's like in Oz in February, it's bloody murder driving for six hours and 400 miles with no air conditioning in your car in a suit. But I was going to see the Stones.

I arrived at the Capitol Theatre for the second show with just 10 minutes to spare. I was offered a programme at the door but didn't buy one. I just wanted to be seated and relaxed for the show. I got my seat just six rows from the front, slightly left of centre – perfect. Security was lined up shoulder to shoulder across the front of the stage and I thought about shows of the Stones I had read about in the paper. We didn't have TV where I lived. A local support band kicked things off. I forget who they were but they were not too bad.

Roy Orbison kicked off the second half of the show and I became embarrassed. He never finished his set because the girls were screaming 'we want the Stones' while he was performing. He gave up and gave over to the Stones.

While things got organised, the emcee informed the audience very forcefully that if any person left their seat and entered the aisles the show would be shut down. And there was enough security there to see it shut down. He left the stage and the Stones began to play 'Everybody Needs Somebody to Love' as the curtain went up.

The girls went berserk screaming.

The band sounded perfect. I could not believe the adrenalin I felt. At one point Charlie got to announce the next song. No one could understand a word he said.

Then there was a slight break in the performance and I took a chance and yelled out "Empty Heart'!' Mick replied, 'Steady on, mate,' not knowing, of course, who yelled it.

After another couple of numbers, Mick turned towards Brian and Bill, said a few words and then they played 'Empty Heart'. I could not believe it. Then the show was over and it was time to leave. Security was moving up from the front to clear everyone. I said to one security guard, 'How about letting me through to back stage as I have just travelled 400 miles to see them?' His reply was, 'You now have 400 miles to go home.'

I had parked the car next door in an underground car park. When I got to my car I noticed there was an open door at the bottom of some stairs. Could this be a fire escape for the Embassy Ballroom, which was between the car park and the Capitol Theatre? I took a chance and went up some stairs and a couple of passage ways.

There were a few doors leading off it. I don't know what the door was that someone opened – maybe a toilet – but the person who opened it was Brian Jones. 'Fuck,' I said, 'thanks for the great show.' He said, 'Glad you liked it.' He was a bit stand-offish. I can't blame him. He must have thought I was a weirdo. At that moment a bloke too big to argue with came around the corner and I turned and left. He must have thought I was official as I had my suit on.

---

*After shows in Australia, New Zealand and Singapore, the Stones began another UK tour in March 1965. This tour, with the Stones headlining, supported by Dave Berry and the Cruisers, and The Hollies, coincided with the release of 'The Last Time', which was to become their third British No.1 single.*

---

# EMPIRE THEATRE
## 6 MARCH 1965, LIVERPOOL, UK

**I WAS THERE: TREFOR JONES**

The Stones were now more popular. I sent for two tickets and took my girlfriend Beth, but we had to sit high up in the gods at the back of the Empire because the best tickets were gone. We counted ourselves lucky to be there. On arriving at the Empire there were hundreds of fans gathered outside, guys selling posters of the Stones, and girls galore! After this, every time the Stones were due to do a show nearby and someone said, 'Are you going?' I would say, 'Nah, I've seen them twice already.' The songs that seemed to stand out from this show were 'It's Alright' and 'Everybody Needs Somebody to Love', but the screaming girls spoilt a lot of them.

THE ROLLING STONES IN THE SIXTIES: A PEOPLE'S HISTORY

# PALACE THEATRE
## 7 MARCH 1965, MANCHESTER, UK

### I WAS THERE: MIKE GIBSON

I went there with a schoolmate from Moss House Secondary School, Mike Lightfoot. We'd previously queued for hours on a school day for tickets, someone reported us and we ended up getting the strap the next day for our troubles. On the previous performance a girl had fallen off the balcony and was reported in the papers as 'the girl in the gods.' The show included Goldie and the Gingerbreads, Emile Ford and the Checkmates, Dave Berry and the Cruisers, and we were told the Stones recorded 'The Last Time' live on the show.

### I WAS THERE: CHRISTINE MCDERMOTT, AGE 13

I had a seat in the stalls - C6 – for this show. Like most groups, when the Stones were in Manchester, they used to appear on Granada's early evening TV programme. It was an easy bus ride from school down to the city centre and over to the Granada studios on Quay Street. One time as they came out in their car, we chased it up to the traffic lights, which as luck would have it were on red. Amazingly, they had the rear off-side window down ,and I launched myself through it and got Keith Richards', Brian Jones', Charlie Watts', and Bill Wyman's autographs. Mick was driving, so I didn't get his. When the lights changed the car drove off and turned right with me still half in, half out of the window. Mick pulled over, let me out, and off they drove.

### I WAS THERE: JUNE LOMAS, AGE 20

I worked at the Blood Transfusion Service as a nurse. My three friends and I worked late and went straight to the Palace in our uniforms. Our seats were in the circle at the front. Dave Berry was first on and sang the 'Crying Game'. The noise was deafening then. When the Stones including Brian Jones came on it was impossible to hear anything for the constant screaming. The girls were climbing onto the stage and were being thrown off the stage by the dozen by bouncers.

After several attempts the Stones finally started to perform, but it was mayhem with girls screaming and fainting. Then to my shock a girl came running past me, stood on the balcony in front of me then launched herself off, shouting 'Mick!' People expected us as nurses to help her, but we were unable to get down because of the crowds. I read in the paper the following day that she only received minor injuries. She was so lucky. Despite all the drama and hardly being able to hear, it was still a great night and one I won't forget.

## I WAS THERE: JEAN WALKER

We found out they were staying at the Plaza in Piccadilly. Hundreds of us ran to Piccadilly and they came on to the balcony at the Plaza Hotel waving at all us screaming girls. My boyfriend wasn't too pleased, but did I care? No way! Best years of my life.

## I WAS THERE: PENNY WHITNEY

I went to the first performance at 6pm, and paid nine shillings (45p) to go in the circle. We went by train from Knutsford to Manchester. I have no idea how I came by the tickets. My brother Richard said he remembers going to a Stones concert with The Hollies supporting them and says he queued all night for tickets. I found that hard to believe as he'd only have been 14, but maybe he was with some 15-year-old friends. It's difficult to imagine parents letting that happen.

I was wearing a light grey flannel skirt and knee-high white socks with red and black stripes round the top, over American tan tights and my navy leather three-quarter coat. Dead cool - I followed fashion in *Honey* magazine. My stand-out memory of the concert was Goldie and the Gingerbreads singing 'Baby, baby, can't you hear my heartbeat?' They were wearing light blue satin bell-bottoms.

I cannot remember anything specific about the Stones themselves other than that it was great to be there. They'd only had a couple of albums at that stage and were only on stage a short time as there were about half a dozen supporting acts.

## I WAS THERE: MARTIN RILEY, AGE 17

I think some of this concert featured on the Stones' EP *Got Live If You Want It*. I went on my own to see them and had an upstairs seat. I remember the support acts, as it was a package tour. Goldie & the

Gingerbreads were an all-women band, unusual at the time, and they had a hit record out. The Hollies had Graham Nash in the line-up. I remember Dave Berry & the Cruisers slowly coming out on to a pitch-black stage, guitarist Frank White using a white double-necked Gibson guitar, specially ordered from America. You could not hear the Stones because of the screaming going on. I came out onto Oxford Street afterwards deaf because of this.

# ODEON THEATRE
## 9 MARCH 1965, SUNDERLAND, UK

**I WAS THERE: WILLIAM RICHARDSON**
I was a sixth former at Houghton-le-Spring Grammar School, County Durham. My classmate Barry Jones told me he had two tickets to see the Stones at a local cinema and did I want to go. I said yes. Another classmate found out I was going to see the Stones and issued me with this warning. He said that due to the screaming girl fans at these gigs I would not hear a note the band played, or a word Mick Jagger sang. I replied, 'They have large amplifiers and powerful speakers, how can that happen?' He said, 'Wait and see!'

Barry and I caught the bus to Sunderland and went into the cinema. Some of the supporting acts were Sounds Incorporated, The Checkmates, Goldie and the Gingerbreads, and The Hollies. Some months before, The Beatles said they liked jelly babies, and when they appeared fans threw them on stage at the group. The fans threw sweets at the performers at the Stones show too and I watched one large one in the spotlight thrown at the stage from upstairs. It was going towards the head of Bobby Elliott, drummer with the Hollies. He continued to play and moved his head a couple of inches as it whizzed by.

Eventually, the Stones appeared on stage. The screaming reached fever pitch, as predicted by my classmate, and I never heard a note the band played or a word Mick Jagger sang. I told Barry what a waste of money it had been. We caught the bus back home and two hours later my ears popped back to normal.

In 1973, I saw the Rolling Stones at Newcastle City Hall. The screaming had stopped and I heard every word sung and every sound from the band. It was then that I began to appreciate how great a drummer Charlie Watts was. In my student days in Coventry in the Sixties, I managed to see a few groups and bands, including Ginger Baker from Cream and jazz drummers Louie Bellson, and the great Buddy Rich. Charlie Watts was not out of place in that company.

**I WAS THERE: GILL DODD, AGE 17**
I worked at the Odeon. I was working my week's notice as I had another job to start. The next day when I went to work I was given a minute's notice because the boss said I had just stood watching the Stones all night. It was worth it though, they were brill - they had just found out 'The Last Time' had gone to the top of the charts. The supporting cast were The Hollies, Dave Berry, and Goldie and the Gingerbreads.

I was an usherette but that night I was selling ices from a tray at the intervals, as you did then. I remember on the afternoon the Stones were on, The Hollies were walking up the rink passage, which was not to be used by the public. The manager told me to stop them from coming in that way. They waved to me as they passed, and I just stood there and couldn't say a word. I think that was one of the few times I saw Mr Ray the manager smile.

## ABC THEATRE (AKA RITZ)
### 10 MARCH 1965, HUDDERSFIELD, UK

**I WAS THERE: JENIFER TAYLOR**
I remember very well going to the Ritz, sometimes to see the concert and often just to hang around the back doors with my friends to see if we could get to see the stars. We did see quite a few this way, but more often than not handed our autograph books over and they came back out with signatures in them. I still have my autograph book. I was lucky enough to see The Beatles, Cliff Richard and the Shadows, Adam Faith, The Bachelors, Dave Berry, and many more. I was still at school during this period of pop history and, because tickets went on sale early on a given day, I remember the queues starting the day before, certainly

for the Stones and The Beatles. So to make sure we had a place in the queue for the Rolling Stones, we set up a rota system from our school, Huddersfield High School at Salendine Nook, whereby those of us who had free periods in classes would go into town on the bus and hold the place in the queue, then they would be replaced at regular intervals by other girls when they had to be back at school. It worked fine, and all this long before we had mobile phones. Of course, when the doors opened on the morning of the sale, it was a free-for-all and the orderly queue nearly turned into a rugby scrum.

I remember they opened all the doors across the front of the Ritz and there were then many queues instead of just the one for ticket sales. A bit dumb, we thought. In the end I missed out on the Stones concert because both my best friend and I got the measles two days before. We were gutted. I remember pleading with my mum from my sickbed to let me go, but to no avail. It was probably the right decision considering, but I've never seen them despite being a huge fan in those early days, with pictures all over my bedroom walls and ceiling. My mum did take our tickets down to the Ritz to sell them back however. I don't know how she managed it, but I guess there would still be plenty of kids wanting tickets.

## I WAS THERE: PAUL RAYNER, AGE 14

In those days you were either Beatles or Stones. I was always Stones, right from the first chords of 'Come On'. My brother's girlfriend worked for the local council and got me a ticket from work, so no queue. Only one ticket, so I was alone, surrounded by teenage girls. Wow! I got all their records up to *Exile*, but for me they were never the same after 1969 when we lost Brian.

## I WAS THERE: LAURIE STEAD

I was backstage at the ABC interviewing them all, plus Dave Berry. It's a long time ago and as it was such a daunting experience - I was very new to interviewing – any memory of the event is difficult to recall, such was the madness backstage. But I have the proof of doing the interviews in the photos a friend took of us. There is no photo of the group all together, but there are of me interviewing them individually.

# THE ROLLING STONES IN THE SIXTIES: A PEOPLE'S HISTORY

Laurie Stead interviews Bill Wyman backstage at Huddersfield ABC

Laurie Stead interviews Brian Jones backstage at Huddersfield ABC

Laurie Stead interviews Mick Jagger backstage at Huddersfield ABC

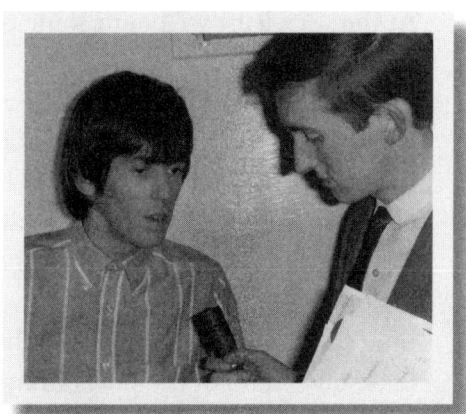

Laurie Stead interviews Keith Richards backstage at Huddersfield ABC

Laurie Stead interviews Charlie Watts backstage at Huddersfield ABC

# THE ROLLING STONES IN THE SIXTIES: A PEOPLE'S HISTORY

## WAS THERE: JENNY MASKELL, AGE 17

I went with my mother, who was only 35 and a great fan. My father couldn't understand why we liked them, but we did, having previously seen The Beatles there. We queued all night for good tickets and again my father wasn't impressed. We had front-row seats in the circle but it was so noisy we didn't know if they were actually singing or not. We were there though. That was important to us, even just to see them. I have never forgotten that night.

## I WAS THERE: GRAHAME NASEY, AGE 13

I attended the evening concert with my 65-year-old grandmother. I attended several other concerts with my gran, and this was the best. At the very least we heard some of the music - at The Beatles it was drowned out by the screaming.

I had Stones records and the way they belted them out was great. We had a great night and returned home on the No.60 bus to Crosland Moor, where we both lived, and had fish and chips in the paper from Gibson's shop at Park Road. I have two original official programmes from the concert. One of them has the autographs of all the Stones, including Brian Jones. My uncle, Denis Morris, had a local group at the time called Denny and the Witchdoctors. Uncle Denny managed to get backstage and got the programme signed.

## I WAS THERE: ANGELA BATTY, AGE 13

I went along with my 14-year-old cousin Susan and sister Judith, aged 11. Tickets cost 10 shillings and sixpence (53p) and the seats were up in the circle. I just could not believe all these famous people I had only seen on television were actually on stage before my eyes. When the Rolling Stones came on the place just erupted. Everyone began screaming. I had never done this before but I joined in with the rest of them and the next day I could hardly talk. Oh, but what a night. The atmosphere and excitement were just something you had to be there to experience. A memory I will never forget is that after the show we ran to the back of the building shouting for Mick, and he opened the window and sat for a while talking, laughing and shouting down to the crowd. He was really nice and had a lovely brown corduroy jacket on, which I thought was fab. There was also a small window at the back of the theatre which my cousin said my sister, being small, would be able to climb in, so we hoisted her up. But a man shouted to us to get down, so that plan was foiled.

# CITY HALL
## 11 MARCH 1965, SHEFFIELD, UK

### I WAS THERE: CAROL OWEN, AGE 16, & BARBARA SYKES, AGE 17

Our dad was commissionaire at the City Hall. We used to get into concerts for free. We used to go straight from school. We saw every pop group possible. For a good five years we were going to City Hall once a month or maybe twice a month. At City Hall they had seats on the stage so we had to sit on the front seats and behave, and when our dad wasn't looking, we would scream. When we saw the Stones we were sat on the stage. They'd turn round and sing to you and wave and things. Because we were young girls as well they weren't really interested in us as such. There was screaming from the start of the show to the finish.

Barbara Sykes, her and Carol's dad was the City Hall commissionaire

Dad managed to get us into the dressing room with the Rolling Stones. They were smoking and drinking and, with Dad being the commissionaire, he said, 'Come on, hurry up and get out, girls' because he didn't want us to be a nuisance to them. They signed autograph books for us. They were friendly enough. We liked Brian Jones best, better than Mick Jagger. When we came out of the show our ears were buzzing from the noise of all the screaming.

THE ROLLING STONES IN THE SIXTIES: A PEOPLE'S HISTORY

# ODEON THEATRE
## 14 MARCH 1965, ROCHESTER, UK

### I WAS THERE: CHRIS WALLEDGE, AGE 16

My friend's father was the manager, so we got in the back circle for free. Goldie and the Gingerbreads were one of the supports. We were sick of the girls screaming out to the male acts, so I shouted out in a high-pitched voice, 'We love you, Goldie!' To two teenage boys that was funny at the time.

The other memory I have was when the Stones appeared. I heard the intro to 'Satisfaction' but then the screaming drowned out every note and every word for the remainder of the show. It was like watching TV with the sound turned off, so I was glad I hadn't paid. Later I met a girl I knew who was in raptures because she'd seen Mick Jagger going in the back door so rushed up and touched him on the side. I was completely underwhelmed.

### I WAS THERE: DIANE MERRICK, AGE 12

I went with my best school friend Lynne Butler. We walked to the theatre as there was no extra money after buying the tickets. We sat downstairs in the stalls and my friend and most of the audience spent the time standing and screaming at the Stones. Eventually I had to join the throng. It was a really great evening and amazing that, at the tender age of 12, I was able to see such an upwardly famous group.

*Diane Merrick went with a school friend*

### I WAS THERE: MARGARET MADGE (NÉE GRACE), AGE 16

I saw the evening show. I had not long started working for Sainsburys. They had organised the tickets. I went with my older sister Susan, who was 17, and cousin Anthea, who was 16. We really enjoyed the evening. It was the first live show we had seen and I really loved Brian Jones and was very sad when he died.

The best song was 'The Last Time'. I don't think we realised they would still be performing 50 years on as we saw them run down the steps of the Odeon and climb into a really scruffy old van. Of all the shows I have seen since, that one sticks in the mind.

*After their fifth UK tour, the Stones played shows in Europe and then North America.*

# L'OLYMPIA
## 16 - 18 APRIL 1965, PARIS, FRANCE

### I WAS THERE: STASH KLOSSOWSKI DE ROLA

I was playing with a guy called Vince Taylor, the inspiration for David Bowie's Ziggy Stardust. He was a black leather Rocker and was rather fantastic. He had this hit called 'Brand New Cadillac', which The Clash and many other bands have covered. I was in his band from '64 onwards.

The first Rolling Stone I met was Charlie Watts, who came to Paris to be with our drummer, a very famous guy called Bobbie Woodman Clarke, who played with all the early greats - the likes of Billy Fury and so on. He was the first person to play double bass drums in rock 'n' roll. People like Ringo and Charlie very much respected him as a drummer and Charlie came and spent a night partying with us. So I'd met him before. But he was the only one I'd had some acquaintance with.

We were absolute rivals with the Stones in a battle of the bands. We played the Easter weekend of 1965 against them, as it were - with them and against them. And their fans took to us like fish to water. We had a very sexy show and were a great, great live band. A very good visual presentation. It wasn't just standing around singing and playing songs. It was a very dynamic sort of thing. We were able to do our entire act just like the Stones. Then there would be an intermission and the Stones came on. We started on Good Friday and ended up on Easter Monday having done all these different shows, including an Easter Sunday matinee. You can imagine how much interaction there was.

The first gig we did with them they stood in the wings watching like hawks and as we came off we were drenched with sweat. Mick Jagger tartly asked Vince, 'You been on?' 'No, no. We've been rehearsing.' And he blew right past him, we just smirked at them and walked on. Their fans were totally besotted with us. Young girls and so on. The Stones in those days only did 20 minutes. We did 20 minutes and they did 20 minutes. We often reminisced with Keith about those good old days when you could get away with doing just 20 minutes.

Any garage band now has almost better equipment in terms of amplification that was available in those days. PAs were especially poor, the returns non-existent. All these kids who missed seeing Brian on stage, for the most part they would have been terribly disappointed because you couldn't hear anything. In Paris you could to some extent, and we certainly could hear them very well. The Beatles found it impossible and gave up touring because it was so bad with the screaming. It was quite exciting but musically speaking it wasn't much of an experience because you couldn't hear what the other people were playing, and it was very hard to know where you were at. So the live gigs were exciting in a way but also lacked a great part of the professionalism that is required today on the stage.

## I WAS THERE: DOMINIC LAMBLIN

The second time they came to Paris they were massive. They were doing three nights so stayed longer, and we spent even more time together and had a very good relationship. In 1965 we were giving up the idea of entering the Olympia through the backstage entrance, because it was so crowded. The fans knew about this entrance just like in London everybody knows where the backstage entrance is for the Palladium, the Roundhouse or other concert halls. What we would do was wait for the show to start and wait for the supporting artists to be on stage, when everything was dark in the theatre. Then we would walk through the main entrance, through the Olympia, and go to the door closest to the stage where you can access backstage. That was funny because it would take about a second for people to realise the Stones are actually right up close and had just walked or run by them, so there'd be excitement but it was too late - we had already disappeared backstage. It was pretty funny to see the crowd reaction.

## THE ROLLING STONES IN THE SIXTIES: A PEOPLE'S HISTORY

In 1965 we went for a soundcheck in the paddy wagon and when we finished we found out there was no police car to take us back to the hotel and there were 200 kids around the entrance. So I told them, 'You know, the only way we can get out of here I can think of is my car, parked right across the street.' It was a Simca 1000. 'I think I'll get it out.' The minute I parked in front of the entrance I just revved, starting my car, and we drove away. There was myself driving and five Stones crammed in the Simca 1000, basically built for four people. It was pretty exciting.

I'd see them every time they'd come to Paris to visit. I would spend time with Brian when he was coming over to see a couple of girlfriends. He'd be coming to Paris pretty often. Same with Keith. All of them would come to Paris. We all know the aim of every Englishman is to finish his life in France, or retire in France, especially the south of France. Keith owns a place, Mick owns a place, I think Bill sold his house in the south of France. Charlie, I'm not sure. I kept on working with them. I was the head of Rolling Stones Records in France in the Seventies.

When they signed with Atlantic Records in 1971 there was a provision in the contract that in each of the major territories, they should have their own label manager, so they said, 'Well, in France why don't you hire Dominic? We've known him six or seven years and we've always worked well with him.'

*April 1965 saw the Stones return to North America for their third tour.*

# ARENA MAURICE-RICHARD
## 23 APRIL 1965, MONTREAL, CANADA

### I WAS THERE: GINETTE LÉONARD, AGE 16

I was 16 years old in 1965 when the Stones played at the Arena Maurice-Richard. They were the second act on, after a young French singer. And they came back in '66 to the Forum de Montreal. They hired dockers for security because the stage was only about one metre high. They played for about 30 minutes, then a riot started. The girls were crying, yelling and one girl fainted near Keith. That stopped the show. My life took another way after I first

Ginette Léonard saw the Stones in Montreal

saw them. We started hanging with English boys, listening to all the beautiful new music that was playing. With every new week there was a new hit on radio. I'm so glad to have lived through those years.

## MAPLE LEAF GARDENS
### 25 APRIL 1965, TORONTO, CANADA

### I WAS THERE: DUVIDOO

The first time I saw them they hadn't really had any hits here, except 'Not Fade Away'. From that show I recall them doing 'Fortune Teller'. There was a lot less screaming than for The Beatles when they played the same venue. You could actually hear the music.

Another time I saw them, Brian was dressed just like on the cover of the *High Tides* album. His hair looked almost white in the lighting. There was none of that zowie stage stuff like late. Mick wasn't doing much dancing around and Keef seemed fixated on Charlie. I wasn't aware of Brian doing any singing, although Bill did from time to time. I can't remember Brian playing harmonica, but he must have. Mostly I remember the drone Bill and Brian were able to set up.

### I WAS THERE: MARGARET MCGOWAN

My first concert was Cliff Richard in September 1959 at the Glasgow Empire. We had seats so high up I was terrified I would go over the balcony. I'm pleased to say my taste in music improved over the years. In September 1964 I saw The Beatles at Maple Leaf Gardens, Toronto,

THE ROLLING STONES IN THE SIXTIES: A PEOPLE'S HISTORY

then the Stones at the same venue in April 1965. I will never forget it. You could hardly hear a single song for the noise us females were making. A couple of girls tried to get on stage by sliding along the curtains and dropping down. It was absolutely crazy.

# PALACE THEATER
## 29 APRIL 1965, ALBANY, NEW YORK

### I WAS THERE: SCOTT MINER

I was a sophomore at Niskayuna High School. It was afternoon, I was home from school but hadn't had dinner. The phone rang. It was my best friend Jeff. 'Hey Scott, you wanna go see the Rolling Stones?' 'What? Are you kidding? Hell yeah!' That was my first reaction, quickly followed by the thought that my mother would never let me go. Jeff and I managed to get into enough trouble together during our freshman year to last 10 lifetimes. At one point I was forbidden to hang around him,

Scott Miner had an offer he couldn't refuse

which only made it more inevitable that I would. 'Hang on man, let me ask.' I turned with the phone in my hand to ask my mother, standing at the kitchen sink washing vegetables for dinner. To my shock she agreed with a minimum of explaining, just wanting to be sure Jeff's mother would be driving us. I quickly told Jeff I could go and within minutes was streaking down the street to his house, three blocks away.

This was during the wave of English bands in the early Sixties that would be known as the British Invasion. After The Beatles played the *Ed Sullivan Show*, it seemed like everybody was washing the Brylcreem out of their hair and forming rock bands. Anything and everything English was totally cool, and the Rolling Stones were right behind The Beatles in popularity.

I wasn't Jeff's first choice to go. He asked a girl named Denise to go with him. I found out a few months ago when I spoke to Denise for the

# THE ROLLING STONES IN THE SIXTIES: A PEOPLE'S HISTORY

first time in 50-odd years she was grounded. Her loss, my gain.

I could hardly contain my excitement on the ride to the Palace. Jeff's mother dropped us at the entrance with instructions to call her when the concert was over. We bolted out of the car into a loud animated crowd of teenagers hanging around the closed doors waiting admittance. The doors soon opened and the crowd surged inside. We managed not to get trampled as we fought our way up to the balcony. We had just gotten settled in our seats when the MC announced the first of the opening acts, local band The Sundowners. They opened with a cover of The Beatles' 'Ticket to Ride' and the screaming began. Everywhere were girls with teased black bouffant hairdos that resembled The Ronettes. Girls didn't look like that in our high school! This was heady stuff for a couple of suburban kids from Niskayuna. The Sundowners played several excellent cover songs popular on the radio before giving way to the second opening act, another local band, Buddy Randell and the Knickerbockers. They had a radio hit called 'Lies' that sounded a lot like The Beatles, which didn't hurt airplay at all. They played several songs, all to screaming girls, before the MC came back on to announce, 'the Rolling Stones!'

It was non-stop shrieking after that. The Stones were dressed similar to their photo on the cover of greatest hits LP *High Tide and Green Grass*. The screaming was so loud I could barely hear Mick Jagger's vocals. It was only by listening to the guitars that I knew what songs were being played. It didn't matter, though. There onstage were my long-haired heroes, the Rolling Stones. I noticed that many of the guys in the audience were throwing pennies at the stage. Not knowing why - this was my first concert after all - I found a few in my pockets and threw them as well, but I'm sure that with my weak arm strength and the distance to the stage I didn't put Mick's eye out. Jeff and I couldn't stop grinning at each other. It would be years before I'd attend another rock concert … but in 1965 I saw the Rolling Stones!

## I WAS THERE: MICHAEL JAY

I was there with my brother. Buddy Randell and the Knickerbockers opened and were great. I remember the Stones were having sound system problems and Mick got frustrated and did a mic drop.

# THE ROLLING STONES IN THE SIXTIES: A PEOPLE'S HISTORY

## I WAS THERE: RALPH MICHAEL SPILLENGER

I went with a couple of my fellow 13-year- old aspiring musicians. 'The Last Time' was their only American hit at the time. I did not become a fan until *Aftermath* as I didn't get into R&B until later. The sound system was useless. All we heard were girls screaming. The only tune I recognized was 'The Last Time', because of the opening lick, and 'Everybody Needs Somebody to Love' because Jagger pointed each time he said, 'I need YOU, YOU, YOU.'

## I WAS THERE: MARY-EILEEN COX, AGE 15

I had front-row seats and backstage passes to meet them. It was an afternoon show and tickets were around $3. At the time, my girlfriend and I truly had no idea this was going to be such a big deal. We lived in Castleton-on-Hudson, New York and would take the bus into Albany. Somehow, we got the nerve to go to the *Times Union* newspaper office and found a sweet man called Joe Higgins (I have no idea how I remember his name after 42 years), who I think was going to be taking pictures at the concert. We simply asked him if we could meet them. I remember standing outside the theatre waiting to go in. Back then, there was no assigned seating. I remember grabbing onto Marcia's belt when the doors opened and just running, sometimes over people, and we got front row. We giggled so hard because as we looked back there were kids all over the aisles.

Just before the show was going to begin, we saw Joe on the right front entrance to the upstairs rooms. We, along with others, followed up the stairs and a group of maybe seven or less concertgoers were put into small rooms to wait for the band. To our surprise, each Stone came in separately, signed autographs, took pictures and went to another room. Not thinking this was such a big deal, I remember looking out the window, seeing my brother on the sidewalk with friends and yelling down to them. They did not have tickets, so they were not happy to see us laughing at them from the windows.

## I WAS THERE: MARCIA PAPPAS, AGE 15

It was a crazy time, those days in the Sixties. It was during the years of the British Invasion. Everyone was in frenzy over British music. The

# THE ROLLING STONES IN THE SIXTIES: A PEOPLE'S HISTORY

Beatles had become famous and many groups followed after that. We had heard some of the Stones' music. Several of us decided we were going to go to this concert. I think the ticket was $2. Here we were, 15 years old, first in line because we wanted to be in the front row.

As soon as the doors opened there was a rush of people. We fell down and tripped over each other but got up and kept on running down the aisle. We got into the first row to see them. It was really chaotic.

We had contacted a reporter at the *Times-Union* called Joe Higgins and he got us backstage passes to go and meet the Rolling Stones. We were standing there and they came into the room and, of course, they were very young as well. We were wide-eyed, awestruck by these people that were famous coming into the room and giving their autographs. We really didn't know what to say to them. We were just young kids. So we just stood there and stared at them. It was very exciting just to say 'hello'. I got their autographs but who knows what happened to them? My mother was probably cleaning out and threw some things away.

There were hordes of people everywhere. We were in the front row and the crowd was out of control. Women and girls were fainting everywhere and being hauled off as they tried to revive them. We just went with the excitement. It carried us away.

I remember being so close to them. In the Palace Theatre, the front row is only 10ft away from the stage. Being that close is unheard of now. There was lots of screaming, and in those days the sound systems were terrible. They didn't have the technology they have now. You could barely hear them, but you could hear them enough to know what they were singing.

When I look back, and when I see they're still performing and drawing such big crowds, I realise we were so lucky to be part of those years. They were so talented, to be able to capture the attention of the American public, and at such a young age. There were several British bands that came that were immediately popular but then faded away. But the Stones had something that really captured the American public's attention, as The Beatles did, and they continued to do so throughout the years where other bands just faded away. I think it was a presence they had. They worked so well together. You could tell they were meant to be together on stage. All their talent came together in this one moment, this

# THE ROLLING STONES IN THE SIXTIES: A PEOPLE'S HISTORY

one brief time that they were on stage performing.

Mick Jagger was my favourite Stone. He was so animated on stage and had that charisma. He drew you right to him. You couldn't take your eyes off him. He has that charisma to this day.

## I WAS THERE: DAVID LOEHR

Early in 1965 radio station WTRY in Albany, New York announced they would be presenting the Rolling Stones at the Palace Theater, Albany. I was 15 and in high school in Pittsfield, Massachusetts, an hour away. Myself and a few friends were hardcore Stones fans, including my best friend, Mick Valenti. We would have arguments at school with a couple other guys as to who was better - the Rolling Stones or Roy Orbison. Mick would always say, 'Them Stones are tough.'

As the day approached, we got more and more excited. There were 6.45pm and 8.45pm shows, with two opening acts, The Sundowners and The Knickerbockers. They had two hours for the three bands to do their sets, get the first crowd out and the second crowd in. Since it was a Thursday, a school day, Mick, Puggy Demary and myself skipped school and got a Greyhound bus from Pittsfield to Albany earlier that day. We wandered around and got something to eat in a diner. Our hair was beginning to get long for the first time, especially Mick's, and at one point a group of girls were chasing us around the streets.

Since the show was at the Palace Theater, they stuck to their daily movie schedule during the afternoon. We had already purchased tickets in advance at Sammy Vincent's Music Store in Pittsfield, which were general admission and cost $2 plus 10 cents federal tax, but we had the bright idea to pay to go to the late afternoon film screening. I don't even recall what the movie was. When it ended we hid under our seats until the moviegoers were all out. It remained dark and we crept around down by the floor, going from aisle to aisle until we got down to the front. At the orchestra pit, we could hear English accents talking and equipment being set up behind the curtain, 20ft away. It was really exciting, and we were tempted to climb the few stairs at the side of the stage and just walk back there. We probably should have - we may have been welcomed.

An usher spotted us and said we had to leave. We hemmed and hawed and moved slowly, not being very cooperative. When they got us to the front lobby and two front glass doors we could see the huge crowd outside waiting to get in. The line went halfway around the theatre. When security was trying to push us out the front doors, the crowd pulled the doors open and it was like opening a flood gate. The crowd pushed through and rushed into the theatre, us being pushed to the very front. Everyone was running and scrambling to get good seats, and we ended up third-row centre. It was utter pandemonium. There was a girl sat right in front of me who had done a really nice oil portrait of Mick Jagger, and was able to get signed by him.

The WTRY disc jockeys were all on stage to do the introductions. The Sundowners, a top-notch regional band, opened and did about four songs, then The Knickerbockers came on and did a few, including Beatles-esque sound-alike hit, 'Lies'. The curtain opened and closed between acts, and the atmosphere was tense. Finally, DJ's Lee Grey and Bob Fuller did the introduction and there they were, the Rolling Stones! The screams and the roar of the crowd, mostly kids in their mid- to early teens, was deafening. They opened with 'It's Alright', the heavy bass riff being almost all you could hear. They were using The Sundowners' amplifiers, and there were only a few of them. It looked like a garage band set-up by today's standards. I later heard from Sundowner Bobby Dick that the Stones had blown out their amps and they were never replaced or paid for, but they could still say they opened for the Rolling Stones, quite a feather in their cap. Mick shuffled his feet and danced around like a combination of Little Richard and Chuck Berry. Brian Jones played his white tear-shaped guitar, and Charlie, Keith and Bill were smiling and just rocking away.

The Stones' entire set lasted no more than 45 minutes and they played their most recent hits, 'Time Is on My Side' and 'Heart of Stone'. Eleven days later they would record '(I Can't Get No) Satisfaction' and it would be released six weeks after, ending up being the No.1 song of the year. The show was totally exciting. Everyone was standing and screaming the whole time, kids filling the aisles and rushing the stage. My first real rock concert. The only time I'd seen anything even remotely close was during a screening of *Rock Around The Clock* at Union Square Theater when the kids were dancing in the aisles. At the Peter, Paul and Mary show and The Dick Clark Caravan of Stars show, the audience sat politely and applauded after each show. This was crazy stuff, and I loved it.

Mick had on a pair of brown, wide wale corduroy pants and a brown jacket with a belt attached which dangled by his sides. A few days later, I went into the Toggery Shop in Pittsfield and asked owner Sam Sukal if he could get wide wale corduroys and after a few weeks he had some in stock and I was one of the first in line to buy them. Sam was very hip to the teen scene and was soon carrying all the new British styles, including paisley shirts and men's ruffled shirts. It wasn't long after that I found a brown jacket with hanging belts.

Back at school the next day, I ran into Sunny Lloyd, who would become my high school sweetheart and Senior Prom date. She also attended the Stones show, with her friend Cande Grieve. She pulled out a little piece of paper to show me and it had all five Stones' signatures on it. She and Cande were somehow able to get backstage. She also managed to end up with one of Mick's maracas. Looking at photos later, we believed it was one Mick used while in the studio recording 'Not Fade Away'.

The experience of that show made a lasting impression on me. I would continue to see the Rolling Stones perform live in concert more than a dozen times over the next 50 years, including shows in England, Wales and Tokyo, culminating with their landmark show at the Indianapolis Motor Speedway on the 4th of July 2015, where I'd end up being eight feet from the stage.

## I WAS THERE: BOBBY DICK

I was a member of a band called The Sundowners who, along with our friendly rival band The Knickerbockers, opened for the Rolling Stones at the Palace Theater in April 1965. There were only AM radio stations back in the Sixties and they sponsored a lot of concerts throughout the country. This one was sponsored by WTRY out of Troy, New York. We were a big fish in a little pond and they asked if we wanted to open for the Rolling Stones. The ticket was $2.50, including 16c tax.

The Palace is in downtown Albany and was one of those theatres used back before microphones were available, when vaudevillians and everybody else would go through there, and acoustically it was absolutely magnificent. They didn't supply their own sound system. I don't know if there was a miscommunication between the radio station and the Stones' manager, but they showed up with their Vox amplifiers. They used our sound system, which was one little cabinet with four 6 by 9 speakers and a Bogen 35w amplifier you normally use for school announcements for lunch and recess. So it was rather bizarre.

The Rolling Stones when they arrived backstage looked absolutely terrible. Having slept on the side of a bus window you get 'hat head' or 'car head'. You're a little groggy from all those miles on the road. I said, 'We really should give them a little slack.' I don't know if they were driving up from Manhattan to Montreal or Buffalo. They were en route somewhere. The Knickerbockers went on and The Sundowners were backstage and the Rolling Stones came down from their dressing room and looked worse than when they got off their bus. The nice thing about Keith Richards is that he looked 75 years old when he was 25. He never really aged.

The Stones were bigger in England at that time than in America. 'Satisfaction' had not come out. But it was sold out. Their audience was totally crazy compared to The Beatles - much louder and much more raucous. And other than Bill Wyman's booming bass, because he showed up with a big Vox bass amplifier with two 18-inch speakers, you didn't hear any vocals. But it didn't matter. We were having a little trouble with the sound system. So Mick was a bit snooty. But I think some of it might have been his displeasure with a minor glitch in the sound system and the fact I was not familiar with the London accent. It can sound a little uppity. But they did put on a great show.

Mick was Mick. They opened with 'Not Fade Away'. He came out with about 10 maracas in each hand. We noticed the girls in the front row had their panties in their hand. I don't know if they brought extra panties or they just took their panties off, but they were throwing them up at the stage. And the only way they could do that was by putting a couple of jellybeans in the panties to give them some heft. Mick got hit in the side of the head with one of these panties with three jellybeans in it. Mick said, 'Would you mind not throwing your panties?'. Because the three jellybeans flung at a pretty high speed can really smart a bit.

We didn't realise how big the Rolling Stones were going to become. The summer of '65, when 'Satisfaction' came out, made them monumental. Superstars. It was just one of those songs. You could call 'The Last Time' a recipe for Top 40 success. But 'Satisfaction' had that unusual basic animal rock 'n' roll beat. It was so basic. I didn't really understand their popularity. I just thought they were so rudimentary. I was looking for great vocals and harmonies and the Rolling Stones were none of that, so I didn't respect what they were doing.

If you listen to the harmonies of what's going on with The Beatles, augmented sevenths and ninths and things like that, you could see where they were going. As much as Keith is great on guitar, I don't think he could play an augmented seventh chord. But they had that animal thing going on around four chords and only incidental harmonies. It was all Mick and his showmanship and ability to project a song and entertain the crowd. The music and vocals didn't matter. It was the energy from the band and from the crowd, feeding off each other. Now I understand it.

In 1966 we played the Red Velvet Club on Sunset Boulevard. On Monday nights, during 1966 and the Summer of Love in 1967, it was the place to be in Hollywood. Mick and Keith came to see us and remembered us. We lived up above the nightclub and they came up to our room. They wanted to sing Beach Boy harmonies and I remember we were singing 'In My Room'. Mick was sitting on our bed and Keith was singing these songs. It was just a crazy time. I wish I'd had a camera.

## I WAS THERE: MIKE ELMENDORF

They played Albany in 2005. On the night of the concert I went with the Mayor of Albany and we presented the key to the city to the band. When we were with the band making the presentation, Mick Jagger was joking about the fact they hadn't been there since 1960-whatever, when they played the Palace Theater. He was joking about the fact that tickets were $3 and the price had gone up slightly since the last time they were here.

---

*I met Mick Jagger in 2005 and he joked about how tickets weren't $3 anymore*

---

THE ROLLING STONES IN THE SIXTIES: A PEOPLE'S HISTORY

# MEMORIAL AUDITORIUM
## 30 APRIL 1965, WORCESTER, MASSACHUSETTS

### I WAS THERE: JOANNE MONINSKI IRISH, AGE 16

I was a junior in high school. We would save our allowance and part-time job dollars and buy records. My parents allowed us to purchase records at The Mart, a Grafton MA department store. I assume it was okay with them because, thinking back, my parents had a small record collection, so must also have enjoyed current favourites during their youth.

When the Stones were on Ed Sullivan, we sat a foot away from the TV watching this phenomenon. It was something I will never forget. My father was pretty strict, not even allowing us to date then. However, he allowed us to go to a Rolling Stones concert.

We bought tickets for the show from M. Steinert & Sons ticket agency in Worcester, the place to buy tickets. I didn't have my driver's license yet, so my father drove my sister and me to the concert and dropped us off in the front of the Auditorium. My sister Nancy remembers running up the stairs to the Auditorium. We had pretty good tickets and were close to the stage. I yelled and screamed my lungs out until I couldn't speak, losing my voice. The actual concert didn't start until 'past our bedtimes' and the dancers and singers prior to the Stones drove us crazy. We didn't want to see them and couldn't wait until they got off the stage and our loves - Mick, Brian, Charlie and Keith - performed for us. I think they were local cheerleader girls who danced.

I remember they sang 'Time is on My Side' and 'Little Red Rooster'. Most of the songs were drowned out by the screaming of us all, including boys in the audience. I took a photo at the concert on my Kodak Instamatic camera. It wasn't very good, but it is evidence that I was there and sat pretty close to the stage. Those days were so different when it came to attending concerts. They weren't the Las Vegas type of performances that take place now. They were just concerts - the

*Joanne Moninski Irish, a foot away from the TV for the Stones when the appeared on The Ed Sullivan Show*

performers on stage without a lot of hype. My regret today is that I didn't keep all the albums and also take pictures of all the concerts I attended. It would be nice to have photos of the people and places from that time in my life. Some I'm sure I probably wouldn't have shown my parents at the time ... if you know what I mean.

## I WAS THERE: SHARON ANN HARMON (NÉE MCGRAIL), AGE 15

Alaric Mills got tickets for me, himself and my best girlfriends, Donna Sherman and Donna Olson. We loved the Stones and none of us ever got to see The Beatles so we thought this was the next best thing. There were so many girls screaming, we couldn't believe our eyes and ears. We sat to the right of the stage, maybe five or six rows back. They were great seats. We didn't scream - I thought it was rather silly and I wanted to hear them sing.

When Mick came out on stage I was thrilled and also rather

*Sharon Ann Harmon went to see the 'next best thing' after The Beatles*

surprised he was so short and slight. He was also dressed in what we called preppy attire. He had a checked shirt, which might have been green, plain pants, and his hair wasn't very long. His eyes were riveting. Screaming continued throughout the whole concert. There was one part where a girl was screaming and I think some guy who was her boyfriend and who was jealous ran up on stage and tried to grab Mick, but security guards pulled him off. That was exciting. Alaric took a home movie of the whole event. Sadly, he passed away and I never got a copy of it.

## I WAS THERE: KEVIN HARVEY, AGE 17

There were only a couple of people in front of me in line that morning and I was terrified it would sell out before me. Top seats going for three and a half bucks, and a copy of the newly-released *The Rolling Stones*

# THE ROLLING STONES IN THE SIXTIES: A PEOPLE'S HISTORY

*Now*! After waiting in the rain outside of the long-gone Ladd's Music I bought two tickets within the first 10 rows. What amazed me that night was that the hall wasn't sold out. At least the last dozen rows on the floor were empty. I didn't check on the balcony.

The set opened with 'Everybody Needs Somebody to Love', Jagger pointing out to each person, 'I need YOU, YOU, YOU.' I recall him taking off his sport jacket, gesturing as if to throw it into the audience and deciding after all to keep it. Brian Jones, with his other-worldly hair and teardrop-shaped guitar, was the visual centre of the band. Jagger moved very little in those days, choosing to work the mic and actually sing. The highlight of the set was a mesmerising 'Little Red Rooster'. They closed with 'I'm Moving On', and they did.

Kevin Harvey got two tickets in the front 10 rows

The Worcester show, pre-aerobics workout and fireworks, remains a black and white marvel of a memory. As the saying goes, you really had to be there. My father, a Worcester police officer who had the evening off, suited up and without informing me of his plans went backstage and watched the show from the wings. 'These guys aren't like you think they are,' he said. 'They're very quiet and don't eat the cookies and cakes the fans send back for them.' I was stunned mute with this. He returned with four of the five band members' autographs, Brian Jones' included, scrawled across a long since missing police report. Ah, well. Ladd's Music, a temple in its day, is also sadly long gone, as is the very street upon which it stood.

## I WAS THERE: RAY LAROCQUE

My father, E Raymond LaRocque, worked for the *Worcester Telegram* and wrote weekly album music reviews. His tastes ran mostly to classical, jazz and pop, including Elvis but not long-haired rock singers like the Rolling Stones. When the weekly boxes of records came from whatever record companies wanted a nice review done, he'd go through the albums, keep the classical and jazz for himself and give me the rock albums. It was late

# THE ROLLING STONES IN THE SIXTIES: A PEOPLE'S HISTORY

March or early April '65 when we got a copy of *The Rolling Stones, Now*, their third album. My father then asked if I wanted to type up a review on the new Stones album. I typed up a good review where I said I hoped the Stones played as well on stage in Worcester for their upcoming show as they did on their new album. I played the album every day, along with Bob Dylan's *Bringing It All Back Home* and the first albums by The Yardbirds and The Byrds. I remember my dad liking 'Down the Road Apiece' by the Stones, which he remembered from the old days.

For my 18th birthday on 30 March, I asked for tickets to the Stones show the following month, and got them. I asked friends for two weeks to go with me and, because the Stones weren't that popular yet, couldn't find anyone to go. This was still a month before 'Satisfaction was released. A friend from my senior high school class, Paul Rastad, then said he'd go, and we drove to the show. Our seats were the best in the house - balcony seats almost overhanging the stage. I remember the girls screaming - it never stopped! A policeman gave a girl near us a cigarette butt from the Stones and she passed right out. I was hanging over the balcony railing yelling 'MICK!' every time he'd shimmy his way over near our seats. And 3,000 girls can really yell. I had a headache for two hours after.

A good show and I never saw another like it until March 1968, when Jimi Hendrix caught us sneaking into Clark University Auditorium, Worcester and let us stay for two shows.

## I WAS THERE: ANN LIVINGSTON, AGE 17

This was my first concert. I went with two or three of my girlfriends. I was about to graduate from high school. We sat on the first level, even with the stage, in the last row and the Stones appeared to be about two inches high. The concert went by fairly quickly and we stood the whole time on top of our seats.

## I WAS THERE: MAUREEN GROGAN, AGE 14

The Auditorium was an old building with fancy seats and balconies - opera house or music hall style. I was there with my then best friend Lynne, her sister Kathy, and one of her schoolfriends. Lynne had just turned 14, Kathy was 12 going on 13. Gosh, we were babies! This was of course less than 15 months after The Beatles came to America and were on *Ed Sullivan*. My sister and I along with Lynne and my friend Darlene - my best friend to this day - were all insanely in love with The Beatles and as Beatlemaniacs had become obsessed with all things British. Hair. Clothes. Make-up. And of course, bands.

It was the height of the British Invasion, we were totally swept up in it, and consequently I only wanted to see the Stones - the next big thing from England. We were way too young to get their more obvious sexuality. My favourite as of the concert date was Brian Jones - sadly not for his talent but because of his hair. But once there I was caught up by the music. I've always remembered Mick singing 'Little Red Rooster' and 'Time Is on My Side'. We were in Row I - which I assume was 9 - but during the show managed to get into empty seats in the centre section, a few rows closer.

It was my first but far from last concert standing on the seat screaming my brains out, until the cops kept making us sit down.

Brian Jones was Maureen Grogan's favourite

Maureen Grogan's ticket

I also remember the rest having more of a folk or blues club look with the turtlenecks, tight pants, and jackets on … all but Mick. They all had such beautifully shiny long hair - much longer than The Beatles at that time. I remember a boy jumping onto the stage as we were directly centre in the fifth or so row by then. I've never understood all the media claims that no one in the audience could hear the music or knew what songs were being performed. Totally not true. We always wrote down the list of songs that had been played after a show.

# THE ROLLING STONES IN THE SIXTIES: A PEOPLE'S HISTORY

## I WAS THERE: ANDREA BONOLDI
My friend Kevin Driscoll and I were seated in the second aisle, centre row, to the right of someone who got so excited and riled up he ended up jumping on the stage.

## I WAS THERE: GARY MORRISON, AGE 16
I was in high school and the guitar player in a band of four called The Ravens. Myself, my fellow band members and my girlfriend went to the show. We all lived in Clinton, Massachusetts, twelve or so miles from Worcester. We sat in the balcony to the right from the stage. I don't remember too much about the music with all the excitement. But I do remember a lot of flashbulbs being thrown at the stage, Mick Jagger being skinny and not a James Bond type, and a good-looking blonde standing on her seat in front of us wearing 'These Boots are Made for Walking' white boots and a minidress, very stylish for the times. It being our first concert, it all went down too quickly but it gave for a lot of conversation with family and friends for a week or so. I'm still a guitar player now, and still very fond of the British Invasion music that changed my life.

## I WAS THERE: MARTHA (HAMM) SERAFIN, AGE 14
I was in Row 14. We went to lots of concerts then. I was in high school and the Stones were not exactly approved of by the nuns at our Catholic girls high school, but that didn't stop us. I doubt we paid more than $5 for tickets. I don't remember much else except Mick threw a tie into the audience and we made chains out of Black Jack gum wrappers to throw to Charlie Watts. It was kind of a big deal but I didn't realize

Martha (Hamm) Serafin was in Row 14

how much of a big deal until years later.

I also saw The Beatles at Boston Garden but was nowhere near as close as I was to the Stones. Most people are surprised the Stones were at the little Auditorium but in those days all the popular bands came to Worcester. And we could actually afford to see them.

### I WAS THERE: DEBRA BOLZ, AGE 12

I will never forget my mother made me wear a pink and white seersucker suit with a skirt. I was not happy. She said if I dressed like a lady, I would be treated like one. I have no memories of the actual show. I do remember running to the stage after and scraping my hands over it. Then I made my father drive me to Harry's Drive-In in Shrewsbury, because rumour had it the Stones stopped there to eat.

### I WAS THERE: KAREN MACARTHUR APOLLONIO, AGE 9

My mother, brother and I attended. I was nine years old. My father was a local disc jockey in Worcester at WORC, going by the name Bob Mack. He and an associate, maybe Dick Smith, booked the Stones for the concert through the William Morris Agency in New York. I remember a lot of people, teenagers, milling around everywhere outside and in the auditorium. We went to get some pizza before the show somewhere nearby and it was jammed with Stones fans. At one point, the owner (or at least a guy working there) said he just saw the Stones go by. Needless to say, the place emptied as screaming young fans ran to check it out. I looked at my mom, not quite understanding what had happened, and she just said the man wanted them to leave the pizza place because it was so crowded.

We sat on the left side of the auditorium, maybe about 20 rows back from the stage. My father wanted to take then 15-year-old brother and I backstage to meet the Stones but said it was too hectic. That was fine with me, as I was too young to understand the magnitude of the moment, or the band for that matter.

My most vivid recollection? The screaming young girls … some of them crying, so excited. And I specifically remember seeing a father come in and drag his daughter out, pulling her by the hair. I was a few years away from getting what all the hysteria was about.

A friend of my dad's, Johnny Sullivan, had a daughter he was trying to get started in the music business as a singer. That's how Little Jonna Jaye ended up opening for the Stones. I remember I had her record, 'Put Up or Shut Up', which Dad had given me a copy of. I wish I still had the fan book I bought at the show. It was full of band photos, etc.

### I WAS THERE: PAM BRALEY

I was 14 years old. I went with five friends from school. We were on the third row, very close to the stage. We could hear the music. I remember Brian was dressed much better than the others, wearing a suit with a white turtle-neck sweater. He played his white Vox guitar and tambourines. Mick didn't move around as much as he does today. The place was not packed; there were a lot of empty seats. I think they were just starting to get some attention in the States. I took pictures, including some good ones of Brian and Mick, but let a friend borrow them and never got them back.

One song I remember from the concert is 'It's All Over Now'. I saw them again in Boston in November the same year. That was a bigger concert than the Worcester one. The last time I saw them was November 29, 1969. There was a lot of open marijuana smoking amongst the crowd, and concerts were changing so much. I never went back to see them again, because I didn't like them without Brian. They never sounded the same without him. He gave the Stones unique sounds with all the instruments he played. I don't think they have really ever given the guy his due credit. I absolutely loved their earlier music.

### I WAS THERE: GARY DOMBROWSKI, AGE 15

It's hard to believe this was my first concert. The Auditorium wasn't a great place to see a show but it was great to me. 'Route 66', 'Not Fade Away' … My mom wouldn't let me go unless I brought my younger sisters, aged 14 and twelve. Great memories.

### I WAS THERE: GARY SHUSA, AGE 18

I was a senior at North High School, practically next door, and went to the concert with a group of friends. If memory serves me well the hall was mostly full. Subdued quiet-type girls I went to high school with were

# THE ROLLING STONES IN THE SIXTIES: A PEOPLE'S HISTORY

screaming their collective brains out. It was the first time I ever saw such a reaction.

The Stones were great - not a long concert, but electric. Worcester obviously made a good impression on them as they came back years later to record and do another concert in a small local venue. After the concert I went looking for my friends at the local Friendly's hamburger joint. Just as I was about to enter, two slightly older guys who I didn't know from Adam, grabbed me and asked me to help them with a big problem they had. It seems they had picked up three young ladies at the concert who wanted to 'party' but would only agree to do so if there was a third guy. Lucky me. I became long lost cousin Gary!

Gary Shusa went onto a hamburger joint, and his luck was in

## I WAS THERE: DAVE GREENSLIT, AGE 14

I played drums in garage band, the Nozmo Kings - a play on the no-smoking sign in my friend's garage where we practised - and our group idolized the Stones. We covered many of their songs and the songs they covered.

I attended the Auditorium show with a friend. If memory serves (and frankly, at my age, often it doesn't), my buddy and I bought tickets for about $5, which got us seats in the back of the cavernous hall. I believe the Stones opened with 'Everybody Needs Somebody to Love.' My friend claims it was 'Not Fade Away', because Mick Jagger was playing maracas. As soon as the curtain rose, the screaming drowned out the music. The acoustics in the auditorium were awful anyway.

The next year we hitchhiked to Hartford for an outdoor show by the Stones, which lasted about as long as the Worcester gig, according to the lead guitarist of our band, who said when we recently talked about the show Brian Jones was too shit-faced to play. The Stones were our favourite band because they were edgy and represented the spirit of the times for kids like us in the Sixties. While my parents acknowledged The Beatles could at least sing, they did not like the Stones. No adults did.

## I WAS THERE: BEVERLY PAQUETTE, AGE 15

I was with my friend Linda. I truly enjoyed the screaming and the concert. I was seated in an aisle seat toward the front and Mick Jagger and the Stones were running up the aisle to get to the stage. I screamed, 'Mick! Mick!' and Mick stopped and shook my hand. I'll never forget that as long as I live.

## I WAS THERE: JEN FORSBERG, AGE 13

I was barely 13 and my brother barely 14. My sister who also attended had just turned 16 and brought her friend, also 16, and her 14 year-old brother. We were dropped off and went up the endless steps into the Auditorium. This was my first concert and all the sounds, sights, emotions and feelings of anticipation left me breathless, anxious and physically excited. We lived only two towns away from Worcester so were in familiar territory. After we found our seats, my sister and her friend disappeared. Although I was curious it just seemed like another chaotic thing that can happen at a concert.

The noise was deafening, several thousand kids, mostly girls, all yelling in unison. Then above all that din there was loud screaming and sobbing from a single girl and when I looked down the aisle behind me I saw my sister and her friend being led back to their seats next to mine by two security guards.

At first I thought she had been hurt, but she was just hysterical. As it turned out they were two of the four girls that had hid out in the Auditorium garage and jumped the Stones. My sister could barely talk but had scratched Mick's hand and grabbed his shoulder. A girl ran up to my hysterical sister, saying, 'Can I touch you? Can I touch you?' My head was spinning as I became catapulted into my sister's experience. And this all happened before the show.

The show itself was simply unbelievable. My sister became famous in our small town for a while amongst our peers. In 1969 I saw the Stones again at the Boston Garden with my best friend and our boyfriends. Although it was a longer concert and much, much bigger and very exciting, it didn't come close to matching the Worcester concert, which had a more innocent air about it. Music was an absolute necessity for us, as it was truly all we had.

# THE ROLLING STONES IN THE SIXTIES: A PEOPLE'S HISTORY

### I WAS THERE: CHESTER CLARKE, AGE 14

I attended with my friend Larry. Local top-40 radio station WORC, often credited with breaking The Beatles in America, ran a contest giving away every Rolling Stones album up to that point to the person who came closest to naming, in order, the first twelve songs the Stones played. Unfortunately, they didn't make it through twelve songs - there were too many girls rushing the stage. It really didn't matter to me. I couldn't name the six or seven songs they did get through, as I couldn't hear much over the screaming crowd. I recognized a little of 'The Last Time', and nothing else.

### I WAS THERE: DENISE QUARANTA, AGE 14

I was attending my very first concert. I remember the excitement because I sat in the second row on the left side of the stage. The ticket price was $10. The anticipation of seeing a British group was cool. The audience-goers were in control but when the curtain opened I heard approximately four chords to 'Mona' and the screaming was deafening. I stood on my seat but could not see well because the crowd ran towards the stage and others stood on the backs of their seats. You could only hear screaming and an occasional note.

### I WAS THERE: RON WHITTLE

When we found out the Stones were coming to Worcester, we did everything we could to get tickets. We had balcony seats near the left side of the stage. I remember more screaming than I had ever heard before and it made it even more exciting to be there to witness it. It was an event to be seen at and something to brag about at school.

I still can see Mick Jagger mouthing the words and being able to hear maybe every fourth or fifth word above the screaming. I remember leaving the Auditorium with my friend singing the Stones' songs with the crowd on the front steps after the show, waiting for our ride home. I loved it. It was a time in my life I will never forget. It was a time rock 'n' roll history was made in Worcester.

### I WAS THERE: KENNETH BOUTHOT, AGE 13

Our local radio station, WORC AM radio - '1310 on your dial,' as they advertised in a jingle - during the British Invasion was at the forefront

# THE ROLLING STONES IN THE SIXTIES: A PEOPLE'S HISTORY

of featuring the rock talents just starting to release singles in the United States for radio airplay. I would be up early before school and listen in, which was very receptive to accepting calls on the request hotline, and remember phoning in, asking politely to hear anything by The Beatles or Rolling Stones, and the Dave Clark Five. I would record them from the portable radio speaker with a small compact reel-to-reel my dad had passed down to me. That was limited to the ever so small 3½ inch reels but – hey - at least I had access to some free songs.

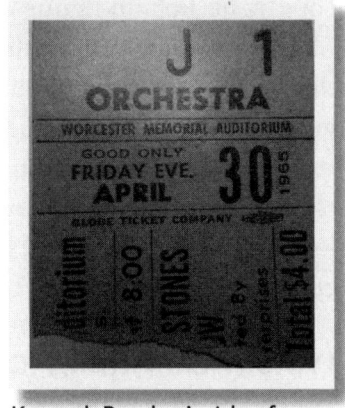

Kenneth Bouthot's ticket from the night

I am sure I heard about the future visit to and concert by the Stones in Worcester as a result of this station's promotions. They had a semi-famous disc jockey, Dick 'the Derby' Smith, known to have bragging claims as one of the very first jocks to play music by The Beatles on American airwaves. I remember clearly walking downtown after school to buy a pair of tickets for the event at a spot called Ladd's Music Shop, located within 100 yards of Worcester City Hall, after somehow amassing the staggering sum of $8 for a pair of tickets, as no way would I be allowed to go alone.

Outrageous add-ons like a service fee or convenience fee for tickets was pretty much unheard of. One thing was for sure - there was no chance of Dad ever having the money to take me, so I bought his ticket. The Worcester Memorial Auditorium later became a favourite place for pro wrestling competitions where, thankfully, sonic quality and acoustics are not of prime importance. The venue featured an oval balcony which in hindsight may have been a better choice for me, but I figured I would get as close as possible to the stage.

As I recall, it was an absolutely flat listening floor, meaning no slope at all. So if you were, like me, maybe 5ft 2 ins, your line of sight might not be premium seating on anyone's scale. I remember a rather brief performance to say the least, lasting not more than maybe 11 songs, most songs running maybe two minutes 35 in length, with deafening screams between. I recall a fellow trying to rush the stage who was grabbed by cops by his belt and flung off the elevated stage in a not so gentle manner.

I think they played 'Little Red Rooster' as I recall the rather violent slide-guitar action of Brian Jones back and forth on the neck of the guitar. If I had any ringing in the ears the next day, it was from the incessant screaming and not because the public address system was loud or even adequate, as it was surely not. I remember the band's amplifiers looking mighty small and few in number, the smaller Vox amps with criss-cross grill cloths the band used most of the time.

### I WAS THERE: ROSE MORTON, AGE 13

We had backstage passes to meet the Stones thanks to my friend's father, who worked in the music business. Myself and Pam Farrell presented a cake to Charlie Watts. It was pretty overwhelming. There was a lot of press there. It was probably one of the most exciting moments of my life to actually meet the Stones.

### I WAS THERE: ROSEMARY AHMADI, AGE 7

I remember being backstage. I was a little disappointed it wasn't The Beatles but remember how friendly the group was. I had two pictures taken with Mick Jagger, but over the years the photos have disappeared. I stood in the wings of the stage and could not hear any lyrics whatsoever. I was, however, able to see the audience and remember how crazy they were for the Stones with cheering and shouting - it really made quite an impression on me.

### I WAS THERE: CLEMENT PORTER, AGE 19

I had a band called Group Therapy and we appeared at the Auditorium a few months before the Stones' concert in a 'battle of the bands'. My cousin worked with the stage manager, setting up concerts, and gave me a call the day before the Stones show to see if my band would be interested in bringing our equipment backstage and possibly playing as an opening act if there was a problem, i.e. an opening act cancellation or the Stones being delayed. The next day we brought in our PA system and amplifiers. We never got the nod but left our equipment there just in case a last-minute unforeseen thing happened. I purchased my Stones tickets weeks before the concert on the third row back from the stage.

# THE ROLLING STONES IN THE SIXTIES: A PEOPLE'S HISTORY

The opening acts were done - now the big event.

The announcement over the PA system came, 'Ladies and gentlemen, the Rolling Stones.' The curtains were closed, but we could hear the music starting behind the curtain. This went on for a couple of minutes, then suddenly Mick Jagger pulled the curtain back just enough to walk out with microphone in hand. Then the curtain gradually and slowly moved back to reveal Brian Jones, who was my favourite, Keith Richards, Bill Wyman, and Charlie Watts.

A few days later my cousin called for us to pick up our equipment at the Auditorium. I was shocked when he told me, 'Guess what? Mick Jagger used your microphone.' They had a problem with their PA system. A friend who was with me but in a different seat took a great picture of the Stones on stage that night. He had also taken pictures of my band on the same stage in the battle of the bands, so I have the pictures of Mick and me, both on the same stage, although at different times, using this good old-fashioned mic.

## I WAS THERE: MICHELLE WELLEN, AGE 14

My father drove myself and a few friends to Worcester, and dropped us off at the Auditorium. We had balcony seats in the front row and made a big sign. All you could hear was girls screaming. My dad came back at 11pm and picked us up. No violence, no fear. It was fun but you could not hear the band. And they looked very small.

## I WAS THERE: ROSE FITZGERALD, AGE 12

I was there in the front row. I went with my mom. She loved Mick Jagger - she loved all music. I also had a friend with me the same age. We sat in the front row at $4.50 a ticket. I remember the show starting and someone ran up on stage. The curtain came down, but it continued. Brian Jones was with them, and to me that was awesome.

My dad was from Italy and very old-fashioned but did allow us to listen for a time. He didn't like it loud, so we had to tone it down. It's funny the music I listened to. My kids grew up with it too, as I always had

Rose Fitzgerald felt it was awesome to see Brian Jones

something playing in my house. To this day I still love the Stones. My mom, God rest her soul, still loved to listen to them too. She died in 2012 at 99.

### I WAS THERE: JODY TUBERT, AGE 14

I have a photo of me and two schoolfriends in our seats, screaming. My brother Mark was backstage meeting them with my father. It was a priceless time.

I also saw The Beatles at the Boston Garden in September 1964 along with three other siblings. My father, Jack Tubert, was in the interview room with The Beatles and got them to sign our programmes. I also got to meet Herman and the Hermits, The Beach Boys, The Searchers, and Bobby Sherman. It was wonderful to have a father whose assignment was 'go cover those mop-heads'.

### I WAS THERE: JEAN JOHNSON, AGE 14

I went with a girlfriend. Our parents dropped us off and picked us up after. It was great. There were many rock concerts at the Auditorium in the Sixties. We saw the Stones just once, but The Beach Boys three or four times, Gerry and the Pacemakers, Sonny and Cher, Peter and Gordon, and others.

Jean Johnson was dropped off by her parents

The building is still there, but unfortunately in a state of disrepair, unused as a theatre for many years. I still live in the area, and it brings back memories every time I drive by.

### I WAS THERE: JOANNE FERRECCHIA WILLIS, AGE 14

My father would not allow me to attend The Beatles' concert in Boston for fear of unruly crowds. But somehow the Stones seemed less of a threat - perhaps parents were not quite as aware of the other groups in the British Invasion. I went along with three girlfriends, all aged 14, and one of their brothers and his friend. We all hailed from Marlborough, about 18 miles east of Worcester. Our front-row balcony seats cost $4 each.

# THE ROLLING STONES IN THE SIXTIES: A PEOPLE'S HISTORY

When the Stones appeared on stage, the screaming and frenzy began immediately. We girls stood screaming and shouting, as did the two boys with us. We heard 'Satisfaction' and instinctively knew a hit was on its way. If you can believe, little attention was paid to Mick Jagger. Brian Jones, dressed nattily and with a gorgeous head of blond hair, garnered the most attention, the most screams. He seemed to smile knowingly.

## I WAS THERE: COLLEEN OLIVER, AGE 13

I went with Patti, a friend from seventh grade. We both told our parents we were going with the other's parents so we could sneak off alone. Of course, our parents met at parent/teachers night and our plot was revealed - we were in big trouble and I think our punishment was a ban on concerts for a while. Luckily, the Stones had already appeared.

We had balcony or loge seats close to the stage on the left side of the house. Looking down at the auditorium, there was a walkway or aisle about halfway back from right to left. It was shocking to see the second section was barely occupied but it was also exciting that we were seeing the Stones before others really knew about them. When the last song, 'The Last Time', started we ran downstairs to the hallway leading to the dressing rooms. The police were not prepared. They set up folding tables between us and them for security. My friend was from the Bronx and considered very worldly, so I followed her lead, flipping the tables over on the police. When they fell, we ran toward the dressing rooms. We were not successful, however, and were immediately removed, so we ran to the garage and watched the performers leaving instead.

## I WAS THERE: NEIL FAUGNO

I was at that concert with a group of guys. We arrived very close to the beginning and the place was jumping with mostly young females. A local DJ introduced some acts of local and regional talent, but in between these acts with the curtain closed you would hear a guitar playing the beginning of a Stones song only to be told another performer was coming on. It was a big tease. Finally, the Stones were introduced and the roar was deafening. Girls were screaming and the small arena shook with excitement.

At the end of their performance a young guy made his way to the stage, but a Worcester policeman lunged at him to keep him from reaching Mick and ended up straight arming him across the throat. Mick saw this and started to move towards the altercation but a hand - I believe it was Keith - grabbed Mick and pulled him behind the curtain.

After the last song ended the crowd ran to an area where they thought the Stones would be exiting, but they never showed and the crowd dispersed. Quite a night.

### I WAS THERE: DIANE GRANGER, AGE 14

I remember standing in line waiting to buy my ticket. I was saving a place for my friend, Margie, who had to return a birdcage and use the refund to buy her ticket. I had my babysitting money.

Later, Margie had a chance to get a ticket closer to the stage than ours so she sold her ticket to my older sister, 20 at the time and glad for the opportunity to go. We lived within walking distance of the Auditorium and walked to and from the show. A newspaper article said the performance was only 23 minutes, but to me it seemed much longer. I remember the ringing in my ears all the way home. A few years ago, I found my stub to the concert and brought it to work to show my co-workers I saw the Rolling Stones back when it only cost $4 to do so. They were impressed.

### I WAS THERE: GAIL NASON, AGE 17

I went with high school friends Alberta Martelli and Betty Rolls. We sat in the balcony and were able to hear them. I thought Mick Jagger was very young looking, even to me, and was quite thin and had a good voice. Of course, as now, his singing was very sensual. They of course had a tougher look than The Beatles.

What an exciting time for music, so lively and upbeat, just what we needed. Except, of course, our parents, who hated the look and the sound. I remember my poor brother Mick being so upset when my father shaved his long hair and gave him a 'butch', so he wouldn't look like a 'freak'. Now that is what you call a generation gap! I will never forget those years.

Gail Nason went with two high school friends

# THE ROLLING STONES IN THE SIXTIES: A PEOPLE'S HISTORY

## I WAS THERE: LYNN COUTURE, AGE 16

The Rolling Stones were coming to Worcester, of all places. This was something I was not going to miss. I had already seen them on the *Ed Sullivan Show* and was totally smitten. I had an after-school job working as a dishwasher and kitchen assistant. At the end of my day, I would return home greasy, sweaty and smelly. I used the money I made (50 cents an hour) and diligently saved to purchase my ticket. I did not hesitate to spend $12 on my ticket (10th row, slightly left of stage).

Lynn Couture was smitten by the Stones

I went with one of my friends. With a mouthful of metal braces and a head full of frizzy hair, I sat composed in my seat while young girls screamed throughout their set. Juvenile screeching was not for me. I took two photographs with my Brownie camera. My only disappointment was that Keith was situated on the other side of the stage. During the performance, Mick sang and gyrated toward our side of the stage. It seemed as though he was looking directly at me. Would I be invited backstage? How many other delusional girls thought the same? The night was wonderful and exciting, and I had no regrets having spent my hard-earned money.

## I WAS THERE: BRIAN BARLOW, AGE 16

My first experience with music came with Ricky Nelson and Connie Francis. That's what I first got inspired by. Then Roy Orbison came out. Roy was my guy and I went to see him in 1962 and couldn't believe how great he was. Then The Beatles changed everything. That killed me. I was in my car one day and all of a sudden they were playing 'Love Me Do'. I said, 'What is this?' Then 'She Loves You' came out shortly thereafter, so I was done.

Brian Barlow already owned two Stones records

Like many teens in the early Sixties, I was obsessed with the new sound out of England, my radio was on all day to local station WORC to hear more of this magical sound. I don't know what it was about the music, but it was great energy.

On 4 June 1964 I had my first taste of the British Invasion with a concert at the Worcester Auditorium featuring The Searchers. They were great and brought the new 'jangly sound' I loved from Britain. I have a magazine I bought in '64 and on the back of the cover it shows up and coming band the Rolling Stones. I'd never heard of them. It was mostly The Beatles and American groups.

They were just kids. They were teenagers. America - the industry here – didn't want that music. They thought guitar bands were dead. They played the Loews, about 20 miles from me, in 1964 and got hassle with the police for having long hair in the pool. They were playing to a half-filled football stadium and then got in trouble at the hotel because you were not allowed to have long hair in pools at that time. You had to wear bathing caps in this country.

When WORC announced the Rolling Stones were coming in April 1965 to the same auditorium I already owned two records by them, 'Time Is on My Side' and 'The Last Time'. I was so excited that I played the 45 of 'The Last Time' over and over in my room. I could not believe that my father, a big jazz fan, commented how much he liked the tune. I was vindicated.

My parents drove me and my brother, Stephen, to the auditorium, where I would meet my cousin Linda and her girlfriend. I was let in early by the manager as he was a close family friend. My mom was concerned about the crowds and potential trouble. I sat down in the front with about 10-15 others in a very calm environment when suddenly the doors opened and crowds of young girls raced in, hustling and jockeying for seats.

In those days a DJ often introduced the band in front of a curtain, and I believe the promoter of the show, Dick 'the Derby' Smith, was that man. He told me later he paid the band $3,000. He added he wanted to bring them back the following year, but the price was $30,000! Anyway, the big maroon curtain opened, and there they were.

While there was a lot of screaming it always came at the end or beginning of a song or with some gesture by Jagger. One could barely hear him sing but the band came through. That show was one of the best I ever heard in terms of how exciting it was and how tight the band was. It did not last long, and we all dispersed to our rides home with a brief but amazing memory.

### I WAS THERE: STEVE SMITH
While I was too young to go to the show, my father Dick Smith, a disc jockey and music director at radio station WORC, was one of the producers of the concert. It was his only venture into concert promotion, and he barely broke even that night. I know there were a lot of unsold tickets around the house.

### I WAS THERE: PAT BRUEMMER
The police actually threatened to shut down the show when Mick started to take off his sports jacket!

### I WAS THERE: BARBARA ANDERSON, AGE 14
Can you believe the price of the ticket? I remember going with girlfriends from school, and someone's parents drove us there. I assume my parents didn't mind as they let me go and undoubtedly paid for the ticket. I recall the excitement of being there, the electricity in the air and being a part of the screaming crowd.

### I WAS THERE: JACK MURRAY
I was on crutches at the time and was allowed to enter the building via a ramp where vehicles would enter. Once inside we found ourselves next a limo. Once the door opened, I was face to face with Brian Jones. A quick 'hello' and he was whisked away...

### I WAS THERE: KERRY PARSLOW, AGE 14
I was two months shy of 15 years old, living in Waltham, a suburb of Boston, when I found out the Stones would be playing just west of us in Worcester. The band was not yet popular in our Beatles-obsessed schools, but two of my best friends and I were fans of the Stones.

The very first LP I bought was the Decca UK

*Kerry Parslow was 14 when she first got to see the Stones*

# THE ROLLING STONES IN THE SIXTIES: A PEOPLE'S HISTORY

release of the Stones' first album - the one with the dark portrait of the band on the cover but without *England's Newest Hitmakers* splayed across the top. It had 'Mona' on it instead of 'Not Fade Away'. The LP had unaccountably shown up in a bin of 'remaindered' assorted records at the corner Rexall drug store. How it got there I will never know, but I paid $1.88 for it. Unfortunately, that LP disappeared many years and many college roommates ago, but I played the heck out of it while I had it.

We three girls got tickets for the Stones show, which I believe only cost $2.50 each. It sounds crazy today, but since I only earned 50 cents an hour for babysitting and my allowance was $2 per week, this amounted to five hours' wages for me. The ticket I bought for the Stones concert in 2015 cost $180, which was only four hours of my adult wages, so I can't really complain about ticket price inflation.

The dad of my friend Sue drove us to the concert, about 30 miles away. He went and hung out at a bar until it was time to pick us up afterwards. People were less attentive about drunken driving back then, it seems. I recall he seemed awfully jolly when he arrived to chauffeur us home.

I remember going up the front steps of the columned theatre and how old and dark it looked inside. There was a decent sized crowd, but the theatre was not completely filled and it was nothing like the mob of hysterically screaming and crying girls we encountered seven months earlier when we saw The Beatles live at Boston Garden. Though the audience for the Stones was clearly excited, I recall there being more guys in the fan-base as well as somewhat older kids, and not as many pre-teen or younger types. I liked that - I was a bit of a hipster snob even back at that tender age and felt superior to my Beatles-crazed peers for having such sophisticated taste to like the Stones.

A solo singer did the warmup. It wasn't anyone we were familiar with, but we were all so hyped on the British sound that they got a good reaction from the pumped-up crowd. Before the Stones started, an announcer invited people sitting in the rear seats to come down towards the front and fill in empty seats, because they had apparently not sold out. I later heard the audience was less than 3,000.

Unlike audiences of today, everybody pretty much stayed in their seats, even when the Stones came out to play their set, though some kids stood up and a few danced in the aisles towards the end. The stage was very plain, as rock shows typically were in those days - just a curtained backdrop with the band standing towards the front of the bare stage.

Our seats were about eight rows back, just right of centre. I remember being only about 20ft from Mick Jagger while he sang and was very excited to see him perform so close by. He looked younger and skinnier in person than he had on *Ed Sullivan* and did a lot of Elvis-like gyrating with the mic stand.

He didn't prance around and across the stage as he would later in his career. He was wearing black and white houndstooth-check pegged pants, black boots and a snug black short-sleeved jersey with a collar. Teenage girls tend to remember that stuff vividly - and I admit I was staring at his crotch, which was pretty well outlined in those pants!

The other band members pretty much stood in place during the set. They gave a respectably good show, but I did not get the feeling they were delighted to be there. In retrospect, they had just played two shows the day before in Albany after having bussed down from Canada, having to leave for New York City right after the concert, so were probably a little fagged.

The Stones remain among my top 10 performers of all time, perhaps even the top five. How could they not be?

## I WAS THERE: STEPHEN BAKER

My best friend's uncle managed the Worcester Auditorium and got us second-row seats. My only clear memories are that they opened with 'Everybody Needs Somebody to Love' and I recalled they all wore jackets and ties. I don't remember anyone getting out of their seats or rushing the stage.

## I WAS THERE: JAY ROMASCO, AGE 15

I went with my sister Fran. We were nuts about the Stones, even more so than The Beatles, who I also saw. Fran pushed to find the tickets. I'm not sure how she did it, but she was always out front on the

Siblings Fran and Jay Romasco were nuts about the Stones

Stones shows and we went each year in Massachusetts in the mid-Sixties, seeing them at the Boston Garden and the Lynn Bowl.

My uncle drove us up to the Auditorium along with my cousin, who was Fran's age. It was a beautiful spring night in central Massachusetts. The Auditorium was buzzing like crazy with anticipation. This area was soul and blues territory. The Auditorium was a central venue for anything show-wise or sports-wise in Worcester County. It was a very simple theatre stage, maybe six feet high, and they had folding chairs on the floor.

There was no one like the Stones then – there still isn't - with their hardcore sound and their attitude. We could not get enough of that whole R&B sound and their image. The Beatles were cool, but the Stones had something far cooler going on than any other band, including The Beatles.

We were in the balcony that surrounded the floor in a U-shape. The floor and balcony were packed. We were on the left facing the stage. The place was frantic to hear and see the Stones. There was a theatre curtain on the stage and the crowd went absolutely nuts when the curtain opened.

Fran started screaming and kept screaming throughout the show. I didn't care because every girl it seemed was screaming and, like all guys, I was glued to the sight of the Stones on stage and mesmerized by the sound of their fresh, infectious R&B. We knew every note by heart, so the noise of the crowd didn't matter. Their sound was fantastic despite that.

Bill Wyman, always on the left on bass, with Brian Jones between him, Mick centre, Charlie behind Mick on the drums, and Keith to the right. The whole band had amazing presence. The set-up was so simple, with one big amp for each of them, sitting out cleanly on the big stage and with mics in front of them to the main PA. It was a great, clear sound, even with the screaming.

At one point in the show Mick took off his jacket, folded it up and pretended to throw it into the crowd, but flung it behind him on stage. He was incredible as the leader, gyrating like crazy while the crowd went wild. Keith was incredible singing harmony while he played. We loved Mick but were nuts for Keith. Fran actually got a fan letter back from him that year.

They closed the curtain during 'The Last Time' but the Stones kept playing and they opened the curtain again, causing the crowd to go absolutely berserk. My memory is that they played for at least an hour. It was tremendously satisfying and worth every penny of our $3 tickets. Yes, $3! We were beyond happy when we filed out and my uncle picked us up in his Dodge, right near the Auditorium. I went back to my little high school band and told the guys we should play only Stones tunes. Fran and I continued to wear new grooves in those London LPs.

## I WAS THERE: FRANCES ROMASCO, AGE 14

My brother Jay and I were very lucky because our parents let us listen to music all the time. I knew many young people who were not allowed to listen to the radio at all because their parents didn't approve of it or who were restricted in their listening time because of their schoolwork. Our father was a very well-known singer in our area. He sung with Charlie Barnett's band and others in the Thirties and Forties. While we were growing up, he was always singing at many different functions and was choirmaster at our church.

I remember hearing music in our house from the time I was very little. Dad liked to listen to jazzier stuff, like Sarah Vaughn. My older sisters watched *American Bandstand* in the afternoons after school, and later we all watched the *Dick Clark Show* on Saturday nights. My sisters always fought about which radio station to listen to – WBZ (Boston) or WORC. AM radio at that time played everything from pop music to show tunes to movie themes, so we were exposed to many types of music. And the radio was always on, in the car and in the house.

Jay and I were huge Stones fans from the first time we heard them. They were very different from The Beatles, who we really loved. The Stones played rhythm and blues. They introduced us to the kind of music our own country had not let us hear - the Chicago blues sound and soul music. Their music had an entirely new emphasis on the guitar instead of the voices. It wasn't as much about the harmony in the songs, like The Beatles were doing, and their lead singer had a very distinct sound.

And for me, the lead singer had it all. By this time, I had amassed a very large collection of pictures and playing cards of John Lennon and Paul McCartney, but when the Stones hit, that instantly changed to Mick and Keith.

# THE ROLLING STONES IN THE SIXTIES: A PEOPLE'S HISTORY

I'm sure we first got word about the Worcester concert from the radio station, WORC. We listened to it constantly on our little transistor radios. I think the first hit song the Stones had in our area was 'It's All Over Now', with its clapping, jangling guitar opening.

I overheard a girl talking about the upcoming Stones concert at a school function. She was my age. I immediately started talking to her about the concert and she told me how she had gotten the tickets. That girl became my best friend and remained a good friend for the next 45 years.

There were two things in my life of equal importance at that time – music and fashion, as they still are now. Deciding what to wear to a Stones concert was of ultimate importance to me. For that concert, I chose a pair of stone-coloured jeans, a turtle-neck jersey and a very cool Madras jacket and matching Madras newsboy cap, like the ones John Lennon and Mick were wearing. I thought I looked totally fab.

I don't remember who we went with, but most likely our little sister Terry came along, and one of the guys in Jay's band. Jay, of course, remembers the equipment the Stones used. Being in a band, it was very important to know what instruments and amplifiers your idols were using.

I, mostly, remember Mick. He was riveting from the minute he was out on that stage, in constant motion and doing that high step he did, shaking those maracas and grabbing the stand-up microphone, bending it down to the floor. Jagger became the music with his dancing. None of us knew his dance moves were mostly straight out of James Brown's act.

My recollection is that they opened with 'Everybody Needs Somebody to Love' and I remember 'Little Red Rooster', 'Play with Fire' and 'Mona'. I was a screamer; and a damn good one if I say so myself, having been blessed with my father's singing lungs. I screamed through that whole concert. I recall that we were in the front row of the balcony because I remember hanging over it, screaming!

Mick Jagger was electrifying but, as much as I was obsessed with him, I wasn't a screaming teeny-bopper who didn't care about the music. If the Stones didn't play the music they played, I'm sure I would not have been interested in them. The music was what made them all so attractive.

I was totally mesmerised by Mick. But I remember watching Keith and Brian. They were all so cool. I remember seeing my father's car when we emerged from the auditorium. We all ran over to it. I'm sure we talked about the concert all the way home, and my dad was probably having fun hearing all that crazy enthusiasm for the music, even though he'd never have told us that. In fact, once when Dad saw the Stones on the *Ed Sullivan Show*, he said they sounded like a bunch of monkeys singing in a barrel! He liked The Beatles though.

We saw the Stones on every American tour from 1965 through 1975 apart from 1969. Every one of those concerts was a major event in our lives. The Stones' music was as important, or more important, than anything else in our teenage years and beyond. When *Their Satanic Majesties Request* was released, Jay drove us through a blizzard from Uxbridge, MA to Providence, Rhode island to get it! It was always like that: the music was worth it whatever it took to get it. Their music was the air we breathed. It's hard to imagine those years without the music of the Rolling Stones.

# ACADEMY OF MUSIC
## 1 MAY 1965, NEW YORK, NEW YORK

### I WAS THERE: RICK ARRA, AGE 10

My sister got tickets to a Stones concert as a Christmas present, with the stipulation that she had to babysit me!

# JOHN F KENNEDY INTERNATIONAL AIRPORT
## 2 MAY 1965, QUEENS, NEW YORK

### I WAS THERE: JUDIE FORCIER, AGE 16

I met the Stones at Kennedy Airport when they came in to do *The Ed Sullivan Show*. My girlfriend and I managed to get into the area where they were being held before going to their hotel. Andrew was not too pleased we got in there. My girlfriend talked her way in - she was good at that. It was a very short meeting. It was almost like what they call nowadays a 'meet and greet'. It didn't help that I was very shy at that time. I'm more outspoken now.

# THE ROLLING STONES IN THE SIXTIES: A PEOPLE'S HISTORY

# SOUTHERN COLLEGE HANNER GYMNASIUM
## 4 MAY 1965, STATESBORO, GEORGIA

### I WAS THERE: GLENN BRAY, AGE 16

I was a junior at Statesboro High School. My girlfriend and future first wife, Caroline, decided to go to the concert thinking we would never get another chance to see the Rolling Stones. As soon as school dismissed for the day, we headed to Georgia Southern College. We went this early so we could get a spot near the front of the line. We knew we would be in line for three or four hours, but we didn't care.

*Glenn Bray felt the Stones were maybe drunk or stoned*

We were accompanied by Caroline's best friend, Sherry, who passed away several years ago. Her boyfriend played in one of the warmup bands. We were in the first 25 people to enter the gymnasium that night and got great seats. The concert was sponsored and arranged by a local fraternity at the college, Sigma Epsilon Xi. The Bushmen and the Sons of Bach played first.

When the Stones took the stage, it was obvious from the outset they were drunk or stoned or something. Their performance was raggedy and poorly executed. The music and singing were sloppy and disappointing. After playing three or four songs they left the stage. We all assumed they were taking a break and coming back soon. But they didn't. The MC, president of the fraternity, came on stage to uncomfortably announce the Stones 'had left the building'. I remember there were outcries of booing and unhappiness from the audience.

And that was it. Caroline, Sherry, and I loaded up in my father's 1962 Ford Falcon and went home. I remember being disappointed at the time and thinking the Rolling Stones put on such a poor performance because this was little unimportant Georgia Southern College and Statesboro GA.

# THE ROLLING STONES IN THE SIXTIES: A PEOPLE'S HISTORY

## I WAS THERE: BETTY WICKHAM, AGE 18

I was a sophomore at GA Southern College at the time and my roommate and several friends from my dorm attended. My mother was tolerant of all music and knew I was infatuated with boy groups like The Beatles as well as 'my' Lettermen and Paul Anka. She wanted me to experience a concert. In those days the Student Activity fee was part of tuition, so I don't think I had to purchase a ticket, but you had to fight for one. I did purchase the programme, which I still have, profiling all five of them with some backstage and recording studio pictures. This was by Peter Jones. I somehow knew to hold onto it, even though it was a substantial part of my entire allowance.

As for the concert itself, it was dismal. They surely expected a large concert arena instead of a small gymnasium seating maybe 2,500. We were told some of their equipment did not arrive from Savannah and, to make matters worse, this was a dry county. So no booze within a 20-mile area and very little weed to be found. They were very pissed off when they heard this. Supposedly they were drinking and smoking pot on the way over in the limo and were already high on the trip over.

Mick Jagger could hardly stand when they finally got out there and no one was together, presumably using some of the other groups' amps and sound equipment. They 'performed' maybe three songs and were being heckled because they were so vulgar and incoherent. The other groups filled in some but mostly we all left very unhappy. But with the music scene headed in a different direction we all knew this was not the last we would hear of them.

## I WAS THERE: PHIL BLANCHARD, AGE 20

There was lots of talk on campus about the Stones appearing. I didn't actually purchase a ticket. A friend, Billy Massey, and I decided we would go to the Banner Gym to see if we could get tickets at the door. When we arrived a girl told us a friend had heard the band was seen outside the rear door of the gym. Billy and I wanted to see if they were still outside. We headed for the back door and there they were!

Phil Blanchard somehow got to blend in backstage

# THE ROLLING STONES IN THE SIXTIES: A PEOPLE'S HISTORY

Apparently they were trying to get a little fresh air as the gym was not air-conditioned and it was May in South Georgia. After hearing those accents, we knew it was the Stones. Minutes later they began to make their way back toward their dressing room.

Billy was the first to reach the door and was turned away by security. I was in the middle of the group and had longish hair. I think that's why I was able to get by security - I blended. After we got in the dressing room I asked if they needed anything. I think they assumed I was supposed to be there to assist them, as they never questioned my presence. Mick Jagger replied, 'Yes, a towel. It's fucking 'ot as 'ell in 'ere!' I had to go across to another locker room to get the towel. I returned, tossed the towel to Mick, and he said 'thanks an 'eap.' I noticed a fifth of bourbon next to a locker. One of the group asked if I would pour drinks. I, of course, complied. The fifth didn't survive too long.

They changed guitar strings and Bill Wyman gave me the used ones. When I got back to my room, I put these things on a closet shelf. At the end of the quarter, when I packed to go home, the items had disappeared. Back at the gym front entrance Billy told a couple of co-eds I had gotten into the Stones dressing room. Moments later, girls were outside the window screaming to get my attention. Of course, they wanted autographs. Not expecting a positive response, I asked if they would sign autographs for my friends. I was surprised when they said yes.

I located my registration form in my wallet, tore it in into several pieces, and thrilled my co-ed friends with their autographs. I later found a couple of autographs – Mick Jagger and Bill Wyman - on the floor. We chatted about their appearance on the *Ed Sullivan Show*. They asked if I was going into the concert, and I said yes. They said for me to just follow them in. I did and found a great spot on the floor in front of the spectator seats. The volume was so loud they didn't realise their microphones were not on, but that was soon corrected. Also, the girls were screaming so loudly it made it difficult to hear the singing. Many of the guys began to boo in response to the screams, and that continued through to their final number.

### I WAS THERE: MARY TOM VARN, AGE 18

I was a freshman at Georgia Southern College when the Rolling Stones appeared there. I was 18 and got to go backstage and meet them personally. I even got Mick's autograph on a matchbook. I was dating someone in the fraternity that sponsored the concert and he got tickets for me and friends. All the guys were busy helping that night, so I went with my roommate and a group of girls. Tickets were only $2.50, $3 at the door.

## JACK RUSSELL STADIUM
### 6 MAY 1965, CLEARWATER, FLORIDA

### I WAS THERE: BOB MCCOMB, AGE 13

Supposedly, the night Keith woke up and recorded the chords for 'Satisfaction' into his tape recorder, the Stones only played four songs because of rowdy fans. It was still amazing because we had just seen them on *Ed Sullivan* the previous Sunday singing 'Little Red Rooster'.

*Bob McComb had just seen the Stones on The Ed Sullivan Show*

## JACKSONVILLE COLISEUM
### 8 MAY 1965, JACKSONVILLE, FLORIDA

### I WAS THERE: GREG DINSMORE, AGE 12

I grew up in Jacksonville, Florida where we had radio station WAPE. They brought all the big 1960s bands to town, everyone from The Beatles to The Monkees. The Jacksonville Coliseum was a sports arena, with a small basic stage used by the bands. There were no strobe lights or

*Greg Dinsmore was mesmerised watching Brian play his white teardrop Vox*

special effects, just pure rock 'n' roll. The warmup bands played four or five songs highlighting their hit singles, and the headliner played about 45 minutes - a far cry from today's sets. The shows usually started at 8pm and the headliner took the stage at 10pm. The shows back then had several supporting acts. The Stones' show had the Righteous Brothers, Sir Douglas Quintet, and Sam the Sham and the Pharaohs on the bill, among others. The best seats in the house cost approximately $3.50 and general admission $1.50 or $2.

I went to the show with my 14-year-old brother. We had general admission seats. Since we were there when the doors opened, we got the primo general admission seats. These were upper seats surrounding the stage. We were no more than ten to twelve feet from the band, although we had to look down as we were located about ten feet above the stage.

I remember the Stones playing 'Time is on My Side', 'Little Red Rooster' and 'Around and Around'. Before 'Little Red Rooster', Mick had Charlie walk to the front of the stage and introduce the song. Also, I remember them play 'The Last Time', their current hit. They sung it on The Ed Sullivan Show earlier that week. The video is on YouTube and reflects exactly how the band looked when I saw them.

About midway through the Stones set, the ushers were not as attentive as earlier in the evening. As a result, I told my brother 'follow me' and proceeded to work our way down to the reserved seats on the Coliseum floor. In those days, if you had a floor seat you could work your way up to the stage. From that vantage point, you could look up and see the guys only a matter of feet away. One distinct memory I still have all these years later is of standing on the floor at the foot of the stage and watching Brian play his white teardrop Vox guitar. I was mesmerised. I was there a minute or two before the ushers told us to take our seats. At one point, Brian looked down and saw how into the music I was and briefly smiled at me. I will never forget that moment.

About 20 years ago, I was with my ex at the Hard Rock Café on Thanksgiving Day. On the video screens was a clip of the early Stones. I proceeded to tell my ex about my experience of seeing the Stones in 1965. The Hard Rock's manager overheard my story and offered us a tour of the Hard Rock vault after our meal.

We took the tour and the final item the manager showed me was

## THE ROLLING STONES IN THE SIXTIES: A PEOPLE'S HISTORY

Brian's Vox white teardrop guitar, the very same guitar I saw Brian play back in 1965. I really felt like things had come full circle. Needless to say, that was a magical moment.

### I WAS THERE: RICK DOESCHLER

I grew up listening to British Invasion bands. Seeing the Beatles in 1964 changed everything for me. I was hooked on music and the guitar. I formed a four-piece band in junior high school at Lake Shore Junior High. One day at school, the girl sitting next to me said, 'My boyfriend saw your band and wants to be your singer.' I thought, 'Well, OK.' So we set up a meeting, he tried out and was very good. He was two years older and had a car. He had never been in a band before and hadn't been a singer, but we didn't like to sing so the match was perfect. My band US was playing songs by The Beatles, Rolling Stones, The Kinks, etc.

Rick Doeschler went to see the Stones in the singer in his band's Mustang

One day it was announced the Rolling Stones were coming to Jacksonville to play at the Coliseum. We were very excited. I was, even at that time, a complete Brian Jones fan. No one else in the band mattered. I got it that Brian was the band, no question. As a player, even at my young age, I could tell this by how many instruments he played, and his arrangements were superb. Our singer had a red Mustang and drove us to see the Rolling Stones. Another life-changing experience. It was also a life-changing experience for our singer. Our band decided to break up as we entered high school. I kept playing, but not in any bands. Our singer did form another band and made it big. We were all friends, and I'm so glad they decided to keep with it and follow their dreams.

The singer's name? Ronnie Van Zant. His band became Lynyrd Skynyrd, who years later opened for the Stones at Knebworth in 1976. Can you imagine that?

THE ROLLING STONES IN THE SIXTIES: A PEOPLE'S HISTORY

# LONG BEACH ARENA
## 16 MAY 1965, LONG BEACH, CALIFORNIA

### I WAS THERE: KRIS GOLLON

My husband and I went to lunch with friends and were telling stories. They are very impressed by my husband's amazing experiences and concert attendance. I saved my only story for another time, but decided to make sure of the date and found your article calling anyone and everyone who saw the Rolling Stones at the Arena in '64 or '65. Thought you might be amused.

Since those were such early days of the phenomenal reactions to these groups, my girlfriend and I were innocent, as well as ignorant of what happened at concerts before taking on this adventure. My girlfriend had gotten several press passes from magazines like *Teen Beat*, and we went to this afternoon concert, haunting the back halls and hoping to catch a glimpse of someone. Of course, we got caught, were asked to leave since we had no tickets and were escorted to the back door. As we were standing at the top of the huge ramp, the Stones limo burst out of the underground garage. Screeching to a halt next to us, the rear doors flew open and a thick cloud of fragrant smoke (ripe with BO) rolled out. We all looked at each other for what seemed like a long moment, then I waved my hand in front of my nose and coughed. The door slammed shut and they started to drive off, but the screaming crowd had flowed around the Arena on the lawn and began flinging themselves from the cement ramp walls onto the limo. Fortunately, they were able to get away before the limo was completely surrounded and engulfed. It was also fortunate for the Rolling Stones that we didn't get into the limo. I was just 14 and my girlfriend was 16. Our parents had no idea we had ridden the bus from Compton to Long Beach to sneak into the Arena.

### I WAS THERE: MICHAEL SHAW, AGE 18

I went with my high school girlfriend. I would have just turned 18 and was soon to graduate. When we exited the concert hall into the round building foyer, there was a trapped limousine with the Stones inside being mobbed by kids. Think the limo was finally able to move off, but it took a while. I saw the Rolling Stones again when they played in Los Angeles. Ike and Tina Turner also played. I do not remember the date, but I remember Tina Turner - wow!

# THE ROLLING STONES IN THE SIXTIES: A PEOPLE'S HISTORY

## I WAS THERE: JANET GUDINO

I remember a girl climbed down the curtain from the balcony, landed on the stage and grabbed Mick Jagger in a huge bear-hug.

## I WAS THERE: MAUREEN ORCUTT, AGE 12

There were many bands that day, but we were there for the bad boys. Girls were screaming – me too! Girls were running on the stage and climbing down the red velvet curtains trying their hardest to get the band's attention.

The grand finale was being up close and personal to the car as it was leaving the arena. I touched it as I was pulled away by security. I was so thrilled to be part of the scene and did not know at the time, but my mom had got tickets for four days later to see the Stones with Sonny and Cher on the TV show *Shindig*! We were up front for that show and saw them when they came out in a Rolls Royce to do '(I Can't Get No) Satisfaction'. What a week.

## I WAS THERE: ANDREA TARR

The Long Beach Arena show seemed tamer than the Civic Auditorium show six months before. My friend's mother again came along. Like the Auditorium show it was packed out, but the Long Beach Arena seemed to hold more people than the other venue.

## I WAS THERE: ANNE STASKEWICZ-BOJOV

I was in that pile of girls who swarmed the car at the Arena concert. However, it was my compatriot who got the worst of it. The stories get embellished over the years, but I believe my friend was clubbed off the car by the police. No hospital, though, just a bad headache. Exciting times.

We have stories about all the concerts in the LA area – all three Beatles concerts, the last Doors show at the Bowl, Country Joe, the Stones all-nighter at the Forum, Buffalo Springfield at Cal Poly

Anne Staskewicz-Bojov was among those who swarmed the Stones' car

# THE ROLLING STONES IN THE SIXTIES: A PEOPLE'S HISTORY

Pomona, the Mothers at the Shrine dancehall, Cream at the Forum, Hendrix in the Valley, and many, many more. Ah, the Sixties in Los Angeles. It was like nothing else.

## I WAS THERE: KIKI MORISHITA, AGE 12

I liberated a copy of *Aftermath* from Thrifty's, a neighbourhood drugstore that had some bins of albums before Virgin Records or other popular record shops existed. A former fellow student called Janna says we went to the Stones together. We were seventh or eighth grade. The show was very exciting and I remember the tumultuous energy throughout, with the passionate outpouring from the audience never subsiding, and in particular the last song being 'The Last Time', their big hit at the time. The mass hysteria sensed it was their final song and immediately began leaving for the exits.

My mother had driven her very cool Corvair to pick us up after. She told me she had driven past the limo with the Stones inside and saw Mick at the window, then the hordes of fans rushed past her, in pursuit.

## I WAS THERE: VICTORIA SMITH, AGE 12

Having been a Beatlemaniac but liking the Stones as well, they were for me the rebels and I found much exhilaration in songs such as 'Satisfaction', 'Under My Thumb', '19th Nervous Breakdown', and 'Time is On My Side'.

I think it was 1965 when I actually 'liberated' the album *Aftermath* from Thrifty's, a neighbourhood drugstore that had some bins of albums before Virgin Records or other popular record shops existed. So you could perhaps attribute this teenage 'lifting' to them. I couldn't recall who had gone with me to see the Rolling Stones but a few years ago a former fellow student at that time called Janna said it was her. We were seventh or eighth grade.

The show was very exciting and I remember the tumultuous energy throughout, with the passionate outpouring from the audience never subsiding, and in particular the last song being 'The Last Time', their big hit at the time. When they began that, the mass hysteria sensed it was their final song and immediately began leaving their seats for the exits.

# THE ROLLING STONES IN THE SIXTIES: A PEOPLE'S HISTORY

Since my parents had divorced, I was living with my mother who was somewhat of a free spirit, of Japanese descent. She had driven her very cool Corvair to pick us up after the concert was over. She told me she had driven past the limo with the Stones inside and saw Mick at the window, then the horde of fans rushed past her in pursuit of the limo.

## I WAS THERE: WALT TURLEY

My father was a plain-clothes police officer working this concert and was able to get me and my brother in. Now, reflecting back, this concert was pretty unreal. It was The Animals, Paul Revere and the Raiders, The Byrds, and the Rolling Stones. I remember standing near the stage, people sliding down the curtain trying to get on stage, going crazy over the Stones.

## I WAS THERE: JOHN TURLEY

I was one of the police officers in charge of outside security at the Stones concert. Their limo was parked on the west side parking lot, and we ran with the Stones to the west exit and got them into their limo. There was already a large group of kids there. In order to move the limo, with it being already surrounded, I sat on the hood of it as it moved very slowly with me using my feet to push the ones in front away. We finally made it to the foot of Linden Avenue and the driver must have panicked as he drove really fast up the hill to Ocean Boulevard. It was a scary ride. I was still on the hood when he made a left turn onto Ocean Boulevard. I had nothing to hold on to except my fingernails in the grooves of the hood. At a high rate of speed he drove fast along Ocean Boulevard, not stopping for signals at several intersections.

At Golden Avenue he made another sharp turn to go south down a grade to where there was a helicopter waiting on the beach front. My intention was to drag out the chauffeur and do whatever to him. However, I had to hustle the Stones to the helicopter. When I then looked for the driver, he was long gone. Not too many people know this story and if I told this to anyone, they would not have believed me anyway. I still do not know how I hung onto the hood of that limo. I guess my legs hanging over the front helped.

## THE ROLLING STONES IN THE SIXTIES: A PEOPLE'S HISTORY

### I WAS THERE: PEGGY JONES, AGE 16

I was a complete Rolling Stones fan and in the early days it was still possible to run into them - with a lot of pluck and determination. I went to this show with my best friend, Marsha. I wore a dress that my mom made for me, and I felt very groovy. I saw there was an empty mezzanine level behind the stage with a curtain hanging from it that went all the way to the stage. I decided to get up there and slide down to the curtain so I could hug Mick Jagger. I was able to do it, although I fell about halfway down and sprained my ankle. I was about two feet from Mick when the security guys jumped me and carried me off stage, kicking and fighting to get loose. All my high school friends who were there couldn't believe what they just saw. It was a very big curtain. It must have been the adrenaline that made me do it.

Marsha and I heard on radio station KRLA that the Stones were staying at the Beverly Hills Hotel, so we drove there to see if we could see them. Imagine our surprise as we were waiting in the lobby of the hotel trying to act cool, when the elevator doors opened and all five Stones walked out, unattended, to the valet waiting area and sat on the bench, waiting for their car pick-up. We casually followed them and, when I walked out of the doors, I heard Mick say, 'That bird has nice legs!' We sat alongside them. I don't remember saying anything, but we were so excited to have another close encounter with our Rolling Stones.

*Peggy Jones' home-made dress made her feel quite groovy*

THE ROLLING STONES IN THE SIXTIES: A PEOPLE'S HISTORY

# COMMUNITY CONCOURSE CONVENTION HALL
## 17 MAY 1965, SAN DIEGO, CALIFORNIA

**I WAS THERE: CATHY MCCONNELL ARDANS**

My friend Nikki Smith, president of the fan club, got to meet Mick backstage. Sadly, I've lost the photos of that meeting. It was a crazy concert. I think they only played for about 25 minutes. They started the show with 'Not Fade Away' and the crowd went crazy. I was sitting in the front row and we immediately got pushed to the front of the stage. It was total chaos. Brian had his ribs taped from having been pulled off the stage in San Francisco a day or two earlier. A girl tried to grab him again this night. They ended up closing the show down because it was out of control. I talked to a friend of mine who sat further back, and where he was everyone was calmly sat in their seats.

---

*I was sitting in the front row and got pushed to the front of the stage*

---

The local paper printed a couple of photos from that show. There's one of the audience taken before the Stones came on. The opening act was The Byrds and I'm in the photo, looking like I'm grabbing my crotch! We saw the curtains part and all jumped up to see if we could see backstage. That's when the photo was taken. I was in the middle of loading film in my camera. I was clutching at my camera in my lap, not my crotch!

I only got a couple of photos. My camera got knocked out of my hands and that was it. Luckily, my friend who was with me grabbed my camera off the floor, so I least got these.

My favourite Stones are still the early Stones with Brian. As a young teen, I was a serious blues fan. My brother, who played guitar, turned me on to Lightnin' Hopkins, Muddy Waters, Howlin' Wolf, etc. I loved the blues influence of the early Stones.

# THE ROLLING STONES IN THE SIXTIES: A PEOPLE'S HISTORY
# ACADEMY OF MUSIC
## 29 MAY 1965, NEW YORK, NEW YORK

### I WAS THERE: LYNDA SMITH, AGE 15

I went with a girlfriend who also loved the Stones sound. I did not tell my parents I was going to the concert until after. They were a little upset I had taken the bus into NYC without telling them. I was living in the suburbs, about an hour bus ride into the city. I remember the really loud screaming and carrying on of the largely teenage girl audience over Brian Jones. The screaming was so loud it was hard to hear the music. And the pushing of the audience as the girls tried to get up to the stage was very annoying.

The concert was held in the 14th Street Academy of Music, an old-time movie theatre with floor seats and a balcony, so it was really easy for the audience to get out of hand. The Stones were the first group I got into that incorporated American blues with rock 'n' roll. I loved both forms of music and could not get enough of the Stones. As soon as a new album was released, I was always sure to get it. It was so long ago but, as it was the first Stones concert I went to, the memories are still clear.

### I WAS THERE: JOANNE BROOKLYN, AGE 15

The Stones played the Academy of Music, NYC in October 1964 on Bill Wyman's birthday. I was going to go but my brother decided to get married that day and I was a bridesmaid. I was 14 and very disappointed. In May 1965 I finally got to see the Rolling Stones at that venue. I was over the moon when Brian Jones and I coincidentally wore the same outfit - white pants and a black sweater. I was sure it was a sign we were meant to be together. He was already 23.

---

*Following their third US tour, the Stones returned to the UK to take to the stage in Scotland in June 1965.*

---

# ODEON THEATRE
## 15 JUNE 1965, GLASGOW, UK

### I WAS THERE: DAVID PATERSON, AGE 13

I first saw them at the Odeon, Glasgow in 1965. The main thing I remember was the atmosphere inside the Odeon before the show began. It was electric. The Hollies were the main support act, Graham Nash wearing a suit and bow tie. The screaming started with them but that was nothing compared to the arrival of the Stones on stage. It was complete bedlam and even all the guys in the audience were caught up in it. My seat was in the rear stalls and their first song was 'Everybody Needs Somebody to Love'. If you listen to *Got Live If You Want It*, that pretty well sums up the vibes. I was only 13 but this experience has never faded from my memory and I love the Stones to this day.

# CAIRD HALL
## 18 JUNE 1965, DUNDEE, UK

### I WAS THERE: MARGARET MACLEOD

My friend and I worked in Wilsons Restaurant then, and were asked to go along to the concert with sandwiches, etc, for the Rolling Stones and The Hollies, which we did with a police escort. We were allowed in the Stones and Hollies dressing rooms. I got all their autographs and foolishly gave them away, which I now regret. We also got to watch the show from the side of the stage. It was a night to remember, and we will never forget it.

### I WAS THERE: DOROTHY THOMSON, AGE 17

It was my first live concert. Although I was mad about Cliff Richard, I was also mad about the Stones. What a contrast! I went to the Saturday show with a couple of friends. We were upstairs at the side, overlooking the stage. When Charlie Watts led them on stage, I grabbed the nearest steward and almost threw him over the balcony. And, yes, I screamed all the way through but loved every minute.

# THE ROLLING STONES IN THE SIXTIES: A PEOPLE'S HISTORY

## I WAS THERE: BRENDA WILSON, AGE 18

I was there, near the front with a group of Bell Street College of Technology students. I was a student nurse at Dundee Royal Infirmary. I remember Mick Jagger strolling on stage. I was so close I could see him very well. The others sort of straggled on. I don't remember a screaming frenzy - not like The Beatles, where the noise was deafening. The whole concert struck me as rather sedate. I remember clapping in time to the music, especially to 'Satisfaction'.

Bill Wyman and Charlie Watts hardly moved a facial muscle. I was fascinated by Mick Jagger. I had never seen such a performance on stage. The singing, the posturing, the movements, the music - I was hooked! It didn't appear overly loud, and I could make out the words of his songs. I think they played 'Little Red Rooster'. Keith Richards just stared at Mick, occasionally coming up front to sing his bit. Brian Jones looked bored, as if playing to a rural backwater was not his scene. I remember clapping politely to the music. I even kept my coat on.

## I WAS THERE: MARI PHILLIPS

I was in the second row, having saved my milk-round money up for the ticket, and was still a fourth-year pupil. The band so nonchalantly strolled on, one by one. So cool then. Mick's cool moves. Bill Wyman deadpan, guitar held high, Charlie Watts. The late but oh so talented Brian Jones, and, of course, Keith Richards.

I recall the screaming and also a St John Ambulancemen looking stunned at the hysterical audience. I also recall going home to my teenage years' home, in a poor housing estate in Dundee, on cloud nine. No one I have ever spoken to about their Caird Hall gig seems to remember how they simply and casually strolled on to that stage and then that bass guitar started up. Something big was happening outside Dundee in the rock world and I, a screaming teenager, had just been part of it. It is a night I just never forgot.

*At the end of June 1965, the Stones embarked upon a short Scandinavian tour, taking in Norway, Finland, Denmark and Sweden, before a further UK tour in July.*

# THE ROLLING STONES IN THE SIXTIES: A PEOPLE'S HISTORY

# ODEON THEATRE
## 16 JULY 1965, EXETER, UK

**I WAS THERE: PAUL WALTERS**

Me, and a guy called Charlie, who looked a bit like the comedian Charlie Drake, were doing tabs. When the curtains open or close at either side of the stage, you hold the tab as it goes across, and any microphones it's going to knock over as it goes across you just pull back out the way so the tabs open and close cleanly. So we were expected to stand behind the curtains and make sure they didn't knock the microphone stands over as they opened.

*Paul Walters backstage at the Odeon Theatre, Exeter, with Lulu*

It must have been the first show of the evening. Looking from the stage to the audience, I was on the left-hand tab and Charlie was on the right-hand curtain. I was tall and skinny and gangly, Charlie was this little guy with a bald head. Mick was doing these warming-up exercises. He was quite into that, stretching and doing all this sort of thing. He came up to me and said, 'Look, would you mind changing sides with this other guy?' I said, 'No, that's absolutely fine. I'll do the right-hand tab and he'll do the left.' Mick said, 'That's absolutely brilliant.' I said to Charlie, 'I've no idea why he wants us to do this, but he wants us to change sides.' Mick had one of these big old-fashioned mics, uni-directional, with a big chrome head on it. He went up to Charlie and said, 'Charlie, can you hold this? Because what I'm going to do, I'm going to do some exercises. I'm going to come up, I'm going to grab the mic from you and, as the curtains go back, I'll be invigorated, and I'll walk on to the middle of the stage.' Charlie said, 'Yeah, that's ok, no problem.' So Mick gave him the mic and Mick said, 'Don't forget. Don't move. As the curtains open, I'll grab the mic and come out.'

So the curtains were closed and they started up with 'Satisfaction'. And Mick was dancing about. Charlie was thinking, 'OK, come on then,

Mick. When are you going to come up?' The curtains started opening. I walked back with my side. Charlie was in the middle of the stage now, holding this mic and thinking, 'Shit, what am I doing here?' Mick came up, calmly took the mic from him, kissed him on the head in full view of the whole audience, and started singing. The band were killing themselves laughing.

# GUILDHALL
## 17 JULY 1965, PORTSMOUTH, UK

**I WAS THERE: BRUCE HORN**
I had previously seen them at the Gaumont in Southampton. By the time of the Portsmouth show, they had learnt some crowd control and said they wouldn't start the next song until the crowd was quiet.

**I WAS THERE: MICHAEL SMITH**
They played 12 tunes. You could just make out 'Satisfaction' and 'The Last Time', but the others I don't think anybody knew what they were playing because of all the stupid girls screaming their heads off all the time. In the run-up they only had to mention the Rolling Stones and that set the screamers off again. But the band just came on, jumped about and played the music. They weren't worried about all the noise.

# GAUMONT THEATRE
## 18 JULY 1965, BOURNEMOUTH, UK

**I WAS THERE: MICK MILLER, AGE 19**
The bill included The Paramounts, who later became Procol Harum. I used to dance to The Paramounts in Southend-on-Sea, Essex every weekend in the early Sixties. I was working on the Swanage Railway as a fireman and was lodging in Swanage.

When I saw the Stones were doing a gig at Bournemouth, I and a pal went to see them. We managed to get backstage to visit the boys from Essex, and Mick Jagger was in their dressing room. After talking to Gary

Brooker and Robin Trower from the Paramounts, Mick asked if we would like to meet the rest of his group. We jumped at the chance, and he took us across the back of the stage to their dressing room on the other side. All the other Stones were there. Charlie came over to me, said, 'I've just split my trousers under the crutch' then showed me the repair he had done with pink cotton. I got all the Stones' autographs that day only to lose them later that evening showing them off to some girls in a pub. One of the girls snatched the autographs from me, the girls and the autographs never to be seen again.

Steam loco fireman Mick Miller was stoked up by the Stones

# ABC THEATRE
## 25 JULY 1965, GREAT YARMOUTH, UK

### I WAS THERE: WENDY QUILLIAM

My brother and I were there by a freak of nature that occurred in either my mother or father's brain whilst holidaying at Golden Sands Caravan Park in Great Yarmouth. Mick Jagger was going out with Marianne Faithfull at the time, and she performed as well. We had really good seats in the theatre.

### I WAS THERE: ADRIAN HOOD, AGE 14

My memories are of Mick Jagger's hypnotic move across the stage and the fantastic groove that was created. I also recall a very tall guy ran down the auditorium and leapt over the orchestra pit and got on stage. He then proceeded to hug Mick Jagger, until two guys came on stage and pulled him off.

# THE ROLLING STONES IN THE SIXTIES: A PEOPLE'S HISTORY

## I WAS THERE: SHEILA ROLL

Unlike when we saw them in Lowestoft a year before, here we were sitting – well, standing and screaming from our cinema seats – with no chance of getting near them. The cinema was full of screaming girls. The best song was 'Everybody Needs Somebody to Love'. Mick Jagger bent down and pointed as he sang, 'I need you, you, you, and I need you, you, you.' There were incredible screams every time he did it. Each girl hoped he meant them. Wonderful. We couldn't get anywhere near them that time, so I treasure my autographs from 1964.

## I WAS THERE: DAVID TATE, AGE 22

I worked at the ABC Regal for several years as a film projectionist then a follow spot operator, controlling the stage sound and lighting, until I eventually became the stage manager.

On the day the Rolling Stones played there I was on the sound desk at the rear of the stalls. The in-house sound system was very basic compared to modern-day sound rigs. It only amplified the vocals. There were six on-stage mics, one off stage, and three rising mics. Stage monitors, now a very important part of a sound rig, were limited to one off-stage speaker. Drum kits were not miked up and the guitars relied on the amps brought in by the bands. Successful bands like the Stones had roadies, but many turned up in an old Transit style van and humped the gear in themselves, with our help.

David Tate, third right, worked at the ABC Regal

Each of the two Rolling Stones performances had around 1,400 screaming fans drowning out the sound of the band. It was all about atmosphere, not sound quality. My wife also worked at the theatre, doing several duties, including box office and secretarial work for the artists. On the evening of the Stones concert, working as an usherette, the theatre management required her and other staff members to stand at the front of the balcony to stop crazed female fans jumping down into the stalls. They had all decided to stand aside if this happened, fearing for their own safety. Fortunately, it did not happen. It was quite a high balcony with a steep seating area, providing good sight-lines. A team of first aiders were at the front of the stalls rescuing fainting fans from being trampled upon. After being revived in the orchestra pit, the fans were placed back among the seething mob.

At the stage door, fans crowded around and a group of young girls removed a double extension ladder from the back wall of the theatre. They then attempted to gain access to the dressing rooms. Order was restored by theatre staff and, again, fortunately no one was hurt. Overall, it was quite a night.

### I WAS THERE: CAROL SCOTT, AGE 15

I went with a school friend and we went to the early show as we had school the next day. It was amazing - the first gig I had been to. We sat about five rows from the front.

I remember Mick Jagger walked down from the stage and we all tried to move from our seats to go and touch him, but so did half the audience. They were so good live even in those days. I can't remember each song they sang but they did my favourite, 'Satisfaction', and I'm sure they were looking at me whilst singing. After the show we went to the stage door to try and see them leave, but were told they had already gone.

### I WAS THERE: JOHN BULLOCK, AGE 16

I had just started work at a shipping company in 1965, and in the evenings - to earn extra money to buy a Mini - I worked at a holiday camp in Hopton-on-Sea. The boss' daughter Susan Caster, sweet 16, came with me to the Rolling Stones gig. As I did not have a car at the time, we caught the bus and Susan's mum took us back to the holiday camp after the concert.

I remember just walking into the booking office and buying two tickets for the circle - numbers A1 and A2 - with an excellent view of the stage. Bill Wyman started off with 'Everybody Needs Somebody to Love' on his haunting bass guitar, smoking a cigarette, which he placed in the upper neck between drags. I am sure the show also finished with Wyman again playing the same number as Mick and the rest of the band disappeared through the stage door. We both enjoyed the whole evening, people were dancing in the aisles to quite a few numbers.

### I WAS THERE: HELEN PLANE, AGE 14

I was there along with my cousin Wendy. I remember queuing early in the morning and my mother getting in the queue for me as I had to go to school. We sat five rows back. Wendy swapped her own maracas at the stage door for Mick's. I have the programme - Bill Wyman's head has black pen round it. He was my favourite Stone. I have two records - *Got Live If You Want It* and *Five by Five*. They've not been played for 40 years or more.

### I WAS THERE: WENDY WILLIAMS (NÉE BETTS), AGE 15

I went with my cousin Helen. I had, prior to the concert, bought a new pair of green maracas out of my pocket money in a music shop in Regent Road, Great Yarmouth in the hope of swapping them for Mick Jagger's. After the concert, I went to the stage door at the rear of the building and the road manager came out, so I asked if he would swap mine for Mick's, which he did. Mine were green and new, Mick's were red with a hole in one of them. I have them to this day.

Wendy Williams swapped maracas with Mick

## FUTURIST THEATRE
## 22 AUGUST 1965, SCARBOROUGH, UK

### I WAS THERE: DEREK COOK

My sister Pam worked in the booking office at the Futurist Theatre and, partly because of her, my band The Methods played on the same bill. Also on the bill were The Roving Kind, Keith Powell, and Lulu and the Luvvers. Alan Field was the compere.

We actually did two spots. We opened because somebody didn't turn up. Lulu was fantastic and the Stones couldn't be heard vocally because of the lousy cinema PA system and the girls screaming. A gig to remember. My drummer at the time, Kelvin Robertson, enjoyed a good chat with Charlie about drums and drumming.

The Methods and their van. On the same bill as the Stones, drummer Kelvin Robertson enjoyed a good chat with Charlie about drums and drumming

### I WAS THERE: KELVIN ROBERTSON, AGE 17

I was in a band and we did a gig at the Futurist in Scarborough as the stocking-filler. They wanted a cheap local band to start each show off. We did 20 minutes at each show and in the interval, I sat on Charlie Watt's drums and chatted with him. I think he was new to independents, which is the art of playing something different with each hand … and feet when you are up to speed. I demonstrated the technique as I played it for 'Pink Champagne'. Charlie had a band of his own playing jazz and, who knows, maybe I was his inspiration. Lulu was the closing act for the first half and kept calling them the 'Rowlin' Bownes.'

### I WAS THERE: PAM HAYDEN, AGE 18

I met them in the theatre I was working in. The Futurist Theatre could hold about two and a half thousand. They put on pop shows following the wrestling craze. I met the Stones as they were preparing to do a show (my brother Derek was on the same show). They were asked to find a local band to appear and somebody came up with Derek's group. They went down a storm as they were well known in Scarborough.

The show was a sell-out but if there were any cancellations they needed somebody to sell the tickets. That's when they'd come in and have a chat. One of them chatted me up – Charlie, the drummer. He was married at the time, so I told him where to go. I was surprised how scruffy they all were when they came in. We thought they were going to get changed, but they never did. They went on stage as they came. It was a bit of a let-down.

## PALACE BALLROOM
### 8 SEPTEMBER 1965, DOUGLAS, ISLE OF MAN, UK

**I WAS THERE: PHILIP RYDER, AGE 10**

My recollection is of meeting the Stones in 1965 at the Castle Mona hotel on the Isle of Man. I was 10 and we arrived on the Saturday to start a week's holiday with my grandparents.

During the afternoon we went to the gardens of the hotel and the Stones were there having afternoon tea. My cousin and I approached them nervously and asked for their autographs, which they gave us. We then sold them to the fans waiting outside for 2/6d (13p) and spent our profits at the toy shop. What fools. If only we had kept them.

The Stones on the day of their Palace Ballroom show on the Isle of Man

## HALLE MÜNSTERLAND
### 11 SEPTEMBER 1965, MÜNSTER, WEST GERMANY

**I WAS THERE: HANNS PETER BUSHOFF, AGE 14**

I was living with my parents in Münster when the Rolling Stones played their first ever German concerts, one at 5pm and one at 8pm. It was my first concert and I had to beg my parents for weeks to go there. I went to the afternoon show, a package show with some other bands, and later I read the Stones played only half an hour or so. For me it was an eternity. I don't have the ticket stub anymore and didn't take pictures. I wish I had, but I would have been far too excited to hold the camera straight.

# THE ROLLING STONES IN THE SIXTIES: A PEOPLE'S HISTORY

## COLSTON HALL
### 26 SEPTEMBER 1965, BRISTOL, UK

**I WAS THERE: JOHN LEIGHTON, AGE 14**
I lived in Bath at the time. My uncle who lived in Bristol bought tickets for me at the Colston Hall and it just sort of blew me away. I had good seats in the upper circle, and it was when 'Satisfaction' had just come out.

It was absolutely amazing. Brian Jones was still with them and I remember Mick wearing these white jeans and this t-shirt with horizontal blue and white stripes. That's all I wanted to buy afterwards. The support band was Unit Four + 2 and they were good, but no one was interested.

It was absolute pandemonium. The Stones were only on for about an hour. It was just screaming girls and people trying to get on the stage and everything. But where we sat we had good vision, reasonably good sound, and it was absolutely fantastic.

Because all you'd ever seen was grainy black and white images on TV and you'd be listening to Radio Luxembourg at night to the Teen and Twenty Disc Club, or whatever. As a 14-year-old you just go home with it in your head and I had to go and get one of those t-shirts. I had to get the white jeans. That's all I wore. It was superb.

On the back of that I bought their first album. It left a lasting impression on me. I've taken my boys to see them. I took them to Wembley in '95 and my eldest son decided he had to play guitar. He picked up the guitar, got a few chords. I bought him an electric one and now he earns a living playing guitar. And a lot of his stuff is Stones based. I've been following the Stones ever since. The buggers have cost me a fortune.

## ODEON THEATRE
### 27 SEPTEMBER 1965, CHELTENHAM, UK

**I WAS THERE: JOAN HEMMING, AGE 17**
I saw them twice at the Odeon. Brian Jones' grave is in the cemetery in Cheltenham. I often park alongside the grave when I go to any funeral there.

# GRANADA THEATRE
## 29 SEPTEMBER 1965, SHREWSBURY, UK

**I WAS THERE: ELIZABETH DAY (NÉE MORGAN)**

I attended a Rolling Stones concert in Shrewsbury. The bus was organised by the Young Conservatives and as we had to leave Ludlow early, some of the young men, who I think were bank clerks, were still in formal suits and looked over-dressed. As I had just left college and started work, I went along more out of curiosity and as a means of getting to know people than as a fan of the Stones.

We were seated in rows in the theatre and, as the evening warmed up, some of the girls in the audience showed their appreciation and were getting rather noisy. The most memorable part of the evening for me was when a girl sat behind me leaned forward, tapped me on the shoulder, and asked, 'Why aren't you screaming?' Every time I hear the Rolling Stones or see their picture in the papers now, I visualise Mick Jagger performing somewhere on a stage below me and remember that nameless girl and her comment.

# ABC THEATRE
## 1 OCTOBER 1965, CHESTER, UK

**I WAS THERE: ALAN POWELL, AGE 14**

Years ago I bought and started a Beatles scrapbook. I painstakingly cut out everything I could find on the Fab Four. Then one day I was hit by a bolt from the blue and, reversing the scrapbook, I started pasting in cuttings of the Rolling Stones.

I used to watch *Top of the Pops* avidly but was mocked by my father, who derided all the acts as rubbish - especially 'the bloody Rolling Twerps' as he called them. Then it was announced they were going to play the ABC Theatre in Chester and a big boy I knew said he was going to bunk off school and go for tickets. I begged and pleaded, and he got me one. I still have the ticket, which cost twelve shillings and sixpence (63p).

I got the bus from Ellesmere Port. You didn't want to miss the last one back or you'd be stranded in Chester - the big city! There were two performances and my ticket was for the second - front stalls, seat H2. The audience was a mixture of boys and girls. There was a full supporting cast of The End, The Original Checkmates, The Moody Blues, The Habits, Charles Dickens, and the Spencer Davis Group, with teenage prodigy Stevie Winwood.

The Stones went down a storm. The screaming - from boys as well as girls - was deafening. All too quickly they finished with 'Satisfaction' and people tried to rush the stage. We were so close. The side doors opened and we rushed out for the last bus, separated only by a line of bobbies parallel to us as the Stones ran to their car. We stretched our arms. Brian was right in front of us, laughing as he dived into the car.

Oh yes - we got the last bus! I have the cutting from the Chester paper the following week. I wrote the track-list down in my special exercise book. Years later I met Bill Wyman and he read through the set-list, nodded, ticked my work, and signed the page.

## ODEON THEATRE
### 3 OCTOBER 1965, MANCHESTER, UK

**I WAS THERE: BERNARD CASWELL**
I think I paid 12/6 (63p) for my seat on the front row of the balcony. Contrast that with what you have to pay now to see them. I can't for the life of me remember who - or indeed if - there were any supporting acts. My main memory of that night is of the loud, incessant screaming from the girls in the audience, which I didn't really expect.

I saw The Beatles at the Apollo in Ardwick the previous year and, although the screaming there was loud and to be expected, the noise at the Odeon was louder. However, the songs could be heard despite the cacophony, and I thoroughly enjoyed the night. They played all their hits, but the only one that sticks in my mind is 'It's All Over Now' and its fantastic guitar riff intro, still one of my favourite intros of theirs. My one regret is not keeping the ticket stub or programme. The money I'd get for them now would be a very welcome supplement to my pension.

## GAUMONT THEATRE
### 4 OCTOBER 1965, BRADFORD, UK

**I WAS THERE: CHRISTOPHER ROPER**

My father dropped me off in town outside the then Gaumont, as he had the previous year for the Beatles. He had a Morris Minor with trafficators coming out of the side.

Paul and Barry Ryan were one of the support acts - I had been at the same school as them for a couple of years a short time previously. I attended the show alone and was downstairs in an end of aisle seat, about halfway from the stage.

## ABC THEATRE
### 5 OCTOBER 1965, CARLISLE, UK

**I WAS THERE: DEANNA SARGENT (NÉE BOERTIEN), AGE 14**

I went with my friend Jennifer Hyslop. It was a school day and we could barely concentrate on our work. We were from outlying villages so had to be transported each way and therefore couldn't hang around for a glimpse of their arrival at the ABC. However, as it turned out they were late as their car broke down on the motorway. Meanwhile, the supporting groups were in place, including Paul and Barry Ryan. During their performance one of the brothers dropped his microphone next to his brother, who was lying on the stage singing and walked off in a fit of jealousy.

*Deanna Sargent went with her pal, Jennifer Hyslop*

After what seemed hours there they were – Mick Jagger made his apologies and their performance was in no way affected by the delay.

We thought they were fantastic. We were quite near the front, and I remember thinking how young they looked. They were a bit more reserved in their appearance in those days. There was no trouble, no drugs, no alcohol. I don't even recall seeing a policeman. It was great.

## CITY HALL
## 7 OCTOBER 1965, NEWCASTLE-UPON-TYNE, UK

### I WAS THERE: PHILIP JOPLING, AGE 16

My girlfriend at the time, who went to the concert with me, was older. We went with two other couples. I remember our seats were midway from the stage in the stalls, but everyone was standing on their seats for the whole of the concert - you simply could not see anything when seated. In addition, the noise of everyone screaming drowned out the music, but the atmosphere was still fantastic.

## GLOBE THEATRE
## 8 OCTOBER 1965, STOCKTON-ON-TEES, UK

### I WAS THERE: IAN GILFELLAN, AGE 15

Jagger was hit in the eye by a coin at one of the concerts. PP Arnold was in The Ikettes, with a cast on her arm. The Spencer Davis group were still unknown, and someone came on dressed as a Dalek!

### I WAS THERE: DAVID CARTER, AGE 15

The Stones were supported by the Spencer Davis Group, and Unit Four + 2. The compere was Ted Rogers, later a TV host. Someone threw a coin on the stage which hit Jagger just above his eye, but he carried on while throwing blooded tissues into the crowd. What a night.

### I WAS THERE: SHEILA SOLBERG (NÉE EVENDEN)

We went to see the Stones twice at Stockton. Some idiot threw coins at the stage, cutting Mick on his forehead. We couldn't wait to get the *Gazette* to see the pictures of the show and find out what happened to Mick.

I remember seeing The Yardbirds, Spencer Davis Group, and other acts. Ike and Tina Turner were amazing, the energy was such I half expected her to run up the wall at some point.

I went with my friends Anne Hall and Jan Phillips. At the opening bars of 'Little Red Rooster', Jan fainted. We spent the next five minutes dragging her into the aisle for the bouncers to revive her.

### I WAS THERE: BARRY PARKIN, AGE 18

On the same bill as the Stones was a young Marianne Faithfull. As the Stones finished their spot, Mick Jagger introduced her. As he walked off stage she walked on and he gave her a kiss in the middle of the stage. Rumours were around that they were seeing each other, so you can imagine the reaction from the crowd.

# ODEON THEATRE
## 9 OCTOBER 1965, LEEDS, UK

### I WAS THERE: PAULINE GERRARD, AGE 17

My then boyfriend Tony Oliver and I begged and borrowed cash from our parents to buy two tickets in the front stalls. The begging was so worthwhile. After taking a two-hour journey involving three bus changes from Royston to Leeds, we joined the long queue at the theatre to see our favourite band.

The atmosphere was electric and when the Stones, dressed in their bizarre outfits, bounced onto the stage they could scarcely be heard above the screams and excitement of the audience. Jagger was phenomenal, covering every inch of the stage whilst performing his outlandish moves, but the loudest outburst came when Brian Jones was introduced - sultry, smiling, hair flopping over his eyes. Every female in the audience immediately fell in love with this broody guy.

They played all their well-known songs but it was hard to decipher which song was being sung above the screaming audience. I had already seen The Beatles, but the Stones gave them a good run for their money and I don't think one person in the audience that night regretted the price paid, the long journey, the queuing, or hearing only snatches of songs. Everyone left the theatre on a high.

## GAUMONT THEATRE
### 11 OCTOBER 1965, SHEFFIELD, UK

**I WAS THERE: ANDY THOMPSON, AGE 16**
I remember Unit Four + 2 were on with them, and maybe the Nashville Teens. At that time Jagger was wearing the sweatshirt with horizontal lines on. I remember them doing 'Johnny was a rockin' ('Around and Around'). Brian Jones wore a white polo-neck sweater. The screaming was slightly toned down compared with 1964. You could actually hear them.

## DE MONTFORT HALL
### 13 OCTOBER 1965, LEICESTER, UK

**I WAS THERE: KAREN SMITH, AGE 13**
A little group of us went. A friend's dad took us. I had been on holiday and bought one of those great big novelty combs you can buy at the seaside. I'd got this comb with me because it was all about their hair. The Beatles and the Stones were always being got at for their hair. I threw the comb on stage as a bit of a joke, and Mick Jagger picked it up and did his hair with it!

**I WAS THERE: MARILYN TAYLOR, AGE 16**
Although I was about three rows from the front, not a sound of their music could be heard. The only noise I could hear was screaming, myself included. It was as if they were miming. I was surprised but didn't care as I was 16 and had just had the best night of my life.

## ODEON THEATRE
### 14 OCTOBER 1965, BIRMINGHAM, UK

**I WAS THERE: JOHN BATES**
I remember the Stones' appearance at the Odeon in Birmingham. They had the Spencer Davis Group, The Checkmates, and Unit 4+2 as support, a Canadian comedian called Ray Cameron compering. The

audience were as energetic as for The Beatles but a little more wild, such was the reputation of both group and fans. The Stones were only on stage for about 30 or 40 minutes.

### I WAS THERE: LIZ WOLSEY, AGE 12
I was on the third row. All I remember is Mick Jagger taking off his tie, throwing it into the audience, and girls going crazy.

# ABC THEATRE
## 16 OCTOBER 1965, NORTHAMPTON, UK

### I WAS THERE: GEORGINA JEYES
As schoolgirls aged 13 and 14, we hardly missed a concert - The Beatles, the Stones, Gene Pitney, The Kinks, etc. I remember sticking my long fringe down at night with Sellotape in order to look like Cathy McGowan … in my dreams!

You were either a Beatles fan or the more rebellious were Stones fans. By the time the Stones came to the ABC, I was going out with Bob, who was 15 or 16, and we sat sedately in our seats at the front whilst the rest of the audience were on their seats screaming. I suppose I didn't fancy any of the Stones, and Mick Jagger did an amazing impersonation of our budgie, Bobby, and therefore made me laugh.

### I WAS THERE: KEITH SHURVILLE
I became a Spencer Davis fan in 1965. They appeared at the ABC as support for the Rolling Stones, when Keith Richard was hit by an apple and the Stones left the stage for a while. The chants of 'bring back Spencer Davis' did not go down well with the females close to us.

### I WAS THERE: PAULINE LEVER, AGE 14
I had just fallen head over heels in love with Brian Jones and the music and singing of the Rolling Stones. I lived in a small village seven miles from Northampton. The Rolling Stones were coming to town and a lady in our village had arranged a coachload of us to go and see the Stones perform. I remember I was so excited I felt as though I

would burst. My friend Kay was in love with Mick, so we were beside ourselves. We had seen other groups perform in town - even The Beatles - but no group or pop singer had ever made us feel like the Stones. We loved the rebellious attitude, the casual look and long hair, growing all the time. The music was sensational.

Once inside we sat through a good lineup, which we didn't really appreciate at the time. Unit Four + 2 were on and to be honest we hardly listened to them. Charles Dickens and another group called The Habits performed, and the Spencer Davis Group were on and very good. Stevie Winwood sang 'Every Little Bit Hurts'. But they had the job of performing just before the Stones, and by then we were at bursting point.

Suddenly, towards the end of the second half, compere Ray Cameron started to whip up the crowd saying, 'Come on, let's have a great big welcome for the Rolling Stones.' We all erupted into a frenzy, screaming and shouting. We found ourselves joining in with the hysteria that threatened.

The curtains came up and there they were - our idols, the best-ever group, and the most gorgeous boy I had ever set eyes on. We screamed and shouted and my eyes were firmly on Brian. Things were being thrown on stage and suddenly I was aware that Keith Richards had collapsed on stage, face down. Brian called for the curtains to close, Mick ran over, and Bill turned off the electrical equipment. We didn't know what had happened. Our hearts were pounding, and we were horrified at the thought that they wouldn't come back on.

The crowd sort of hushed, although there was a shout of 'fake!' from somewhere, and Ray Cameron came on and said Keith was fine, ad-libbing some jokes of sorts.

Then the curtain went up again, we screamed, and suddenly I had the urge to get to Brian. I was about five feet tall but could run and climb so I vaulted the stage and hoisted myself up - I can't imagine trying that now. A policeman grabbed my foot and pulled and I was aware he was determined to get me off, and it would hurt. The stage was almost my height and there was just a hard floor beneath me so, aware that I could be seriously injured if he was going to pull me off the stage, legs first, I waved to him and said I would get down.

He helped me down, threatened me and then went after some other hysterical girl. Subdued, I stayed close to the stage, eyes fixed on Brian, still screaming. The bouncers and police were very rough, but I suppose they had not come across this sort of adulation before and were unsure what to do.

One girl lay on her back kicking her legs screaming for Mick, and some bouncers sat on girls to keep them down. After the show, totally exhausted and still hyped up, we were ushered back to the bus. My friend and I sat and sort of cried and giggled and hugged each other, making little sense.

When I got in, my mum came and said, 'Well, was it good?' The adrenalin was settling and I was in a cold sweat and squeaked an answer at her. I could hardly speak. I remember Mum saying, 'You silly little devil, what a state to get yourself into. Whatever will Mrs Hayward think?' Mrs Hayward was the lady who always organised the coaches and tickets. The newspaper report the next day stated that it was not a bad show at all and the Rolling Stones stole the limelight but the fantastic performing audience came a close second.

## GRANADA THEATRE
### 17 OCTOBER 1965, TOOTING, LONDON, UK

**I WAS THERE: JANET HOBSON, AGE 19**
It was in Tooting Broadway at a cinema, very plush inside. I went with my girlfriend and we had to queue for tickets on a previous day. I wore a grey mini-dress with Peter Pan collar. It was a great night, with lots of screaming. Mick Jagger was jumping around on stage – as he still is – and Charlie Watts with that deadpan face. I kept the tickets for years but have misplaced them now.

*Following their sixth British tour, the Rolling Stones returned to the USA and Canada for their sixth North American tour.*

# WAR MEMORIAL
## 29 OCTOBER 1965, SYRACUSE, NEW YORK

### I WAS THERE: MIKE OTIS

I attended two Brian Jones-era Rolling Stones shows in Syracuse, New York, both at the War Memorial. The first was in October 1965 and had the Stones sharing a bill with the Ramrods, the Marathons, Patti LaBelle and the Bluebells, Monti Rock III and local band, Ed Wool and the Nomads. Seats were ticketed and tickets were $2. My memories include screaming, fainting girls and a very brief Stones set, lasting no more than 25 minutes.

# MAPLE LEAF GARDENS
## 31 OCTOBER 1965, TORONTO, CANADA

### I WAS THERE: DAVID SHAW

The first time I saw them there was screaming, but not bad compared to The Beatles, when hearing what was being played was an impossibility. Problem was, I had no Stones albums yet so had very little idea what was played that night. The main thing I picked up on was the fabulous drone put on by Brian and Bill. Keith Richards had his back to the audience for much of the show, seemingly keeping an eye on Charlie Watts, and Mick Jagger was quite sedate.

They returned less than a year later. They'd had some hits then and I had a much better grasp of what they were playing. 'It's All Over Now' was a standout, with Mick doing some amazingly acrobatic dance moves, seemingly levitating from one side of the stage to the other, and Brian and Bill providing an even better drone effect than the previous time. Brian was playing a Vox teardrop guitar and was dressed in black turtleneck and red cords, as he appears on the *High Tide and Green Grass* album cover. Keith still had his back to the audience most of the time. Mick was much more active than he had been during that earlier show.

### I WAS THERE: ROB SULLIVAN

I was at a few Stones concerts back then. My father knew a scalper who worked for hotels and always had extra tickets. We usually sat around fifth row centre, very good as the stage was about 10ft high, so our view was perfect. Once was with Brian Jones playing sitar, sitting lotus position on a dais in the middle of the stage. The stage was surrounded by security police and the venue turned on the lights after the show started, because they were afraid of a riot. Of course, it didn't happen. Another time I watched Keith walk up to the mic and touch it with his lips. The electricity wasn't sorted and he got a nice bright flash of blue light and got knocked on his back. Pretty scary. When 'Satisfaction' came out, they started a concert with that, and Keith's Maestro Fuzz-Tone crapped out in the middle of the intro. He picked it up and tossed it while Mick sat on the front of the stage with his feet dangling over the crowd's heads, all screaming of course. A roadie plugged in a spare Fuzz-Tone and all went as planned.

# ACADEMY OF MUSIC
## 6 NOVEMBER 1965, NEW YORK, NEW YORK

**I WAS THERE: ELLEN BEDELL**
I heard 'Not Fade Away' on the radio and that was it. My older brother got tickets to the Academy of Music show on 14th Street, Manhattan. We lived about an hour away. We got three tickets, so I had to sit alone – great. It was a smallish venue and I was in about the 10th row in the floor area. I had a very clear view of Mick. He wore his favourite old striped sweatshirt. They did 'Everybody Needs Somebody to Love' and got to the 'I need you, you, YOU' part, Mick pointing straight at me. I blew him a kiss. Girls around me were screaming, which I found annoying as I wanted to hear the band. I don't scream at concerts. The last song they played was 'The Last Time'. Well, it certainly wasn't the last time, because I saw them twice more, but I'll never forget the first. The Stones are a lifelong love.

*The Rolling Stones went on to play a second show that day in Phildelphia, PA.*

THE ROLLING STONES IN THE SIXTIES: A PEOPLE'S HISTORY

# CONVENTION HALL
## 6 NOVEMBER 1965, PHILADELPHIA, PENNSYLVANIA

**I WAS THERE:
TOM SHEEHY, AGE 15**

I never felt more alive than on the night I saw the Rolling Stones at the Convention Hall. I was planning on going with my friend Jim Fury, but at the last minute he had a hot date so bowed out. I went to the show solo. Opening the concert were Philadelphia's own Patti and the Bluebells. Patti would go on to become a superstar as Patti LaBelle, and Bluebell Sara Dash would years later join Keith Richard's X-Pensive Winos side-project. Keith once remarked he had his eye on Sara ever since that night in Philly.

It was my very first rock 'n' roll show. Needless to say, I was consumed with anxiety, because I sensed something significant was about to happen in my young life. From the moment the lights went down and I heard the opening chords of 'Everybody Needs Somebody to Love', my heart started pumping and didn't slow down until I got home. The Stones not only sounded amazing, they looked mesmerising as well.

Mick Jagger kept pointing to girls in the audience and calling out 'I need you, you, you!' which caused young women to scream, rush the stage, climb upon it and grab Jagger. Brian Jones was my fave member of the band and looked so cool in black turtleneck sweater and striped plaid trousers. Both Bill Wyman and Charlie Watts came off as the pensive lot, as they made very little facial moves, suggesting they were just taking it all in. Then there was Keith Richards flailing away at his Gibson, smiling at the audience continuously.

*Brian Jones, on stage in Philadelphia*

*Convention Hall attendee Tom Sheehy with Keith Richards*

Highlights were 'That's How Strong My Love Is', where Jagger fell to the stage, laid on it and sang from the floor, James Brown style. I was blown away when I heard the opening notes of 'The Last Time', because I could clearly see it was Brian who played the lead on that song, Keith supplying the rhythm parts. As the set progressed, it was quite obvious they were saving the best for last. They closed the show with '(I Can't Get No) Satisfaction'. I saw Keith step on a guitar pedal in front of him on the floor, which I later found out was a Fuzz-Tone, then he hit those immortal opening notes. It was the most powerful moment of the evening, and when I got home and my family asked how the show was, they all laughed at me because I think I was speaking in tongues, as someone might do when they just went through a dramatic religious experience.

# LINCOLN MOTOR INN
## 9 NOVEMBER 1965, NEW YORK, NEW YORK

**I WAS THERE: BARBARA NEUMANN BEALS**
I think they were staying at the Lincoln Motor Inn this time. And my sister said, 'Would you like to meet them?' I said, 'Are you kidding? Of course!' She didn't have to ask twice. She said, 'Just dress nicely and act calm. Don't act like you're about to meet the Stones.' Which was very difficult to do.

We went upstairs and went inside, and I was knock-kneed and frozen. They were five storeys up and had a little terrace outside. They'd been throwing things down at the fans. Mick Jagger appeared at the window. He knocked at the door. Apparently he was locked out. So my first vision was Mick Jagger, those blue eyes and that stunning face. He was pointing at the door to me, you know, 'Can you unlock it?' and I couldn't move. I literally froze to the spot.

Someone else had gotten up and opened the door, and he said to me, 'Cat got your tongue? But you do have nice knickers.' He was very charming. He could see I was nervous as hell. I'd never met anyone famous before and he was just trying to talk to me. I didn't even get to tell him how I danced like him. In my mind beforehand I was thinking, 'oh, I'll show him a few moves.' Ha ha! I couldn't even move. I was so stunned. And then I met Charlie, Keith and Bill.

On our way out, my sister knocked at Brian's door. Oh my God - that was bizarre. That was when he was with Anita Pallenberg and they had those famous fights. He answered the door with little more than his underwear on. You know, people used to call me Brian because I had the same hair, the same blonde hair and bangs and everything. It was like, he looked at me for a second and was like, 'Is that my doppelganger?' but then he went on, 'I can't talk now – we're fighting, we're having a big fight.' And when they did play next time he had a broken rib.

## REYNOLDS COLISEUM
### 10 NOVEMBER 1965, RALEIGH, NORTH CAROLINA

**I WAS THERE: AL SLAUGHTER, AGE 16**

I went with a buddy of mine, Sonny Watkins. We were best buddies. I lost my driving license and couldn't drive for 60 days on suspension. He hauled me around everywhere and told me he had tickets to go and see the Rolling Stones, and I said, 'Well, we might as well.' I worked at an A&P store for 90 cents an hour. We'd save up our money and go to soul shows like James Brown. Around here we were big into R&B and rock 'n' roll and soul music then. We were a couple of farm boys who got tickets by accident and went over there. We'd heard of them. We'd seen The Beatles.

They were really great tickets for a couple of high school kids. We were amazed how little they were. They were so small. We were 16, 6ft tall and 180lbs. They were a different breed. All those guys. The Rolling Stones were totally different. It was just an atmosphere that night. It was quite a treat to get a free ticket from your best buddy who hauled you around when you didn't have a driver's license.

# COLISEUM
## 12 NOVEMBER 1965, GREENSBORO, NORTH CAROLINA

**I WAS THERE: CATHERINE COCHRAN, AGE 13**

I was so lucky to see them. I won two fifth-row tickets through the local radio station. I had seen Herman's Hermits a few months before - my first concert - so went with my 11-year-old brother. I liked The Beatles, but when I heard 'Around and Around', that was so rocking compared to them.

Also, at that time the stage came down so low that the stage was only about a foot off the floor. But the clincher for me to be a loyal fan for 50-plus years was when Mick sang 'Everybody Needs Somebody to Love', looked me straight in the eye, pointed at me, and said, 'I need you!' It was instant love for me. I have seen them now more than 10 times. My room is a shrine, just like I was still 13. It was a dream come true to be in my Sixties and still see them live. They are like family to me.

# WASHINGTON COLISEUM
## 13 NOVEMBER 1965, WASHINGTON DC

**I WAS THERE: BILL CURRIER, AGE 17**

I was 17 and a high school junior. I had all the albums released, *England's Newest Hit Makers*, *12 X 5*, *The Rolling Stones Now!* and *Out of Our Heads*. I took a city bus in the morning to the event alone. None of my friends wanted to see this English group but me. I purchased a ticket at the door for $4.50. I was only making $1.25 an hour, so it was like a half day's work.

The show was early in the day - the Stones had to get out of town

*None of Bill Currier's friends wanted to catch the Stones with him*

and play in Baltimore that same night. The crowd was on its feet the whole time. I don't think it was sold out. The Coliseum was in the ghetto, the slum area of DC, and held about 9,000 people. The sound system wasn't great. It was a Sixties show and I was about 20 rows away and the thing you could hear was guitars, drums, and a very loud crowd.

Brian was jumping all over the place and awesome on the harmonica. What I remember was his hair was so neat and clean looking, like a perm, compared to Jagger and Richards. I loved every second. Just me and the Stones and about 8,000 crazies. It was my first concert and, like a first girlfriend, one you never forget.

### I WAS THERE: JACKI REESE, AGE 11

I turned 11 on 10 November, so was just a youngster. My sister is six years older, so it was she who listened to the Stones - and The Beatles of course - so I listened to them too. The first LP I bought was *Big Hits (High Tide and Green Grass)*.

I don't remember a whole lot about the concert but can truthfully say I don't remember seeing any other Stone but Brian. I sat and looked at him the entire time. He was wearing his tartan trousers and a brown turtleneck. I had a programme from that concert, which cost $1. I no longer have it. For some reason, my sister has no recollection of the concert.

## CIVIC COLISEUM
## 14 NOVEMBER 1965, KNOXVILLE, TENNESSEE

### I WAS THERE: SONNY THROWER, AGE 11

I got to see a lot of acts through having a dad with two radio stations. There were about 250 people there for the Stones show - East Tennessee hadn't really gotten into them yet. Brian was there with his white Vox Teardrop. I was hypnotised.

I was already in a band and studied the Stones appearances on *The Ed Sullivan Show*, *Shindig!*, *Hullabaloo*, etc. so knew what to expect. But getting to see Brian was miraculous.

His stage presence was almost spiritual and it took some doing to get the live focus off him. His hair and style really made him stand out, in spite of Mick's dancing. Brian had a glow around him somehow and his spirit and passion were undeniable in that live stage performance. It was a life-altering experience to be remembered with perfect clarity forever. Brian exuded such elegant class and grace; he was clearly the Stones creator and different from the rest. It's burned into my memory like it was yesterday. I have seen the Stones numerous times with Mick Taylor and with Ronnie, but seeing Brian … wow!

## I WAS THERE: ROBERT PEGUES

I began my sophomore year at UT in August 1965, found about a Rolling Stones concert in November and decided I had to go. I went down to the Civic Coliseum and asked for the best tickets they had. The seats were less than 10 rows from the stage and cost about $10 each. I then got a date with a girl - I think named Charlotte - who knew nothing about the Stones and didn't really want to go. My bet is she's changed her mind since.

The concert occurred on the day 'Get Off of My Cloud' became the No.1 song in the country. On the day, we went down to the venue at the announced time and were told there would be a delay. No reason was given. This only increased my date's apprehension. We killed two to four hours in downtown Knoxville and returned in the evening.

The crowd was very sparse, perhaps 1,000 people. I don't think many tickets were sold to begin with and a lot of people never returned after the delay. The audience was dead. The crowd was not into the Stones – I think they were expecting a Beatles clone - and the Stones were definitely not into the crowd.

*The audience was dead - the crowd was not into the Stones*

Jagger and the Stones hardly moved on stage at all during the show. They ran through their set and left with no encores. Despite the negatives, I thought it was wonderful and my lifelong fandom was reinforced. I also remember Charlotte was singularly unimpressed and we returned to her dorm soon afterwards – needless to say, there was no goodnight kiss.

THE ROLLING STONES IN THE SIXTIES: A PEOPLE'S HISTORY

# STATE FAIR YOUTH CENTER
## 20 NOVEMBER 1965, SHREVEPORT, LOUISIANA

**I WAS THERE: DEBBIE ALLEN**

It was a Saturday. I was very young, only 11 that year, and my older cousins took me. There was an underage limit. But I got all my height early… by twelve years I was bending over to put my head on the shoulders of boys to slow dance at parties. So my height made me look older than I was.

It was a very short set the Stones played that night… only about 30 minutes. Hit songs (and stage sets) were very short in length then. They only played four songs, but they were good ones: 'Play with Fire', 'Satisfaction', 'Get Off of My Cloud', 'Out of Time'. This was my first rock concert, and after seeing them at that age, the songs in their set that night hold an extra bit of magic for me when I hear them now. It was amazing.

I spent the next two years fighting with my mother over my haircut. I wanted my bangs long, in my eyes like Brian Jones wore his. I got a brown corduroy Mod cap and wore it everywhere, because I had seen pictures of the Stones wearing them. It was very much all about London in those years. A week later the Dave Clark Five played there. They were huge then. I was 'Glad All Over' about that show too. In my memory, it remains a very magical autumn. Alchemy indeed for a young girl who dreamed of becoming a singer.

# WILL ROGERS COLISEUM
## 21 NOVEMBER 1965, FORT WORTH, TEXAS

**I WAS THERE: ELAINE MCAFEE BENDER**

I arrived early and took my seat in a folding chair on the floor in front of a built up, temporary stage. Typically, this venue was used for rodeos and livestock shows. There was permanent, elevated seating around the periphery of the building.

KFJZ Radio sponsored this show, as was typical of most rock concerts in Fort Worth. I worked for KFJZ Radio after school (I was a high school sophomore) and worked many of the shows as a hospitality hostess. I was told no underage girls would be allowed to work backstage at this particular show but was given a complimentary ticket and VIP seat to watch the show.

As I took my seat, I looked around at the audience, made up of mostly teen girls and the rest teen boys. A group of girls near me were holding signs declaring love for Brian Jones: 'Brian Baby!'

An armoured car approached from the back of the audience and drove all the way down the centre-aisle to the stage. Policemen seemed to be everywhere. One opened the door of the armoured car and out stepped Brian Jones, followed by Keith Richards, Mick Jagger, Charlie Watts, and Bill Wyman. Girls screamed and pushed forward, and police kept the crowd away from the performers.

There were several opening acts, the Stones on the stage less than an hour. That's pretty much how most rock concerts were in those days. I was quite taken with the brilliance of Brian Jones' abilities as a multi-instrumentalist. Mick Jagger strutted, and what girl could resist watching him. As an aside, when I did meet Mick Jagger several years later, he was quite a gentleman. Charlie Watts was one of the best drummers I've ever seen live. Keith Richards flirted with the audience and laughed with Mick, while Bill Wyman quietly killed it on the bass.

They only played about 10 songs that night. I have seen the Rolling Stones many times since. While I have enjoyed them at each and every show, that day in 1965 was the best. Five musicians, a tight rock band, some rhythm and blues and no frills - just raw enough, straight up rock 'n' roll at its finest.

## I WAS THERE: MIKE HICKS

On November 21, 1965 at Will Rogers Coliseum, I attended my very first concert. I was in my junior year of high school (11th grade). It was a Sunday afternoon and I went by myself. Beatlemania was in full swing, with the full-blown British Invasion - The Animals, Gerry and the Pacemakers, Dave Clark Five, The Yardbirds, and more. I had been able to see The Beatles when they came through Dallas.

I knew even then the Stones were an important band and too important to miss. It seems like there were some hot R&B acts that opened, but I'm a little foggy on that. What I do remember is that even though the crowd was relatively small, the Stones were delivered to the stage via armoured car, just like they carry gold in. It seems like they were mostly dressed in black, as was very popular, especially for rock groups. But I don't know if that's an actual memory, or if the memory itself is by now black and white.

What I do know is they played a great set, including all their early hits. 'Satisfaction' had come out about four months previous and was a gigantic hit. And, if memory serves, they also played 'The Last Time', 'Mercy, Mercy', 'Get Off My Cloud', 'Hitch Hike', and maybe a half-dozen more.

I enjoyed the concert tremendously. Thus started my 'concert years'. Which were many, and filled with some of the greatest acts the world would ever see. Later I worked in the music business as a promotion man and had the pleasure of seeing and even meeting lots of great talent. My wife and I have compiled a list of shows we saw, easily numbering over 400. We recently sold our very large ticket stub collection.

When I saw the Stones that afternoon, they had the original lineup, including Brian, Mick, Keith, Bill and Charlie. Brian played his unusual assortment of strange instruments. I remember the odd-looking white electric guitar in particular. They sort of took my breath away, since I'd seen them on TV and heard them on radio, but this was my first such experience live, and it was a great one to start with.

I saw the Stones three more times over the next couple of decades. They were all great shows, especially one in San Antonio on June 3, 1975 at the Hemisfair Arena, when they got into trouble for whipping out their giant inflatable penis!

## I WAS THERE: FREDERICK GOGGANS, AGE 15

Fort Worth was my hometown, where I grew up. I went with a girlfriend. The Will Rogers Center was known as being the location of the world's first indoor rodeo with professional cowboys and all that every January. And the arena was set up like a pavilion for the rodeo. It's a kind of elliptical building

Frederick Goggans saw the Stones in his hometown

and normally has a dirt floor where the cowboys ride the broncos and things of that nature. At one end of it are gates where they have chutes for the animals that the cowboy comes out on top of a horse or a bull or whatnot. So one end is where everything comes into the arena.

This concert was in November so three months before all that. I remember they used it all for various other performances and the dirt was all taken out and they put sheets down on the floor. My recollection of the Stones concert is that they had a platform or a stage that was circular and rotated and it was in the middle of this arena. There were chairs and the Stones arrived in a Brinks armoured car through a little pathway through the crowd.

The crowd was quite enthusiastic. There were lots of girls screaming. I think it was much more of a mixed audience than you'd find at a Beatles concert. The armoured car was there for protection. There might have been a theatrical component to it. They departed in the same vehicle.

## I WAS THERE: RODGER W BROWNLEE

Totally sold out? Far from it! I should know - I was there, and spent a little time with the Stones before the concert while they waited to go on stage. I was a member of a local band, ThElite, and we were slated to open for the Stones at this appearance.

The concert was sponsored by KFJZ radio and their top DJ Mark Stevens, who happened to be our local handler, negotiating with the promoters to have ThElite open the show. At the time we were playing numerous venues sponsored by KFJZ and MC'd by Mark and were a top draw. We could put 1,500/2,000 people in one of their venues and I'm sure that was part of his reasoning. Plus, being one of his bands, he wanted us to get this exposure.

A day or two before the concert, Mark contacted us and said, 'Madison Avenue types from New York blew in and nixed it.' So we were out – they didn't want any local band. Disappointed, we nevertheless decided to go. Having played at the Will Rogers complex on numerous occasions, we knew most of the Fort Worth cops who pulled security, so when we showed up at a back door, they opened it for us. We walked into the area that was used as stock pens for the rodeos, one of which had recently concluded - the smell still lingering strongly in the air. It was mostly dark but we headed for a light coming from one of the tack room doors. We went in and there were the Stones waiting to go on. They looked somewhat dishevelled and tired and complained of being hungry. They sent an old porter out for food.

We chatted them up and took a few photos. They were all nice, quiet, hungry guys - not all that different from ourselves.

When the armoured car arrived at the tack room, we decided to make our way into the Coliseum and find a good vantage point to watch the concert. What we saw from an upper tier of seating was almost stunning; rather than the sold-out concert everyone expected, turnout was dismal. We guesstimated there were fewer than a thousand people. The floor seating was not even full, much less the tiers of balcony seating around the arena. When the armoured car came out of the end of the arena through the gates usually used for the rodeo grand entry, there were screaming girls alright, but the armoured car was hardly needed. There was no crush of female humanity.

Throughout their performance there were screaming girls around the stage, but the concert overall was a disappointment from an attendance standpoint. At the end of the show, it was widely rumoured that Mick Jagger stated, 'I'm never coming back to this fucking hick town' or words to that affect, and they didn't for another seven years.

ThElite subsequently made numerous appearances at the Will Rogers Coliseum, opening for the like of The Beach Boys and The Byrds among many other top groups. Most of those shows were sold out but, sadly, not for the Stones on their first trip to Cowtown.

## ARENA AUDITORIUM
### 25 NOVEMBER 1965, MILWAUKEE, WISCONSIN

**I WAS THERE: DENNIS KOERS**
I was in high school when I saw an advertisement that the Rolling Stones were coming to the Arena in Milwaukee, and their opening act was The Buckinghams, who had a hit with 'Kind of a Drag'. The Arena holds 12,000 people and there couldn't have been more than 200 or 300 people there. After The Buckinghams came on, the Stones came on, and

Jagger looked around the Arena and said he wouldn't start playing until everybody moved up, regardless of ticket price. I went with a friend and was about 15ft from the stage. It was great.

The set-list contained the usual stuff. I think they finished with 'Satisfaction'. They didn't play too long. I think they did ten or twelve songs. I remember there was a young woman up at the front row and she had this huge rabbit or teddy bear. It must have been 4ft tall, and she threw it on the stage and almost hit Brian Jones in the head. He had to duck out of the way. It's probably the second-best concert I've ever seen. The best? That was James Brown, and you could see where Mick had stolen the moves off him. I remember Mick saying the biggest mistake he made was following James Brown on at the TAMI Show. He thought that took the real steam out of their performance.

I live in a little town called Gwinn, Michigan in the upper peninsula. It's very isolated. A guy lived about 30 miles from here, in Marquette, Michigan, called Chuch Magee. He was the guitar tech for the Stones until he died. A friend of his who's a friend of mine, and who's pretty good with his hands, constructed a foot pedal for Charlie Watts. The day of Chuch's funeral, Mick, Keith, Charlie and Ronnie Wood came up in a big black limousine, went to Chuch's funeral service, and sang 'Amazing Grace'.

## THE GARDENS
### 27 NOVEMBER 1965, CINCINATTI, OHIO

**I WAS THERE: PAULA BROCK, AGE 12**
This venue was used a lot for basketball games and sporting events. What sticks in my mind the most just a little over a year from seeing The Beatles at the same venue is that it was sold out for The Beatles and we had to sit in the seats that were assigned to us. At the Stones concert it must have been more than half empty.

After first sitting in our assigned seats we realised we could sit anywhere we wanted because there were so many empty seats. There were seats each side of the stage with only a metal railing separating us from them. I sat on the right side with my older sister and her best friend. We happened to be on Bill Wyman's side of the stage, much to my disappointment as I was in love with Brian Jones. Brian was on the left, Mick in the middle, Keith and Bill on the right, and Charlie in the back. There were only a few yards between us and them. There were no security guards or police on the stage or near us. Their current hit on the US charts was 'Get Off of My Cloud'.

I am not sure just how long they played, but it was probably about 30 minutes. I remember while they were playing they turned on the spotlight and shone it around the seats and it showed off the pitifully half-empty arena. Even though the place was not sold out by any means, the crowd was loud and the girls, including myself, were going crazy. I have no idea to this day what made us girls scream and cry when we saw them or The Beatles. It was just a natural reaction.

Paula Brock's sister's best friend jumped the railing

My sister's best friend told her she was going to jump over the railing after their last song. I will never forget her going over, her bright red satin slip showing as she vaulted the railing. She liked Keith the best and disappeared behind the curtain so fast following the boys that I didn't even realise it at first. It all happened so fast. I remember my sister and I going outside and waiting to see if we could find her. I remember crying hysterically over Brian and knowing I was so close to him but didn't get to touch him. Our friend finally showed up outside and was so excited. She told us she ran backstage after Keith and grabbed onto him, around his waist. She said a cop was trying to pull her off and she said Keith told him to leave her alone. I will never know if that really happened for sure, but I really think it did. She was as quick as a rabbit vaulting over that railing.

THE ROLLING STONES IN THE SIXTIES: A PEOPLE'S HISTORY

# ARIE CROWN THEATRE
## 28 NOVEMBER 1965, CHICAGO, ILLINOIS

**I WAS THERE: MARY GLUSAK**

It all started in February 1964: the dark ages. We were five relatively normal freshmen at a Catholic high school in Chicago: Diane, Donna, Lin, Mary (me) and Pat. We all loved music and would alternate Sundays at each other's homes to watch *The Ed Sullivan Show*: it was the way we would see the latest British Invasion musical groups. We heard who would be Ed's guests from local rock radio station WLS. Sundays were the best day of the week. The Beatles were our first obsession. The next group we watched was the Dave Clark Five, but they were 'fake Beatles', and didn't tug at our heartstrings. Gerry and the Pacemakers were bland.

Enter the Stones in October 1964: five teenage girls sitting there totally mesmerised. Hypnotised. They were nothing like we had ever seen. Beatles? Who were The Beatles? They were completely forgotten: a distant memory. The Stones changed our lives and made us hungry for their raw blues/rock music. Nothing vanilla here. It oozed with passion. It burned through our souls. It was an influence that would cover decades. We had all-girl parties at my house, playing Stones records and with Lin dancing like Mick, holding a turkey baster for a microphone. Damn, she was good: she even looked a little like him.

We were relentless in seeing them live, buying outrageously priced tickets ($5.50 was the top price - a kingly sum). The radio gods would divulge when tickets would go on sale and where they would be playing. If they were coming, we were going!

We staked out McCormick Place, home to the Arie Crown Theatre. The auto exit ramp was the best place to see them. We saw their limo speed off. We stalked the Sheraton Chicago Hotel for glimpses.

I worked for a while as an Andy Frain usherette. Backstage, Keith Richards grabbed my long, blonde ponytail and said, 'Guys, I'm taking this one home with me.' At age 17, I panicked. 'Nooo, I can't… Mom will kill me.' He smiled but figured he couldn't be bothered babysitting. That job ended because I couldn't stand spiked high heels and a straight wool-skirted uniform. Even the Stones weren't worth a potential broken ankle.

Time changed a few things: graduation, college, marriage, children, but the love of the Stones remained for me and Lin. After one concert at the Chicago Stadium (the 'Star Star' phallus show in '75) we had such a contact high that, in leaving, I took a short cut and drove down a sidewalk to escape the crowd and chase their limo. Sadly, they eluded us.

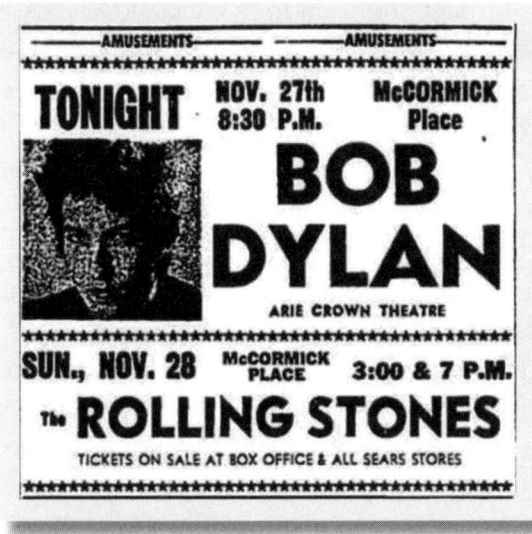

We travelled to other cities, stayed in their hotels, met some of the band and hung out after shows. I lost count after 60 shows, during the *Steel Wheels* tour. My hubby, John, promised front-row tickets to the *Voodoo Lounge* tour: our first time. It was amazing. Mick came walking out on the empty stage with a single spotlight. He bowed to the audience and Linda nearly fainted.

The Stones were at the Crown shortly after another rising Sixties act

John would hunt ticket brokers to procure those precious front-row tickets. He's a sweetheart: thanks to his perseverance with ticket brokers, Lin and I saw 14 more concerts from the front row. Knowing Keith's love for Marlboro cigarettes, I would hand him a carton at each show. He would sometimes kiss my hand, but always gave me a guitar pick. The picks are framed along with some of my pirated photographs.

Most of the shows were very good, but a bad one comes to mind: Milwaukee. We had lower balcony seats, overlooking part of backstage. Blondie Chaplin was playing for Ronnie behind the curtain. We walked out.

One of our most memorable adventures was in Cleveland at the Ritz Carlton. We arrived in the early evening after a miserable flight and a worse cab ride from the airport. We had arranged for the hotel to send a limo. It never arrived. The front desk attendant was most apologetic and asked how they could improve the Ritz experience. I said an upgrade to the Club Floor would be nice: my request was fulfilled. We dropped our bags and went for a cocktail. As we were pouring drinks, Mick came into the dining room, smiled and said, 'Good evening, ladies.' Lin's hand shook so badly she splashed cognac all over her hand. Mick didn't see the exhibition of nerves.

And I remember Blondie Chaplin singing happy birthday to my hubby in Cleveland, having breakfast next to Charlie and Shirley at the Ritz in Chicago, and Keith and I riding in an elevator together.

All good things ultimately come to an end. My sister Lin passed away in 2008. I don't get front-row tickets any longer because they are obscenely priced, but I still go to Stones concerts with good seats with Donna, my friend from Pittsburgh. We've stayed at Stones hotels (wherever there is a Ritz Carlton) and partied with other die-hard Stones fans and supporting artists. Perhaps that was how support artists got drinks. It doesn't matter, it was fun. The Stones were seldom seen. Some things have changed, and many have remained the same, but the fun and Stones mania continues.

## I WAS THERE: PAUL PETRATIS

I was fascinated by the Rolling Stones. I read on the back of their second album they were recording in Chicago, so I took the bus down to Chess and hoped to run into them. But I never did. I saw them twice. For my first show, Brian came out of the orchestra pit on a little riser. He was wearing a red suit that day. It was a very flash sort of thing to do. He'd spent the day in the hospital and that was one of the days the Stones recorded at Chess without him.

Keith was playing bass slide parts on his guitar. He often covered for Brian in the early years. He'd say it wasn't important who played what, it was the overall sound that mattered, but Brian wasn't showing up for all the gigs.

As a budding harmonica player, I was always intrigued by 'Not Fade Away'. I couldn't figure out how Brian did it, then I sussed out he was using two harmonicas. He was always intriguing, with that and the slide guitar. Even though I lived in Chicago, the first slide-guitar I heard was Brian – before I heard Muddy, Earl Hooker or Son House. It was seeing Brian play 'Little Red Rooster' that allowed me to work out how to play open tuning in E. I knew that couldn't be a regular guitar. Arguably,

Brian was the first chap to play slide-guitar in the UK, after hearing a DJ play an Elmore James album around '61/'62.

When you go back and listen, you realise some of the really cool parts are Brian's. It wasn't all Keith. Brian played really aggressive English-style rhythm. Of all the things British musicians gave the world, it's that really hard-driving, trebly, rhythm guitar – that 'chunk-chunk-chunk' - which enabled the band to get on doing whatever they were doing. Then Brian got distracted and interested in things other than the guitar. But I picture Brian and Keith in that horrible Edith Grove flat, just living for guitar.

And Brian was a fashion plate. Who was wearing scarves first? It was Brian, a media beacon. He got more attention than all the rest of them. And I guess his relationships suffered as a result of the paparazzi and all that. You didn't know where to look when you saw them live. You had Brian one side of the stage, Keith on the other throwing shapes, and then that guy singing. You didn't know what to make of him. Iggy Pop once said, 'The Stones taught us how to sing, how to play and how to dress.'

## COLISEUM AUDITORIUM
### 29 NOVEMBER 1965, DENVER, COLORADO

**I WAS THERE: K ARLAN EBEL, AGE 14**

I was just learning to play guitar. The Stones were my favourite band. I had the first three albums and *Out of Our Heads* had just come out. As we were being let into the auditorium proper there was a stampede of rushing, screaming kids and my friend got knocked down and almost trampled. It took all of my 14-year-old strength to lift him safely onto his feet. We were drenched with sweat before the show even began.

The opening band was The Ramrods. They all had dark curly hair

K Arlan Ebel remembers a fans' stampede

and wore jean jackets. They mostly did Dylan covers, including 'Like A Rolling Stone', recently released. They were actually pretty good. What I remember most clearly is Brian Jones' hair and how well he played the harmonica. I was enthralled by the guitar playing, but couldn't always tell who was playing what between Brian and Keith since we were a little ways back from the stage. I loved the concert. They played all my favourites except for 'Little Red Rooster'. And I remember that we had a good laugh because on the way to the concert, we saw a place called the Rolling Stone Motel. One of the kids said, 'That's probably where they're staying.' We all cracked up.

# ARIZONA VETERANS MEMORIAL COLISEUM
## 30 NOVEMBER 1965, PHOENIX, ARIZONA

### I WAS THERE: DENNIS DUNAWAY, ALICE COOPER BAND

In the mid-Sixties, the drab isolated scene in Phoenix, Arizona had been thoroughly shattered and brought back to vivid life by the British Invasion. My high school buddies and I had started a band called the Spiders and had gotten good enough to be the house band in a popular local teen club. We had just bought new Fender amplifiers and the payments left us broke.

When we heard the Rolling Stones would be doing a show at the Phoenix Coliseum, our guitar player Glen Buxton and I got the idea to go to Montgomery Wards and buy some dirt-cheap cardboard guitar cases.

Early in the afternoon of the concert, we went to the backside of the Coliseum and knocked on the artist's entrance until someone finally opened. Back then, few guys in Phoenix had long hair, and with our guitar cases in hand, it was easy to convince the guy we were the Rolling Stones. He let us in. We stashed our cardboard cases behind the bleachers and hung out until people started filing into the arena. Soon, the large room was packed. Everybody was there.

The opening band was the Rockin' Ramrods, who I'd never heard of before (or since) but I liked their solid rock style. The next act was Patti LaBelle and the Bluebelles, who weren't my taste in music (at that time) but they were great singers and put on an impressive high-energy show.

Then it was time for the Stones. The crowd waited and waited. It was a solid hour before they finally exploded onto the stage. The music started. Bill Wyman with his stoic stance seemed like he was made of stone. Charlie Watts' expression was stone-like as well. Mick Jagger and Keith Richards moved around the stage rapid-fire, while Brian Jones looked more like a model posing for photos, yet stood out from a distance because of his blond hair and iconic white Vox teardrop guitar.

I knew all the songs and loved them all, but the music was just the soundtrack to the raw excitement of the performance. Girls screamed fanatically. They had seen girls do that on the *Ed Sullivan Show*, but there seemed to be genuine emotions behind it. And it was infectious throughout the arena.

Suddenly, the Stones finished and walked off. The set was surprisingly short, but the impact left us reeling. Somehow, we felt the whole world had changed. The Fifties were over, and the Rolling Stones were a big part of that.

They represented something important. They were rebellious and the music was more than the combination of the instruments - their combined sound blended into one big moving force that hit you in the chest and below the belt. It grabbed you by the gut and swept you away from the teenage world of school, parents, and jobs. The Rolling Stones represented fun, freedom, and something new.

## MEMORIAL AUDITORIUM
### 3 DECEMBER 1965, SACRAMENTO, CALIFORNIA

**I WAS THERE: MICHAEL LAZARUS SCOTT**

Ed Takitch and I were at the Sacramento Memorial Auditorium and saw Keith Richards get electrocuted on stage. Ed and I had seen the Stones about six months previously at this same venue. It was the concert that forever changed my life. This time round they were performing two shows, so we decided to attend both. The first one was, as always, exhilarating. The second began with even more energy and sheer rock 'n' roll abandon.

About a half-hour into the show, Keith stepped up to a mic to sing backup. His ungrounded guitar inadvertently touched the mic stand and sparks flew as Keith rather gracefully collapsed onto the stage floor. Mick, being closest, immediately ran to his side, followed by Brian. The stage curtains closed, and all bedlam broke out. Girls were screaming and crying. Some boys were pissed. The announcer came out and said the show was over and to please vacate the building.

Ed and I hightailed it around to the back of the auditorium where, with some other fans, we watched as an old-style Cadillac ambulance backed into a rear exit. We were right next to the back side of the Caddy, with other kids around on both sides. They promptly brought Keith out walking, his arms around the shoulders of two medics. He looked badly shaken and when he saw all of us, he got a look on his young face I'll never forget. It firmly stated, 'Don't fuck with me now!' We all froze - no one moved a muscle. He totally polarised us. The next night Keith was back on stage in San Jose. You can't stop rock 'n' roll.

## I WAS THERE: TIKEY KREST

I grew up in Sacramento, California and saw a lot of concerts, from the Stones to The Beach Boys, and Frank Zappa and the Mothers of Invention. In the Sixties I saw the Rolling Stones at Memorial Auditorium in Sacramento. As the Stones launched into 'The Last Time', Keith Richards' guitar hit the microphone stand, which gave him an electric shock. He landed on his butt, and they shut the show down.

*Keith's guitar gave him an electric shock*

## I WAS THERE: MICK MARTIN

I was right in the front row, in front of Keith. I saw the blue light. I literally saw Keith fly into the air backward. I thought he was dead. I was horrified. We all were. Silence fell over the crowd. They carried him out with oxygen tubes, and he was semi-conscious. I patted him on the shoulders and said, 'I hope you're going to be okay'

THE ROLLING STONES IN THE SIXTIES: A PEOPLE'S HISTORY

# CIVIC AUDITORIUM
## 4 DECEMBER 1965, SAN JOSE, CALIFORNIA

**I WAS THERE: BOBBY ASEA, AGE 12**

Before the British Invasion I was fortunate enough to have an older sister in her teens and very much a fan of the most popular band around at the time - The Beach Boys. Having moved from the East Coast to the West Coast in Northern California it wasn't long before both of us got bit by the surf sound bug. The Beach Boys were our idols. Luckily for me, the band came to our town and my sister was nice enough to bring me along to see them in concert twice; pretty good for a 10-year-old in 1963. For me the Beach Boys were kings.

Then out of the blue came this new group called The Beatles from Liverpool,

Bobby Asea was a Stones fanatic

England that everyone was talking about. They were going to appear on *The Ed Sullivan Show* the next Sunday night. Being open enough to check it out but not mature enough to accept their greatness I, along with the rest of the country, tuned in. We were truly blown away. The memories of that night will stay with me forever. But in spite of how great and interesting those four lads were, I was determined to stay true to my idols, The Beach Boys. In my head I was thinking 'how dare these foreigners come here to this country and take over with their popularity and No.1 hits?' Inside I knew they were great, and I dug them. I just didn't want to admit it.

This behaviour carried on for a while until I heard of the Rolling Stones. When I heard their music and saw their performances on shows like *Hollywood Palace, Shindig!, Hullabaloo* and *The Ed Sullivan Show*, I thought this British band was like no other. I fell in love with their music and everything about them from that day. My life was changed. My sister Dorothy still preferred The Beach Boys so when the Rolling Stones came to town I didn't have a chaperone to escort me to the concert in the

# THE ROLLING STONES IN THE SIXTIES: A PEOPLE'S HISTORY

spring of 1965. Luckily for me, they came back to San Jose in December that year. By then I was the ripe old age of twelve and a veteran of the concert scene thanks to my sister.

Somehow my parents allowed me to go with best friend Joe, who was also a Stones fanatic. The Civic Auditorium holds around 3,000 and they played two shows. We went to the early one. With the stage curtains closed behind him, as the announcer was in the process of introducing the Stones, it seemed Mick and Keith were tugging at the curtains, which in turn made the young audience react in a wall of screams.

The place was sold out and, like Beatlemania, us Rolling Stones fans screamed our lungs out. Even though there was a lot of screaming going on, I remember being able to hear the music. 'Satisfaction' was their latest hit and of course they played it live. Other songs I remember clearly are 'That's How Strong My Love Is', with Brian playing electric organ, 'Get Off of My Cloud', 'Mercy Mercy', 'Play with Fire' and 'The Last Time'. Bill was on the far left, Brian next to him, Keith far right, Charlie on a platform, and Mick all over the place.

Brian seemed to be enjoying himself. I distinctly remember Mick doing his James Brown imitation dance, going from one end of the stage to the other. At one point he took off his jacket, stood on the edge of the stage and swung it out towards the audience as if he was going to fling it to a lucky fan in the seats. He didn't, and the jacket kept going until it landed on his shoulder. I think he fooled everyone. The show was all too short – about twelve songs.

On our way out we ran into friends waiting in line for the next show. We were so excited to tell them about the greatest show we had ever seen.

## I WAS THERE: MICHAEL FUNKE, AGE 18

That 1965 US tour promoted their fourth US LP *Out of Our Heads* and a few of the stops included two shows in one night. San Jose was one. My friend Glenn and I had tickets to the first show. I still have the $5.50 ticket stub - Section 209, Row D, Seat 5 in the balcony, facing the stage. I was a bigger Stones fan than Glenn, but it was his first Stones show, and we were a pair of excited 18-year-old white bread suburban kids that night. Glenn favoured Keith. I was and still am a Brian Jones fan.

While we knew what marijuana smelled like neither of us had smoked

# THE ROLLING STONES IN THE SIXTIES: A PEOPLE'S HISTORY

pot (yet) and our first trip to a psychedelic dance hall was three months away. We were there for the music, for the Stones, and restlessly sat through several opening acts - the Rocking Ramrods, the Embers, Vibrations, Patti LaBelle and the Blue Belles, and more. And, finally, the Stones! 'Dam deedle dee dam dam, little girl where did you come from?'

They quickly rolled through a dozen songs, ending with their huge 1965 hit 'Satisfaction' a little over 30 minutes after they kicked it off with 'She Said Yeah'. I'm not sure what happened next. We were simultaneously pumped about

Michael Funke stuck around for the next show

the show and disappointed it was so short. It was probably Glenn who suggested we try to find a place to hide while ushers cleared the auditorium for the second show. Anyway, we ended up in a men's rest room with maybe half a dozen other guys. We were all milling around, talking excitedly, determined to find a place to hide but clueless about where that might be. Suddenly a guy wearing black engineer boots, a black leather jacket and sporting a ducktail - a 'greaser' in the language of the Fifties - strutted in and up to a small square door in the far wall. He lifted his leg and kicked the door open. We all piled in. The greaser - our hero now - and a few other guys pressed their bodies against the door and told us to shut up. We sat mutely, looking up at the tiered seats of the balcony above us. Finally, we heard someone enter the rest room. We all seemed to press forward against the door and held our breath. There was a rap on the door. Another one. A grunt as someone pushed against it. Then footsteps, followed by silence.

I don't know how long we waited, but eventually we all piled out, smiled at one another in the bright lights of the restroom and went our separate ways. Glenn and I headed back to the balcony. The seats were rapidly filling up. We gazed down at our shoes and tried to look inconspicuous as ushers checked ticket stubs and rent-a-cops stood by. We stood in an aisle, so we weren't blocking anyone's view and watched as the opening acts paraded out and performed identical short sets to kick off the second show. It seemed to go on forever. Finally, Patti LaBelle and the Blue Belles closed their set with 'I Sold My Heart to the Junkman', just as they had less than two hours earlier.

By now Glenn and I were vibrating with anticipation. This, we said, is going to be so cool. The auditorium was packed, everyone ready to rock with the Stones. Finally, there they were back on stage. 'Dam deedle dee dam dam, little girl where did you come from?' Mick was prancing around like crazy. Actually, pretty much exactly like he'd pranced around in the first show. Wait a minute. Didn't he twirl the microphone cord at exactly the same time in the first show?

Some twelve songs later, after the last fuzzy tone of 'Satisfaction' faded away, Glenn and I looked at one another and essentially said, 'What a gyp.' We knew next to nothing about the music scene and never considered the Rolling Stones would be playing the same set night after night on their tour of the States. We know better now. But despite the brief and repetitive shows, Glenn and I were more than satisfied. It was the Stones, after all, and we had heard some great tunes – 'Hitch Hike', 'Mercy Mercy', 'The Last Time', and their latest single 'Get Off of My Cloud.'

For two guys who had never smoked pot we were feeling pretty high as we hit the street, where we were suddenly surrounded by crazed, boisterous people, their faces painted day-glo, dressed up like clowns. The Merry Pranksters. They were passing out wildly drawn handbills that asked, 'Can you pass the Acid Test?' Even though we had never smoked dope we knew what that was about, and our answer was, 'Fuck, no.'

# SPORTS ARENA
## 5 DECEMBER 1965, LOS ANGELES, CALIFORNIA

**I WAS THERE: CYNTHIA PORTER, AGE 14**
I went with my friend Jackie. Tickets were $5.50 and we didn't have a lot of money so I pulled weeds in my neighbours' yards at 25 cents an hour. I also cleaned hotel rooms. My mom drove us and went for a coffee

# THE ROLLING STONES IN THE SIXTIES: A PEOPLE'S HISTORY

across the street while she waited for the show to finish.

I think the reason I liked the Stones was because Mick was so weird. The other bands were in suits, but the Stones wore t-shirts and sweatshirts. We were trying to get on stage but the security pushed us back. They were very gentle, not like they are today. I threw my bracelet at Mick. I would have thrown my bra on stage if I'd been wearing one, but at 14 I didn't have any boobs. I didn't like Brian because his hair made him look like a Beatle. I loved Mick. I still do.

Cynthia Porter loved Mick Jagger's weird ways

## I WAS THERE: DEEDEE KEEL

In December 1965, the Rolling Stones were scheduled to perform at Los Angeles Sports Arena. I had met a girl at school who shared my love of the band and unbelievably her father was the general manager of the arena - just how lucky could I be? We were taken to the show by her father and put into incredible seats right up front. The size of the arena and number of people in attendance at this show was so amazing. This show was much more intense than the first I'd seen in Long Beach. There was a huge amount of anticipation in the air. The stage was much higher and when the band came on the roar was nearly deafening. The quality of the sound this time seemed deep and full. This time I paid much more attention to the musicianship and stage moves. The only song I remember from this show is 'Get Off of My Cloud'. It was like a dream and there was magic in the air.

When the show ended my friend and I had to stay and wait until her father got the arena cleared. We were allowed to walk through the rows of seats and play around as we watched the stagehands take down the equipment. On the floor we discovered many items that had been thrown at the Stones and began to pick them up. It was surprising what fans had tried to get up there - jewelry, signs, stuffed animals, clothing, and – yes – underwear! We gathered up as many 'souvenirs' as we could before we were told we must come to the area behind the stage to wait for my girlfriend's father to finish up and take us home.

Very shortly a huge hangar door opened and in drove a big shiny bus. Within minutes we saw a group of people come from another area and head toward the bus. Unbelievably, amongst them were the Rolling Stones! I was shocked to see them heading in our direction and began walking closer. I locked eyes with Bill Wyman and felt like I was going to faint on the spot. As they began to walk onto the bus, Bill turned to me and said, 'Hey little girl, wanna come on the bus?' Oh, my goodness. Yes, I did! But no sooner had it been said than we heard a voice approaching that called out 'no!' It was Father, and it was definitely time to leave…

This was the last time I would ever see the Rolling Stones live, but the experiences and memories are clear and live in my head.

---

*1966 started quietly for the Rolling Stones, with no performances until they arrived in Australia in February for their second tour Down Under. It was to be a quieter year generally, with fewer than 90 shows worldwide and only 23 in Britain. Something of a contrast to the height of their gigging activity in 1963 and 1964, when they routinely played more than 25 shows a month.*

---

## KINGSFORD SMITH AIRPORT
### 16 FEBRUARY 1966, SYDNEY, AUSTRALIA

**I WAS THERE: LOUISE MORRIS (NÉE FERRIER)**
I saw the Stones in Sydney. Mick arrived in Sydney by helicopter in a pink satin suit, singing, 'Hey, you, get off of my cloud!'

---

*Mick arrived by helicopter in a pink satin suit*

THE ROLLING STONES IN THE SIXTIES: A PEOPLE'S HISTORY

# COMMEMORATIVE AUDITORIUM SHOWGROUNDS
## 18 – 19 FEBRUARY 1966, SYDNEY, AUSTRALIA

### I WAS THERE: JOHN DILLIMORE, AGE 18

I was born in England but living in Sydney, Australia. I took a girl called Bridget. I recall a large crowd lining up to get in and an exciting atmosphere. I had good seats and was only rows from the stage. The Searchers were the support band, quite big at that time, and sang 'Needles and Pins', a hit in those days. But primarily we were there to see the Stones and it was electric when they did come on. They wore white pants. Mick played tambourine. They sang '19th Nervous Breakdown' and 'Satisfaction'. Everyone was stoked and happy at that gig. Wish I still had my ticket.

### I WAS THERE: MARGARET VINCENT

Their second tour seemed like only a short time after the first. Like the first time I went on a Saturday afternoon, this time without my sister. The show was being filmed for some reason and, whilst I could still only afford cheap seats, the venue was only half full. Everyone was moved up close to the front and we had a great view. I have seen them every time they have played Sydney, except in 1973 when they played Randwick Racecourse.

I had just given birth to my first child and was in hospital. However, the hospital was only a short distance from the racecourse so we all sat out on the balcony and heard most of the show. On their last tour I was part of a medical team, there to look after the artists and crew. I met Mick and got a wave from Ronnie and a wink from Keith, although my jealous brother-in-law swore it was a nervous tic.

# CITY HALL
## 21 FEBRUARY 1966, BRISBANE, AUSTRALIA

### I WAS THERE: PAUL CHESHER, AGE 15

It was my first ever concert. It was held at the Milton tennis courts in Brisbane, an open-air concert with the stage at one end of the arena. I was in the stand directly in front of the stage and we were so excited. The first set was fantastic, and the crowd went wild. During the second set it started to rain. The Stones kept playing for a few minutes and then stopped.

We were sitting in the rain wondering if it would be cancelled, then Mick Jagger came on stage and said, 'If you guys can sit and listen in the rain, then we will play in the rain.' The crowd erupted. Despite the obvious dangers - the roadies must have been working feverishly to keep the electrics dry - they finished the concert with Jagger singing in the rain for the rest of the concert. We were all soaked to the skin but on such a music high. It was one of my most memorable experiences and demonstrated the group's dedication to their fans.

# CENTENNIAL HALL
## 22 FEBRUARY 1966, ADELAIDE, AUSTRALIA

**I WAS THERE: GUS HOWARD**

The band was more confident, had bigger amps and seemed more business-like. They played 'That's How Strong My Love Is', 'Mercy Mercy', 'Get Off of My Cloud', 'She Said Yeah', '19th Nervous Breakdown', 'The Spider and the Fly', 'Play with Fire', 'Satisfaction', and 'Not Fade Away' - slightly more original Stones material this time, but still some covers.

I remember Brian had that same odd insecure look, like he'd just stolen something. There was nothing in the show or his playing that indicated the wide variety of instrumentation he was introducing to the recorded material of the band at the time. I half remember seeing him on that stage with a sitar, but I am not sure that's reliable. They must have been incredible pressurised then. The shows were sandwiched by a just few days between appearing on *The Ed Sullivan Show* in New York and returning to LA to complete the sessions for *Aftermath*, so the flat-out professional Stones stage delivery may have also carried a bit of a 'where are we?' element.

THE ROLLING STONES IN THE SIXTIES: A PEOPLE'S HISTORY

# PALAIS THEATRE
## 24 FEBRUARY 1966, MELBOURNE, AUSTRALIA

**I WAS THERE: DAVID N PEPPERELL**

The Stones clearly did not want to be in Australia in 1966. Certainly their press conferences set new standards for contempt for local media. Then again, things had changed a lot for them in the year since they last played Melbourne.

They had challenged the Beatles for popularity and had made themselves a firm No.2 in the world - of course the Mop-Tops were unapproachable. Their single 'Satisfaction' had topped the charts everywhere, including the US, confirming their status as the other major group in the current pop stratosphere. It was possible they were not accorded the same recompense, lifestyle and accommodation in Australia that they received in the United States.

Staying in Melbourne at the John Batman again, a very small cheap motel, must have rankled them and was certainly not up to what they would expect in their newfound status as pop icons. Also, possibly there was nowhere to score any dope in Melbourne, so they spent their entire stay here drinking day and night to alleviate the boredom. It was obvious from Mick's opening remarks, 'We're so glad to be back in Melbourne, pig's arse,' and Brian Jones' repeated spitting on the front row and his advice to, 'Go home, you fucking Colonials, we've got your money' - which I heard clearly from my third-row seat - that they were pissed off at something.

Still, after sitting through local acts the Moods, Twilights, New Zealand's Max Merritt and the Meteors, and from the UK, The Searchers, who were OK, it was still such a blast to see the Stones begin their set with a blistering 'The Last Time', 'Mercy, Mercy' and 'That's How Strong My Love Is' showed us they had a soulful side whilst rhythm rockers like 'She Said Yeah' and 'Not Fade Away' lifted us out of our seats and on to our feet. 'Play With Fire' even succeeded in lowering the decibel rate of the screamers for a short time.

Mick sang 'Spider and The Fly' in a slurring vocal only demonstrating the state he was in, but his harmonica playing was straight from the Delta and everyone knows booze and Blues belong together. All eyes were on Brian as usual, dressed in a girl's bone jumper, red elephant corduroy pants and sporting a sunburst Gibson Firebird. Keith remained the quiet achiever, but their sound relies so much on his chunky fills and bee-sting leads, he is probably the group's most important member.

When the Stones are on song there is no band in the world that can touch them. The last three numbers, a kind of Stones mid-Sixties' trilogy – 'Get Off of My Cloud', '19th Nervous Breakdown' and the stellar 'Satisfaction' wiped all feelings about their stage demeanour from my mind... and I think from everyone else's.

This was indeed the fabulous Rolling Stones, the Greatest Rock 'n' Roll Band in the World, and we fell in supplication at their feet once again. They could be nasty boys, but who really cares? It's the music that matters, and the Stones are always about the music first and everything else second. I left the theatre loving Mick Jagger, Keith Richards, Brian Jones, Bill Wyman, and Charlie Watts, and that love will be with me to the day I die.

---

*After Australia, the Stones were back on tour in continental Europe in March and April, then off to the USA again in June.*

---

## MANNING BOWL
### 24 JUNE 1966, LYNN, MASSACHUSETTS

**I WAS THERE: BRIAN GRANGE, AGE 14**
It was drizzling a little and they were getting shocked with their guitars. They tear-gassed the crowd and the wind blew the tear gas back to the stage. I saw Keith push a cop off the stage. Chairs were flying. Headlines the next day said, 'Stones get stoned' because rocks were being thrown at the limo when they left. The stage was rushed twice. After the first time the local radio DJ grabbed the mic and said if that happens again the Rolling Stones will fly back to London. They played 10 songs, 30 minutes, and it was over.

When we were walking in, the limo passed us. I could see Charlie in the back seat next to the window on the driver's side. Like Jagger said later, 'It wasn't very secure.' Great show.

# THE ROLLING STONES IN THE SIXTIES: A PEOPLE'S HISTORY

## I WAS THERE: ART DANSKER, AGE 16

I lived one town over from Lynn, Massachusetts. Myself and two friends decided to drive to Manning Bowl to see what the outdoor concert spectacle was. We did not have tickets, nor did we expect to attend. We found a parking space quite near the back entrance to the stadium, which proved to be the backstage entrance. My friends and I, along with probably another 20 or 30 people, were just hanging out at the closed gate. We didn't really know what we were looking at. We could hear The McCoys playing and, I think, The Standells. About 10 or so minutes before the Rolling Stones took the stage, a police officer opened the back gate and told all of us standing there we were welcome to go on in.

Because we were entering the stadium from behind the makeshift stage, we were led out in front of the crowd that was already there, so we were in about the second or third row from the stage. The Stones started playing. It was great. But after about five or so songs, the crowd screaming their approval, during 'Paint It, Black' the cops seemed to get nervous and for no particular reason started throwing tear gas grenades into the crowd. As soon as that started happening, we made a dash for the gate we came in - probably seconds behind the Stones exiting the same gate in their limos - and jumped into our cars and left. The biggest take away that I got from the experience is that the Lynn police had planned on the tear gas attack well before the show. That's why the police officer opened the back gate and let us in for free.

## I WAS THERE: GARY DOMBROWSKI, AGE 15

What I remember most about that show was standing on the folding chairs watching Brian Jones sitting on the stage with his sitar, Mick announcing to the crowd, 'Lady Jane in the rain', and the smell of tear gas.

## I WAS THERE: COLLEEN OLIVER, AGE 14

My parents drove me, and my best friend, Arlene, to Lynn to see the Stones and planned to have dinner out while we were at the concert. Our seats were terrible - far back and on the ground. We couldn't see anything. I think it was during the intro for the Standells that the announcer said the concert would be called off if people left their seats. That was like our signal to go up front before everyone else did, and that's exactly what happened. We were right in front and there were only horses and police between us, and the Stones. Back then the stages were very low so we felt like we could almost touch them. What an experience.

I vaguely remember them saying they were cutting it short due to the rain, but I can't swear to it. What I do remember is the crowd pushing forward and us being pushed into the police. The next thing we knew, tear gas was being thrown and we had no way to escape it - the crowd was behind us and the police and Stones in front of us. The tear gas was awful. I was separated from my friend, and we spent hours looking for her. My poor parents were beside themselves, but all ended well thankfully. At the time, there was a photo published where we could pick ourselves out of the crowd. I don't think it exists anymore. We were also getting a reputation. What fun.

### I WAS THERE: DICK NORTON

My recollection is that the Stones bolted during 'Satisfaction'. The rain was more a heavy mist. I recall Jagger pulling his jacket up over his head and telling the crowd, 'You should be home in bed.' The sound system was terrifically awful. I recall also that the band piled into limos parked behind the stage. The next day I went out and bought *Aftermath*.

## DILLON STADIUM
## 27 JUNE 1966, HARTFORD, CONNECTICUT

### I WAS THERE: GARY GERARD

1966 was on the cusp of the really large venues like Shea Stadium, so you could get reasonable tickets easily to see just about anybody. I was in a working garage band at the time. The guys in the band were going, not necessarily together, to see the Stones. Tickets were $5 general admission. Opening act was a band called North Atlantic Invasion Force, known as NAIF to everyone who saw them. They were a well-known local group that had had one local hit. They never got very big but they were a good cover group. I think the McCoys were there too.

It was a warm evening. The crowd got really boisterous and unruly, yelling and chanting, 'We want the Stones! We want the Stones!' over the top of the opening bands. You couldn't hear anything. Then they started crowding together. The lead singer of NAIF got so mad because he couldn't even hear himself. He said, 'You want the Stones? OK, we'll give you the Stones' and started to play 'Paint It, Black', a song that they did extremely well.

They played that and the crowd was then a combination of screaming 'yes' because they loved it and the other half just booing. And it just got louder and louder. That was the last song NAIF played.

Everything was late and the Stones came on late. It was not well organised. The Stones played maybe half a dozen songs. When they started 'Satisfaction' the crowd surged forward and broke through the barriers at the front and rushed the stage. At that point, the power went out and the whole thing went to hell. The Stones' security rushed them off the stage into the waiting cars and off they went.

And that was it. In just a split second the whole thing was over.

There was an interesting conversation between George Morgio from NAIF and the Stones manager as NAIF came off stage. With a few expletives, Andrew Loog Oldham basically asked George how dare they play a Stones song and said he was going to smear their name all over the industry. George said, 'Make sure you spell it right.'

### I WAS THERE: TONY A

I was the keyboard player in opening act NAIF, or The North Atlantic Invasion Force. I didn't get to meet the Stones. They came in unmarked plain wrapper white vans - and bolted after the show.

### I WAS THERE: DON MASSEY, 18

I was a high school student, and we were all caught up in the British mania of the period, rightly so. Dillon was at that time a rather simple stadium of rather small dimensions and nothing close to what is now defined as stadium or arena that would be appropriate for shows, just a small bleacher-seat space overlooking a field that was often used for high school football games and the like. There were no performance spaces suitable for shows in Hartford. It would be a number of years before a civic centre would be built. The excitement for Connecticut fans like me and my friends grew pre-show, as one would expect. The very idea that a British group would appear in our humble capital city was amazing itself. The fact it was going to be a Rolling Stones concert made the atmosphere thick with tension and pleasure.

By today's standards, there were relatively

Don Massey on bass guitar in the Shandells

few uniformed officers arrayed around the stage, but they were not likely to be pressed by crushing crowds, since those in attendance were really quite tame. I recall thinking the crowd was not very loud or rambunctious and I guess I expected we would all combine our excitement into one powerful rush of sound, coupled with a rising tide of motion toward the stage, but there was very little of the sort. Frankly, that surprised me. This was the Stones and they were right there in front of us.

The Stones took the stage and it was obvious that the crowd was delighted. As bands go, they were as good as one would expect, their talent and execution honed very well by live shows in prior years in Britain. They looked as we expected – a touch of Carnaby Street evident in their costume choices. Sadly, the show did not go its full length.

From the very first the speaker system was quirky and irritating, prone to intermittent cut-outs that left Mick Jagger singing largely to himself at stage front. A number of times the vocal audio simply stopped, and each successive time made Jagger more and more frustrated. Even from my bleacher seat halfway back, it was obvious to me that Mick wanted a better sound system than was present that night, and his irritation grew with every interruption. I have read that it was primarily because of the fans pressing toward the stage that led police to request the show be terminated.

I recall nothing intrinsically dangerous or threatening to either Mick or the fans down front that would have led a wary police force to cut the show early. In fact, Jagger voiced his displeasure with the sound system several times during the show, well before the culminating moment. I felt for Jagger and his bandmates because the desire to provide the best show possible was being thwarted by the sound system. Each effort to correct it failed. So, having reached his limit, Jagger simply stopped singing, tossed the mic stand into the crowd below and left the stage in a huff.

The band never said anything to us before leaving the stage – they simply walked off. They were at the mercy of the production team who provided the sound. Stunned as we were to realise the show had come to a premature halt, we accepted it and filed out of the bleachers. Of course, a mic stand being thrown from the stage by a rowdy British singer whose anger was evident even 50 yards from the stage was a new thing for us. In my case, I empathised with Jagger and clung to the memory of his having tossed the stand from the stage as an appropriate gesture of his frustration and outrage.

Now the police might have contributed to the decision to end the show early, but the Stones were never in any physical danger and the crowd loved their work. I could not have accepted the sound issue if I were on stage to perform. The show ended because of the sound, that's all there is to it. Am I glad they came to our city? Yes. Am I glad I went to the show? Absolutely. Each time they return to Hartford or a nearby city, I am led to the memory of the Dillon show and the first evidence of Jagger's sexy surly nature that would contribute to the definition of the man and the band in coming years.

## I WAS THERE: ROB MARONA, AGE 16

My band decided to go see the Stones. The oldest of us had just turned 16 and nobody had a driver's license yet and none of our parents had volunteered to take us, so we hitchhiked all the way, just like the song. It was to be our first concert, with our No.1 heroes. What could be better than that? The concert was at a college football stadium. Stones concerts in stadiums bring back memories for hundreds of thousands, if not millions, of people. But this had to be one of the worst concerts ever. It was the middle of the afternoon in the blazing sun, and only about 200 people came. The stage was set up in the bleachers at the 50-yard line and the audience was made to sit in the bleachers on the opposite side with the empty field in between. There were a couple opening acts, which we weren't interested in, then the Stones arrived.

Three limousines drove out onto the field to the front of the stage and out they came. Apparently, they were already experiencing conflicting ego problems. Surely they all could have fitted in one or at most two limos? Or maybe they had one as a decoy. They had to run for their lives from the girls sometimes back then. But not this day.

They started playing and it soon became obvious, even from that distance, that something was wrong with Brian Jones. They played 'The Last Time' and he just couldn't play the signature guitar lick right. And that seemed to amuse him. They played three, maybe four, songs. After about 10 or twelve minutes they quit, got back in the limos and left.

I was very disappointed. I guess that's the way they did shows back then but by today's standards, and even then, it seemed like a rip-off. None of us remembers exactly how we got home that day, but we got right back to practicing, undaunted by the experience, and no less committed to learning Stones tunes.

## I WAS THERE: HOLLISTER LOWE

They arrived on the field in a station wagon. It got a little rowdy and the show was cut short, Mick dropping the mic stand off the stage.

## I WAS THERE: BRAD KRONES, AGE 12

We were driving on the highway adjacent to Dillon Stadium as I heard a commercial on the radio, WPOP AM, for the upcoming concert. I begged my mother to get tickets and she agreed to. I ended up going with my stepsister, who was about my age. We had the better tickets which were $5 each. The cheap seats were $2.50. We were seated near the back of the section but had a good view of the stage. The radio DJ came out in a tux to introduce the bands and there were several warmup bands, including The Syndicate of Sound, The McCoys, and as I recall two more.

The Association was supposed to perform, but we were told one or more band members were ill. The Stones were fabulous. Brian Jones was wearing the same outfit he wore on the cover of *High Tides, Green Grass*. The crowd was noisy as hell, but you could still hear the music.

# THE ROLLING STONES IN THE SIXTIES: A PEOPLE'S HISTORY

The place was jumping but I do not remember any disturbances, as newspaper reports of the time alleged. I read that the police chief signalled the group to leave early but have no memory of anything like that. The two songs that stick out in my memory are 'Satisfaction' and 'Paint It, Black'.

Mick announced during the show this had been the largest crowd the group had every performed for, yet the place was so small, considering what was to come in the music world. Compared to later concerts and events, this early production had an aura of innocence to it, as if the genre was so new that nobody knew what to do other than to try and duplicate the type of staged shows that typified the industry back in the big band era, hence the radio guy in the tux, for example. Looking back on it, that was ridiculous. And why did they imagine they needed four warmup bands to draw a crowd? Another amazing aspect was that, at age twelve, I was permitted to go to such an event without supervision. My parents were divorced, and my mother was very progressive in her outlook.

## I WAS THERE: JANE THOMPSON

It was my very first concert without my parents. I was used to going to the Grand Old Opry, when it came to the Armory in Hartford, to see Ernest Tubb and Minnie Pearl, but nothing like the Stones. I don't know how my best friend Kathi and I talked our parents into letting us go, but I'd guess they were just thankful it wasn't The Beatles, because they weren't loving them.

My best friend since we were five years old and I were so close. When we were 10, we started riding our bikes to each other's houses, mostly hers because she had a larger, friendlier family than mine. I have no idea how we scored the tickets, but we may have won them from WTIC or the other radio station we used to listen to. We had just gotten out of our second year of high school the week before the concert. We were too young to have jobs so were free on a Monday night to go to a concert.

Kathi's father didn't work Mondays, because he worked as buyer at G. Fox and Co., about a mile away, Tuesday through Saturday. Our hometown of Meriden was about 18 miles away. They were just putting I-91 together, to bypass the Berlin Turnpike, the way we always got to Hartford. It would open just after I got my driver's license a year later. It was so exciting.

I don't remember a single song they played, but it was loud for those days, although nothing like what they grew to be when I saw them 25 years later. I'm not sure they even brought their own sound systems. There sure weren't any visual effects, big screens, or projectors. It was all about the music. It was magical!

They were huge at the time, totally neck-and-neck with The Beatles. The incident at the end was weird. I missed what was thrown - somehow, I've always remembered it as a guitar - although I was sure that Mick Jagger had thrown it and a bunch of people rushed the stage. Since it was an athletic field, and they didn't really fill in the entire field with chairs, there was plenty of room for everybody to rush the stage and start throwing chairs around. I was totally freaked out. I knew I would be in so much trouble if I got involved with that.

The police went forward, and my friend and I ran for the gates. We got out and waited for her dad, and I honestly don't remember any details after that. Looking at their schedule, they were just probably exhausted and pissed off because it was in an open-air stadium with no security to speak of. I remember the crowd being rude. I'd be touchy if this was my sixth concert in four days in six cities. That was a lot of travelling.

Despite the fogginess of my memories, this event changed my life. It was a week or two later that the *Sunday Parade* magazine ran an article about the 'filthy' lyrics of '(I Can't Get No) Satisfaction'.

That day I came biking home from my friend's house just before dinner and my father was waiting for me to yell about the smut I had been listening to. He raved on and on for a bit and, when he paused for air, I made a crack about his favourite, Peggy Lee, and her song 'You Made Me Love You'. Well, I got a slap across my face that near cracked a tooth and I gave him the look that I would kill him if he ever did it again. I turned and walked upstairs. To say it changed our relationship might start a clue. I made sure to be smart enough to go to college on my own merits after that. I was gone a couple of years later, on scholarship.

## I WAS THERE: JOHN HANNON, AGE 15

My parents dropped me off because I was too young to drive. I didn't have a date - probably no one else wanted to go. I remember the stage being set up in the middle of the field. There was no encore – a station wagon backed up to the stage after the concert and drove off with the band. The announcer went on the PA, 'The Rolling Stones have left the stadium.' A great experience.

## I WAS THERE: ALAN BUDNEY

When we were walking to the stadium from where we parked, we passed a factory, and several workers were on break outside. They were teasing and mocking. One of them said, 'Hey, you want to see Rolling Stones for free? Watch this,' proceeding to roll a fistful of stones down the road. What a joker. We had field seats and the concert was great, with amazing riffs on 'Satisfaction'. Apparently, there was a bit of a scuffle at the end, but we saw only a little of all that.

## I WAS THERE: HAROLD MONTGOMERY, AGE 15

I first heard 'Not Fade Away' on the radio, then saw the Stones on *The Hollywood Palace* TV show. They sang 'I Just Want to Make Love to You'. Dean Martin was hosting. I remember him being rude to them. I was a hardcore Beatlemaniac too. This was when you couldn't be a Beatles fan and a Rolling Stones fan at the same time. Add the Supremes to that mix (especially in a racist state like Florida) and my friends thought I was dead nuts. I had a Beatle fan penpal in the UK who'd trade me the monthly *The Rolling Stones Book* for American Beatles stuff. I have them all bar the last one. I went to the Dillon show with a schoolmate named Daniel. We bought our tickets at a record store. Brian was my favourite Stone. I thought it was magical that he could play the harmonica, guitar, dulcimer, flute and sitar. Two months after the Stones at Dillon Stadium, I saw The Beatles in Boston, Massachusetts, making 1966 a very golden year.

## I WAS THERE: TOM CUBETA, AGE 14

I was 14 years old and my friend was 15. I think I paid $6 for the ticket. My friend had a girlfriend with an older brother who also liked the Stones. He drove us to the concert and then, when the concert was over, we met him at the car to go back home to Middletown. It's been a few years, but I remember rushing the stage for the last few songs. We were ten to 20 feet from the stage and I remember yelling out to Mick Jagger.

# THE ROLLING STONES IN THE SIXTIES: A PEOPLE'S HISTORY

We were so close to the stage. I don't recall any security trying to keep anyone away. No fights, no real pushing or shoving, just a bunch of kids having a good time watching their favourite band.

### I WAS THERE: ROGER WILEY
The Rolling Stones arrived by helicopter. A very strange young woman dressed totally in black sat next to me and made very dark pronouncements to nobody in particular. I suspect she may have been a prototype for the Goth era.

### I WAS THERE: LINDA RINALDI, AGE 15
Our music shop in Meriden, Connecticut organised a bus trip to Dillon Stadium, about half an hour away. I remember folding chairs lined up neatly on the outside ball field. Everyone sat quietly, very well behaved, so different from a few years later when concerts were a free-for-all.

### I WAS THERE: CHUCK SHEKETOFF, AGE 11
That was my first concert. My father took my brother and me. I was only 11 and my brother was almost 13. My dad was sitting with us smoking one of his cigars while older kids around us smoked pot.

### I WAS THERE: PETER ZONI, AGE 15
I went with my friend Michael Fallon, who had moved to Hartford from Forestville, Connecticut. I had never been to a rock concert, but my mom let me go. The concert was for the newly-released Stones album, which featured 'Mother's Little Helper'. The last song before the stage was rushed was 'Satisfaction'. The crowd went berserk and flooded towards the stage. I got my leg caught in a folding chair and it was crushed. I cut it pretty bad.

   I had brought a Hohner Marine Band harmonica with me from home to the concert. I was walking near the concert after we had all left the stadium. At a traffic light, a car full of four girls and one guy, all at least six to eight years older than Michael or I, was stopped on red. They saw blood on my pants leg as they were stopped and inquired as to what had caused such an injury. They also saw the harmonica in my hand and asked where it was from. I told them that I had taken it off the stage floor

## THE ROLLING STONES IN THE SIXTIES: A PEOPLE'S HISTORY

when Mick and company had rushed from the stage at the surge of the crowd. The guy pulled out a $20 bill, which in 1966 was a good amount of money for a 15-year-old. I sold him the harmonica.

**I WAS THERE: SHEILA MAYO**
I had great seats, front row and centre. My father, Glendon R Mayo, was Director of Licences in Hartford, Connecticut and gave them the permit to have the concert at Dillon Stadium, so they comped him the tickets. The Stones were late arriving, and the crowd was very worked up. I seem to recall them arriving in a helicopter behind the stage. The stage was set up on the field with fold-up chairs arranged in rows in front of it. Each row of the chairs was connected so when one chair in a row was folded, the whole row folded with it - an important fact once the riot started. The announcer introduced the Rolling Stones and Mick started singing 'Satisfaction'. A girl with long, stringy brown hair jumped up from a stadium seat, high in the rows above my seats, and ran down onto the field. She ran right down the aisle next to me and up onto the stage and grabbed Mick Jagger. I remember being amazed at how little resistance she encountered, all the way down and all the way up to the stage. There was some security present in the form of the police present, but they appeared totally unprepared for this kind of action. The crowd surged forward onto the field. The chairs folded and a wave of people came towards us. The Stones stopped playing and left. My older sister pushed me forward into the oncoming crowd saying, 'Tell them you're going to throw up, it will part the crowd.' It did, and we got out quickly and safely. And as long as my father was in that government position, there were no more concerts at Dillion Stadium.

# STEEL PIER MARINE BALLROOM
## 1 JULY 1966, ATLANTIC CITY, NEW JERSEY

**I WAS THERE: MARY JONES**
My Mom said I could go because she felt bad that I wasn't allowed to see The Beatles in 1964 in Philly. Six of us went. My friend Char said we took two buses to get there. It probably took us three hours. Normally

it would be one and a half hours by car. Peter and Gordon opened and were watching the show. At the intermission we ran so fast to see if the Rolling Stones were with them and all our food dropped as we were running. What a day.

## FOREST HILLS MUSIC FESTIVAL, FOREST HILLS TENNIS STADIUMS
### 2 JULY 1966, QUEENS, NEW YORK

### I WAS THERE: CURT ANGELIDES

The very first time I heard the Rolling Stones on the radio at home, the first few bars stopped me dead in my tracks. From there I did two things I had never done before. The first was to turn up the family radio, the second was to stop performing the chore I was involved in. What I heard was so full of energy, colour and joy that it blew away any thoughts of maintaining a stance within the grey, quiet, old world that up until that point was what appeared to be all that the world had to offer. Sure, there were The Beatles and Bob Dylan, but the Rolling Stones said it all so much better than anybody else.

I grew up in New York City in the Bronx. In 1966 I was in junior high school, old enough to be out in the evenings on dates, visiting friends for the sake of studying school material or going downtown to take sitar lessons. I was able to afford dates, records and tickets because of a regular self-employment situation. I knew when the Rolling Stones would be playing in the city. Because I was a regular customer of this band's records at a particular shop, when I asked about getting a ticket, the person behind the counter gave me the needed information to easily obtain a ticket in a timely manner. Another point in my favour of being able to attend this show was that it did not clash with other planned activities, like being at the beach with the family two days later on July 4th.

One point that was not in favour of my attendance was that the Rolling Stones were not particularly well received by family members, or society in general. They were viewed as scruffy, unkempt and rude, or even downright ill-mannered and obnoxious. The lyrics of some of the songs were not well received. Then there were the riots that periodically erupted when they played one place or another. If their songs happened to come on the radio or television, there was really no limit placed on that, but too much enthusiasm would garner odd looks and wisecracks. The adults did not favour the band or the music, the long hair and manner of dress. It was said they were a bad influence and trouble. My older sister thought Elvis was a better singer, with better songs.

I figured that it would serve no good purpose to announce I had any interest in going to a Rolling Stones concert. I had to come up with a good cover story as to why I was going out that night. In the few weeks between getting my ticket and attending, I spent more than the usual amount of time hanging out with my best friend Tommy. Because it was summertime, his brother's band had more time for practise, and they even played at events in a park and a block party in Harlem. It was my good fortune that they had an engagement on the same night as the Stones gig. We worked out the details with the adults in both households, with the agreement that we would all be back home no later than midnight. My friends and I also worked out the details between us and firmly agreed to be back at the station by where we lived no later than 11.30pm.

On July 2$^{nd}$, shortly before seven, Tommy, his brother Jeff and I were observed leaving the block we lived on, heading for the train station. They were going to an open-air bandstand where a number of folk music acts would perform in the grounds of a schoolyard. My friends knew I had somewhere else to be. When the D train got to 7$^{th}$ Avenue, I switched to the E train heading into Queens. When I got out at the stop for the venue, I walked to the proper entry gate and went in at about 8.10pm.

There were four acts that evening: The Tradewinds, The Standells and The McCoys were the opening acts, and the Rolling Stones were headliners and main attraction. It wasn't until 10.15pm that they appeared, and in a very energetic fashion went through a 10-song set in just over 30 minutes. They opened with one of my favourite songs, 'Not Fade Away', and closed with 'Satisfaction'. Among the remaining eight songs they played three – 'Stupid Girl', 'Lady Jane' and 'Paint It Black' – from the new album, released the same day. The sound level in the place was something else, certainly louder than a radio or television set or any other concert setting I had been to up until then. The band, however, were at times having to compete with the sound of the audience. The show seemed to end abruptly, which was good because I had just enough time to get home by the agreed upon hour, if I was really lucky. 'Satisfaction' ended and I ran from my seat to the train station, put my token in the turnstile as the train pulled into the platform and barely got through the doors as they closed.

It was an anti-climactic end to an energising and inspiring night, knowing that even if I caught the next train with no waiting time, I would miss my friends by at least 15 minutes. I got out of the train thinking my cover story was sunk. I turned to head for the exit and, two cars down, saw my friends get off the train. Three minutes later, I waved goodnight to Tommy's mother and two minutes after that I was home with 10 minutes to spare. All in all, it was a great night out, and no one at home was any the wiser as to where I'd spent the evening.

### MY MOM WAS THERE: STEPHEN CONN

My mother, Natasha Conn, saw the Stones in concert in Forest Hills. Her girlfriend threw flashbulbs to make a couple dancing in front of them sit down and afterwards they noticed many dolled-up girls waiting to be let into the band's hotel.

Natasha Conn remembered thrown flashbulbs in Queens, NYC

## CONVENTION HALL
### 3 JULY 1966, ASBURY PARK, NEW JERSEY

### I WAS THERE: PATRICIA CESTARE

I saw the Stones with Brian when they played the Convention Hall at Asbury Park, New Jersey. I was just graduated from elementary school. I remember Brian was sitting down and playing a dulcimer that he had in his lap.

THE ROLLING STONES IN THE SIXTIES: A PEOPLE'S HISTORY

# ONONDAGA COUNTY WAR MEMORIAL
## 6 JULY 1966, SYRACUSE, NEW YORK

**I WAS THERE: MIKE OTIS**

When they returned to Syracuse in 1966, they topped a bill which included the McCoys, The Standells and The Tradewinds, along with local band The Monterays. This concert was festival seating so the swift of foot got the best seats. The shows were low tech, with small amps and no special lights, effects or flashy costumes, all of which endeared them to me in those pre-stadium days. I recall that one's eyes fell upon Brian as upon Mick. Brian was my favourite, Charlie next. Brian had a pinstripe suit in 1966 and his sitting to play the dulcimer was electric.

This concert was on a sweltering hot rainy day. An American flag had been brought in to dry. It was draped on a chair backstage to dry. Brian took it and reportedly 'dragged it' behind him. After the concert, the band was taken under the War Memorial through a tunnel to the Public Safety Building to be questioned, where the matter was resolved. It took another 16 years for the band to return to Syracuse.

I still have the concert programmes from both 1965 and '66, costing only a few dollars. Photo buttons were sold too, this before all souvenirs were made in China, $50 t-shirts and all.

I have been to 15 Stones concerts, the last of which was in 2015. The Stones have appeared in Syracuse 10 times and I've also seen them in Buffalo and Albany plus Hartford, Connecticut, which was a smaller show with little staging on a brief tour, so a flashback to the early days.

I didn't see Mick Taylor with the band but did see him as a solo artist years later: he pitched a fit with his band and stormed off. I have all the LPs, cassettes, 8-tracks, CDs, VHS tapes and DVDs, plus all the US tour programmes and a myriad of t-shirts and books. I have an autographed photo with a provenance from 1966, and Ron Wood's and Mick Taylor's autographs. The 2021 tour cities were a bit out of reach for me in terms of both distance and cost. I think the tour should have been cancelled and they should be calling it a day, post-Charlie....

### I WAS THERE: BRAD CLARRY

This was their second concert here in nine months. Brian Jones was arrested for 'defacing' an American flag. He had picked up a flag and dragged it about 20 feet, rolling it up as he walked. Jones later apologised and told police he wanted the flag as a souvenir, and the case was dismissed.

I was 15 and my ticket was $3.50. It was the first concert of my life. I was also interviewed by the local newspaper about the concert around 20 years ago.

## ARIE CROWN THEATRE
### 10 JULY 1966, CHICAGO, ILLINOIS

### I WAS THERE: BILL CLARK

Two years after first seeing them in Milwaukee, my best friend and I went to Chicago to see them at the Arie Crown Theatre in McCormack Place. They were touring in support of *Aftermath*. The Standells and The McCoys opened. Brian was present but the band was not tight. I recall a Chuck Berry cover, maybe 'Around and Around', in which Keith and Brian seemed out of sync and exchanged glances. Mick invited Charlie to the microphone to announce 'Lady Jane'. I think they were playing two shows that day.

## KIEL CONVENTION HALL
### 12 JULY 1966, ST LOUIS, MISSOURI

### I WAS THERE: KATY MCLEOD

I've followed them since 1964, when they first came on the radio. I was twelve. DJs loved the British Invasion music. I had a favourite DJ who was on the radio at seven o'clock every night, Johnny Rabbit on KXOK. He would play all that stuff. 'Time is on My Side' is my very first recollection, along with 'Play with Fire'. I went to see the TAMI Show at a movie theatre in 1964. We had to wait far too long to see them in concert. They were on the coast in New York, and went to Chicago to record at Chess Records. It took two years to get them to St Louis, but my little girl heart was pumping for Mick months before that. I was already having conversations with my girlfriends at slumber parties about Mick Jagger. But it wasn't just Mick. It was all of them. It was their long hair, their sloppy clothes. They were different from The Beatles. They had a little bit more of the bad boy image about them, and I was already deep into fan magazines like *16 Magazine*, with all the gossip – their favourite colour and so on. Whatever you could read about them, I would read about them. Mick had sex appeal. I don't know if I even knew the word back then.

By 1965 I'd already seen The Beatles. I was invited to go to a Beatles press conference and travelled 300 miles on a bus to see them. I got to ask George Harrison a question and it opened the world for me. I met these kids in Chicago who were the hugest Stones fans. One of them had a Charlie Watts fan club button. They were so far ahead of me. They'd already seen them in concert and seen a press conference the Stones did right on the street on Michigan Avenue, in the middle of downtown for everybody to see. My brand-new friend I met on that trip to Chicago had already met Brian Jones at a party. I caught that wave. I was a groupie and proud of it. The term 'groupie' didn't have all the modern-day associations then.

When they came to St Louis, She Panitz, Linda Thaw and I went to see them arrive on their private plane. It was 108 degrees outside but we had our best mini skirts on and only two flight techs to keep us company. The airport was a ghost town as there was a commercial airline strike going on. We didn't mind waiting for four hours because the man in the FAA control tower assured us the Stones were flying in from Houston, even giving us the number of the plane. They arrived at 4am and we watched them walk down the stairs, one by one. Mick was wearing white bell bottom pants and a summer tank top but Brian was wearing a three-piece pin striped suit like he just walked off stage. They climbed into the waiting limos and Linda went over and talked to Keith.

Our seats for the show were off the floor but it was really easy to get downstairs and go up the front. Nobody really stopped you. The Kiel Auditorium seated 14,000 people and years later I read a news article that said it was only half full and there were a lot of empty seats. I didn't notice that. When you're young and caught up in a frenzy at the front of the stage, all you hear are screams and all you see is excitement. The rest of it you just block out.

# WINNIPEG ARENA
## 14 JULY 1966, WINNIPEG, CANADA, AGE 19

**I WAS THERE: HOWARD MARKSON**
I was in a rock 'n' roll group in Winnipeg for a couple of years, The Male Gender. We did many Stones tunes. I went to see the Stones with my buddy Billy. Our seats were pretty decent. I went. The big buzz was how the group could be rowdy and egg on their fans, so I watched not only the show but how it played out. I remember Mick wore a tight pair of white pants, and shook his butt impishly and provocatively. One male fan jumped from the balcony onto a curtain that was behind the group. He crawled down onto the stage, only to be greeted by security. I considered this the greatest concert I had ever been to, until I saw them in Vancouver in June 1972.

# MEMORIAL AUDITORIUM
## 22 JULY 1966, SACRAMENTO, CALIFORNIA

**I WAS THERE: MARK HALVERSON, AGE 15**
By the time I first saw the Rolling Stones live and in person, a month shy of my 16th birthday, the quintessential bad-boy quintet had already altered my DNA. Hunkered down in tight-quarter bedrooms and living rooms sporadically devoid of parents in suburban North Highlands, California, my buddies and I relentlessly spun the band's early LPs on small mono portable turntables and bulky TV-phonograph consoles. The music whetted my appetite not only for more rock 'n' roll but also more criminally-neglected American rhythm and blues. And I hungrily devoured all album liner notes in search of my own gateway to musical maturation and peer group hipness.

The back of the Stones' first US release, *England's Newest Hitmakers*, in 1964, heightened my percolating testosterone with an introductory carrot for all impressionable, rudderless souls: 'The Rolling Stones are more than a group - they are a way of life.' Subversive and tribal. Seductive. The music felt like a seamless weave of the old and new that propelled me into Tower Records listening booths to unearth its fountainhead.

# THE ROLLING STONES IN THE SIXTIES: A PEOPLE'S HISTORY

My high school rock band heavily featured early Stones tunes alongside those from The Yardbirds, The Animals, The Beatles and other AM radio hitmakers of the day. The Stones' second US album, *12 x 5*, unveiled instrumental '2120 South Michigan Avenue', named after the home of legendary Chess Records, a song I can never hear enough of to this day. And 1965's *The Rolling Stones, Now!* was a motherlode of cover material, with 'Everybody Needs Somebody to Love' inspiring me to catch Solomon Burke live. Playing 'Off the Hook' at a high school rally launched my band's first and only standing ovation. And *Out of Our Heads* gave birth to the single '(I Can't Get No) Satisfaction', which a student brought to our ninth-grade class on the last day, transforming our final two hours into an impromptu one-song sock hop.

While vinyl provided rock 'n' roll sustenance, it was the Stones' TV appearances on which I really feasted. Each family viewing of them on *The Ed Sullivan Show* brought disparaging remarks from my father – 'ugly English kids trying to sound black, who can understand their lyrics?' – and polite smiles from my mother. And the Stones used variety show *Shindig!* to not only publicly debut 'Satisfaction' but also introduce Howlin' Wolf (who performed 'How Many More Years') to mainstream TV audiences. All this left me wanting more … and more.

To see the Stones perform at the Sacramento Memorial Auditorium was more a pilgrimage than a musical event. I'd only seen two previous live shows: organist Korla Pandit, a turban-topped, light-skinned African-American known as the Godfather of Exotica, and Jimmy Durante, known for his prominent schnozzola and exuberant vaudeville schtick. Neither event nor the Stones TV appearances fully prepped me for the reciprocating sonic booms ignited by the live Stones and their writhing, screaming fans.

The Tradewinds, The Standells and The McCoys opened with sets that included their current radio hits before Mick Jagger and company upgraded the opening chords of 'Not Fade Away' into a tsunami of swagger, big beats, pelvic thrusts, galvanizing musicianship and theatrical cavorting. With stacked amps battling the rabid bursts and a general roar from the Mod and Rocker- influenced crowd for dominance, the Stones quieted briefly for an elegant 'Lady Jane' and capped the evening with a muscular '19th Nervous Breakdown' and the suitably transcendental 'Satisfaction'.

THE ROLLING STONES IN THE SIXTIES: A PEOPLE'S HISTORY

# CIVIC AUDITORIUM
## 24 JULY 1966, BAKERSFIELD, CALIFORNIA

**I WAS THERE: LIZ BEAVERS**

My memories of the Stones at the Bakersfield concert in the Sixties were not that fond. Mick wore a white t-shirt and pink trousers. The singing was great but Mick sang with his back to the audience almost the entire time. He would prance back and forth occasionally and briefly turn around. I took it as a snub to Bakersfield. But that was also back in the day when you expected a performer to face the audience. I think Johnny Cash was the first one to turn his back on the audience while singing.

**I WAS THERE: MIKE BAILEY**

In 1966 I had just graduated from high school. Many artists, rock and country, came through Bakersfield back then. I saw many concerts then. Still do. The Rolling Stones were probably the most famous at that time. On July 24, I went to the first of the two shows that night.

A local group opened with three songs. Then the Tradewinds came on. They had one hit, 'New York's a Lonely Town (When You're the Only Surfer Boy Around)'. Of course, California surfers didn't look like they looked. They looked like the Stones. After them came the Standells, with the hit, 'Dirty Water'. They were great and put on quite a show. They even did James Brown's 'Please, Please, Please, Please'. Very entertaining. Then came The McCoys with 'Hang on Sloopy!'. Rick Derringer (back then he was still Zerringer) was fantastic. Great show.

Then the Stones came on. Jagger in a pink sports coat and Brian Jones in a Union Jack suit. The crowd went crazy. They opened with 'Not Fade Away'. But because the Fuzz-Tone pedal for 'Satisfaction' was inadvertently on, it sounded crap. Keith was growing angry with the sound, then Ian Stewart walked out, made eye contact with Keith, then pushed the off switch with his finger, then smirked at Keith. Their latest hit had been 'Get Off of My Cloud'. They played their hits and introduced a new song, 'Lady Jane', with Brian on dulcimer.

It was a short but decent show. What I remember most is that the only time they talked to the audience was when Charlie introduced a song. And none of them smiled, not even once. They seemed bored and tired.

And they were probably both.

One more thing: because I got tickets to see a top group like the Stones, I got a date with the prettiest girl in school.

# HOLLYWOOD BOWL
## 25 JULY 1966, LOS ANGELES, CALIFORNIA

**I WAS THERE: IRA KNOPF**

Their performance only lasted about 30 minutes, give or take, the set-list including 'Not Fade Away', 'The Last Time', 'Stupid Girl', 'Time is on My Side', 'Get Off of My Cloud', 'Paint It, Black' and closer 'Satisfaction'. Sadly this turned out to be almost the last ever live performance with Brian Jones, as the Stones were not to reappear in concert in LA until November 1969, when Mick Taylor had replaced Brian. Ticket prices for their Hollywood Bowl concert were $5, $4 and $3.50.

**I WAS THERE: CYNTHIA PORTER**

I wasn't near the front when I saw them at the Hollywood Bowl. I was sat next to Humble Harv, a DJ with Radio KHJ, Los Angeles who used to play 'Goin' Home' by the Stones on his radio show every night at a quarter to midnight. It was 15 minutes long and he'd close the show with it.

I remember cruising along Downey Boulevard to the first ever McDonalds listening to 'Goin' Home'. I think the reason I didn't try to get on the stage at this show was because I was sat next to Humble Harv. I had him sign my playbill. To begin with I thought, 'I don't want this messing up,' then I thought, 'But it's Humble Harv!'

# COW PALACE
## 26 JULY 1966, SAN FRANCISCO, CALIFORNIA

**I WAS THERE: BETH ELLIOTT**

My town sponsored a youth group outing and hired a bus to take us into San Francisco for the show. The show was in the Cow Palace, which has always hosted a major regional stock show and rodeo. The format was

# THE ROLLING STONES IN THE SIXTIES: A PEOPLE'S HISTORY

the old rock 'n' roll revue for the first half, a number of bands beginning with a couple of one-hit wonders, leading up to a decent set by pre-Grace Slick Jefferson Airplane, folk rock edging toward psychedelia. The second set was the Stones, and by this time they had enough Top-40 hits to put on a show without doing anything experimental. I remember Mick Jagger turning away from the audience, waving a tambourine between his legs, and wiggling his bum. That was about the extent of the stagecraft; and era-appropriate.

Beth Elliott went on a bus trip to the Cow Palace

### I WAS THERE: JO D'ANNA, AGE 16

I was on one of my first dates with my first boyfriend and it was all a blur. I remember it being extremely crowded and smoky inside. I was very impressed, but I guess I was focusing more on my new boyfriend. It was his idea to take me to the Stones, so I wasn't really aware of who they were, since I was only 16 and very naive musically, only really knowing The Beatles and The Beach Boys.

### I WAS THERE: CHARLIE GREENE, AGE 14

The summer of 1966 is where it all began. I had just graduated from Catholic grammar school and was ready to rock at 14 years old. Like everyone else, I was introduced to rock 'n' roll when The Beatles hit *Ed Sullivan*. Then another band on a later show caught my eye. Their music was R&B, and they weren't dressed in suits like The Beatles and all the other British bands. They were the Rolling Stones, which I thought was a trés cool name. I found out later that Brian got it from a Muddy Waters song, 'I'm a Man'. I could tell they were rebels.

In 1966, my best friend and I would hang out at the Matrix in my neighbourhood in San Francisco. Marty Balin started the club with his band, the Jefferson Airplane. All the SF bands played there, including the Grateful Dead, Big Brother and the Holding Company (Janis Joplin), Steppenwolf (then called Sparrow), the Steve Miller Blues Band, et al. I also used to see them all play for free at Golden Gate Park. I saw the Jimi Hendrix Experience play there in 1967.

My older sister and I saw the Rolling Stones at the Cow Palace on what was Mick's 23rd birthday. It was an awesome gig, but the sound was like the *Got Live If You Want It* LP, with the girls all screaming. Brian played his red twelve-string Rickenbacker guitar, and sitar on 'Lady Jane'. The coolest thing I remember about the gig was Mick swinging his jacket to the audience over and over like he was going to throw it to them, moving forward with every swing. He eventually swung it over his shoulder and took off, dancing. Trés cool, Mick.

### I WAS THERE: RANDY STANLEY, AGE 13

I was born and grew up in the Bay Area, about 30 miles south of San Francisco, now the heart of Silicon Valley. My younger sister had the *Meet The Beatles* album, which I occasionally heard her playing. It was OK, but I was not moved. Around the middle of '65 I was at my older cousins' house. On this visit they were playing music, it was definitely not The Beatles. I asked, 'What is that?' I was moved. It was *The Rolling Stones, Now!* - much rougher and more raw than The Beatles. For me it was like, 'Holy crap, I've got to have more of this.' From then on, I was hooked, and it was the Stones only for me. I started buying their albums, and in '66 saw them for the first time at the Cow Palace in Daly City. My dad took me and three friends. I was 13, turning 14 that October. It was the only time I saw Brian Jones, but it's a great memory.

# HONOLULU INTERNATIONAL CENTER
## 28 JULY 1966, HONOLULU, HAWAII

### I WAS THERE: BRIAN JARVIS

I saw them in Honolulu in the summer of 1966. There were only 8,000 people at the show. There were three or four warmup bands, then the Stones played last. They only played for half an hour. The show was broadcast live on radio station KPOI FM.

*The Stones stayed in the United States following the end of the tour, recording tracks at RCA Studios in Hollywood that would later feature on Between the Buttons.*

## ED SULLIVAN THEATER
### 11 SEPTEMBER 1966, NEW YORK, NEW YORK

**I WAS THERE: JOANNE ROGERS**

I saw them with Brian at the Ed Sullivan Theater. For some reason I remember Tom Jones being on the same bill. If you look it up it says they were on the same bill together on 2 May 1965, but I know I did not go that day as it was my brother's birthday. In an Italian family – mine, anyway - you celebrated each other's birthday.

We had no tickets to get in but waited outside to see them. I remember a police officer grabbing Brian's long blond hair as he mistakenly thought he was a female fan trying to run in the entrance of the theatre. Of course, seeing the Stones without the whole entourage they travel with now was so refreshingly beautiful. Just them and their music.

*The Stones returned to the UK to perform 23 concerts, in what would prove to be their last British tour of the Sixties.*

## ROYAL ALBERT HALL
### 23 SEPTEMBER 1966, LONDON, UK

**I WAS THERE: STEPHEN MOYCE, AGE 16**

I was 16 in September 1966 when I paid the then exorbitant sum of £5 to see the Stones play at the Royal Albert Hall in London. The package tour mindset still existed then and supporting the Stones were, incredibly, The Yardbirds, featuring both Jeff Beck and Jimmy Page, plus Ike and Tina Turner.

# THE ROLLING STONES IN THE SIXTIES: A PEOPLE'S HISTORY

As the evening progressed, the atmosphere and tension building up in the hall was almost palpable – we were going to see the Stones for real! Seeing them on TV and playing their records was great, but this was different. At last, they were on – the hall erupted in total chaos with deafening noise from the screaming girls, many of whom rushed the stage. They were continually repelled by security guys and, amazingly, concert promoter Tito Burns.

The Stones played on regardless. My seat was about 30ft from the stage and I could clearly see Brian Jones, resplendent in a purple velvet jacket. He was smiling at all the mayhem as his rhythm guitar chords helped power along all the hits, the Stones having notched up six No 1's since 1964.

The vocals were virtually inaudible. The venue in 1966 had yet to receive the necessary saucer-shaped acoustic baffles, and Mick Jagger's best efforts just disappeared into the vast roof space, but it didn't matter. The experience of it all was totally overwhelming. What a time to be a teenager. The next twelve months would see the Stones embroiled in the *Satanic Majesties* album and Brian's sad decline accelerate alarmingly. But on that early autumn evening they were peerless – and I was there!

## I WAS THERE: HELEN LOCK, AGE 14

The first time I saw the Stones was in 1966 at the Royal Albert Hall, six months after my first ever concert, seeing Dylan in the same venue. I was 14 and thus I spent so long pondering my wardrobe that I still remember what I wore. I went with a friend and we were in about the 20th row, on the aisle. It was a great seat, which was actually pretty irrelevant since the moment the band came on stage, we all stood on our seats and screamed. I remember doing this because I was caught up in the fact that everybody was doing it,

Helen Lock's Stones journey started at the Royal Albert Hall

437

not because it was my natural response, but I was undeniably incredibly excited at the idea of being in the same space as the Stones.

They came on and did a few songs. I remember being so relieved that I could more or less see, as I'm only five feet tall, and then some girls got on stage and tried to pull Brian off. Or maybe it was Mick - it's all on grainy black and white film on Youtube somewhere.

I just remember being amazed watching this girl grabbing him, then security hauling her off. The show was halted for a while and in the crowd there was a mixture of anxiety that they wouldn't return and a vague sort of excitement that we'd been part of some newsworthy sort of event. They did finish up the show. I loved it - it was the day 'Have You Seen Your Mother, Baby' was released and we were excited to hear it - and as always I wrote about it in my diary when I got home. You'd think a first-hand account so soon after the show would be pretty accurate, but apparently not. For example, I listed that they played 'Who's Driving Your Plane?' and I all but remember them playing it, but to this day people tell me I'm wrong. I must have confused it with another slow blues number, as I did when trying to compile the Hyde Park set-list.

## I WAS THERE: BRENDA PARKER

Brian just stood quietly playing his guitar and staring up at the ceiling, seemingly in a world of his own. Mick was the centre of attention and now he had his James Brown moves down pat, he was the one everyone looked at and the others just played behind him, almost as if they were his backing group. Not that it mattered as before they'd even played a note everyone was already screaming at the top of their lungs.

## I WAS THERE: STASH KLOSSOWSKI DE ROLA

There was a famous show I went to (at the Albert Hall) with the band, where the girls stormed the stage immediately and it was over in a matter of moments. Very often they ended like that. They totally lacked crowd control, so it just turned into a mess.

I've seen them dozens and dozens of times in various venues. I don't go anymore. Mick Jagger was wondering why I hadn't come when they played Rome in 2014 and I said, 'Well, you know, if he wanted me to come he should have made special arrangements, including sending a limo to pick me up here at Montecalvello.' Because I wasn't about to brave those crowds to go to a Stones gig.

The last time I went to a Stones gig was in LA for *A Bigger Bang*. And although I was invited it took me two hours to get to the gig, when it should have taken an hour from my house. It took an extra hour to approach and find a place to park. There was a special VIP section with the sound box, and it was great to see the show. But either you went with them in buses for the guests and then you had to miss three or four numbers, or you went with your own transport, but then it took you another couple of hours to get to where you were going. By the time I went to the hotel, Keith had gone to bed.

# ODEON THEATRE
## 24 SEPTEMBER 1966, LEEDS, UK

### I WAS THERE: BRIAN ROBINSON

My job was travelling all around the country, and I happened to be in Leeds in 1966 selling decorating materials and all that sort of stuff. We were in a hotel and saw the Rolling Stones were on in a cinema round the corner. It was probably ten shillings to see them, and it was the Stones, Ike and Tina Turner, and The Beach Boys.

We were sitting on the second row and when they'd finished the concert, we were very close to the emergency exit doors on the side, and me and two mates I was working with opened the doors because we wanted to get out quick. There was an alleyway down the side and a big stretch limo, and I ran out first and bumped straight into Keith Richards. They got in the limo and drove off.

# EMPIRE THEATRE
## 25 SEPTEMBER 1966, LIVERPOOL, UK

### I WAS THERE: ALAN POWELL, AGE 15

I was in row V. The price was 17 shillings (85p). Well, they had to pay for those outrageous clothes somehow. The opening acts were Ike and Tina

Turner and the Ikettes, The Yardbirds with Jeff Beck and Jimmy Page on guitar, Peter Jay and the New Jaywalkers, and Long John Baldry.

The Stones played tracks off *Aftermath* and were awesome. I remember the lighting was very good. Charlie introduced 'Lady Jane' and Brian, his hand bandaged, played his dulcimer with a big white feather. They had so much energy. The place was bouncing and it was over too soon. We later saw the footage of the Royal Albert Hall gig from the same tour and it brought it all back.

# ABC THEATRE
## 28 SEPTEMBER 1966, ARDWICK, MANCHESTER, UK

### I WAS THERE: CHRISTINE MCDERMOTT, AGE 14

I was sat in the stalls – seat E2. The Stones had Ike and Tina Turner as one of the support acts. Having been to see The Beatles twice in Ardwick, when it came to the Stones concert I knew that for artists to get away from the theatre quickly they went out of the stage door and through the back yard of a terraced house that backed on to the theatre and out through their front door where their car was waiting for them. I found this out because I was friends with the sister of Eric Stewart (of the Mindbenders). They lived near me in Ardwick and Eric went to school with my cousin. Knowing this we were able to get out of the theatre and round to the house just as they were coming out into their car.

Like most of the concerts back then you didn't hear much of the music for all the screaming, but the Stones were one of the bands you wanted to hear so the later ones weren't too noisy that you could hear quite a bit of the songs. I count myself lucky to have been a teenager and lived in Manchester during that period. It was such an amazing place for music, clubs and concerts. I prize my autographs, especially the Brian Jones one. I also have Otis Redding's autograph, seeing him at the Ardwick ABC on his last tour before he died.

# GLOBE THEATRE (AKA ABC THEATRE)
## 29 SEPTEMBER 1966, STOCKTON-ON-TEES, UK

### I WAS THERE: IAN GILFELLAN, AGE 16

I had to hitch a ride from work to buy the tickets as I only had enough for them and no fare to Stockton - that was in July, about the same time as the World Cup finals. Jimmy Page and Jeff Beck were in The Yardbirds, and I remember Jeff tried playing his guitar over his head and not noticing he'd pulled his lead out. We ended walking back to Middlesbrough.

### I WAS THERE: GEORGE MORLAND, AGE 17

After seeing them in 1964, the next time I saw the Stones was at the ABC in 1966, ticket price 15/- (75p), where I went with my girlfriend - now my wife – and we sat in the circle. The show was excellent … apart from the non-stop screaming when the Stones came on.

### I WAS THERE: BARBARA GIBBON, AGE 19

My friend Jean and I were at the Globe when they played with The Yardbirds, Ike and Tina Turner, and I'm sure Billy J Kramer and The Dakotas were also on that night. We decided to go to Stockton early on the morning of the Stones gig. We walked from Middlesbrough. Venues for groups and artists in the Sixties weren't large arenas like today, and you were quite close to the artists in the theatres.

We decided to go early to find a way into the building so we could see and talk to the Stones, and mainly Mick Jagger. Our plan went really well. We sneaked in and looked round the place. The only place we could find where we could hide and not be seen was a dressing room with a washbasin, with a curtain round it. We got under and pulled the curtain over. We hid there for quite a while, then some people came in and were talking. We don't know what they were doing but later assumed they were getting ready for the show because all of a sudden the curtain was pulled back and there was Keith Relf of The Yardbirds with a drier in his hand. He must have been looking for somewhere to plug it into. We just crouched there looking amazed, and never said a word. Neither did Keith – he just walked away. We weren't bothered about The Yardbirds at the time, all we wanted was to see Mick Jagger, just like we had seen Keith. A good few minutes later some man who worked in the Globe came in, pulled back the curtain and told us we weren't allowed in the dressing rooms or anywhere else in the theatre until the doors opened for the show. He took us to the stage door entrance and said that was the best he could do.

It was okay with us as when the Stones did arrive, although there were other screaming fans with us by then, we got to see them close up and touch them. It was a brilliant time. We had tickets four rows from the front. What a good view we had. Of course, we were all screaming so you couldn't hear the words of the songs.

When the Stones had finished, girls were throwing things on the stage to them. I had nothing to throw so took one of my shoes off and threw that. Mick picked it up and threw it back. Was I glad. Not only had Mick Jagger touched my shoe and thrown it back, but it had never entered my head as to how I would have walked back to Middlesbrough with only one shoe.

## ODEON THEATRE
### 30 SEPTEMBER 1966, GLASGOW, UK

**I WAS THERE: GORDON RENNIE, AGE 16**
I saw the Rolling Stones at the Odeon Cinema in Renfield Street. Long John Baldry compered the show. The support acts were Peter Jay and the New Jaywalkers, The Yardbirds, and finally the Ike and Tina Turner Revue - quite a line-up. I don't think I heard much of the Stones due to the screaming. The cost of this show was 12/6, about 63p in today's money.

## CITY HALL
### 1 OCTOBER 1966, NEWCASTLE-UPON-TYNE, UK

**I WAS THERE: RITA MANN (NÉE JOPLING), AGE 16**
I went on a school cruise in 1964 and played 'Not Fade Away' on the jukebox all the time. I added it to my record collection, where it joined

'It's All Over Now.' My mam specially ordered 'Come On' for me and I avidly followed the Stones after that. I ordered 'The Last Time' without even listening to it. My friend and I knew we would love it. It cost either six shillings and thruppence (31p) or six and eightpence (33p). You could buy three singles for one pound in those days.

The first concert I went to was the Rolling Stones at the City Hall in Newcastle with Kathleen, a friend from school, although I was working by this time. One of the support acts was the Ike and Tina Turner Revue. They were backed by the Ikettes, who were dressed in green and were three of the thinnest girls I have ever seen. I remember Tina singing 'River Deep, Mountain High'. Peter Jay and the Jaywalkers were also on as were, I think, The Yardbirds, although I've no recollection whatsoever as to what they performed. Like every teenage girl, I was chanting and chanting, 'We want the Stones!' We sat about five rows from the front. There were barriers up. They came in from the right side of the stage and the place erupted. I can't tell you what they performed. I was too busy staring, and screaming.

Rita Mann was chanting, 'We want the Stones'

## ODEON THEATRE
### 6 OCTOBER 1966, BIRMINGHAM, UK

**I WAS THERE: PENNY EDWARDS, AGE 14**
There were no big venues or anything like the NEC, etc. like today. This was held at the Odeon Cinema on New Street in Birmingham city centre. It's still there. The Stones were very scruffy and still are, but the sound – wow! I was with a girlfriend, we stood at the side of the cinema, perhaps because it was cheaper, but rocked for three hours. The most vivid memory was being deaf for three days afterwards. No health and safety spoiling your fun in those days. Plus, we couldn't hear our parents moaning.

# THE ROLLING STONES IN THE SIXTIES: A PEOPLE'S HISTORY

## I WAS THERE: LIZ WOLSEY, AGE 12

They were playing with Ike and Tina Turner, and maybe The Yardbirds. I so wish I had written it all down. I was nearly 13 years old, and it was so exciting. I was on the third row but all I remember is Mick Jagger taking off his tie and throwing it into the audience, and girls going crazy.

## I WAS THERE: PAULINE LEVER, AGE 16

After seeing the Stones in Northampton in 1965, my friend Kay and I were itching for more. We looked at tour dates and discovered they were appearing at Birmingham Odeon in October. We booked tickets and thought we would worry about getting there nearer the time. As time drew near, we asked my friend's dad for a lift. He refused, my parents didn't have a car, and we were getting concerned. My boyfriend at the time came up with an idea and the day before the concert we spent an agonising few hours waiting to see if his friend could find somewhere to hire a car. He was 17 and most places said no. However, he did get one and on the day we were picked up at 5.15pm and were on our way. The lad put his foot down on the motorway and we drove at speed towards Birmingham.

Kay and I soon found the Odeon and we snooped about trying to find some way to perhaps get into the building. We were moved on a few times and eventually tried to get into a pub close by. Once inside I looked around and noticed a blond young man standing with a group by the bar. My heart almost stopped, but a closer look revealed he was not Brian. I said to my friends, 'He looks like Keith (Relf) of The Yardbirds (who were also appearing), but his hair is too short.'

Later at the show it was revealed Keith had in fact had his hair cut shorter. It must have been him. However, we were soon spotted and thrown out of the pub. Time soon came around for the concert to start and we went into the Odeon, hearts beating and feeling very excited, the only thing was that we were not in the stalls but upstairs in the circle.

The show itself was very good. The line-up included Long John Baldry, Peter Jay and the New Jaywalkers, The Yardbirds, and Ike and Tina Turner. But we had come to see The Stones, and the others were poor comparison. However, Ike and Tina were fantastic, and The Yardbirds were also very good.

# THE ROLLING STONES IN THE SIXTIES: A PEOPLE'S HISTORY

The tension inside us was building up, and when the Stones came on we almost burst with excitement. My eyes fixed on Brian, and I screamed and shouted and just ran for the edge of the circle. I remember looking down at the stalls and longing to be there. I actually remember wondering if I could climb down and even, 'if I jumped would I be OK?' Which of course was silly - I would probably have been killed. A bouncer came and grabbed me, said, 'I hope you're not thinking of jumping.' He sent me to my seat, saying if I moved he would throw me out.

The Stones were fantastic. They sang 'The Last Time', 'Paint It, Black', 'Lady Jane', 'Under My Thumb', 'Get Off of My Cloud', and 'Satisfaction'. Towards the end other girls from the circle started to go to the edge. We also went and stood by the edge, waved and screamed. Downstairs all hell had let loose, and we longed to be there.

The show came to an end and we filed outside where people were selling posters. I queued, watching as the posters of Brian were disappearing quickly, but purchased my prize and we met the boys. This was the Sixties and the drink-driving law hadn't come in. The boys had been drinking and were listening to our constant talk about the show, which probably distracted the driver. He went out of a side-road and we saw a bus coming and knew there was no way we were going to miss it. We went straight into the bus, causing a huge dent, and skidded to a halt. The police arrived and were lovely. They made a huge fuss of Kay and I, and laughed because I was crying and saying, 'I've creased my poster of Brian.' We were basically unhurt - just bumps and bruises. They took us to a garage and the car was towed there.

When we arrived, they made us sweet tea and arranged for someone from the hire company to come and get us. They asked if we should phone home and I suddenly realised I had lied to my parents, and they thought Kay's father was taking us. They would not have let us go with the boys. We got home about 5.30am and immediately Mum asked if Kay's dad and the car were OK, and I had to come clean. The car was written off and something was mentioned about a court case, but I don't remember anything about whether it took place.

I got into a lot of trouble for lying, but we had seen the Stones again, and survived the crash. After sleeping for about an hour I was dragged out of bed to go to work - at 16 I had been working for about six months. What an experience we had, but it was all worth it to see the Stones, the best ever group, and my blond hero, albeit from a distance.

# GAUMONT THEATRE
## 9 OCTOBER 1966, SOUTHAMPTON, UK

### I WAS THERE: MICHAEL SMITH, AGE 24

It's now called the Mayflower, but it was the Gaumont then. They had a bit more stage presence by then, because Mick just turned round and said, 'Shut up everyone, otherwise I shan't sing any more. And I wanna do a quiet one.' It was 'Lady Jane' and he got absolute quiet before he started. It was just all these screamers, and they didn't worry about being able to hear what they were playing. There were a lot of girls there.

At the time you were either a Beatles or a Rolling Stones fan. The Beatles were all right to start with but to me they just went off. When they got to *Sgt. Pepper*, I thought that was a load of rubbish. I liked the Stones right from the start and stuck with them. My girlfriend was more into classical music. I said, 'I've managed to get tickets for the Rolling Stones.' Her reaction? 'I don't like the Rolling Stones.' I said, 'Well, I've got tickets now, so we're going!' 'Well,' she said, 'I'll come with you on one condition - that you come with me to a concert I want to go to.' And I said, 'Yeah, fine.' So I had to sit through the Vienna Boys' Choir. At half time when the lights came up, I sank down in the seat so no one could see me, in case anybody I knew was there and thought, 'What's he doing there?' Some of it was in English and some in Austrian. So I took Sally to see the Rolling Stones, then had to put up with the Vienna Boys' Choir. It was worth it to see the Stones though.

# MAYFAIR, LONDON

### I WAS THERE: JIM GLEESON

I worked at One Stop Records in Mayfair, London from 1966 until 1974. During the mid-Sixties (I can't be sure of the exact date), I was working in the shop one Saturday afternoon, and on this day we closed a little early, and were getting ready to leave when a limo pulled up outside and in walked all five members of the Rolling Stones! They stayed for a about half an hour and bought loads of records. I was gobsmacked to see them all in the shop. The two things I remember were how small all the guys were and how nice they all were. They made an awestruck teen feel very cool.

I later saw them at the Hyde Park memorial show. Cool times!

*While 1966 saw the end of the Rolling Stones' extensive touring schedule within the UK, 1967 was to be another quiet year for the group in terms of live performances. Apart from a 27-show tour of Continental Europe, including the first performances by a Western rock music band behind the Iron Curtain, the Stones did not play live. Instead, recording and other off-stage interests increasingly preoccupied the different band members.*

*American TV host Ed Sullivan objects to the Stones performing 'Let's Spend the Night Together', with Mick forced to change the lyrics to 'spend some time together'.*

# THE ED SULLIVAN SHOW
# MAXINE ELLIOTT THEATRE
## 15 JANUARY 1967, NEW YORK, NEW YORK

### I WAS THERE; MICHAEL ACKERMAN, AGE 4
I remember a great deal of that day seeing the Stones on *The Ed Sullivan Show*. I was already a fan, so that probably helped. But I was also a fan of Petula Clark and have only a vague recollection of her performance, even though she sang one of my favourite songs, 'Elusive Butterfly' by Bob Lind, so that's kind of surprising.

# THE ROLLING STONES IN THE SIXTIES: A PEOPLE'S HISTORY

I would swear the Stones did a song other than 'Ruby Tuesday' and 'Let's Spend Some Time Together', but I've never been able to confirm that. I've asked Andrew Loog Oldham, have the DVD of the dress rehearsal I saw, and I guess I could ask Bill Wyman, but I haven't gone that far yet. But it would make sense, because if the Sullivan show would not let them do 'Let's Spend the Night Together' and the Stones refused to do 'Let's Spend Some Time Together', or it didn't work, they'd have another song to perform. My recollection is that they did 'She Said Yeah' or 'It's Alright', but I don't remember and maybe I'm misremembering completely.

After the dress rehearsal my mother and I went to a nearby restaurant (Childs, a couple of blocks away) and in returning to our car, parked in the garage on 53rd Street, we walked past the Ed Sullivan Theater again and the Rolling Stones were outside on 53rd Street at the stage door. I'd never seen anyone who looked like Brian Jones before. He shone as though he was either lit by the sun or was plugged in electrically. He was the most rock star-looking rock star I've ever seen. They were signing autographs and posing for photos, and I said to my mother, 'Let's go get their autograph.' She replied, 'It wouldn't be worth it,' presumably referring to the crowd of people around them.

Two important things happened out of that experience. Firstly, my mother became the anti-barometer; if she said 'don't do it' I thought about doing it, while if she said 'let's do this' I was sceptical. Secondly, for the very first time I realised famous people like the Stones or The Beatles were people, just like me. I had never once thought that before, because I had only seen the Stones on album covers, in magazines and on television, so they were like gods to me. In fact, they were humans, just like the four-year-old looking at them. It changed the way I view celebrities, and I carry that with me to this day.

## I WAS THERE: BARBARA NEUMANN BEALS

My sister Lynne became quite chummy with the Stones. She dated Keith for a while, but it wasn't a great love affair or anything like that. And I think she ended up really liking Andrew Oldham. But just for those few years, a period of about four years, I got to meet them.

Lynne took us to the hotel where the Stones were staying, and they were not there. So she said, 'Just poke around, take anything you want.' I was like, 'what?' So we each took a pack of cigarettes, and I just happened to take Mick Jagger's harmonica. I still have it proudly in my room and can't believe I did that when I was – what – 14, 15 years old. But I did. And I think we each took one little bit of clothing.

We didn't steal money or anything like that. Just little mementoes. Then we had to hurry and got in the audience for *Ed Sullivan*, that famous night the Singing Nuns refused to go on. They were to appear the same night as the Stones but took offence at the lyrics for 'Let's Spend the Night Together' and told Ed Sullivan they would not go on unless the lyrics were changed. I got to hear all this going on. It was fascinating. And finally, they changed the lyrics. But Mick leered at the camera when he said, 'Let's spend some time together.' It was absolutely hilarious. And of course, the audience was in on the whole thing, so we just continued screaming, 'Mick! Keith!'

Lynne made herself very useful to cement the friendship between her and the Stones. She invited Charlie's wife Shirley to go clothes shopping. They went to Bloomingdales – naturally - and Arnold Constable, which is now defunct but was very popular at the time. Lynne told me Shirley was very shy, very sweet and overwhelmed by the fans, none of whom recognised her. They had a great time. She'd do small errands for various Stones, since it was hard for them to sneak out. She went with them to Arthur's, near the 59th St Bridge, one of the first huge clubs for rock stars. She brought my brother Eric to meet them there, before he shipped out to Vietnam. Obviously, he was thrilled and brought me a souvenir - an Arthur's ashtray.

I always wanted to meet Keith in the 1990s or 2000s to present him with this rare souvenir. Unfortunately, it broke recently, so that's that. I have nothing but wonderful memories of that magical time, actually meeting the Stones, long before it became synonymous with the name groupie or other derogatory assumptions. For Lynne and me it was such a special time during the Swinging Sixties, wearing the Carnaby Street look and being the envy of friends.

They were just charming and smart and it was just nice. They couldn't have been more polite. That's what struck me. So nice, and I think at that time they had a lot of respect for younger fans and knew I was a rabid fan.

# THE ROLLING STONES IN THE SIXTIES: A PEOPLE'S HISTORY

My sister told them she had to do the talking for me. Because I literally just couldn't speak. I was so scared. They were joking around saying, 'Come on'. There were no drugs, not that I saw. It's not like they were offering me drugs. It was all very sweet and very innocent.

I talked to Keith on the phone one night. He had a blackout back then and my sister was there and said, 'Keith has nothing to do, I thought we'd give you a call.' I said, 'What?' I was on the phone with Keith for about half an hour, thinking, 'Who's going to believe I'm talking to Keith Richards?' I was trying to sound like I knew what I was talking about. I did grow up with the old blues, so we were talking about blues and Muddy Waters. He said, 'Oh, you like that stuff?' and I said, 'Yeah, I sort of grew up with it. We loved that stuff. My parents used to go to the Cotton Club.' He was intrigued and was so nice. They were all so nice. There was never anything like, 'Oh, I'd like to screw your sister.' There was never ever anything like that. It wasn't raunchy. It was just the early stages. They just wanted to know how they were doing.

*I was on the phone with Keith for about half an hour*

They were hoping that they'd be a bigger success. When that happened we absolutely lost touch with them. As my sister went on to other groups and they became more famous, it all kind of faded away, little by little. The minute they became so big, it was a whole different world. For those few years of the early Swinging Sixties, with the English Mods and the early part of the British Invasion - when we tried to dress like Patti Boyd or Jane Asher or Marianne Faithfull - it was quite a charming and relatively innocent time. It was quite a thrill. But my sister went on from there to meet Eric Clapton, The Animals, and The Kinks. All I know is I remember getting a lot of front row centre seats for a lot of concerts that were pretty darned good. I just consider myself very lucky. I haven't gotten any big phone calls from Keith lately, but that one phone call I treasure. Those were really special times. I'd like to thank the Stones for changing our lives in the most positive, friendly way.

## I WAS THERE: CAROL SIEGEL

I met the Stones outside Colony Records in New York City a couple of hours after *The Ed Sullivan Show* when they had to change the lyrics to 'Let's Spend the Night Together'.

Carol Siegel had her photo taken with both Keith and Brian in NYC

---

In March 1967, the Rolling Stones embarked on what would prove to be their final concert tour with Brian Jones, playing shows in Continental Europe.

---

# PALAZZO DELLO SPORT
## 6 APRIL 1967, ROME, ITALY

### I WAS THERE: STASH KLOSSOWSKI DE ROLA

Brian was with Anita, so I saw a lot of the other Rolling Stones as well throughout '66. In the fall I went to Rome and then in '67 the Stones came to Rome. I went with them to the gig at Pallazo Dello Sport in Rome, a big gig. It was memorable. It was a very good live concert. The sound was very good. There was still some screaming but the hysteria had somewhat subsided and you could actually hear the songs.

I remember how everyone was impressed with Brian playing the dulcimer and all these different instruments. I rode in their car with them. In fact, I was expecting to go up with them at one point, play with them on stage, but in the excitement it just didn't happen.

There we stood with Gina Lollobrigida. It was wild. Then the management of the Piper Club said, 'Oh, you're friends with the Stones.

Can you invite them down on our behalf?' And we all ended up staying, with the exception of Keith, who took a plane and went straight back after the gig to be with Anita (when that split had occurred between Brian and Anita). So there was some tension.

I was going to do a film in America with my then fiancée Romina Power, Tyrone Power's daughter. She'd gone on ahead to America. I was supposed to do a picture with her and John Huston. Brian said, 'Listen, we're going on to Greece. If you're stopping in London, stay at my house and I'll put my car and driver at your disposition.' Brian then asked me to go with him to Cannes, to delay my departure. That otherwise he wouldn't go, and did I think he had a chance to get Anita back. I believed he did. So we went to Cannes and it was fun, although it didn't quite work out as Brian had hoped. Then Brian and I went back to Paris. We'd both been flirting with Suki and called her and made her join us in Paris at the Lancaster Hotel. Then Suki and Brian went together, and then we went back to London. Brian and I were alone, and I was preparing for my last few days in London when we were busted, and history was completely changed.

# HALLAND,
## JUNE 1967, LEWES, EAST SUSSEX, UK

### I WAS THERE: BOB FAIRWEATHER

My brother and I were asked to erect a prefabricated building for Charlie Watts at his home in Halland, Sussex. We found his house and woke Charlie up and he made us a cup of tea. He showed us where he wanted the building erected.

The prefab was for Charlie's wife to do her sculpturing. It was a carry of about 75 yards through mud. As the prefab weighed about seven and a half tons in all, we were not happy. I said if he helped us, we would do it, and he agreed. I must mention here that Charlie was an animal lover and had dogs of every breed running around. We worked until midday, when he had to go off for a recording session. His wife took him to Uckfield station, because Charlie couldn't drive. Before he went, he lent me his wellies as the sole had come off my shoe. I had to telephone my firm at two o'clock and he said I could use the phone in his house and had left the door undone for me.

At 2pm I went down to the house, opened the door and was confronted by white carpets, so had to take my wellies off. I made the call, opened the door to come out and was met by Charlie's dogs. They were snarling and wouldn't let me get to his wellies. They had followed me most of the day with no trouble and it suddenly dawned on me it was Charlie's wellies they liked, not me. Once I took them off, I was doomed.

I had to make my way through the house and get out through a window. I ran back up to the prefab in my socks and got up on the roof, where I stayed until they lost interest and wandered off. While we were unloading the prefab, Charlie told us that when Keith Richards used to call he would drive his Jag up the drive at 100mph and do a handbrake turn, scattering gravel all over his flower beds.

In the newspaper that morning was an article saying the Stones had become millionaires. I told Charlie this and he just shrugged. I don't think money meant that much to him. He also told me he used to live in a prefab with his parents. He had no airs and graces. He was one of the nicest blokes I ever met.

# MONTEREY POP FESTIVAL
## 18 JUNE 1967, MONTEREY, CALIFORNIA

**I WAS THERE: STASH KLOSSOWSKI DE ROLA**
Brian got to go to Monterey, and it was a brief respite. When he came back, he was extremely paranoid. He lowered the flag, admitted defeat, and said, 'They're too strong for us, you'll see.' I was staying with Paul McCartney, and Paul had been boosting me up, saying, 'No, no, you've got to fight. Even if you were guilty, which you're not, you should say, 'Well, see what you've caught me doing - it's nonsense!' But Brian was terribly despondent, and that's what led to his ultimate downfall. And that's what the fans of Brian Jones don't realise.

## A COFFEE SHOP, KING'S ROAD
### JULY 1967, CHELSEA, LONDON, UK

**MY MOTHER WAS THERE: STEPHEN CONN**
In 1967, my mother Natasha Conn was living in London to study ballet. One day, sitting in a coffee shop on the King's Road, she overheard some schoolgirls say, 'Oh look, a Rolling Stone! A Rolling Stone!' and turned to see Brian Jones talking to Russian dancer, Rudolf Nureyev. While she found Nureyev the more magnetic of the two, she distinctly remembers Brian wearing a purple jacket, with white cuffs practically flowing to the floor.

## COURTFIELD ROAD
### SEPTEMBER 1967, SOUTH KENSINGTON, LONDON, UK

**I WAS THERE: DAVID KIRCH**
The Rolling Stones rented a large flat from me in Courtfield Road, South Kensington, London. The living room was oak panelled and it must have been at the time they were accused of taking drugs, because there was a raid at my flat, which involved the removal of the panelling, as presumably drugs might have been hidden behind it. No drugs were found, with the panelling put back again. And they paid all their rent, so it was not really a problem to me.

## LONDON CLINIC
### NOVEMBER 1967, LONDON, UK

**I WAS THERE: ANNETTE WILLIAMS**
I'm from Western Australia and came to the UK for six months, staying 13 years. Most of the Sixties I spent in London, working as a nurse at the London Clinic. In November 1967 I looked after Linda Keith, and Brian Jones was a frequent visitor. At that time I was - and still am - a Beatles fan, but my 12-year-old brother Denis back in

Australia was a Rolling Stones fan.

I bought a Stones 45 record for him with a view to asking Brian to autograph it for Denis. When I saw Brian on his visit to Linda, I asked him if he would autograph the 45. He looked at the record, then said, 'I'll give you a special sleeve and autograph it.' A few days later Brian came in to see Linda. He gave me the sleeve and autographed it for me. The sleeve was for '2000 Light Years from Home'.

Long afterwards, I discovered that the first 45 I asked him to autograph was by someone called Paul Jones. I admire Brian and what a gentleman to save me from acute embarrassment, then giving me his own sleeve, that he had designed. He was truly a kind person and a dedicated musician. I left the UK in 1971 to return home. In 1991 I read Bill Wyman's *Stone Alone* and was amazed to read about the sleeve Brian gave me. Later I was in need of a new stereo system and thought, 'I'm sure Brian would not mind' so I put the sleeve up for auction. It went for $1,400 and I received a cheque for $1,000 and bought a great stereo. Thanks Brian - I really enjoy my music.

# EMPIRE POOL
## 12 MAY 1968, WEMBLEY, LONDON, UK

*As the band increasingly experimented with drugs, much of the latter part of 1967 and early 1968 was taken up with police interest and media scrutiny of the band's off-stage interests, including occasional court appearances. Time spent in the recording studio, not always productively, outweighed that spent performing live. Then in May 1968, the Rolling Stones made a surprise and unbilled appearance at the annual New Musical Express Poll-Winners' Concert, performing 'Jumpin' Jack Flash' and '(I Can't Get No) Satisfaction'. It was their first live performance anywhere in the world in over a year.*

# THE ROLLING STONES IN THE SIXTIES: A PEOPLE'S HISTORY

## I WAS THERE: PAULINE LEVER

I don't think the Stones were expected to appear. We went on a coach trip which a friend had arranged. He lived in the next village and my friend Brenda's Dad drove us to Roade, where we got on the bus. Always travel sick, I hated the journey. It was a big deal going to London and we were country girls in the city, a little out of our depth.

Roger Moore was there at the concert. I remember because I always found him creepy. Status Quo were on, and Amen Corner and Scott Walker, which in my eyes was dreadful, because I always loved John. I remember Dusty Springfield's hair. I always thought she was old-fashioned. When the Stones came on, there was a roar and I screamed and shouted, but Brenda didn't. It was dreadfully disappointing because we just couldn't see them. We did not have good seats. They were way back. People towered in front of us. It was so frustrating. I'd heard the rumours about Brian leaving and chose to bury my head in the sand and pretend it wasn't going to happen. They weren't on long. They sang 'Jumpin' Jack Flash' and 'Satisfaction'.

After the show, Brenda and I went off to find some London nightlife. We found a nightclub in the West End, where two black men asked us to dance. We felt very pleased with ourselves and were a little mesmerised by it, as it seemed so different to the discos and things we were used to around our scene, where we knew loads of boys and girls wherever we went. We left it until the last minute before going to find the bus. We were nearly an hour late. The bus was just moving off. It stopped to let us get on. We were not very popular, sitting very quietly on the way home, smirking to each other.

---

*The Rolling Stones decided to produce a concert film based around a live band performance with a circus theme. The aim was to make a full-length TV show that would provide sufficient transmittable footage, such that the band would not need to travel to TV studios around the world to perform, a task made more onerous by the convictions for drug-related offences that Mick, Keith and particularly Brian had accumulated in the two years they had been away from live performance. It was to be Brian's last public appearance as a member of the Stones.*

---

# THE ROLLING STONES IN THE SIXTIES: A PEOPLE'S HISTORY

# ROCK 'N' ROLL CIRCUS, INTERTEL STUDIOS

## 10, 11 & 12 DECEMBER 1968, WEMBLEY, LONDON, UK

### I WASN'T THERE: PATRICK TIERNAN

Back in '67 I was at Nuneaton College. There were a lot of Coventry students there too. Amongst them was a girl called Celia Thomlinson. She was quite a character, with long wild hair, not academic. She said she was a Stones fan. In fact, she said she knew them. We all took that with a pinch of salt until one day she brought in a pile of photos, and there she was with the Stones. I remember seeing a photo of her with Mick's parents and brother Chris. I also remember seeing a photo of Brian standing in a lounge in an SS uniform, reading a magazine. Celia could do a very accurate impression of Mick's dance moves. One day she asked me to go with her to a private gig in a circus tent. I don't remember why but I said I couldn't go. When I saw her next time, she was raving about it. When I realised what I'd missed I could have wept.

If ever you see the film, Celia is at the front. She takes off her cape and she's wearing a blue dress with a white collar. She was in the studio when the Stones recorded 'Sympathy for the Devil' too. Mick mentions her name right at the end. 'Tell me, Celia, what's my name?' When I left college, I lost contact with her. I caught sight of her about two years later. She looked wasted; I hope it wasn't drugs. She met all The Beatles and got me The Who's autographs. I often wonder what happened to her.

### I WAS THERE: IAN ANDERSON, JETHRO TULL

At one of our final concerts with Mick Abrahams, the opening act was a band called Earth, from Birmingham. What struck me about them was Tony Iommi's guitar playing. It was very forceful, it was simple, it was direct, it didn't have complicated chords. It was just open fifths and very simple direct music, and he had a good strong tone. And it wasn't a blues band, it was something else. It was a precursor to their later name change to Black Sabbath. It was the same guys.

# THE ROLLING STONES IN THE SIXTIES: A PEOPLE'S HISTORY

I somehow got in touch with Tony and asked if he'd like to come down to London and have a play about with us in rehearsal. You couldn't call it an audition because it wasn't as cold-hearted and as functional as that. It was just a get-together to try a few things out. I ran a few songs by Tony which he didn't find that easy to cope with. I didn't realise until later that the reason was that he'd lost the tips off a couple of fingers of his hand, so certain chord shapes were very difficult or impossible for him to play, which is why he developed the style he did, which of course is what made Tony unique and Black Sabbath a huge hit. So Tony's limitations turned into Tony's strengths, much as they did in a way for Django Reinhardt, similarly afflicted by a lack of digital possibilities due to finger damage.

Tony was a nice guy. We got on well, but it clearly wasn't right for him to join Jethro Tull, and he went back to his pals in Black Sabbath. But we called him back to do the *Rolling Stones Rock and Roll Circus* with us, because he was the only guy that we knew really. We said, 'Would you mind coming down to do the Rolling Stones TV show?' We weren't playing live. We were just miming to a backing track. There was no time to learn, and I don't think Tony played bottleneck guitar anyway. It was a particular piece of music that required a different guitar approach, so Tony mimed to the backing track. I sang and played live, and the others were Memorex. They were battery-powered!

I asked Charlie Watts and Bill Wyman how it was that we were invited to take part in the *Rock and Roll Circus* and, according to them, they were the architects of our appearance at short notice on that show. They'd seen us play somewhere, perhaps at the Marquee Club, and recommended us as a potential guest act to Mick Jagger and the show's producer, Michael Lindsay Hogg. The Stones were trying to get a very broad mixture of musical talent, from a classical violinist to the screeching Yoko Ono and appearances by John Lennon and The Who, who were the major draw after the Rolling Stones, and a few other folks. Jethro Tull were the rookies, the new kids on the block no one had heard of, that rounded out the broad balance of musical talent.

We went along and felt a bit awkward and out of place, but did what was asked of us. Then the show was shelved for many years because of the death of Brian Jones and, so rumour has it, because the Stones – or at least Mick Jagger – were not very happy with their performance. The Stones perhaps ended up looking a little ragged compared to the full-on performance of The Who, who were combat ready. The Who had been on tour and were fighting fit, whereas the Stones had been off the road for a long time and had muddled through an album called *Beggar's Banquet*, actually a very good album. The TV show was a promotional vehicle for that album release.

But Brian Jones by then was somewhat marginalised from the band and not really a full participant. I remember he sat down to begin the rehearsals and was fumbling in his pocket, then came over to me and said, 'I don't suppose you've got a plectrum I could borrow? I mean, a guitar pick.' I thought that was interesting. I'm not playing the guitar. I'm the flute player. But I just happened to have a plectrum with me, so I gave it to him. He then attempted to join in, playing whatever they were rehearsing.

## I WAS THERE: STASH KLOSSOWSKI DE ROLA

It was really, really tragic with Brian, because downers make you lose your ability and he lost musical ability, considerable musical ability, in that process. It didn't get any better. He had sparkling moments. He played brilliantly on 'No Expectations'. But to me it's very painful to watch *The Rolling Stones Rock 'n' Roll Circus* because Brian is a shadow of himself. He doesn't do any of the introductions properly. I'm just aghast when I see him on that. He can barely hold it together. Brian, this amazing force, this amazing beacon of light he had been, was a sorry caricature. I miss him a great deal. I loved the guy.

*Brian had been this amazing beacon of light but he became a shadow of himself*

# THE ROLLING STONES IN THE SIXTIES: A PEOPLE'S HISTORY

*After their May 1968 appearance at Wembley, the Rolling Stones did not perform live in front of a paying audience for the remainder of 1968 or the first six months of 1969. Recording for their next album, Let It Bleed, took up much of the early part of the year, although sessions were sporadic, band members arriving at different times. Brian Jones, increasingly ostracised by Mick Jagger and Keith Richards, made only limited contributions to the new album. Mick and Keith, wanting to tour the USA again but aware that Brian's drug convictions meant he was unlikely to obtain a visa enabling him to appear with the band, took the decision to sack Brian and, along with Charlie, visited Brian at his home in Sussex to break the news. Brian left the group in June 1969 and announced he would instead devote his energies to other musical projects.*

## I WAS THERE: CANDY EVANS

Candy Evans is my maiden name. I was raised by a Welsh father, so Brian liked that as well as the music factor. I saw the Rolling Stones in Dallas, Texas, when Brian was with them. I met Brian at Monterey Pop Festival. My brother was a studio musician and knew Jimi Hendrix plus many other musicians. So I met Brian because of my brother. I was introduced to Brian, Jimi Hendrix, Janis Joplin and Mama Cass. I was going on 19 years old. My brother is seven years older, he and Brian a year apart. Brian was very, very polite and charming.

We talked and walked together through the fairgrounds, just the two of us. We talked about music. I was raised in a family that played and loved music, classical, country, rock 'n' roll. He asked me about Texas and did I like country music. He liked Ernest Tubbs and Bob Wills - swing music - and liked country music. His voice was very soft. He seemed to enjoy talking about music. Because of my brother, he felt free to talk with me about music. That was the bridge between us.

## THE ROLLING STONES IN THE SIXTIES: A PEOPLE'S HISTORY

I don't have any photographs. I was too self-conscious to get my camera out. I was very aware that this was very special. I felt out of place in a way. I was very young and came from a sheltered environment. I didn't know anything about grass, marijuana, and the entire fairgrounds smelt sweet. I didn't know what was in the air, I learned much, much later. I was very innocent. I had long hair but was not involved in the Hippie movement.

Brian stayed in touch with me by telephone. He liked calling me rather than writing. There was romance. Because I was young, he took time to get to know me. I didn't want anything from him, so we enjoyed our time together. He flew into Los Angeles to meet me at the Hyatt Hotel in either 1967 or 1968. He stayed in touch with me until the end. I have a ring he gave me.

He was miserable. It was Brian who made the Stones. It was rough on him, to have to leave (the group). I talked with Mick a few times. He was curious as to who I was. It was all like being in a dream. Mick was trying to support Brian, because of the busts and possible time in prison. I spoke with Mick off and on, he was very concerned about Brian's state of mind. He knew I was a good support for Brian. Mick encouraged the relationship.

Mick needed Brian in the Rolling Stones and he and the other Stones were trying to help Brian through the difficult times. I'm not sure about Keith though, I know they were close in the early days. Brian needed a lot of support. I talked with Mick enough to know he was a good person. At least that was my own view of Mick, that he was very, very concerned about Brian.

Brian talked about everything with me. I was safe and someone who would not judge him. I don't know much about Nico. Anna Wolin wrote a book, mentioning being pregnant with Brian. He was still in love with Anita, but he put her in a bad way. I can understand why she left him. I am more realistic today. I didn't know any of this when I was with him but have now read a few books. I can piece things together. Brian was fine with me though.

I met him maybe four times. We talked on the phone more. There was definitely a connection between us.

He loved Cotchford Farm. He loved the pool and the woods, all the land. He felt he was in heaven out there. He loved Winnie the Pooh as a child.

He had come to terms with the Stones thing. It weighed heavily on him. I think he was relieved to finally let it all go. It took such a toll on Brian, it wore him down.

The last time I had contact with Brian was the beginning of summer 1969. He was relaxed and didn't seem worried.

I heard about it (his death) on the news, on the TV. My mother knew about my relationship with Brian. She talked with Brian, she liked him very much. Brian was charming and very articulate. Brian spoke well and knew how to speak with people. I had much grief. I had it for years. I am over it now.

---

*In July 1969 the band announced a return to live performance with a free concert in London's Hyde Park. Two days before the concert was due to take place, Brian Jones was found dead in the swimming pool at his home in Sussex, apparently the result of drowning. The band elected to press on with the Hyde Park show. Their last performance in Britain in the Sixties was hastily re-badged as a tribute to Brian, the founding member of the Rolling Stones.*

---

# HYDE PARK
## 5 JULY 1969, LONDON, UK

### I WAS THERE: ELAINE SPINKS, AGE 19

I went to Hyde Park in 1969 the day of the free concert by the Stones, just after Brian Jones had died. The memory of walking in Hyde Park towards the stage with thousands of other fans still brings goosebumps now. The atmosphere in the park that day was amazing - there was no trouble and my friend and I were right at the front side of stage. We saw Mick Jagger and Marianne Faithfull get out of a car backstage, and he waved. There was almost silence when they walked on stage, Mick with his white smock on and new guitarist Mick Taylor. Jagger spoke emotionally about the band's loss, then released some doves - you could have heard a pin drop, then everyone cheered. What a day.

**I WAS THERE: ANDY THOMPSON, AGE 20**
I went down on the midnight train from Sheffield and got to Hyde Park about quarter to seven in the morning. It was a really hot day and we were possibly 80 yards off stage in the park for 6.45am. The Stones didn't come on until around 7pm, a long wait but well worth it. But they were absolutely rubbish that day. They were in an air-conditioned caravan because it was such a hot day and tuned all the guitars, and when they got on stage all the tuning went out. They weren't very good at all.

**I WAS THERE: JILLY WILLIAMSON, AGE 20**
It was a boiling hot day. Anticipating a huge crowd, myself and friends left Aylesbury on the first train, having been up all night to make quite sure we did so. We were at the park well before 8am and found a good position, not too near the stage on a slight rise to give us a good view. There were a few people around the stage and a couple of dog walkers. We slept. I still remember the amazement of waking in a crowd that stretched as far as the eye could see. It was a great show apart from the fainters from the heat, man-handled over heads to I don't know where. I didn't need the loo - which was just as well.

**I WAS THERE: BILL SHELTON**
I was so far back and over the brow of a hill that I gave up and went to the Albert Hall to see Chuck Berry and The Who. When I asked for tickets at the box office, they told me Chuck had been taken ill and would not be appearing, so I gave up and caught the train back early. The following week I read a review in the *Melody Maker* which said Chuck did perform that night, so the day turned out to be a complete flop.

**I WAS THERE: TED GARRATT, AGE 21**
We went to Hyde Park in '69. I was 21 then. I was still single, leading the boy's life, and a car-load of us went down there and parked in an underground car park. We weren't part of the hysteria, in that we

couldn't have been much further away than anybody else in Hyde Park. We could hear the sound wafting over the breeze, but Family, a Leicester band, were on that bill as well. We wanted to see Family so planned on going anyway, but then of course Brian died and he'd been a hero to all of us, partly because he seemed to be the most musical. And because he said very little, even in interviews, you always wondered what made him tick. It was a cultural thing as well as a musical thing to be there.

## I WAS THERE: GUÐBJÖRG ÖGMUNDSDÓTTIR, AGE 17

Nothing could dampen my spirits that day. There was not a cloud in the sky. Within me I still felt the deep sorrow for Brian's sudden passing. But today was a celebration of his life and his music. A Danish friend from work was going with me. When we got out into the street outside the hospital where we had been working, we were filled with suspense and excitement. Almost immediately we noticed the headlines of the day on every other street corner. We stopped and bought some papers and saw pictures of people lying in sleeping bags in front of the enclosure in front of the stage. We had not realised people had started arriving at Hyde Park the evening before and the police, afraid they would have a riot on their hands, would let them stay in the park throughout the night. This was unheard of - Hyde Park was always locked at night.

We hurried down the Underground and made the short journey to the nearest station to where the concert was being held. The trains and sidewalks were filled with young people around our age and some a little older, a few a lot older. Everyone had long hair. We had never seen so many hippies walking along the streets, coming from all directions.

When we reached the area in front of the stage where people were already sitting and lazing in the sunshine, everyone was really cool and friendly. By this time my heart was beating so fast I thought I would have a nervous breakdown. I felt I needed to calm my nerves. To my surprise my friend pulled out a bottle of valium. She said she was going to take one and I took one too. We pulled out a sandwich to eat and a beer to drink with it and some of the people around us broke out in laughter and made some comments at us for being really uncool to have brought beer. We really felt embarrassed. Of course, we had smelled all the incense and joints in the air, and when a joint was handed our way we accepted and took a drag or two and gave out sandwiches or fruit in return. No one wanted our beer.

Everyone was really nice and friendly. It was a tremendous joy to be there among the crowd. I was amazed at the size of the crowd. It went on for as far as you could see. A few guys near us announced they had seen what they had come to see, and it was time to split - the Rolling Stones were sell-outs and not worth listening to anymore. The announcer explained Mick was going to read something for Brian and was asking all of us to be quiet while he did so. Then thousands of white butterflies would be released.

The Rolling Stones walked on stage and the roar of the crowd was unbelievable. They all looked so cool. Mick was wearing this incredible outfit. The next day the headline across the front page of one paper read, 'Where Did He Get That Frock?' He was all dressed in white and when he spoke everyone went quiet. It was the weirdest thing. But he didn't think the crowd was quiet enough. So he said, 'Are you going to shut up or not?' After that you could have heard a pin drop. Then he read Shelley's poem in remembrance of Brian. It was very beautiful. I could feel the pain stinging in my heart. I really felt like crying.

Right afterwards, brown cardboard boxes were brought out and thousands of beautiful white butterflies were released into the air. It looked so fitting and beautiful. I could feel my heart fill with joy. This was a moment in history that would not be forgotten.

The Stones were on stage for over an hour, performing lengthy versions of most of their songs. I felt empty inside after they left the stage. It almost seemed as if the sun had left the sky. Emotion was overcoming me and I suddenly felt all the anticipation, excitement and experience of the day overwhelm me. I staggered off the path and sat down under a great big tree. My friend followed me, and I told her I needed to take a moment to take all this in. Emotions absolutely overtook me, and I started shaking and crying. Tears were streaming down my face. Almost at the same time I started laughing uncontrollably. All the grief of Brian's passing that I had been holding in and the joy of seeing the Stones perform just had to come out. I felt unspeakably happy and sad at the same time. A couple of young guys came by and started asking what was wrong, but I couldn't talk. At last one of them said he thought he knew what I was feeling, that I was crying for Brian and laughing due to the happiness of having just seen the Stones perform.

# THE ROLLING STONES IN THE SIXTIES: A PEOPLE'S HISTORY

## I WAS THERE: HELEN LOCK

By this time, I was 17 and my parents were long used to letting me go to shows by myself, and very patient about being called out to pick me up when I missed the last train home. I usually went by myself, as nobody else liked the same music I did, but I was amazed looking at my diary a few years ago to see I'd gone to Hyde Park with a school friend/acquaintance. I've absolutely no memory of being with anyone else.

The Hyde Park free concerts were big events and I was beyond excited to be going to the Stones show, dressed in my hippie finery. It had been so long since I'd seen them. We spent most of the day at the top of the incline, a pretty long way from the stage but with a perfect view, and with a good view of all the people in trees too.

When the Stones were about to come on, I wanted to get closer (this may be where I parted company with my friend) and wormed my way down toward the front. I was now right in the thick of things but couldn't see a thing. For one thing, the stage was very low. The show started and I was so excited to be hearing them again. The whole thing had the feel of a real occasion, especially with the introduction of Mick Taylor, and with everybody wondering how they would handle mentioning Brian's death.

I was overwhelmed and relieved because the music was so great - despite what naysayers have said in the years since, those of us down there in the crowd were having a blast - and a kind stranger lifted me up onto his shoulders so I could see Mick dancing in the white dress.

Later, all I caught were glimpses, but it was enough. It developed into a real party and the amazing thing is that this is despite the fact that so many of the songs were new to us (hence my problem with the set-list). We didn't know 'Sympathy for the Devil', for example, but I remember everybody picking up cans and bottles and playing percussion on them, and some people actually brought tambourines and were playing them. I also saw butterflies flying around, but no dead ones - that was something I only learned about later. I had an amazing time and got home in time to watch the report of the event on the late-night news. Tired, but happy, as they say.

# THE ROLLING STONES IN THE SIXTIES: A PEOPLE'S HISTORY

## I WAS THERE: BOB LEE

I was working at the AA. I think there was a big football match on at the same time. All the trains and all the coaches were full. So I thought, 'I'm not going to be able to go.' By this time, I was married. And the AA, for reasons I can't understand, had a personnel manager for Manchester who in actual fact lived in London. I knew this and that he commuted back at weekends so I dropped hints like bricks, you know, and he sussed this out and eventually offered to give my wife and myself a lift down when he was going back on Friday. He kindly offered to put us up at his house as well. That's how we managed to get down there. He was a big music fan but a jazz fan.

He ran us into Hyde Park as well. And that, again, was incredible. We didn't see an awful lot because we were quite far back, but you could hear them clear enough. I remember walking round London and hearing this record coming out of somewhere and said, 'Listen to that - it's fantastic.' It was 'Honky Tonk Women', which came out that weekend. That was the first time I heard it, and it just blew me away.

## I WAS THERE: THOMAS MARSCHIK, AGE 20

I had just finished my sophomore year in college. I missed meeting Keith Richards by 15 minutes as he came by the small hotel I was staying in near Paddington Station, about a 10-minute walk to Hyde Park. I slept in Hyde Park the night before the concert. There were perhaps maybe a hundred of us in my area, where they were constructing the stage. Someone had a radio and I must have heard 'Honky Tonk Women' two dozen times that night - the song had been released that Friday. There was also an announcement that because we were orderly the police would not come in and evict us, as Hyde Park at that time was always closed at night and no one was supposed to be there overnight. This caused someone to break apart a lawn chair and build a small fire. Luckily, we were not evicted.

If you watch the concert video on You Tube and freeze it seven seconds in, there is a guy sitting in the middle of the frame in a blue jacket, kind of by himself, from the back. That, I believe, is me. Pretty cool.

# THE ROLLING STONES IN THE SIXTIES: A PEOPLE'S HISTORY

## I WAS THERE: TRISH COLE

I went with a gang of lads; my then boyfriend and three or four of his mates. We drove up from Ashtead in an open-top Land Rover and, if I remember correctly, we were able to drive into the park and leave the Land Rover quite close to the stage. I had long straight hair with a fringe then, and someone yelled, 'It's Marianne Faithfull!'

We were quite near the stage, where the ground began to rise away from the flat. People were mostly sitting and lying on the ground, with the odd person dancing. We were all very aware of the death of Brian Jones and I was interested to see how Mick Taylor would fit in. I remember when the butterflies were released, although I believe that many of the butterflies died. I can't remember anything about the quality of the performance, but I liked Jagger's white 'dress'.

## I WAS THERE: DANY MATER

I was living in Ilford. My friends and I were so excited about the concert. Then there was the shock of the awful shattering news of Brian's death, shortly after he was sacked from the band. The concert was first cancelled, adding to our grief, and then Mick Jagger announced the concert would finally be held in memory of Brian.

We went to Hyde Park hours before the concert was due to start and the weather was just glorious. There were hundreds of thousands of us in a peaceful gathering, between happiness and tears for Brian, and anxious to see Mick Taylor with the Stones. I had seen him before with John Mayall, and he was just an amazing musician. I was about halfway to the stage, near a tree which brought us some shelter from the blistering sun. Then they came on, and Mick read that beautiful poem by Shelley and released thousands of white butterflies (although I later heard they did not survive because they were not adapted to that environment).

Marsha Hunt was standing on the side of the stage at Hyde Park. What a beautiful lady. The whole event was emotion through and through, although it probably wasn't technically their best performance. They'd been away from the stage for quite a while, and they'd also been through rough times. Mick Taylor had only just joined and they had Brian's death to deal with on top of that. But there was a stunning 'Sympathy for the Devil', with wild African drums. I'll never forget that day.

# THE ROLLING STONES IN THE SIXTIES: A PEOPLE'S HISTORY

## I WAS THERE: DAVID ROBINSON

I went with three friends. One of the guys drove us in his convertible Triumph and we went to see a friend who worked in a pub somewhere in central London. We then drove over and parked as close as we could to Hyde Park. When we entered the park, Richie Havens was walking towards us, his guitar resting on his shoulder; it was quite surreal. There was a natural sort of amphitheatre, which overlooked the stage, and we found a spot on the bank approximately 50 yards from the stage. The crowd grew larger and larger as time went by. Eventually, there were around a quarter of a million people there.

There was a wide variety of mainly young people there, ranging from smartly dressed to Rocker types and flower-power types. I was 19 at the time and my friends were a year or two older. There was a fantastic party-type atmosphere. You knew what to expect from the Stones, and they didn't disappoint. It was different from the Blind Faith concert I'd seen earlier in the year in Hyde Park, where people were waiting to hear what they played. After the Stones concert, we hung around for a while then drifted back to the pub where our pal worked, before driving home.

## I WAS THERE: DEN BOUNDY

Hyde Park was a wonderful experience - a lovely warm day with a lot of cool hippies around. There were various reports after that there were between 200,000 and 500,000 people there. My friend and I must have got there fairly early, as we got a good spot not too far from the stage.

It was the only time I saw the Stones. Brian Jones had recently died and Mick released a load of white butterflies in his memory. I was quite shocked at the time that Mick was wearing a white dress. King Crimson played before the Stones came on. Crimson were being lauded by the *Melody Maker* at the time, which encouraged me to buy their first album, *In the Court of the Crimson King*. It was sold out when I first tried to get it and I had to order it from the record shop.

# THE ROLLING STONES IN THE SIXTIES: A PEOPLE'S HISTORY

## I WAS THERE: OLIVER BALL

I had never seen so many people together, we got there late and stood right at the back. Consequently I didn't see much but it felt like you could hear them all over London. There was also something else everyone felt, as though we had been part of something special.

## I WAS THERE: ROWAN WYMARK, AGE 15

I was 15. I'd just started doing drugs in a minor league way and was working my way toward dropping out of school. I wouldn't describe my then self as a hippie - I was a bit too young to have hit the full-blown Woodstock period. The Hyde Park concerts were pretty regular then. Blind Faith made their debut at one in June. I went to the Stones concert with a group of friends and a relatively new boyfriend. We missed all the warmup bands but found a really good space to sit at which had a great view of the stage. I remember Mick in his light green dress, and the butterflies that were released becoming tangled in people's hair. The main thing I remember about the concert was the energy, Mick didn't let up and the whole stage crackled. It was as if sparks flew out and hit us all.

Rowan Wymark was at Hyde Park for the Stones

I knew at the time it was going to be a significant moment in history. I saw a Stones documentary not so long ago that included shots of the concert, and it was odd to realise that one of the 'blobs' that made up the huge audience was me.

## I WAS THERE: BRENDA PARKER

Hyde Park was like closing a chapter and turning the page and moving on into a new and very different decade. Everything had changed by then. It wasn't pop music anymore. Now it was rock, and the Stones truly were 'The Greatest Rock 'n' Roll Band in the World'. The screaming had mercifully stopped and the music was being taken seriously now. Brian's recent departure had been a blow, but word was that he was putting his own band together so that was something to look forward to, and the announcement that the Stones would do a free concert to introduce his replacement was met with great excitement.

My friend Robert and I were really looking forward to it and were eager to see what the new Stones would be like, but of course Mick Taylor's debut was completely overshadowed by the terrible news of Brian's death, and at first no one seemed to know if the concert would take place. When word came that it was going on as planned, albeit now as a tribute to Brian, I felt it was the right thing to do. It was such a strange and surreal day, firstly because the weather was so hot, secondly because I think we were all still trying to process that Brian was dead. We weren't used to our rock stars dying then. Brian was the first, so it was truly shocking.

I remember coming out of Marble Arch tube station, seeing a veritable army of us all in our hippie finery streaming across Park Lane from every direction, heading into the park. I was directly behind someone dressed head to toe in heavy black velvet, maybe in mourning for Brian, and remember thinking, 'She's going to be so uncomfortable in such a heavy outfit in all this heat.'

I don't remember what time the concert was scheduled to begin, but Robert and I got there only a couple of hours before the allotted time and had no trouble finding a place to sit, only a few yards from where the stage was being set up. Everything was so much simpler then - can you imagine doing that now? Then we just sat there and waited for what seemed like forever.

Looking back on it, I can't believe we sat there for all those hours in the boiling heat with no food or drink. And if there were bathrooms set up anywhere, I don't remember seeing them. Yet it didn't bother us at all. As time passed we could see we'd been joined by heaven only knows how many thousands of people, some of whom had climbed trees way behind us. It was literally a sea of people, but everyone was friendly and good natured, although the mood was subdued because of Brian. At the sides of the stage the crew had set up a pair of massive pictures of Brian from the photo session for the inner sleeve of *Beggar's Banquet*, which I thought was an odd choice, but he had a big grin on his face, so I guess that's why they'd been chosen.

It took forever before the Stones finally showed up, and before they

# THE ROLLING STONES IN THE SIXTIES: A PEOPLE'S HISTORY

did we had to endure the Battered Ornaments, The Third Eye Band (or maybe the Third Ear Band? They were so boring I really didn't pay much attention to their name), and Alexis Korner and the New Church, who I found very disappointing. Apparently, King Crimson also played, although I have no recollection of them at all. I remember seeing Marsha Hunt in the area just in front of the stage, all dressed in white-fringed buckskin and looking fabulous, but none of us knew then about the affair she was having with Mick. The security people made her move, and she was obviously annoyed - apparently the security people didn't know about the affair either.

The security people were a bunch of bikers and I've always thought it was because they did the security at this concert that the notoriously bad decision was made to use bikers as security at Altamont. The Brit bikers were pretty harmless, but I don›t think anyone realised the Hell›s Angels in California were just a bunch of vicious thugs and nothing like their UK counterparts.

Anyway, after what seemed like a really, really long time, Sam Cutler finally announced the Stones and out came Mick in his Mr Fish white 'dress'. Knock-offs showed up in the Oxford Street boutiques within days. He looked very serious and said he was going to say a few words for Brian and read a poem by Shelley, but the sound system wasn't great. I think a lot of people thought he said he was going to read a poem by Che. And then the white butterflies were released. It was a nice gesture. I took a picture while they were being released.

A lot of the songs were from *Beggar's Banquet* and *Let it Bleed*, and during 'Midnight Rambler' a bunch of people sat a couple of yards in front of us got up and blocked our view. Everyone was trying to get them to sit down again. When it became apparent they weren't going to, several people began shouting out to Mick, asking him to make them sit. They got Mick's attention, but instead of him shaming the standees he just shimmied his way to the other side of the stage as if to say, 'Hey, not my problem!' Fortunately, they did eventually sit down, but it was no thanks to Mick. By the end of the concert he had ditched the dress in favour of the pale mauve sleeveless t-shirt he was wearing underneath. He was full of energy and running and dancing all over the stage, but the concert itself was a bit ragged and I didn't think Mick Taylor looked very comfortable.

# THE ROLLING STONES IN THE SIXTIES: A PEOPLE'S HISTORY

Then it was over, it had been an emotional and very tiring day but really was the end of an era. I still love the Stones and always will, but I never went to see them again.

## I WAS THERE: JOHN PHILPOTT, AGE 20

My sidekick Chris Poole and I managed to convince the concert organisers, Blackhill Enterprises, our local paper the *Rugby Advertiser* needed to cover the event. Our barefaced cheek paid off as after a few calls two sky blue tickets for the press enclosure arrived in the post. Chris was the main mover here, for he had struck up a friendship with concert promoter Sam Cutler, the man who not only oversaw that historic London gig but went on to become the Stones' chief road manager.

That Saturday Chris and I rose early and made our way to Rugby Midland Station only to find all the Euston-bound trains were full. Somehow we managed to convince a guard our mission was urgent, and he allowed us to ride in the mail carriage. The sky was as blue as our tickets when we joined the crowds heading for Hyde Park. Being in the press enclosure meant we were in the company of the emerging rock aristocracy. In my case, that meant sitting next to pop starlet Marsha Hunt, a vision in white buckskins topped off with an Afro halo of hair. All manner of bands prepared the way for the Stones, most of them now little more than musical memories.

John Philpott, left, was at Hyde Park with the press contingent

Pete Brown's Battered Ornaments, Third Ear Band, Screw... who knows what became of the musicians that helped to make history on that boiling hot day all those years ago?

A crowd of nearly half a million listened to them politely, if a little dutifully, then around mid-afternoon the Stones strode on stage. The footage has been played many times - Jagger in Greek soldier's ceremonial frock, Richards a living skull, and the rest looking rather bewildered. Introduced by Sam Cutler as 'The Greatest Rock 'n' Roll Band in the World', they were hopelessly out of tune, a vision of jaded rebellion that even then was showing signs of being very much part of a new Establishment.

They came and went. As Chris and I filed out of Hyde Park in the dusty heat of that July day, I reflected on the fact that my only sustenance all day had been a hamburger and Coke, both bought for what seemed like an extortionate amount. This had been the first big rock festival and the rip-off merchants had been more interested in LSD of a different kind! We caught the train back to Rugby, suspecting we had witnessed history in the making.

## I WAS THERE: ALAN POWELL, AGE 18

We had to get the bus from Ellesmere Port in Cheshire. It was my first ever trip to London. Hyde Park was packed when we got there - strangely dressed people lying on the floor smoking long roll-ups. There was nothing like that in Ellesmere Port, and no free love either.

We climbed a tree but it didn't help so we sort of wove our way forward, stepping on the occasional ankle. The British Hell's Angels didn't look that tough, a bit like some of the hard knocks at home. We watched the exotic girls climbing up on the stage and sat by them as they played. 'Was that Marianne?' 'There's Suzy Creamcheese!' We saw Keith with the Gibson V - so cool. The press said they were out of tune, that Jagger had a dress on, that the butterflies they planned to release were already dead. But we loved them, and this was a rare chance to see them. They were getting so remote and untouchable. They'd been in the papers, acing jail. We bloody loved them – leave 'em alone!

---

*The press said they were out of tune, that Jagger had a dress on, that the butterflies they planned to release were already dead... But we bloody loved them!*

---

# POSTSCRIPT

Hopefully this book has given the reader a flavour of what it was like to attend one of the early performances given by the Rolling Stones. In compiling this book, I have endeavoured to contact as many people as possible, but in the UK alone the Stones played more than 750 times between 1963 and 1966. There will be many more fans out there whose story hasn't yet been heard. If you witnessed one of those early shows or know someone who did, I'd love to hear those memories and I can be contacted on *iwasatthatgig@gmail.com*.

One of the less pleasant discoveries in researching this book was finding out just how many of Britain's fabulous provincial cinemas and theatres have failed to escape the wrecker's ball over the years. Too many of my contributors concluded their reminiscences of seeing the Stones in their hometown with the words, 'It's not there now.' Even those venues still standing are routinely subjected to redevelopment proposals from avaricious developers who face feeble resistance from overstretched and underfunded local authority planners. Either that or they are boarded up and neglected in the hope that funds will someday arrive to enable them to be restored to their former grandeur.

It is sad and a little ironic that, if the Stones were today to offer to play some of these theatres and donate the fee they can now command to the venue's restoration, the desperate struggle to fund to return some of these magnificent buildings to their former glory would be ended overnight. Mick Jagger has thrown his weight, if not his wallet, behind a few such restoration campaigns but the list of buildings which remain vulnerable to redevelopment remains too long.

# THE ROLLING STONES IN THE SIXTIES: A PEOPLE'S HISTORY
# ACKNOWLEDGEMENTS

I could not have written this book without the help of many people. I am indebted to the many journalists and features editors of local and regional newspapers – in the UK and beyond – who printed my letter or ran a feature on my original plea for fans to come forward with their memories of seeing the Rolling Stones play their local theatre, club or ballroom. I'd like to thank all the people who saw the Rolling Stones in the Sixties and were kind enough to share their memories with me, including those who scoured attic rooms and cardboard boxes for the photographs that appear in this book.

I'd particularly like to thank: Robin Mayhew for his reminiscences about the Red Lion in Sutton and for putting me in touch with others who were able to contribute to this period of the Stones' story; Alan Ford from Stevenage Museum and David Menconi from the *Charlotte News Observer* for doing the same; Sarah Stoner from the *Sunderland Echo* for an early lesson in researching the facts and for making me aware of just how many times the Stones played in the North East of England; Alan True for giving up a slice of his Sunday morning to show me his Stones memorabilia; Martin Culleton for the photos of the Stones backstage at the Parr Hall, Warrington on 25 November 1963; Laurie Stead for photos of the Stones backstage at the Huddersfield ABC on 10 March 1965; the late Dominic Lamblin for the pictures of him with the Stones in Paris in the Sixties.

For permission to reproduce extracts from their memoirs I'd like to thank: Rodger W Brownlee of 'ThElite' © for recollections of the Stones appearing at the Will Rogers Memorial Center, Fort Worth; Dawn Young for permission to reproduce an extract from *Not Fade Away*, her memoir about life with Brian.

I found myself referring to Nico Zentgraf's excellent database about the Stones' early activities more times than I cared to remember, and I would like to thank Pauline Lever, a Brian Jones aficionado and someone who has put me in touch with other fans of Brian, and my long-time writing support group of Jenny Parks and Diane Finlayson. Thanks also to proof-reader extraordinaire Malcolm Wyatt, my editorial assistant Gabriel Smith, design wizard Bruce Graham and web wizard Bruce

Koziarkski.

I would like to especially thank Kate Sullivan for the coffees, meals and all-round love and support that have enabled me to apply myself to the task of writing this book, and Bill Houghton, onto whom I seem to have passed my enthusiasm for, and shared love of, the greatest rock 'n' roll band in the world.

And I must not forget to thank my Mum and Dad. Mum took me to see several pop acts in the Sixties, including The Beatles and Cliff Richard and the Shadows. And had my dad not disliked Mick Jagger so much, I might never have become a Stones fan and so never have thought to write this book.

THE ROLLING STONES IN THE SIXTIES: A PEOPLE'S HISTORY

# SPECIAL THANKS

Special thanks to the following for their support for this book:

Barry Parkin
Richard Luetchford
Graham Day
Mark Halverson
Rita Mann
Pauline Lever
Dane Fernandes
Michael Johnson
Gary Epperson
Tim Croucher
Pamela Barone
Margarita Jones
Ira Knopf
James Bank
Steven Butcher
Sandra Carver
Tom Schutz
Gary Morrison
Chuck Sheketoff
Michael Newell
Ric Arra
Mary Glusak
Julian Hardiman
Randy Stanley
Nigel Molden
Peter Fielding
Aart Boeser
Randi Udelson
Curt Angeledes